The King's, Liverpool Regiment of Foot

The King's, Liverpool Regiment of Foot
A Regimental History from 1685-1881

ILLUSTRATED

Richard Cannon

The King's, Liverpool Regiment of Foot
A Regimental History from 1685-1881
by Richard Cannon

ILLUSTRATED

First published under the title
Historical Record of the King's, Liverpool Regiment of Foot

Leonaur is an imprint of Oakpast Ltd
Copyright in this form © 2021 Oakpast Ltd

ISBN: 978-1-78282-994-2 (hardcover)
ISBN: 978-1-78282-995-9 (softcover)

http://www.leonaur.com

Publisher's Notes

The views expressed in this book are not necessarily those of the publisher.

Contents

The King's, Liverpool Regiment of Foot	7
Prefatory Notice	9
An Epitome of the Story of the 8th The King's Regiment	25
Part 1: Services of the First Battalion, 1685-1880	35
Part 2: Services of the Second Battalion	177
Appendix 1	207
Appendix 2	257
Appendix 3	340
Appendix 4	343
Appendix 5	362
Appendix 6	366

The King's, Liverpool Regiment of Foot

Previous to 1751, and for some years afterwards, when referred to by cotemporaries, the regiment was generally designated by the name of its colonel, and was called first Lord Ferrars', then in succession the Duke of Berwick's, Beaumont's, Webb's, Morrison's, Hotham's, Pocock's, Lenoe's, Onslow's, Wolfe's, and Barrington's Regiment. It was also sometimes called the "King's Royal Hanoverian White Horse Regiment," and in the *Gazette* of 1755 it is styled "His Majesty's Own Regiment of Foot."

In a volume of army uniforms, called *A Representation of the Clothing of H.M. Household and of Great Britain* London, 1742, the King's Regiment is numbered "the Ninth Regiment of Foot." The regiment which immediately precedes it, and which is numbered "the Eighth," has yellow facings: the succession list of its colonels contains the following names:—Colonel Cornwall, 1685; Nicholas, 1688; Cuningham, 1688; General Stuart, 1689; Colonel Campbell, 1715; Cathcart, 1716; Otway, 1718; Kane, 1725; Brigadier-General Hargrave, 1737; Colonel Read, 1739. In the printed Army List of 1740 also "Read's" precedes "Onslow's" regiment, but about the year 1751 the order of precedence of these two regiments was reversed; the King's became the Eighth, and the regiment raised by Colonel Cornwall became the Ninth.

The Regiment,

WHICH FOR THE FUTURE IS TO BEAR THE NAME OF

THE KING'S (LIVERPOOL REGIMENT),

WAS DESIGNATED, FROM 1685 TO 1702,

THE PRINCESS ANNE OF DENMARK'S REGIMENT;

FROM 1702 TO 1716,

THE QUEEN'S REGIMENT;

FROM 1716 TO 1751,

THE KING'S REGIMENT;

FROM 1751 TO 1881,

EIGHTH (THE KING'S REGIMENT).

The Regimental Colour

BEARS

THE WHITE HORSE,

ON A RED FIELD WITHIN THE GARTER, AND AROUND A CRIMSON CIRCLE "LIVERPOOL REGIMENT," ENCIRCLED BY THE UNION WREATH AND SURMOUNTED BY THE

IMPERIAL CROWN;

THE MOTTO

"NEC ASPERA TERRENT"

ON A SCROLL OVER THE ENDS OF THE UNION WREATH;

IN THE FIRST CORNER THE BATTALION NUMBER, IN THE SECOND, THIRD, AND FOURTH,

THE ROYAL CYPHER AND CROWN;

ON EITHER SIDE A LAUREL BRANCH WITH SCROLLS, ON WHICH ARE INSCRIBED THE NAMES OF THE FOLLOWING VICTORIES:—

"BLENHEIM, RAMILLIES, OUDENARDE, MALPLAQUET;"

"DETTINGEN,"

(In commemoration of the battle fought at that place on the 27th June, 1743;)

"MARTINIQUE,"

(For the capture of that Island in 1809;)

"NIAGARA,"

(For distinguished conduct on the Frontiers of Canada in 1814;)

"DELHI AND LUCKNOW,"

(In commemoration of services in restoring order in Her Majesty's Indian Dominions in 1857-58.)

"PEIWAR KOTAL, AFGHANISTAN, 1878-80,"

(In commemoration of gallant behaviour in the Afghan Campaigns.)

AND UNDERNEATH

THE SPHINX, WITH THE WORD "EGYPT,"

(To commemorate services in Egypt in the year 1801.)

Prefatory Notice

This edition consists, first, of a reprint of Mr. Cannon's *Record* of the services of the regiment from its formation in June, 1685, until April, 1843; second, of a continuation, bringing down the record to 1st July, 1881.

★★★★★★

In the Chronological Summary prefixed to the *Records*, the chronology is continued to 9th October, 1882; and later a sheet has been reprinted, in order to insert a note recording certain incidents which occurred after the printing of Appendices 1 and 2 was completed.

★★★★★★

No alterations have been made in the text of the first edition, but it has been divided into sections corresponding to the periods of home and foreign service, and those paragraphs which refer to the services of the second battalions, borne on the establishment of the regiment from 1756, to 1758, and from 1804, to 1815, have been extracted and placed at the commencement of Part 2 of the new edition.

A few notes have been also added, principally derived from some folio volumes belonging to the library of the Royal United Service Institution, containing MS. notes and newspaper cuttings, which record a multitude of incidents illustrative of the services and history of every regiment of the army. I am indebted to the late Mr. Sullivan, the Assistant-Secretary of the Institution, for directing my attention to these volumes, and for valuable advice and assistance, having reference not only to researches connected with the preparation, but also to the arrangements for the publication of the new edition.

The continuation of Mr. Cannon's *Record* embraces an account of the services performed by the regiment during the great *Sepoy* Mutiny of 1857-58, and of its Second Battalion during the Afghan

Campaigns of 1878-79-80. The narrative of those incidents of the *Sepoy* Mutiny in which the regiment took part was contributed by Lieutenant-Colonel J. Millar Bannatyne and Major Reginald Whitting. Lieutenant-Colonel Bannatyne's narrative embraces the period from 13th May, 1857, when a detachment of the King's secured the fort and magazine of Phillour, until 9th February, 1858, when the regiment, which had been reduced to a skeleton, was withdrawn from the field force under Sir Colin Campbell, and sent to occupy the cantonment of Agra (*vide* chapter 1, part 1).

Lieutenant-Colonel Bannatyne served with the regiment as a captain from the outbreak of the Mutiny to the conclusion of the Siege of Delhi; during the subsequent operations he held the appointment of Major of Brigade, first to Colonel Greathed's force, and afterwards to the Third Infantry Brigade; he was therefore thoroughly acquainted with all the details of the incidents he describes. Moreover, the proof-sheets of his MS. were submitted for revision to the following officers:—Generals J. Longfield and Sir E. Greathed; Lieutenant-Generals A. C. Robertson and R, S. Baynes; Major-Generals J. Hinde and E. N. Sandilands; Colonels G. E. Baynes, Webb, Walker, and A. Ross; Lieutenant-Colonels Daniell, Bannatyne, and Beere; Majors McCrea and Stebbing, and Deputy-Inspector General of Hospitals F. Annesley; all these officers served with the regiment during the Mutiny campaigns. General Sir H. Norman was also good enough to read over these proof-sheets, and to contribute several interesting notes to this portion of the *Record*

The narrative of Major R. Whitting describes the sequel of the field services of the regiment during the Mutiny campaigns; it embraces the period between 9th February, 1858, and 28th February, 1859, (chapter 1).

The account of the services of the Second Battalion during the Afghan campaigns of 1878-79-80, was contributed by Captain F. J. Whalley who, during these campaigns, held the appointment of Adjutant of the Battalion; the proof-sheets of his MS. were revised by Colonels F. Barry Drew and K Tanner.

The four plates representing the uniforms worn at different periods by the officers, non-commissioned officers, and privates of the regiment, were lithographed from coloured drawings made by Mr. S. M. Milne, (of Calverley House, near Leeds.) The regiment is also indebted to this gentleman for the very interesting notes on its costume and equipment given in Appendix No. 4. The sketch plans were compiled by Lieutenant James Dallas, Royal Engineers.

The abstract of the services of the Second Royal Lancashire Militia (now the Third and Fourth Battalions of the King's), *vide* Appendix No. 6, was made from a copy of the *Records* of the regiment given me by its colonel commandant, Nicholas Blundell. The proof-sheets of the abstract were submitted for revision to him, and to his adjutant, Major John James Hamilton.

In superintending the preparation of this edition, I have been in constant communication with the officers commanding the two battalions; from them I have received copies of the MS. Records of each battalion, and to one or other of them the proof of each of the printed sheets was submitted for revision and approval.

The completed volume is now presented to those for whom it has been prepared; to readers whom, whatever may be its defects, it is sure to interest; to the survivors of the officers, non-commissioned officers, and soldiers of the King's (many of them my friends and former comrades), whose services it records; to their successors, now serving and who shall hereafter serve in the regiment; may they often look back on the two centuries of noble achievements which this volume commemorates; may it be their good fortune to add many glorious pages to the unwritten annals of the years which are to come.

A. Cuningham Robertson,
(Lieutenant-General, formerly Lieutenant-Colonel,
Eighth, the King's Regiment).

February, 1883.

CHRONOLOGICAL SUMMARY.

Year.
1685. 20th June. Formation of the Regiment, which is styled the Princess Anne of Denmark's Regiment
—— August. Encamped on Hounslow Heath, and twice reviewed by King James II
—— September. Quartered at Chester
1686. February. Changes Quarters from Chester to Berwick. James Fitz-James (Duke of Berwick) appointed Colonel
1687. June. Encamped at Hounslow Heath
—— August. Quartered at Portsmouth
1688. September. The Lieutenant-Colonel and five Captains refuse to receive Roman Catholics into their Companies, and are tried by Court-Martial
1689. 13th June. Inspected at Carlisle by the Commissioners appointed to remodel the Army
—— Moves to Chester, embarks at Highlake, and anchors in the Bay of Carrickfergus on 13th August
—— August. Siege of Carrickfergus
—— September. Encamped near Dundalk
—— Winter Quarters, Green Castle and Rostrevor
1690. In the Spring stationed at Londonderry
—— 1st July. Battle of the Boyne
—— 7th July. Reviewed by King William at Finglass
—— Limerick unsuccessfully besieged
—— September and October. Sieges of Cork and Kinsale. Winter Quarters, Cork
1691. September. Siege and Surrender of Limerick
1692. 16th February. Embarks for England
—— Expedition to the Coast of France disembarks at Ostend in the beginning of September
1693. Returns to England early in the year, and is quartered at Portsmouth
—— April. Changes Quarters to Canterbury and Dover
1694. Quartered in Leicestershire and Nottinghamshire
1696. Embarks for the Netherlands, and garrisons Dendermonde
—— Joins the Army encamped at Gemblours under the command of King William

Year.	
1696.	Detached to Ghent, where it winters
1697.	In the Spring marches to Brabant
——	20th September. Treaty of Ryswick. Regiment returns to England during the Winter
1698 to 1701.	Quartered in Ireland
1701.	15th June. Embarks at the Cove of Cork
——	8th July. Arrives at Helvoetsluys
——	21st September. Reviewed by King William on Breda Heath. Winter Quarters, Geitruydenberg
1702.	March. Leaves Winter Quarters, and encamps near Rosendael
——	8th March. Death of William III, and Accession of Queen Anne. The Regiment is designated "The Queen's Regiment"
——	24th April. Leaves Rosendael and encamps at Cranenburg, covering Siege of Kayserswerth
——	10th June. Retires to Nimeguen
——	September. Siege of Venloo
——	18th September. Storming of Fort St. Michael
——	October. Siege of Ruremonde and Liege
——	23rd October. Grenadiers engaged in storming Citadel of Liege. Winter Quarters in Holland
1703.	April. The Duke of Marlborough reviews the Regiment
——	7th May. The Regiment joins Camp at Macswyck
——	August. Siege of Huy
——	September. Siege of Limburg. Winter Quarters, Breda
1704.	Early in May Regiment leaves Breda, arrives at Mayence in the beginning of June, and joins Army about end of month
——	2nd July. Battle of Schellenberg
——	13th August. Battle of Blenheim
——	October and November. Encamped at Croon-Weissenberg, covering the Siege of Landau. Winter Quarters at Breda
1705.	Early in May the Duke of Marlborough reviews the Regiment in Camp near Limburg
——	July. Siege of Huy
——	18th July. Forcing the French Lines of Mehaigne, near Helixem
——	October. Siege of Sandvliet. Winter Quarters, Breda
1706.	Regiment leaves Breda early in May, and joins Army at Bilsen
——	23rd May. Battle of Ramilies
——	August. Siege of Menin

Year.		
1706.	September. Siege of Aeth. Winter Quarters, Ghent	
1707.	16th May. Leaves Ghent and joins Army near Brussels; in the Autumn again returns to Ghent for Winter Quarters	
1708.	March and April. Regiment embarks at Ostend; arrives at Tynemouth; returns to the Netherlands, and again disembarks at Ostend	
—	The Duke of Marlborough reviews Regiment at Ghent early in May	
—	22nd May. Leaves Ghent and joins Army near Brussels	
—	11th July. Battle of Oudenarde	
—	After the Battle the Regiment was engaged in covering the Siege of Lisle, and in the Relief of Brussels. Winter Quarters, Ghent	
—	28th September. Battle of Wynendale	
1709.	July and August. Siege of Tournay	
—	11th September. Battle of Malplaquet	
—	After Battle, covering Siege of Mons. Winter Quarters, Ghent	
1710.	14th April. Leaves Ghent and rejoins Army	
—	21st April. Passage of French Lines at Pont-à-Vendin	
—	May and June. Covering the Siege of Douay	
—	15th July to 9th November. Encamped at Villers Brulin. Covering Sieges of Bethune, Aire, and St. Venant	
1711.	5th August. Passage of the French Lines at Arleux	
—	Siege of Bouchain	
1713.	14th April. Peace of Utrecht. During Winter Regiment quartered at Ghent	
—	Garrisons the Citadel of Ghent	
1714.	23rd August. Returns to England and is quartered at Berwick	
1715.	April. Is sent to Ireland	
—	October. Embarks for Scotland, and is quartered in Glasgow	
—	11th November. Joins the Army of the Duke of Argyle, near Stirling	
—	13th November. Battle of Dunblane	
1716.	Receives the title of "THE KING'S REGIMENT," and authorised to bear as a Regimental Badge the WHITE HORSE	
1717.	Is sent to Ireland	
1721.	Returns to England, lands near Chester, and marches to Berwick	
1722.	In the Spring marches south, and encamps on Salisbury Plain	

Year.	
1722.	30th August. Reviewed by King George I
——	September. Marches to Worcester and afterwards to Bristol
——	During the Winter is sent to Ireland
1727.	Returns to England, but in the Autumn is sent back to Ireland
1739.	In the Autumn arrives in England
1742.	During the Winter embarks for Flanders and lands at Ostend
1743.	26th June. Battle of Dettingen
1745.	11th May. Battle of Fontenoy
——	Returns to England, and joins Army of Field-Marshal Wade, near Newcastle
——	24th December. Leaves Newcastle and marches to Edinburgh
1746.	17th January. Battle of Falkirk
——	16th April. Battle of Culloden
——	During the Summer embarks for Holland
——	9th October. Arrives at Maestricht
——	11th October. Battle of Roucoux
1747.	1st July. Battle of Val
1748.	18th October. Treaty of Aix-la-Chapelle. During the Winter the Regiment returns to England
1750.	Is sent to Gibraltar
1752.	Returns to England
1756.	Is augmented by a Second Battalion
1757.	Both Battalions are encamped near Dorchester, and are afterwards sent to the Isle of Wight
——	September. Both Battalions embark to make a descent on the Coast of France. Island of Aix captured
1758.	The Second Battalion constituted the Sixty-third Foot
1760.	May. The Regiment embarks for Germany
——	June. Lands at Bremen
——	20th June. Joins Camp near Fritzlar of Allied Armies, commanded by Prince Ferdinand of Brunswick
——	10th July. Battle of Corbach
——	31st July. Battle of Warbourg
——	December. Cantoned in villages near the River Weser
——	5th September. Action of Zirenberg
——	16th October. Action of Campen
1761.	15th–16th July. Battle of Kirch-Denkern
1762.	24th June. Battle of Groebenstein
——	Siege of Cassel
——	8th November. Treaty of Fontainebleau
1763.	Regiment returns to England, and is quartered in Scotland
1765.	Quartered in England

Year.
1766. Reviewed in Hyde Park by King George III
1766–8. Quartered at Dover Castle....
1768. May. Embarks for Canada, and is quartered at Quebec, Montreal, &c.
1773. Proceeds to Upper Canada, and is quartered at Niagara, Detroit, &c. ....
1776. 19th May. Captain G. Foster captures the American Fort of the Cedars....
1777. August. A Detachment assists in the Siege of Fort Stanwix
1785. September. The Regiment returns to England
1786–87. Quartered at Plymouth
1790–91–92. Quartered in Jersey
1793. Quartered in Ireland
—— June–July. The Flank Companies employed at the Capture of Martinique and Guadaloupe
1794. April. The Regiment returns to England
—— June. Embarks for Ostend....
—— Evacuates Ostend, and joins Army of the Duke of York in Holland
—— November. Assists in Defence of Nimeguen
1795. January. Evacuation of Holland and Retreat to Germany
—— May. Embarks at Bremen-Lee, and arrives in England....
—— November. Embarks for the West Indies. Six Companies are driven back by a Storm
1796. March. Six Companies at Newport
—— 24th March. Four Companies land at Grenada, and are present at Capture of Port Royal
—— April. Six Companies quartered at Basingstoke....
—— July. Six Companies quartered in Scotland, where they are joined in October by Four Companies from the West Indies
1799. Quartered in Guernsey
—— 6th May. Embarks for Portsmouth
—— 10th May. Arrives at Spithead
—— 27th May. Sets sail for Minorca
—— 18th June. Disembarks at Port Mahon, and is quartered there until August, 1800
1800. 12th August. Inspected by Sir Ralph Abercrombie
—— 28th August to 7th October. Expedition to Cadiz
—— 22nd October to 4th November. On Board Ship at Gibraltar

* These dates are taken from MS. Journal of the late General Thomas Evans, colonel Eighty-first, then a lieutenant in the King's (*vide* Appendix II, No. 72).

Year.		
1800.	21st November to 21st December. On Board Ship at Malta	*
1801.	1st January to 22nd February. On Board Ship in Bay of Marmorice	*
——	8th March. Lands in Egypt. Battle of Aboukir	
——	13th March. Battle of Mandora	
——	21st March. Battle of Alexandria	
——	19th April to 5th May. Encamped near Rosetta	
——	9th May. Action of Rahmanie	*
——	27th June. Surrender of Cairo	
——	30th August. Surrender of Alexandria	
1802.	In Garrison at Gibraltar	
1803.	August. Returns to England, and lands at Portsmouth	
1804.	27th August. Reviewed at a Camp near Eastbourne by the Duke of York	
——	25th December. Establishment augmented by a Second Battalion	70 and
1805.	January. First Battalion quartered at Colchester, Second Battalion at Doncaster	70 and
——	29th October. First Battalion embarks for the Continent, and lands at Cuxhaven	
1806.	11th February. Embarks for England at Bremen-Lee	
——	26th February. Disembarks at Ramsgate	
——	March. Second Battalion marches from York to Scotland	
——	March. First Battalion embarks at Liverpool for Ireland	
——	December. Second Battalion returns to England	
1807.	23rd July. The First Battalion embarks at Dublin	
——	27th July. It disembarks at Liverpool	
——	16th August. First Battalion having been detailed for expedition against Copenhagen, lands at Wisbech	
——	14th October. Embarks at Copenhagen, and disembarks at Portsmouth in November	
1808.	January. First Battalion embarks for North America	
——	April. Lands at Halifax	
——	November. Embarks for the West Indies	
1809.	29th January. Expedition against Martinique leaves Carlisle Bay	
——	2nd February. Action of the Heights of Surirey	
——	24th February. Surrender of Fort Bourbon	
——	17th April. First Battalion returns to Halifax	
——	May. Second Battalion quartered at Pevensey	

* These dates are taken from MS. Journal of the late General Thomas Evans, colonel Eighty-first, then a lieutenant in the King's (*vide* Appendix II, No. 72).

Year.		
1809.	16th July.	Its flank companies embark at Portsmouth, and land at Walcheren
—	September.	Flank companies return to Portsmouth
—	December.	Second Battalion sent to Jersey
1810.	28th May.	First Battalion lands at Quebec
—	21st June.	Second Battalion lands at Portsmouth
—	August.	Six companies (Second Battalion) embark for Nova Scotia and New Brunswick
1812.	In the Summer First Battalion moved from Quebec to Montreal	
—	In the Autumn moved to Upper Canada	
1813.	13th February.	Attack on Ogdenberg
—	27th April.	Defence of York
—	27th May.	Defence of Fort George
—	29th May.	Attack on Sackett's Harbour
—	5th June.	Surprise of American Camp at Stoney Creek
—	29th December.	Attack on Black Rock
1814.	February.	Winter March of Second Battalion from St. John's, New Brunswick, to Quebec
—	5th July.	Action near Chippawa (First Battalion)
—	23rd July.	Battle of Lundy's Lane (First Battalion)
—	August.	Siege of Fort Erie commenced (First Battalion)
—	6th September.	Battle of Plattsburg (Second Battalion)
—	21st September.	Siege of Fort Erie abandoned. First Battalion sent to Montreal
1815.	June.	Both Battalions embark for England at Quebec
—	July.	First Battalion lands at Portsmouth
—	24th December.	Second Battalion reduced
1816.	February.	Regiment sent to Ireland
1818.	January.	Embarks at Cork for Malta
1819.	19th January.	Leaves Malta and disembarks at Corfu
1824.	June.	Embarks at Cephalonia
—	3rd August.	Disembarks at Portsmouth
1826.	March.	Embarks at Plymouth, and disembarks at Glasgow
1827.	January.	Embarks for Ireland, and disembarks at Belfast
1830.	Service Companies embark for Nova Scotia and disembark at Halifax in July	
—	Depôt Companies embark for England and disembark at Liverpool	
1833.	May.	Service Companies embark at Nova Scotia
—	June.	Disembark at Bermuda
—	July.	Are sent to Jamaica
1835.	30th June.	Depôt Companies disembark at Cork

Year.		
1838.	August.	Depôt Companies change Quarters from Ireland to Guernsey....
1839.	April.	Service Companies embark at Jamaica
——	May.	Disembark at Halifax
1841.		In the Autumn Depôt Companies change Quarters from Guernsey to Ireland
——	2nd December.	Service Companies embark at Halifax ....
——	27th December.	Disembark at Cork
1842.		In the Spring Regiment moves to Dublin ....
1843.	April.	Changes Quarters from Dublin to Manchester ....
——	October.	Changes Quarters from Manchester to Bolton....
1844.	3rd to 9th December.	Changes Quarters from Bolton to Chester
——	26th to 30th December.	Changes Quarters from Chester to Weedon
1845.	13th June.	Changes Quarters from Weedon to Portsmouth
1846.	25th to 30th April.	Embarks for India
——	1st to 29th August.	Disembarks at Bombay, and is quartered at Poona....
1848.	29th September to 18th October.	Changes Quarters from Poona to Kurrachee
1850.	11th November to 19th December.	Changes Quarters from Kurrachee to Deesa
1853.	1st and 4th December.	Regiment leaves Deesa ....
1854.	20th and 24th January.	Arrives at Agra....
1855.	24th November to 30th December.	Changes Quarters from Agra to Jellundur
1857.	10th May.	Sepoy Mutiny breaks out at Meerut ....
——	13th May.	Fort of Phillour secured
——	7th June.	Sepoy troops at Jellundur mutiny
——	14th June.	Regiment leaves Jellundur
——	28th June.	Joins the Army before Delhi....
——	9th July.	Action of Subzee Mundee
——	14th July.	Sortie repulsed ....
——	18th July.	Sortie repulsed ....
——	23rd July.	Sortie repulsed ....
——	12th August.	Attack on post at Ludlow Castle ....
——	7th September.	Ludlow Castle and the Khoodsia-Bagh seized
——	14th September.	Assault of the City
——	15th to 20th September.	Operations in the City.... 123—
——	24th September.	Colonel Greathed's Column crosses the Jumna
——	28th September.	Action of Bulandshahr ....
——	5th October.	Action of Alighur

Year.		
1857.	10th October.	Battle of Agra
—	28th October.	Establishment augmented by a Second Battalion ... 133 and
—	30th October.	First Battalion crosses the Ganges at Cawnpore
—	3rd November.	Action at Marigunj
—	14th November.	Action of Dilkoosha
—	16th to 22nd November.	Relief of Lucknow
—	29th November.	First Battalion recrosses the Ganges
—	2nd to 5th December.	Actions near Cawnpore
—	6th December.	Gwalior Contingent attacked and dispersed
1858.	2nd January.	Action of Khuda Gunj
—	23rd January to 9th February.	First Battalion detached to Agra
—	23rd March.	Second Battalion changes Quarters from Buttevant to Kinsale
—	1st and 2nd July.	Changes Quarters from Kinsale to the Curragh Camp
—	19th to 28th July.	First Battalion changes Quarters from Agra to Futtehghur
—	7th September.	Service Companies of Second Battalion embark at Kingstown. Depôt Companies quartered at Templemore
—	13th September.	Service Companies Second Battalion land at Gibraltar
—	18th October.	First Battalion crosses Ganges at Futtehghur, and joins Column of Brigadier Hale
—	24th October.	Capture of Sandee
1859.	16th January.	Recrosses Ganges and Reoccupies Futtehghur
—	16th November.	Reviewed by Lord Clyde, and Ball given to Lady Canning
—	2nd and 24th December.	Leaves Futtehghur
1860.	31st January, 1st and 13th February.	Arrives at Calcutta
—	5th May.	Headquarters embark at Calcutta
—	5th September.	Disembark at Gosport
1861.	8th August.	1st Battalion changes Quarters from Gosport to Aldershot
1862.	2nd September.	Changes Quarters from Aldershot to Sheffield
1863.	25th September.	Second Battalion embarks at Gibraltar
—	1st October.	Lands at Malta
1864.	12th March.	Bursting of Reservoir and Inundation at Sheffield

Year.		
1864.	22nd July.	First Battalion changes Quarters from Sheffield to Manchester....
1865.		Depôt from Templemore joins Headquarters
——	16th March.	First Battalion embarks at Liverpool
——	17th March.	Disembarks at Kingstown and marches to the Curragh
——	20th and 26th July.	Changes Quarters from Curragh to Dublin
1866.	9th March.	Embarks at Kingstown
——	19th March.	Lands at Malta
1868.	24th February.	Second Battalion embarks at Malta
——	6th March.	Disembarks at Portsmouth, and is moved by Rail to Aldershot
——	10th October.	First Battalion embarks at Malta....
——	3rd November.	Disembarks at Bombay, and is moved to Poona by Rail
1869.	1st April.	Second Battalion is moved by Rail from Aldershot to Portsmouth, and there embarks....
——	10th April.	Disembarks at Liverpool and is moved to Bury
——	17th and 18th November.	First Battalion leaves Poona....
1870.	26th January.	Arrives at Nusseerabad
——	18th October.	Second Battalion changes Quarters from Bury to Manchester
——	24th October.	The Viceroy, Lord Mayo, reviews the First Battalion
1872.	25th January.	First Battalion leaves Nusseerabad
——	3rd and 4th March.	Arrives at Cawnpore....
——	17th July.	Second Battalion changes Quarters from Manchester to Preston ....
1873.	1st April.	The United Kingdom divided into Military Districts and Sub-districts, and the King's Regiment assigned to the 13th or Liverpool Sub-district
——	11th August to 12th September.	Second Battalion encamped at Cannock Chase....
——	12th September.	It embarks at Birkenhead
——	13th September.	Lands at Kingstown, and is moved by Rail to the Curragh Camp....
——	30th September.	Is moved by Rail to Cork
——	24th October.	First Battalion leaves Cawnpore ....
——	27th November.	Joins Camp of Exercise at Bhugwanpoor near Roorkee....
1874.	16th March.	Leaves Camp ....
——	25th and 29th March.	Arrives at Chakrata
1875.	20th April.	Second Battalion is moved by Rail from Cork to Fermoy
——	20th May.	Is moved by Rail from Fermoy to the Curragh

Year.		
1875.	20th September.	Returns to Fermoy
—	15th, 16th, and 17th November.	First Battalion leaves Chakrata
—	11th December.	Joins Camp of Exercise at Bussai near Delhi
1876.	7th January.	Reviewed by the Prince of Wales
—	18th January.	Leaves Camp of Exercise
—	17th March.	Arrives at Peshawur
—	29th May.	Second Battalion embarks at Queenstown
—	31st May.	Disembarks at Portsmouth, and is moved by Rail to Camp at Aldershot
1877.	1st January.	The Queen Proclaimed Empress of India
—	14th February.	First Battalion leaves Peshawur
—	15th February.	Arrives at Nowshera
1877.	10th July.	Second Battalion Reviewed in Windsor Great Park by Queen Victoria
—	21st September.	Embarks at Portsmouth
—	26th October.	Disembarks at Bombay
—	19th November.	The First Battalion leaves Nowshera
—	29th November.	The two Battalions meet on the March at Camp Mundra near Rawal Pindi
—	3rd December.	Second Battalion arrives at Rawal Pindi
1878.	3rd January.	First Battalion embarks at Bombay
—	11th January.	Disembarks at Aden
—	17th April.	Warrington Barracks occupied by Depôt Companies of both Battalions
—	15th October.	Second Battalion leaves Rawal Pindi
—	21st November.	Crosses Afghan Frontier at Thull
—	2nd December.	Battle of the Peiwar Kotal
—	28th December.	First Battalion embarks at Aden
1879.	23rd January.	Disembarks at Portsmouth, and is moved by Rail to Warley
—	24th March.	Second Battalion Inspected by General Sir F. Paul Haines, Commander-in-Chief
—	27th May.	Peace of Gundamuck
—	3rd September.	Massacre at Cabul of the Envoy Sir Louis Cavagnari and Suite
—	14th October.	Attack on Camp at Ali Kheyl repulsed
1880.	21st October.	Second Battalion Recrosses Afghan Frontier at Thull
—	29th November.	Arrives at Meean Meer
—	7th December.	First Battalion moved by Train from Warley to Manchester
1881.	1st July.	The two Battalions of the 2nd Royal Lancashire Militia incorporated with the two of THE KING's, and the four Battalions designated THE KING's (LIVERPOOL REGIMENT)

Year.		
1881.	7th December.	First Battalion moved by Rail from Manchester to Bradford with detachments of two Companies at Tynemouth, one Company at Liverpool, and one Company at the Isle of Man.
1882.	29th April.	Her Majesty's commands given to inscribe on the colours the victories of Blenheim, Ramilies, Oudenarde, and Malplaquet*.
——	29th July.	First Battalion moved by Rail from Bradford, embarked at Liverpool, and on 31st landed at Queenstown; Headquarters and six Companies were quartered at Cork, and two at Haulbowline.
——	23rd August.	Two Companies detached to Fort Carlisle.
——	20th September.	Her Majesty's approval intimated of the Regiment being permitted to bear on its colours the word Dettingen†.
——	9th October.	Detachment at Fort Carlisle rejoins Headquarters at Cork.

---

* 20
Gen. No.
1549.

Horse Guards,
War Office, S.W.,
29th April, 1882.

SIR,

By desire of H.R.H. the Field Marshal Commanding-in-Chief, I have the honour to acquaint you that Her Majesty has been graciously pleased to command that the victories of Blenheim, Ramilies, Oudenarde, and Malplaquet, shall be inscribed on the colours of the Liverpool Regiment, and the same shall be recorded in the next issue of the "Queen's Regulations and Orders for the Army," in addition to the present achievements.

I have the honour to be, &c.,
(Signed)   G. J. WOLSELEY, A.-G.

The Officer Commanding 1st Battalion
Liverpool Regiment, Bradford.

---

† 20
Gen. No.
1470.

Horse Guards,
War Office, S.W.,
20th September, 1882.

SIR,

By desire of H.R.H. the Field Marshal Commanding-in-Chief, I have the honour to acquaint you that Her Majesty has been graciously pleased to approve of the Liverpool Regiment being permitted to bear on its colours the word Dettingen in commemoration of the battle fought at that place on the 27th June, 1743.

I have the honour to be, &c.,
(Signed)   R. G. H. TAYLOR, A.-G.

The Officer Commanding 1st Battalion
Liverpool Regiment, Cork.

An Epitome of the Story of the 8th The King's Regiment

******

This skilfully constructed narrative was contributed to the *Warrington Guardian* of 11th June, 1881, by Mr. H. Manners Chichester, a contributor of long standing to military and scientific periodicals, and is reprinted by his kind permission, and that of the editor of the *Guardian*, In it the most notable incidents of the good, faithful, and gallant services performed by the regiment during a period of nearly two hundred years, the many arduous campaigns, the many memorable victories, the many glorious achievements with which the name of the King's Regiment will for ever be associated, are presented in a very interesting and attractive form, and are grouped together in a manner which renders them easy to be remembered. It therefore seemed to me that Mr. Chichester's narrative would be a most suitable introduction to prefix to the detailed records of the incidents (many of them trivial and uninteresting) of each year of the regimental history.—A. C. R

******

A regiment great in history bears so far a resemblance to the immortal gods as to be old in power and glory, yet to have always the freshness of youth.—*Kinglake* (Vol.V, Chap. 1, sec. 6).

Not alone in their military details, but apart from and beyond these in their wider associations, the careers of our older regiments are replete with meaning to whoever can discern the full scope and reach of British history during the last two hundred years; and of none may this be said more truly than of the brave old corps that forms the subject of the present brief sketch.

The Eighth (the King's) Regiment, which is now localised at Warrington, and has become the King's (Liverpool Regiment), dates its origin from the days of the Duke of Monmouth's rebellion, having been raised by one of King James's courtiers, Robert, Lord Ferrars of Chartley, on 19th June, 1685. It consisted originally of ten companies, which, in the fashion of the day, were composed partly of musketeers, partly of pikemen. Of these, one company was raised by Lord Ferrars personally, in Hertfordshire; another at Derby, by Colonel John Beaumont, a veteran officer who had fought in the wars of Charles I's. reign, and afterwards commanded the regiment at the Battle of the Boyne; a third in the neighbourhood of London, having its quarters in the suburban villages of Islington and Holloway; while the remaining seven were raised in Derbyshire and the country round about. The rendezvous was at Derby.

This same year a camp was formed on Hounslow Heath, where were high revels and much licence, and withal, "divers jealousies and discourses as to the meaning of the array." Among the troops there collected was My Lord Ferrars', now known as the "Princess Anne of Denmark's Regiment," making a brave show, we are told, in the Stuart colours—red coats with bright yellow facings, yellow vests and knickerbockers, and cavalier hats tied up with yellow ribbons. The regiment afterwards returned northwards, and was augmented by a company of grenadiers, raised by Sir John Reresby, M.P., at York. (Some interesting details, military as well as political, will be found in *Sir John Reresby's Diary*, a new and revised edition of which has recently—1881—been published).

In November, 1686, Fitzjames, Buke of Berwick, a natural son of the king, lately returned from the wars in Hungary, was appointed colonel of the regiment, whence arose an incident that caused much stir at the time, although Macaulay accords it but casual mention. Berwick proposed to introduce a certain number of Irish Papists into the regiment as recruits. Colonel Beaumont and five other captains present with the regiment, which then laid at Portsmouth, refused to receive them, and memorialised the king, stating that their companies were at full strength; that they could not discharge good men and Englishmen to make room for "foreigners;" and they claimed the right of choosing their own men or resigning their commissions.

Much incensed, the king despatched a troop of the Blues, to bring the contumacious "Portsmouth Captains," as they were henceforth styled, to Windsor, where they were arraigned before a general court-martial, and found guilty of disobedience; one member of the court, Churchill, afterwards Duke of Marlborough, voting for sentence of death—with the Machiavellian design, some contemporaries alleged, of further increasing the king's unpopularity. The sentence actually passed was that of dismissal from the service, the king refunding, or promising to refund, the sums disbursed by the prisoners in raising their companies. In the next reign one at least of their officers was restored—Beaumont, who fought at the head of the regiment, as before stated, at the passage of the Boyne in 1690. This first page of the regimental history closes with the Revolution of 1688.

With the wiser rule of King William came many innovations and improvements in army discipline. The regiment served through King William's Irish campaigns, from the siege of Carrickfergus to the fall of Limerick. In 1696-97, it was in Flanders. And thither it was sent again in 1701.

When the Princess Anne succeeded to the throne, the regiment, which heretofore had been called after her, was directed to style itself "the Queens," under which designation it appears in the narratives of Marlborough's campaigns, through which it served with the greatest distinction.

★★★★★★

(This title was also conferred at the same time on the present 4th (King's Own), but that corps was serving as marines in the Mediterranean and in Spain, and was not with the Duke of Marlborough.

★★★★★★

The grenadiers of the regiment signalised themselves much at the storming of the citadel of Liege at a very early stage of the war, in 1702, and the regiment subsequently shared in the glories of Blenheim, of Oudenarde, of Ramilies, and of Malplaquet.

★★★★★★

The following list of officers of the King's Regiment who were present at the Battle of Blenheim, and memorandum of casualties, is extracted from an article contributed to the *Broad Arrow* of 21st January, 1882, by Mr. H. Manners Chichester. It was copied by him from a MS., preserved in the public records, which it is believed has hitherto escaped the researches of regimental historians.—A. C. R.

The King's (afterwards Eighth the King's), then Brigadier-General Webb's.—Survivors: Brigadier-General Webb, colonel;

Lieutenant-Colonel Sutton; Major Ramsey; Captains Coulombier, Ra. Congreve, — Hammers, W. Congreve, — Napper, Fielding, Kater, Farcey; Lieutenants E. Loyd, Walker, De Cosne, Adams, Rupton, Balfoure, Clavers, Morton, Goudet, Whitney, Cuttle, Kerr, Bozier (wounded); Ensigns Smith, Paul Lewis, Fletcher, Barton, Hobart, Mason (wounded), Loyd (wounded); Chaplain Reverend George Powell; Adjutant H. Whitney; Quartermaster B. Cuttle; Surgeon John Chambers; Mate Charles Lowndes; thirty-six sergeants, thirty-nine corporals; six hundred and twenty-nine drummers and soldiers. Officers killed; None.

★★★★★★

Under its colonel, Webb, it greatly distinguished itself in the wood of Wynendale during the siege of Lisle, and laboured and fought at many a stubborn siege and in many a hardly-contested field, the names whereof have now well-nigh lost the meaning they once had to English ears. During these campaigns the ancient pike finally gave place to the modern musket; and the flank-sections of pikemen had disappeared from its companies when the regiment returned home in 1714.

In 1715, the regiment was engaged in suppressing the Rebellion in Scotland. At the Battle of Dunblane, while changing front, it was surprised by the furious onset of an immense body of Highlanders armed with claymore and target, the *élite* of the insurgent clans. Before the soldiers had time to level their muskets, the ranks were broken, and all formation and order were lost; the soldiers and Highlanders became a confused crowd of combatants, struggling with desperation for mastery, amongst whom, in some places, might be seen a veteran of the Eighth contending successfully against four or five mountaineers. Brigadier-General the Earl of Forfar, riding at the head of the regiment, was wounded and taken prisoner; Lieutenant-Colonel Hanmer, who commanded it, was surrounded; he held several opponents at bay for a short time, but was overpowered and killed. Six other officers, four sergeants, and ninety-seven privates were likewise slain; many others were wounded, and many taken prisoners. The regiment would have been utterly destroyed had not a very gallant charge of dragoons enabled the survivors to fall back and reform their ranks.

After the suppression of the rebellion, while stationed at Glasgow, King George I. was graciously pleased to reward the regiment with the distinguished title, which it at present bears. The King's Regiment of Foot. The facings were at the same time changed from yellow to blue, and the regiment was authorised to bear as its regimental badge the White Horse, within the garter. This badge was copied from the reverse of a medal struck at Hanover, to commemorate the accession to the electorate of George Lewis, Duke of Hanover, afterwards George I. of England. The White Horse on a field gules has for many centuries been the armorial bearing of the illustrious House of Brunswick. It was assumed by Henry the Proud, in 1123, on his marriage with Gertrude, daughter and heiress of the Emperor Lothaire II., and lineal descendant of Wittekend, the first of the kings of ancient Saxony or Westphalia. The banner of Wittekend bore a *Black* Horse, which, on his conversion to Christianity by Charlemagne, was altered to *White*, as the emblem of the pure faith he had embraced.

It is worthy of notice that a proposal was made about this time to localise particular regiments, on the principle recently adopted, but was negatived on the ground that the system would prevent the employment of the troops in case of insurrections. There was even a plan for erecting barracks for six thousand men in Hyde Park, the designs for which, strangely at variance with modern notions, have lately been disentombed.

And now followed a long interval of twenty-seven years passed at home in the duty of "aiding and abetting the civil magistrates when thereunto required," as the War Office books of the time have it, which appears to have been pretty frequently, although a growing reliance on civil authority is plainly traceable from year to year, in the evident desire to avoid recurring to force.

In a collection of carefully executed drawings of British uniforms about the year 1742, which is preserved in the British Museum, the King's is depicted with facings of a bright lively blue, the veritable heraldic azure, but whether this was a fancy of the artist's or the hue really adopted at first we know not.

The regiment went to the Low Countries in 1742, and made the campaigns in Flanders and Germany. It fought at Dettingen and at Fontenoy; it was among the picked troops hurried home on the news of the Pretender's landing; with Duke William of Cumberland it fought the clans at Falkirk and on Culloden Muir; then, returning to the Low Countries, it shared in the bloody fight at Val and in various other actions, until the peace sent it to Gibraltar, where it served until 1751.

When war with France appeared once more imminent, in 1756,

the King's, in common with certain other old regiments, received instructions to form a second battalion. The regiment was then at Plymouth, and the new battalion, presumably, was raised in the West of England. At any rate, the War Office "Marching Orders" show the recruiting rendezvous to have been at Plymouth. In 1758, it was formed into a separate corps, and has since had a distinguished and eventful career as the 63rd Regiment of Foot, which is now localised at Ashton-under-Lyne, and constitutes one of the line battalions of the Manchester Regiment under the new organisation.

The Eighth King's was with Sir John Mordaunt in the descent on the Isle of Aix in 1757; after which it went to Germany, and fought at Warbourg, Zierenberg, Campen, Kirch-Denkern, Groebenstein, and in sundry other engagements in the Seven Years' War. At the peace it came home.

In 1768, the regiment went to Canada, and for years was distributed in remote detached posts along the shores of the Canadian Lakes. In Canada it remained all through the American War of Independence, in the course of which detachments much distinguished themselves on various occasions. The most notable of the exploits performed by these detachments was the capture of the American Fort of the Cedars, by thirty-eight men of the King's, and a body of Canadian Volunteers and Indians, under the command of Captain George Forster. The garrison, three hundred and ninety strong, surrendered prisoners of war. A few days later, on 27th May, 1766, a flotilla of boats, having on board seven hundred men under command of Colonel Arnold, made an attempt to retake the fort, but these troops were signally repulsed by Captain Forster, and compelled to return to Montreal dispirited and exhausted. In 1785, the regiment again returned home.

At the outbreak of the French Revolutionary War the King's was in Ireland, and its varied record of active service begins with the capture of Martinique and Guadaloupe, at which its flank companies were present in the flank battalions of Sir Charles Grey's force. The rest of the regiment joined the Duke of York's army in Flanders, and served at Neiuport and Nimeguen, in the operations on the Waal, and in the terrible winter retreat through Holland and Westphalia to Bremen. Next it was employed in the West Indies, at the capture of St. Lucia, and in suppressing the insurrection in Grenada. In 1798, it was in Guernsey: in 1799, in Minorca: in 1800, it proceeded to Cadiz and Malta with the troops under Sir Ralph Abercromby, with whom it went to Egypt the year after.

It fought at the landing in the Bay of Aboukir, and in the great battle in front of Alexandria on 21st March, 1801, when the gallant Abercromby fell. It was among the troops under General Hutchinson which captured Rosetta and advanced as far as Ghizeh and Cairo; whence it descended the Nile to take part in the siege of Alexandria, which capitulated on 31st August, 1801. From Egypt the regiment went to Gibraltar, and thence returned home at the peace of Amiens. On renewal of the war with France in 1804, the Eighth King's raised a second battalion of "short service" men from the battalions of the Army of Reserve in the West Riding of Yorkshire and the adjacent parts of Lancashire. The men engaged for the continuance of the war or other period not exceeding seven years.

The First Battalion went with Lord Cathcart to Hanover in 1805; it served at the siege and capture of Copenhagen in 1807; the Second Battalion shared in the deadly Walcheren expedition in 1809.

The First Battalion went out to Nova Scotia in 1808, and thence accompanying the expedition to the West Indies, took part in the reduction of the island of Martinique. From the West Indies it went back to Nova Scotia. In 1810, it was sent to Canada. In 1812 war broke out with the United States, and the regiment, or detached companies belonging to it, were present in nearly all the actions fought on the Canadian frontier in 1812-13-14—at Fort George, Sackett's Harbour, Stoney Creek, Black Rock, Oswego, Chippewa, Lundy's Lane, &c. At the last-named engagement, otherwise known as Niagara, having been fought close to the Falls, the First Battalion of the King's greatly distinguished itself.

Meanwhile, (in 1810), the Second Battalion had been sent out to Nova Scotia and New Brunswick, and six companies thereof, with a party of seamen, under command of Major Evans of the First Battalion, made a memorable march on snow shoes through the backwoods from New Brunswick to Quebec in the winter of 1813-14. This battalion subsequently served in the expedition to Plattsburg.

At the peace of 1815, both battalions were brought home, and the Second Battalion was disbanded at Portsmouth. One who served with it at Plattsburg, the late Lieutenant-Colonel Bayly, lived to fight with the regiment before Delhi forty-three years afterwards It is interesting to note that two officers who fought with the King's in the American campaigns yet remain: Major Weyland, retired, and Lieutenant John Lowry, half-pay Ninety-Fifth Foot, who were then lieutenants.

In 1818, the King's, once more a single battalion corps, went to

Malta, and thence in 1819, to the Ionian Islands, where it continued during the Greek War of Independence. In 1830, it went to Nova Scotia; in 1833, to Bermuda. Thence it proceeded to Jamaica, then deep in the troubles of Abolition, where it served six years; after which, it went back to Nova Scotia, returning home in 1841.

In August, 1846, the regiment embarked for its first tour of service in India. It was at first stationed in the Bombay Presidency, and passed some time in Scinde. Afterwards, it was transferred to Bengal, and at the time of the outbreaks at Meerut and Delhi, in the spring of 1857, had not long removed from Agra to Jellundur in the Punjaub.

Early in the morning of the 13th, (the third day after the Meerut outbreak), a detachment of the regiment under Brevet-Major R. Stuart Barnes rendered an important service by seizing and securing the fort and magazine of Phillour. On the night of 7th June, the *sepoy* troops at Jellundur broke into open mutiny. On the 14th, the regiment received orders to join the force before Delhi. It accomplished the march from Jellundur to Delhi in fourteen days—during which the excessive heat and the forced marching severely tried the endurance of the men—the casualties from sunstroke or fever were Quartermaster Ross and eight men.

All through the three succeeding months of that most memorable siege, in drenching rain and deadly heat, amidst sore privations and in the shadow of death, the King's fought as it had fought on the plains of Flanders one hundred and fifty years before. At the repulse of the sorties of the 9th, 14th, and 18th July, of the attack by the enemy on the 23rd July, at the occupation of the Khoodsiabagh and Ludlow Castle on the 7th September, and in all the other operations up to the storm and capture, the regiment under its Colonel, Greathed, now General Sir E. Greathed, K.C.B., who had succeeded to the command soon after its arrival before Delhi, was in the thickest of the fight. Those who would learn more of this period of the regiment's history should read the stirring details, as given in the first volume of Malleson's *History of the Sepoy Mutiny*.

When the fall of the city struck the first great blow at the rebel cause, the King's formed part of a flying column under Brigadier Greathed, which was pushed on to clear the Doab between the Jumna and the Ganges of the rebel forces, and to reopen communications with Agra and Cawnpore. At Bulandshahr and Alighur Colonel Greathed attacked and dispersed two large bodies of rebels, and at Agra, on 10th October, after a forced march of forty-four miles, he signally repulsed an unexpected onset made on his camp by a force of about seven thousand mutinous *sepoys* from Neemuch, Mhow, Delhi, and Gwalior. In this brilliant action about five hundred of the mutineers were slain, and the whole of their artillery, consisting of twelve guns, was captured.

The regiment was next engaged with the force under Sir Colin Campbell, which relieved Lucknow on the 22nd November, 1857, and with him it returned to Cawnpore after Inglis's heroic garrison had been withdrawn from the Lucknow Residency and Outram reinforced at the Alumbagh. On the arrival of the column at Cawnpore, the garrison was found to be hard pressed by a force of twenty-five thousand mutineers with thirty-six guns. An attack made by the mutineers on the entrenchments on the 2nd December, was beaten off by the King's and other corps of Greathed's brigade, and on the 6th the brigade bore an active part in the crushing defeat inflicted on the enemy, who was driven from Cawnpore in headlong rout. The regiment was also engaged at Khuda Gunj (2nd January, 1858), and subsequently bore its share in the operations in Oude in 1858-59.

At the end of December, 1859, when, to quote the words of Lord Clyde, "the contest was brought to an end, the resistance of one hundred and fifty thousand armed men having been subdued with very moderate loss to Her Majesty's troops and with the most merciful forbearance towards the misguided enemy," the Eighth King's—which afterwards received permission to inscribe the names "Delhi" and "Lucknow" on its colours in memory of its distinguished services—was collected at Futtyghur, whence it subsequently moved to Fort William. In 1860, the regiment returned home, and out of twenty-one officers and five hundred non-commissioned officers and men landed at Portsmouth on 5th September of that year, it was observed that two officers and one hundred and ten non-commissioned officers and men had embarked there for India just fourteen years before.

Meanwhile a second battalion had been formed at Buttevant at the end of 1858. In the following year it embarked for Gibraltar, and from thence, in the autumn of 1863, it was sent on to Malta. At the termination of its tour of home service in March, 1866, the first battalion was also sent to Malta; then, for the first time, the old and new battalions met; and there, for the next two years, the two battalions of the King's served together.

In the spring of 1868, they were again separated. The second battalion returned to England, and the first went on *via* Suez to India, and was among the corps to whose lot it fell to greet the British Heir Apparent on that historic soil. After a turn of service at Aden the battalion returned home in 1879, and is now quartered at Manchester.

The second battalion which, about ten years ago, during its tour of home service, was likewise quartered for some time at Manchester, re-embarked in 1877, proceeding to India, where, on arrival, it was stationed at Rawal Pindee. In 1878, it joined the Kurum Field Force, under General Roberts, and under command of Lieutenant-Colonel Tanner, C.B., now commanding the first battalion at Salford, fought at the storming and capture of the Peiwar Kotal. (Brigadier Cobbe having been wounded during the action, Colonel Barry Drew succeeded to the command of the brigade, and Brevet Lieutenant-Colonel Tanner to the command of the battalion). The battalion continued with the force in the Kurum Valley during the subsequent operations in Afghanistan, and is at present stationed at Mean Meer.

Such, in brief outline, is the story of the King's Regiment from 1685, to the reorganisation of 1881. Military institutions are not exempt from the changes which time brings to all mundane things. Generations pass away and others fill their places—"the old order changeth, giving place to the new"—but the annals of the King's and of other old and famous regiments prove conclusively that brave deeds and soldierly devotion are not the prerogatives of any single generation, or the product of any special tactical system. It remains for the soldiers of the future to enter into the true spirit of their regimental traditions—to emulate the steady discipline which no less than personal valour distinguished those who preceded them—and we may rest assured that whenever opportunities offer they will illustrate anew the motto of the King's Regiment and of the Anglo-Saxon race, "*Nec aspera terrent*"—*No difficulties dismay.*

Part 1: Services of the First Battalion, 1685-1880

SECTION 1.—AT HOME, 1685-1692

1685. James Duke of Monmouth, natural son of King Charles II., erected the ensigns of rebellion in the west of England, in June 1685, and summoned the people to aid him in an attempt to dethrone his uncle, King James II., whose predilection to papacy occasioned the adventurous Monmouth to believe, that a protestant people would not submit to the government of that prince. The din of warlike preparation instantly spread throughout the land; corps of cavalry and infantry were speedily embodied for the support of the crown; and Egbert Lord Ferrars, of Chartly, whose father, Sir Robert Shirley, Baronet, was one of the sufferers in the royal cause in the time of King Charles I., was appointed to the command of one of the corps raised on that occasion; which, having been continued in the service to the present time, now bears the distinguished title of The Eighth, or The King's Regiment of Foot.

The first company was raised by Lord Ferrars, in Hertfordshire; the second by John Beaumont, Esq., in Derbyshire; the third by John Innis, Esq., near London; and the other seven by Rowland Okeover, Charles Chudd, Thomas Paston, William Cook, Simon Packe, Walter Burdet, and Thomas Orme, in Derbyshire: the general rendezvous of the regiment being at Derby. Each company was directed to consist of three officers, three sergeants, three corporals, two drummers, and one hundred private soldiers. Men flocked to the royal standard on this emergency; and such was the success which attended the appeal made to the loyalty of the people, that, although the warrants for raising the regiment were not issued until the 20th of June, on the 26th, one company (Innis's) was complete in numbers, and ordered to march to

Islington and Holloway; and on the 4th of July Lord Ferrars' company was directed to march to St. Albans.

Lord Ferrars had held an appointment in the establishment of Queen Catherine in the preceding reign; he was highly esteemed at court, and his regiment was distinguished with the title of The Princess Anne of Denmark's Regiment of Foot, in honour of the King's second daughter (afterwards Queen Anne), who was married to Prince George of Denmark. (The regiment is styled the Princess Anne of Denmark's Regiment in the order for Major Innis's company to march to Islington and Holloway, 26th June, 1685.) The lieutenant-colonelcy was conferred on John Beaumont, Esq., and the majority on John Innis, Esq.

The captains were armed with pikes; the lieutenants with partisans; the ensigns with half-pikes; the sergeants with halberds; thirty rank and file of each company were pikemen, and seventy-three musketeers; the whole carried swords. The uniform was scarlet, lined and turned up with yellow; yellow waistcoats and breeches, white stockings, and white cravats, with broad-brimmed hats, having the brim turned up on one side, and ornamented with yellow ribands. (For details respecting arms and equipment, *vide* Appendix 4.)

The formation and arming of the regiment were in rapid progress, when the rebel bands were overthrown in a general action at Sedgemoor, on the 6th of July, and the Duke of Monmouth being afterwards captured and beheaded, all further resistance ceased. The several companies of the Princess Anne's regiment were immediately reduced to sixty men each, and on the 25th of July, to two sergeants, three corporals, two drummers, and fifty private soldiers each.

At the same time the eight companies were ordered from Derby, to the vicinity of London, and in the early part of August, the regiment encamped on Hounslow heath, where it was exercised by experienced officers, and twice reviewed by King James II. In September it struck its tents and marched to Chester, where it passed the remainder of the year.

1686. Leaving Chester in February, the regiment marched northwards; and, halting at Berwick, passed the succeeding twelve months in Northumberland; during which period the colonelcy was conferred on James Fitz-James (natural son of the king), a most gallant and enterprising youth, in the seventeenth year of his age, who had returned, a few days before, from the siege of Buda, where he had served with the Imperialists against the Turks.

1687. In the early part of this year, the colonel was created Duke of Berwick, and returned to the seat of war in Hungary. At the same time, the regiment left Berwick, and proceeding southwards, halted a few days in quarters near London. While on the march, the regiment was joined by an independent company of grenadiers, which had been raised at York, by Sir John Reresby, a political character, whose interesting memoirs are an agreeable addition to the history of the period in which he lived.

The regiment, consisting at this period of ten companies of pikemen and musketeers, and one of grenadiers, pitched its tents on Hounslow heath, in June: after taking part in several military spectacles, mock sieges, and battles, which were performed in the presence of the royal family and numerous assemblages of spectators, it marched into garrison at Portsmouth, in August, detaching, at the same time, the grenadier company to York.

On the Duke of Berwick's return from Hungary in the autumn, he was appointed Governor of Portsmouth.

1688. King James having resolved on the introduction of papacy and arbitrary government, determined, as a preliminary step, on the repeal of the penal laws; and the Earl of Oxford refusing to use his influence, as lord-lieutenant of the county of Essex, in procuring petitions in favour of this measure, was deprived of the colonelcy of the Royal Regiment of Horse Guards, which he had commanded twenty-seven years; and was succeeded by the Duke of Berwick, who continued to hold, also, the colonelcy of the Princess Anne's (now The King's) Regiment of Foot.

Thus the command of the eldest regiment of cavalry in the service, one of the most efficient corps of infantry, and the important fortress of Portsmouth, was given to one of the king's natural sons, who (though a gallant soldier and a discreet and trustworthy man) was a stanch papist, and consequently disqualified for these appointments by law; but the king claimed authority to use a dispensing power, by which he could enable his subjects to violate the law with impunity.

During the summer the army was again encamped on Hounslow heath; and King James having discovered that his soldiers had as much aversion to papacy as his other subjects, dismissed the regiments to their quarters, determining on a more general introduction of Roman Catholics into the army.

Commencing with the garrison at Portsmouth, the Duke of Berwick gave orders for a number of Roman Catholics, who had arrived from Ireland as recruits for Colonel Roger McEligott's Regiment, but who were not required for that corps, to be incorporated in the Princess Anne's Regiment (now The King's), of which His Grace was colonel. This proved a most trying occurrence to the officers, who prided themselves in keeping their companies complete, all English, and of stanch Protestant principles; and several of them determined not to contribute to the overthrow of the constitution and laws of their country by tacitly permitting the character of the corps to be thus changed.

The lieutenant-colonel, John Beaumont, and Captains Simon Packe, Thomas Orme, John Porte, William Cook, and Thomas Paston,—gentlemen of a patriotic spirit, resolved to adhere firmly to what appeared to be their duty to their country on this occasion, although it might prove detrimental to their private interests, or even fatal to their lives, and they sent a memorial to the Duke of Berwick, in which they remonstrated against receiving Irishmen into their companies, alleging that their numbers were complete and they had no allowance for supernumeraries; adding, that if an augmentation was ordered, they had sufficient credit in the country to obtain Englishmen; and concluding with a declaration of their determination to resign their commissions rather than receive Roman Catholic recruits into their companies.

The Duke of Berwick forwarded information of this occurrence to the king, and His Majesty was so incensed at their open resistance to his authority, that he commanded a cornet, quartermaster, and twenty *cuirassiers* of the Queen Dowager's Regiment, now Sixth Dragoon Guards, to proceed immediately to Portsmouth with the following mandate:

> James R.,
> Our will and pleasure is, that you forthwith send up unto our court at Whitehall, such officers of our dearest daughter the Princess Anne of Denmark's Regiment of Foot under your command, as have behaved themselves disrespectfully towards you, where they are to answer what shall be objected against them. And you are to cause them to be put into the custody of ten troopers and a quartermaster, who will be relieved by a like number of Major-General Werden's regiment of horse at our town of Godalming, according to our directions in that behalf. Given at our court, at Windsor, the 8th September, 1688.

By His Majesty's command,
William Blathwayt. (Official Records)

To Our dearly beloved natural Son,
James Duke of Berwick,
Governor of our town of Portsmouth.

These patriotic officers were accordingly arrested and sent under the charge of a guard of *cuirassiers* to London, from whence they were removed to Windsor, and on the 10th of September they were brought to trial before a general court-martial, held at Windsor Castle.

★★★★★★

My Lord,   Windsor, 8th September, 1688.
Lieutenant-Colonel Beamont, Captain Paston, Captain Packe, Captain Orme, Captain Port, and Captain Cook, of the Princess of Denmark's regiment of Foot, are to be tried here, Monday next, by a Gñall Court-Martial, for refusing to take forty Irishmen into their companies, as they were directed by their colonel, the Duke of Berwick, and for behaving themselves disrespectfully, both by writing and otherwise, towards His Grace.
    I am, &c.,

William Blathwayt.

To the Lord Langdale.

★★★★★★

Being found guilty of violating the fifteenth article of the regulations established by the king for the government of the army, a distinguished member of the court (Lord Churchill, afterwards Duke of Marlborough), is reported to have voted, from motives which have been variously represented, for passing a sentence of death against the prisoners.

★★★★★★

The following account of this occurrence is copied from the *Life of King James II.*, compiled from the memoirs written with his own hand:

"The Duke of Berwick having directed his Lieftenant-Col. Beamont, to admit some Irish Soldiers for recrutes, he being already engaged in the Prince of Orange's interest, was unwilling to have so many spy's upon him; so refused it, under a pretense that it was a dishonour to the subjects of England, to have recurs to forreigners (as he termed them) to fill up their company's, and proffered to lay down their commissions rather than comply: this refusal was too insolent to go upunished; the col., therefore, and such as joined with him were tried at a Council of war and cashired accordingly: but it was observed and wondered at afterwards, when peoples intentions came to light, that amongst those officers who sat upon them, some, who soon after appeared to be in the same interest with those they condemned, were nevertheless the most severe against them; particularly My Ld. Churchill moved to have them suffer death for their disobedience, foreseeing that such a piece of severity would reflect upon the king and inflame the people."

★★★★★★

But the Roman Catholic party had become alarmed at the news of an armament preparing in Holland, for the support of the Protestant interest in Great Britain, and, fearing to exasperate the people further by an act of cruel severity, the more lenient sentence of being dismissed the service was passed. The king himself had become sensible of the danger of proceeding to extremities, and when he commanded the sentence to be put into execution, he informed the six officers that they should be repaid the expense incurred in raising their companies, or in the purchase of their commissions.

These six gentlemen were viewed by the public as champions for the civil and religious liberties of their country, and as suffering for pure patriotic principles; they were styled the "Six Portsmouth Captains;" ballads were composed in their commendation and sung publicly; and their portraits were engraved and circulated among the zealous opposers of the proceedings of the Jesuitical councils which prevailed at court.

The conduct of the Roman Catholics generally had given rise to feelings of disgust among the Protestants; the soldiers of the regiment appear to have been filled with indignation at the treatment experienced by their officers, and a number of men deserted rather than serve with the Roman Catholic recruits, who had been forced into the regiment. No second attempt of a like character was, however, made; the regiment became more tranquil; Colonel Ramsay was appointed to the lieut-colonelcy; and Lieutenants Barnes, Fielding, Southern, Mackarty, and Fletcher, were promoted captains.

The appearance of the Prince of Orange with a powerful land force to support the Protestant interest, put an end to all farther usurpations; the king discovered that his soldiers would not fight in the cause of papacy, and fled to France, accompanied by the Duke of

Berwick.

The Prince of Orange having assumed the powers of the government, promoted the patriotic Lieutenant-Colonel Beaumont to the colonelcy of the regiment, by commission dated the 31st of December, 1688.

1689. A convention having conferred the crown on William and Mary, Prince and Princess of Orange, some resistance to Their Majesties' authority was experienced in Scotland, and the Princess Anne's Regiment was ordered to the north from its quarters at Southampton, where it was stationed after the flight of King James to France. It halted at Carlisle, and was there inspected on the 13th of June, by the commissioners appointed to re-model the army.

Edinburgh Castle having surrendered to the forces of King William, the regiment did not continue its march to Scotland; but nearly all Ireland having been preserved in the Roman Catholic interest by the Lord-Lieutenant, the Earl Tyrconnel, this was one of the corps selected to proceed thither with the army commanded by the Duke of Schomberg.

After encamping a short time near Chester, the several regiments embarked at Highlake, and anchoring in the Bay of Carrickfergus in the afternoon of the 13th of August, landed immediately and pitched their tents in the fields, near the shore. The siege of Carrickfergus was afterwards commenced; the Princess Anne's Regiment was one of the corps employed in this service, and, before the end of the month, the garrison surrendered.

Advancing from Carrickfergus to Dundalk, the army formed an intrenched camp at that place, on low wet ground: and the weather proving particularly rainy, the health of the soldiers suffered considerably. On the morning of the 21st of September, the camp was suddenly alarmed at the approach of the French and Irish forces, under King James, displaying their royal standard. The British troops stood to their arms, and the regiment was ordered to the trenches beyond the town; but the enemy withdrew without venturing an attack.

After losing a number of men at the unhealthy camp at Dundalk, the regiment marched into winter quarters, and was stationed at the frontier garrisons of Green Castle and Rosstrevor.

1690. In the spring of this year, the Princess Anne's Regiment was stationed at Londonderry; in June, King William arrived in Ireland to command the troops in person, and the officers and soldiers rejoiced at the prospect of having an opportunity of evincing their innate bravery and zeal for the Protestant interest under the eye of their sovereign. At the forcing of the passage of the Boyne, on the 1st of July, the regiment was brought in contact with the troops of King James, whose army was overpowered and driven from the field with loss. The Irish forces fled in dismay; but the French and Swiss retired in good order. The British pursued several miles, and afterwards encamped near the field of battle.

The immediate result of this victory was the capture of Dublin, and the flight of King James to France. The Princess Anne's Regiment was one of the corps reviewed by King William, at Finglass, on the 7th of July, on which occasion it mustered five hundred and twenty-six rank and file, exclusive of officers and non-commissioned officers.

From Dublin the regiment proceeded to Limerick, and was engaged in the siege of this important fortress. Several unfortunate occurrences prevented the capture of the city of Limerick on this occasion; and when the siege was raised, the regiment went into quarters.

Towards the end of September, the Earl of Marlborough arrived with several additional corps from England, and besieged Cork. The Princess Anne's Regiment was called from its quarters to take part in this enterprise, and the city was taken before the end of the month. The siege of Kinsale was afterwards resolved upon, and the attack on the forts was immediately commenced. The old fort was speedily taken, but the new fort held out until the middle of October, when everything being ready for an attack by storm, the garrison surrendered.

After the surrender of Kinsale, the Princess Anne's Regiment was placed in garrison at that town. About the beginning of November, a French ship, of thirty tons, laden with brandy and salt, sailed into the harbour, and anchored under the old fort, supposing the place to be in the hands of King James's adherents; but she was soon boarded and taken.

The garrison of Kinsale was well supplied with provisions; but the soldiers having been in the field in severe weather in September and October, their health suffered severely. On the regiment being removed to Cork, it left two hundred sick men behind; and soon after its arrival at Cork, nearly one hundred men were unfit for service; it, however, received recruits from England, and had above five hundred men fit for garrison duty throughout the winter.

1691. In the spring of this year, when the army took the field under General De Ginkell (afterwards Earl of Athlone), the Princess Anne's Regiment was left in quarters in the county of Cork, to hold the enemy in check on that side, and to secure several small garrisons from the attacks of the enemy; it was, consequently, prevented sharing in the capture of Ballymore and Athlone, in the victory of Aughrim, and in the reduction of Galway and in other places of less note. The wreck of King James's army having rallied at Limerick, where it was resolved to make a final effort to preserve Ireland in his interest, in the hopes of receiving succours from France, the regiments left in quarters in the county of Cork were ordered to join the army. The victorious English Army directed its march towards Limerick; the siege of this very important fortress was commenced, and before the end of September the garrison was forced to surrender.

1692. The reduction of Limerick terminated the contest in Ireland, and on the 16th of February the Princess Anne's Regiment embarked for England.

Shortly after its return from Ireland, the regiment embarked for the Netherlands, to serve with the army commanded by King William in person, against the forces of Louis XIV; but the order was countermanded, the shipping returned to port, and the regiment landed at Gravesend, in consequence of the receipt of information that King James had collected above fourteen thousand English and Irish, to whom the King of France had added several thousand men, under Marshal Belfonds, who were designed to sail from Cherbourg, La Hogue, and some other places in Normandy, under convoy of the French fleet, to land in Sussex, where they expected to be joined by a number of disaffected persons, and advancing immediately to London, to overturn the existing government, and replace King James on the throne.

To ensure success to their designs, a conspiracy was formed on the continent for the assassination of King William. The regiment was consequently detained in England, and preparations were made to repel the invaders; but while the public mind was agitated with various emotions, the French fleet was defeated off La Hogue, by the British and Dutch, and the danger instantly passed away.

Section 2—Abroad, 1692

The destruction of a great part of the French fleet, gave the British and their allies the uncontrolled dominion of the sea; a descent on the coast of France was contemplated; and the Princess Anne's Regiment marched to Portsmouth, where it embarked for this service, under the command of Lieutenant-General the Duke of Leinster. The French coast was menaced for many miles, and considerable alarm and consternation was produced; but a landing was found impracticable, and the fleet sailing to Ostend, the troops disembarked in the beginning of September, 1692, and encamped several days about a league from that place, in the direction of Nieuport, to refresh themselves after being so long on board of ship.

They were subsequently joined by a detachment from the confederate army, commanded by Lieutenant-General Talmash, and having taken possession of Fumes, fortified it against any sudden attack, for a winter cantonment. They afterwards repaired the works of Dixmude; and while this was in progress, the Princess Anne's Regiment was encamped within the ramparts; but on the arrival of five Dutch regiments to garrison the town, this corps marched out, and was subsequently placed in cantonments.

Section 3.—At Home, 1692-1696.

1693. The regiment returned to England during the winter, and was employed in garrison duty at Portsmouth, from whence it was removed in April, to Canterbury and Dover. The army in the Netherlands having suffered severely at the Battle of Landen, the regiment sent a draft of a hundred men to one of the regiments which had sustained a heavy loss.

1694. During this year the regiment was stationed in Leicestershire and Nottinghamshire.

1695. In December Colonel Beaumont was succeeded in the command of the regiment by Colonel John Richmond Webb, a most zealous and meritorious officer, who afterwards acquired considerable reputation in the wars of Queen Anne.

During the campaign of 1695, the French lost Namur, in the Spanish Netherlands, and Cazal in Italy, and these disasters, with their weakness on the Rhine, and in Catalonia, proved that the confederates had obtained a superiority. Louis XIV. resolved on extraordinary efforts, and issued, at the end of the campaign, commissions for raising between forty and fifty additional regiments.

The extensive preparations of the French monarch induced His Britannic Majesty to augment the number of his forces in the Netherlands, and the Princess Anne's was one of the regiments ordered to the seat of war. (The establishment of the regiment at this time was forty-four officers, one hundred and four non-commissioned officers, sixty-nine grenadiers, seven hundred and eighty privates.—*MS. Records, R.U.S.I.*)

Section 4.—Abroad, 1696-1697

1696. The regiment embarked in February; after its arrival in Flanders it was placed in garrison at Dendermonde, a strong town situate in a district of uncommon fertility, at the confluence of the Rivers Scheldt and Dender, eighteen miles south of Antwerp. Here it remained in comfortable quarters until the beginning of June, when it joined the troops under the Duke of Wirtemberg encamped on the banks of the Scheldt, from whence it proceeded to the main army, commanded by King William in person; and arriving at the camp at Gemblours, it was formed in brigade with the Royal Fusiliers, and the regiments of Mackay, Stanley, and Seymour, commanded by Brigadier-General Fitzpatrick.

After serving the campaign of this year, which was passed in marching and manoeuvring without any fighting, excepting a few slight skirmishes between detachments, the regiment was detached from the camp at Gammont, on the 21st of August, towards Ghent, in which city it afterwards passed the winter.

1697. From Ghent, the regiment marched, in the spring to Brabant; and was formed in brigade with a battalion of the (First) Royals, Prince George of Denmark's regiment (now Third Foot), the Royal Fusiliers, and Seymour's regiment, under the command of Brigadier-General O'Hara, afterwards Lord Tyrawley. The contending powers, had, however, become weary of the war; and in September a treaty of peace was signed at Ryswick.

Section 5.—At Home, 1697-1701.

1698. The Princess Anne's Regiment returned to England during the winter; and soon afterwards proceeded to Ireland: at the same time its numbers were reduced to a peace establishment. (Strength, forty-one officers, sixty-eight non-commissioned officers, fifty-four grenadiers, four hundred and sixty-six privates.—*MS. Records R.U.S.I.*)

1700-1701. On the decease of Charles II., king of Spain, without issue, in November, 1700, Louis XIV. procured the accession of his grandson, the Duke of Anjou, to the throne of Spain, to the prejudice of the house of Austria. Hostilities were determined upon; but before any declaration of war was made, a body of British troops was sent to Holland, under Brigadier-General Ingoldsby; the Dutch frontiers being menaced by the French, who detained the Dutch garrisons of the barrier towns of the Spanish Netherlands.

Section 6.—Abroad, 1701-1714.

The Princess Anne's Regiment was selected to proceed abroad; and, having embarked at the Cove of Cork, on the 15th of June, 1701, on board of ships of war, arrived at Helvoetsluys, in South Holland, on the 8th of July, where the officers and men were removed on board of Dutch vessels, and proceeded up the River Maese to Gertruydenberg. Leaving this station in the middle of September, the regiment pitched its tents on Breda heath, where it was reviewed by King William, on the 21st of that month, and subsequently returned to its former quarters.

1702. Great Britain not being then at war with France, the regiment received orders to take the field in the character of a corps of imperialists. It left its winter quarters in March, and traversing the country to Rosendael, encamped on the west bank of the Demer, beyond that town, where information was received of the decease of King William, on the 8th of March, and the accession of Queen Anne. The elevation of the Princess Anne of Denmark to the throne, was followed by the royal authority for this regiment to be designated "The Queen's Regiment." (The Fourth Foot having been designated "The Queen's Regiment" by King James II., continued to hold that title; and during the reign of Queen Anne, two corps were styled "Queen's Regiments." The Fourth served as marines in that reign.)

On the morning of the 24th of April, the regiment struck its tents, and traversing the country to the Duchy of Cleves, encamped at Cranenburg; forming part of the covering army during the siege of Kayserswerth, on the Lower Rhine, by the Germans. In May, Lord Cutts arrived at the camp with information that Great Britain and Holland had declared war against France and Spain. While the regiment lay at this camp, a French force of very superior numbers, commanded by the Duke of Burgundy and Marshal Boufflers, attempted, by a forced march, to cut off the communication of the small army at Cranenburg with Grave and Nimeguen.

The allies, in consequence, struck their tents a little before sunset on the 10th of June, and, marching all night, arrived about eight o'clock on the following morning within sight of Nimeguen; at the same time the French columns appeared on both flanks, marching with all possible expedition to surround the allies.

The main body of the army continued its retreat, and went into position under the walls of Nimeguen. The leading French corps were assailed with a sharp fire of musketry, and the Queen's Regiment (now the King's) was one of the corps which displayed signal intrepidity and firmness on this occasion, holding the enemy in check until the army was safe under the walls of Nimeguen. The movement was effected without much loss; but the commander of the allied army, the Earl of Athlone, was censured for not having better intelligence, as smother half hour's delay would have occasioned a most serious loss.

The Dutch were alarmed at seeing their frontiers menaced by a powerful French force; but the Earl of Marlborough on arriving to assume the command of the allied army, and having assembled additional troops, he advanced boldly against his opponents, and, by skilful movements, forced them to retire.

The enemy avoiding a general engagement, the Queen's Regiment was detached with a considerable body of troops from the main army to besiege Venloo, a strong fortress in the Duchy of Guelderland, situate on the east side of the River Maese. This regiment formed part of the force under Lieutenant-General Lord Cutts, which besieged Fort St. Michael, situate on the west side of the Maese, and connected with the town by a bridge of boats. The trenches were opened on the 7th of September, the batteries commenced firing on the 16th; and on the 18th, the grenadier company, with a small detachment from the battalion companies of the Queen's Regiment, formed part of a storming party designed to make a lodgement on the top of the glacis of Fort St. Michael

The storming party was commanded by Colonel Hamilton, and consisted of the Royal Irish (now Eighteenth) and Hukelom's (Dutch) regiments, with the grenadiers of the Eighth and several other corps, a detachment of musketeers, and three hundred and twenty workmen, under Colonel Blood. Lord Lorne (afterwards Duke of Argyle), the Earl of Huntingdon, Lord Mark Kerr, Sir Richard Temple (afterwards Viscount Cobham), Colonel Webb, of the Eighth, and several other noblemen and officers, served as volunteers on this occasion.

About four in the afternoon, the batteries fired a volley, and the grenadiers and musketeers sprang forward with a shout, and rushing up the covered way, sword in hand, carried it in gallant style. The enemy gave one scattering fire, and fled; Lord Cutts ordered the soldiers to pursue, let the consequence be what it might; and, with an ardour and intrepidity almost unrivalled in the annals of war, they leaped into the covered way, and chased their opponents to a ravelin, which they carried with astonishing resolution, notwithstanding the explosion of a mine. The garrison fled to the rampart, from whence a tremendous fire of musketry was opened on the storming party; but the undaunted British threw forward a shower of hand-grenades, and rushing to a bridge which connected the ravelin with the interior works, they were opposed by ranks of pikemen and a storm of musketry, which they speedily overcame, and forced the bridge before the enemy had time to cut or break it down.

Captain Parker, of the Royal Irish, who was one of the storming party observes:

> Here, like madmen, without fear or wit, we pursued the enemy over the tottering bridge, exposed to the fire of the great and small shot of the body of the fort. However, we got over the *fausse braye*, and then our situation was such that we might take the fort or die. They that fled before us climbed up by the long grass that grew out of the fort, so we climbed after them. Here we were hard put to it to pull out the palisades, which pointed down upon us from the parapet; and was it not for the surprise and consternation of those within, we could never have surmounted this difficulty; but as soon as they saw us at this work, they quitted the rampart and retired down to the parade in the body of the fort, where they laid down their arms.
>
> Part of the garrison in attempting to escape across the Maese, was drowned in the river. Thus, were the unaccountable orders of Lord Cutts as unaccountably executed, to the great surprise of the whole army, and even of ourselves, when we came to reflect on what we had done; however, had not several unforeseen accidents concurred, not a man of us could have escaped. (Parker's *Memoirs*.)

Thus, was Fort St. Michael captured with the loss of one hundred and thirty-six officers and soldiers killed, and one hundred and sixty-one wounded; and the progress of the siege of Venloo was facilitated.

While the Queen's Regiment was before Venloo, the Germans, under Prince Eugene of Savoy, took Landau, and the regiment was called out, with the remainder of the besieging army, to fire three volleys for this event. The garrison and inhabitants imagining the troops were assembling to attack the town by storm, were panic-stricken, and the magistrates begged of the governor to surrender; the first volley augmented the terror and consternation, and the governor immediately capitulated.

Leaving Venloo on the 29th of September, the regiment crossed the Maese, and advancing up the river to Ruremonde, was employed in the siege of that fortress; at the same time, a detachment from the main army besieged Stevenswaert. These two places were captured in the early part of October.

After the capture of Ruremonde, the regiment rejoined the main army, under the Earl of Marlborough, and advanced against the city of Liege. The French retired into the Citadel and Chartreuse, which fortresses were besieged. On the 23rd of October, the grenadiers of the Queen's Regiment were engaged in storming the citadel of Liege, and highly distinguished themselves. The Chartreuse surrendered a few days afterwards.

1703. These important conquests having been achieved, the regiment marched back to Holland, where it passed the winter.

In the spring a body of recruits arrived from England; the establishment at this period was twelve battalion companies, of sixty private men each, and one company of grenadiers, of seventy men; and in April, when the Duke of Marlborough visited the quarters and reviewed the regiment, he complimented the officers on the efficient and soldier-like appearance of the several companies.

The regiment quitted its cantonments on the 30th of April, and on the 7th of May pitched its tents at Maeswyck, where a division of the army was assembled, while the Duke of Marlborough was carrying on the siege of Bonn, with the Dutch and Germans. On the evening of the 8th of May, soon after sunset, the camp was alarmed with the news, that the French Army under Marshals Villeroy and Boufflers was advancing to attack the allies in their dispersed quarters; the soldiers instantly struck their tents, and, marching all night, arrived at the famous city of Maestricht about noon on the following day.

The French marshals were delayed by the steady valour of the British regiments, the present Second Foot, and Elst's, (since disbanded), which held Tongres twenty-four hours against the French Army, and gave time for the allies to assemble at Maestricht, where a line of battle was formed, and the Queen's (now the King's) Regiment was stationed at Lonakin, a village of great strength, situated on a height which commanded the whole plain. From this summit the soldiers looked down on the plain beneath, and espying the French Army approach, in order of battle, they stood to their arms and prepared for action; but, after a short cannonade, the enemy withdrew to Tongres.

Bonn having surrendered, the allied army was united, and the Queen's (Eighth) Regiment was formed in brigade with Barrymore's (Thirteenth), Bridge's (Seventeenth), Hamilton's (Eighteenth), and

Leigh's (afterwards disbanded), under the command of Brigadier-General Frederick Hamilton. The British commander advanced against his opponents, who withdrew behind their fortified lines, and the duke being unable to bring on a general engagement, detached a body of troops to besiege Huy, a strong fortress situate in the valley of the Maese, above the city of Liege. The Queen's Regiment was employed on this service, and took part in the attacks against Fort Picard. The town and forts were speedily reduced, and on the afternoon of the 25th of August, while ladders were being raised against the castle, the garrison beat a parley, and, after some delay, surrendered prisoners of war.

After this success the city of Limburg, in the Spanish Netherlands, was besieged and captured, and the Queen's Regiment subsequently marched to Breda, where it was stationed during the winter.

In the meantime, the Elector of Bavaria had taken arms against the Emperor of Germany, and being joined by a French force under Marshal Villars, he was making considerable progress in the heart of the empire. To uphold the Imperial throne, on which the safety of Europe appeared to depend, the Duke of Marlborough resolved to lead his British bands into Germany, and the Queen's Regiment of Foot was one of the corps which had the honour to be employed on this splendid enterprise.

1704. Before commencing this bold and magnificent undertaking, the regiment detached three hundred men to Maestricht, where extensive works were forming on the heights of Petersburg. In the early part of May, 1704, the regiment traversed the country towards the Rhine, and was joined at Bedburg by the detachment from Maestricht. From Bedburg the troops moved dong the course of the Rhine; crossed that river, and also the Moselle, at Coblentz, and proceeding towards the Maine, arrived at the suburbs of Mayence, in the beginning of June: the route was continued, and before the end of June the British were at the seat of war in Germany.

At three o'clock on the morning of the 2nd of July, the regiment marched in the direction of Donawerth: after traversing many miles of difficult country it arrived opposite the heights of Schellenberg, where a strong division of French and Bavarians, commanded by the Count d'Arco, occupied a formidable entrenched position; and about six in the evening a body of troops, of which a detachment of the Queen's Eighth Regiment formed part, moved forward under a heavy and destructive fire, to storm the enemy's work. This was one of the numerous occasions in which the valour and patient endurance of the British soldier was put to a severe test. The struggle was firm and determined; the result was for some time doubtful; but, the protracted contest having shaken the strength and weakened the resistance of the enemy, at the same time a body of Imperialists arrived to cooperate; the intrenchments were forced, the French and Bavarians were overpowered, and sixteen pieces of cannon, with a number of standards and colours, and the tents and camp-equipage of the enemy, including the Count d'Arco's plate, were the trophies of this victory.

The Queen's Regiment lost on this occasion Ensign Savage and five private men killed; Ensigns Bezier and Mason, two sergeants and thirty-one private soldiers wounded. The conduct of the several corps engaged was highly commended; the Emperor of Germany, in a letter to the British commander, spoke in the warmest terms of "the *wonderful bravery and constancy*" of the troops, which had fought under His Grace's command.

The possession of Donawerth was the immediate result of this victory; and the regiment crossed the Danube and was engaged in operations in Bavaria, which country the Imperialists enveloped in flames, reducing many towns and villages to ashes. After penetrating as far as the city of Augsburg, where the Elector had formed an intrenched camp, which it was found impossible to force, the army retired a few stages, and the Germans, under the Margrave of Baden, commenced the siege of Ingolstadt.

Louis XIV had, in the meantime, sent additional troops to Germany under Marshal Tallard, and the united forces pitched their tents in the valley of the Danube near the village of Blenheim. The British and Dutch, with the Germans under Prince Eugene of Savoy, encamped near the village of Minster, and on the morning of the eventful 13th of August, 1704, they advanced in columns to attack their opponents.

On this memorable day, so glorious to the British arms, and so important to the dynasties of Europe, the soldiers of the Eighth Foot had another opportunity of signalising their innate valour and steady resolution. They were first engaged, under Lieutenant-General Lord Cutts, in supporting the attack on the village of Blenheim, where the enemy had stationed a considerable body of troops, and they took part in the capture of two water-mills on the little River Nebel.

Afterwards crossing the river, they opened their fire on the French line with such perseverance and effect that their opponents gave way and fell back in confusion. The thunder of the artillery, the steady and well-directed fire of the infantry, and the charges of the cavalry were continued until the main body of the French Army was overpowered and chased from the field with great slaughter, many standards, colours, and guns being captured, also a number of officers and soldiers taken prisoners, among whom was the French commander, Marshal Tallard.

The French troops in the village of Blenheim were afterwards surrounded, and twelve squadrons of cavalry, with twenty-four battalions of infantry, were made prisoners of war. Thus was a victory gained over the flower of those powerful French Armies which had marched from conquest to conquest; the legions of the most powerful monarch in the world were vanquished; the wreath of fame was transferred from the French standard to that of the allies, and the house of Austria was preserved on the Imperial throne. The recollection of the field of Blenheim depressed the French soldiers; the name of Marlborough became a watchword of fear among the ranks of the enemy, and the achievements of the British troops were lauded by the sovereigns of Christendom.

The Queen's Regiment of Foot had a number of men killed and wounded; Major Frederick Cornwallis was among the killed: and Captain Leonard Lloyd and Lieutenant Bezier were among the wounded.

******

Major Frederick Cornwallis's name is omitted among the killed and wounded in the *Annals of Queen Anne*; but it is contained in the list of killed in the *London Gazette*; he was omitted by mistake in the list of killed and wounded in the *Record of the First, the Royal Regiment*.

******

The results of this victory were of a most stupendous character; the 16th of August, was kept by the army as a day of solemn thanksgiving; the troops were reviewed, and a triple discharge of cannon and small arms was fired.

Bavaria was subdued, cities and towns submitted to the conquerors, and the army traversed the country to Philipsburg, where it passed the Rhine, and the British troops were encamped at Croon-Weissenberg to cover the siege of Landau, which was undertaken by the Germans. At this camp the Queen's Regiment remained until the middle of November, when, Landau having surrendered, it embarked in skiffs near Philipsburg, and sailing down the Rhine (a river remarkable for the romantic scenery on its banks); it passed thirty cities and towns, and arrived in twelve days at Nimeguen, from whence it marched to Breda, to form part of the garrison of that fortress during the winter;

having travelled a distance of about one thousand one hundred and seventy miles in this one campaign.

1705. A hundred and forty young men from England, who thirsted for the honour of gaining laurels under the renowned Marlborough, replaced the losses of the Queen's Regiment in Germany; and when this distinguished corps took the field, it proceeded to the province of Limburg, and pitched its tents on the left bank of the Maese, where it was reviewed by the Duke of Marlborough, in the early part of May. Having struck its tents on the 15th of May the regiment proceeded to Juliers, from whence it continued its route through a barren and mountainous country, to that part of the valley of the Moselle where stands the ancient city of Treves. The regiment subsequently crossed the Moselle and the Saar, and was employed in the movements made with a design to carry on the war in Alsace. When the British commander found his views frustrated by the tardiness of the Germans, he marched back to the Netherlands.

While the troops were employed up the Moselle, the French had captured Huy; on the 4th of July, the Queen's Regiment was detached from the main army, with several other corps, to retake this fortress, which was accomplished before the middle of the month.

After remaining a few days at Huy, the regiment was directed to rejoin the army, in order to take part in the difficult enterprise of forcing a stupendous line of intrenchments and forts which the enemy had constructed to cover the Spanish Netherlands; the Queen's constituted part of the leading column on this occasion, and was formed in brigade with Prince George of Denmark's Regiment (now Third Foot, or the Buffs), and a Dutch battalion, commanded by Brigadier-General Welderen.

Having menaced the lines on the south of the Mehaine to draw the French troops from the point designed to be attacked, the allies advanced, during the night of the 17th of July, with great secrecy, in the direction of Neer-Hespen and Helixem, and about four o'clock on the following morning the Queen's Regiment, and other corps in advance, approached the lines, at the moment when the French Army was assembled to resist an expected assault many miles from the real point of attack. Being favoured by a thick fog, one column speedily cleared the villages of Neer-Winden and Neer-Hespen, another gained the bridge and village of Helixem, and the third carried the castle of Wange, which covered the passage of the Little Gheet.

The British and Dutch soldiers rushed through the enclosures and marshy grounds; forded the river, and, crowding with enthusiastic ardour over the works, surprised and overpowered the French guards, and drove a detachment of dragoons from its post in a panic. The lines were thus forced; and while the British pioneers were levelling a passage for the cavalry, the Marquis d'Allegre hurried to the spot with twenty battalions of infantry and fifty squadrons of French and Bavarian cavalry. Some sharp fighting took place, and the enemy was repulsed with the loss of many standards, colours, and cannon, and of officers and soldiers taken prisoners.

The Queen's Regiment was afterwards engaged in several movements; but the enemy, having taken a strong position behind the Dyle, near Louvain, the Dutch generals refused to co-operate in forcing the passage of the river, and the plans of the British commander were frustrated. In October the fortress of Sandvliet was besieged and captured; and in the early part of November the British infantry marched back to Holland, and were stationed at Breda, Warcum, Gorcum, &c.

1706. Every campaign was thus marked by success, which added new lustre to the British aims, and the summer of 1706, was distinguished by the acquisition of additional honours. The Queen's Regiment left Breda in the early part of May, and the army, having assembled at Bilsen, advanced, on the 23rd of May, in the direction of Mount St. André. While on the march, the French, Spaniards, and Bavarians, commanded by Marshal Villeroy, and the Elector of Bavaria, were discovered forming in order of battle, with their centre at the village of Ramilies; the British commander made dispositions for attacking the enemy, and the Queen's Regiment was posted on an eminence, near the right of the front line of infantry.

Descending from this height, the British infantry made a demonstration of attacking the enemy's left at the villages of Offuz and Autreglize; when the enemy weakened his centre to support his flank: and the Duke of Marlborough, suspending the attack of the French left, instantly assailed their centre with all the weight and power of infantry, cavalry, and artillery, he could bring to bear on the point: by which bold and masterly movement he succeeded in forcing the centre, and the village of Ramilies was carried. Disorder and confusion became manifest in the French Army: the Queen's Regiment, and several other corps, advanced against the enemy's left, which was speedily broken and routed; and a decisive victory was gained. The pursuit was continued during the night; the enemy's cannon, many standards and colours, and a number of officers and men, were captured.

A splendid French Army was thus annihilated, and the officers and men who had escaped from the field, with the garrisons of the fortified towns, were so amazed, confounded, and panic-stricken, that fortresses of the greatest importance, which had resisted powerful armies for months, were at once delivered up. When the magistrates of Antwerp presented the keys of their city to the British commander, they stated:

> These keys have never been delivered up since they were presented to the great Duke of Parma, and then after a siege of twelve months.

Even the port of Ostend, which once withstood a siege of three years, (See the *Record of the Third Foot, or Buffs*), held out only three days and a few hours after the batteries commenced firing. After taking part in several movements, the Queen's Regiment was detached under Lieutenant-General Lumley, Major-General the Earl of Orkney, and Brigadier-General the Duke of Argyle, from the main army, to engage in the siege of Menin; a fortress of great strength, and considered the key of the French conquests in the Netherlands. Some sharp fighting took place at the opening of the trenches, and at the storming of the counterscarp, in which the British soldiers evinced their native courage and intrepidity; and Ingoldsby's Regiment (Eighteenth) suffered severely. Before the end of August, the garrison surrendered.

In September, Aeth was besieged and taken, which was the last important event of this astonishing campaign; and the British infantry took up their winter quarters at Brussels, Ghent, and Bruges, the Queen's Regiment occupying quarters at Ghent.

1707. On the 16th of May, the regiment marched out of Ghent; and, proceeding to the vicinity of Brussels, where the army was assembled, it was united in brigade with the second battalion of the Royals (First) and the regiments of Ingoldsby (Eighteenth), Tatton (Twenty-Fourth), and Temple (afterwards disbanded), under the orders of Brigadier-General Sir Richard Temple. The campaign was, however, passed without any engagement of importance; and in the autumn the regiment returned to Ghent.

1708. The French monarch, finding his armies beaten and dispirited, and his fortresses wrested from him, meditated the separation of England from the allies, by placing the Pretender on the throne; and an expedition was prepared for this purpose at Dunkirk. The Queen's Eighth Regiment was one of the corps ordered to return to England, to repel the invaders; and having embarked at Ostend, on the 26th of March, arrived at Tynemouth in the beginning of April.

******

A board of general officers, assembled on 8th March of this year, allotted the counties of Essex, Suffolk, Norfolk, and Cambridge as the recruiting district of the King's Regiment.—*MS. Records, R.U.S.I.*

******

Meanwhile, the French fleet, with the Pretender on board, had been chased from the British coast, by the English men-of-war, and forced back to Dunkirk; the Queen's Regiment was, consequently, ordered back to Flanders, and landing at Ostend, proceeded in boats along the canal to Ghent.

Although this project was frustrated, the French court anticipated gaining a decided superiority on the Continent; but the campaign of 1708, proved equally glorious to the British and their allies, as that of preceding years.

The Queen's Eighth Regiment was reviewed at Ghent, in the early part of May, by the Duke of Marlborough, and on the 22nd of that month, commenced its march for the rendezvous of the army near Brussels. Shortly afterwards the French obtained possession of Ghent and Bruges, by treachery; and these acquisitions were preparatory to an attempt on Oudenarde, which fortress, being situated on the Scheldt, and at the verge of the frontier, was a connecting link for the alternate defence of Flanders and Brabant.

Oudenarde was invested on the 9th of July, and the French commanders, the Duke of Burgundy, and Marshal Vendome, designed to occupy the strong camp of Lessines, on the Dender, to cover the siege: but they were opposed by a general, whose promptitude and alacrity have seldom been paralleled, and whose resources were called forth by the magnitude of the stake for which he was contending. By a forced march, the Duke of Marlborough gained the position at Lessines before the French, and disconcerted their plans. Being thus foiled, they relinquished their designs on Oudenarde, and proceeded in the direction of Gavre, where they had prepared bridges for passing the Scheldt. In order to meet the enemy on the march, and bring on a general engagement, the Queen's Regiment was detached, with a number of other corps, under Major-General Cadogan, to throw bridges over the Scheldt near Oudenarde, for the army to pass.

Leaving the camp at dawn, on the 11th of July, the Queen's Regiment arrived at the right bank of the Scheldt, at half-past ten in the morning: the bridges were completed by mid-day, the detachment passed the stream, and the Queen's, with eleven other regiments, formed line on the high ground, between the villages of Eyne and Bevere. The French were, at the same time, passing the river two leagues below: their advance-guard was, soon afterwards, descried on the further side of the plain, and the appearance of the van of the allied army in position in their front, with the remainder hurrying over the river, created a general sensation throughout the French ranks. Seven battalions of the Swiss Regiments of Pfeffer, Villiers, and Guedar, took post at Eyne, with a support of cavalry in their rear, and the main body was put in order for the battle.

While the main body of the allied army was passing the river, Major-General Cadogan seized a favourable moment to strike the first blow at the seven battalions in Eyne; the Queen's (now the King's), with Ingoldsby's (Eighteenth), Sabine's (Twenty-Third), and Meredith's (Thirty-Seventh) regiments, led by Brigadier-General Sabine, and supported by two other brigades, descended the hill, forded a rivulet, and, raising a loud British shout, rushed upon their opponents.

The Queen's, being on the right of the brigade, led the attack in gallant style; plunging into the village, they assailed the Swiss battalions with a destructive fire of musketry, and pressed upon their opponents with the characteristic energy and firmness of British soldiers; while a few squadrons of Hanoverian cavalry made a short detour to gain the rear of the village. The conflict was of short duration; the Swiss were unable to withstand the fury of the British soldiers, and Brigadier-General Pfeffer, and three entire battalions, were taken prisoners: the officers and men of the other four battalions were either killed, or intercepted and made prisoners, in their attempt to escape.

The Queen's stood triumphant in the village of Eyne, their commanding officer received the colours of the Swiss battalions; the captive soldiers were disarmed, and placed in charge of a guard; and thus, an important body of the enemy's infantry was put *hors de combat.*

After this gallant exploit, the regiment halted a short time in the village: it was afterwards ordered to reinforce four battalions, which had taken post behind the hedges near Groenevelde, where the first attack of the enemy was expected; and the officers and soldiers, being elated with their previous success, hurried to the aid of their companions in arms.

The attack had commenced before they could gain their station:

the four battalions boldly disputed the edge of the streamlet, and the Queen's, and other corps ordered to this point, threw themselves into the hedges near Herlehem, and opened a heavy fire against the enemy's centre. The Duke of Argyle brought forward twenty battalions of infantry, and prolonged the line, and the combat of musketry became tremendous: each regiment being engaged separately in the enclosures which border the rivulet.

The Queen's was engaged with the *élite* of the French infantry, and occupying a kind of focus in the centre of the hostile position, they were assailed by very superior numbers, and forced to withdraw, fighting, out of the coverts and avenues near Herlehem, into the plain. Being reinforced, they renewed the conflict, and gained some advantage: the fighting was continued until the shades of evening gathered over the scene, and the combatants could only be discerned by the flashes of musketry. The French were driven from hedge to hedge; their right wing was nearly surrounded; and the streams of fire, indicating the attack of the allies, were seen gathering round the legions of France, whose destruction appeared inevitable.

Darkness having rendered it impossible to distinguish friends from foes, the troops were ordered to cease firing. Crowds of Frenchmen were made prisoners without resistance; others escaped from the field; and before the following morning, the wreck of the French Army had retreated in disorder towards Ghent. Such were the results of the Battle of Oudenarde, in which the Queen's, now Eighth, or, The King's Regiment of Foot, performed so distinguished a part.

Thus, the daring Marlborough, having ventured to outstep the rules of military science, was enabled, by the extraordinary exertions of a brave, experienced, and toil-enduring body of men, to surprise and defeat his antagonists by efforts beyond the calculations of ordinary experience. Soon after the victory of Oudenarde, the arrival of a body of Germans, under Prince Eugene of Savoy, enabled the allied army to undertake the siege of the strong fortress of Lisle, which was the key to the country watered by the Lys and the Scheldt. The Queen's Regiment formed part of the covering army under the Duke of Marlborough, while the siege was carried on by the troops under Prince Eugene and the Prince of Orange: and it was in position when a powerful French Army advanced to relieve the place, which was prevented by the superior skill of the British commander.

The Queen's were repeatedly employed in escorting supplies to the besieging army, and their grenadier company was eventually employed in the siege. The colonel of the regiment, Major-General John Richmond Webb, was detached from the main army, with several regiments of foot and a troop of cavalry, to escort an immense quantity of military stores from Ostend to the besieging army; and being attacked in the woods of Wynendale, by a very superior body of the enemy, under Count de la Motte, he made so excellent a disposition of his troops, and displayed so much skill and valour in repulsing the assaults of the enemy, that he brought off the convoy in safety, and received the thanks of parliament for his distinguished conduct.

When the Elector of Bavaria besieged Brussels, the Queen's were employed in forcing the enemy's strong positions behind the Scheldt, and in compelling the elector to raise the siege and make a precipitate retreat.

After the surrender of the citadel of Lisle, the siege of Ghent was undertaken, and this place was captured in a few days. Bruges was afterwards delivered up; and the Queen's passed the remainder of the winter in quarters at Ghent.

1709. The arrival of new clothing for the regiment, with a supply of accoutrements, and a hundred and fifty recruits, occasioned the Queen's, when they took the field in June, to present so efficient and warlike an appearance, as to elicit the commendations of the Duke of Marlborough, at the general review of the army. The French were commanded by Marshal Villars, who took post behind a line of intrenchments; but he was unable to cope with the British commander, who menaced his lines, which induced him to weaken the garrison of Tournay; afterwards the British invested that fortress.

The Queen's Regiment formed part of the covering army, while the siege of the town of Tournay was in progress; and when the siege of the citadel was commenced, the regiment left the covering army to engage in this service. In carrying the attacks against the citadel of Tournay, the troops had to encounter dangers of a character to which they were not accustomed, from the multiplicity of the subterraneous works, which were more numerous than those above ground. The approaches were carried on by sinking pits several fathoms deep, and working from thence underground, until the soldiers came to the enemy's casemates and mines, which extended a great distance from the body of the citadel; several mines were discovered, and the powder removed.

The British and French soldiers frequently met underground, where they fought with sword, pistol, and bayonet. On several occasions the allies were suffocated with smoke in these dismal labyrinths; and the troops, mistaking friends for foes, sometimes killed their fellow-soldiers. The enemy sprang several mines, which blew up some of the besiegers' batteries, guns, and many men. On one occasion a captain, lieutenant, and thirty men of Ingoldsby's (Eighteenth) regiment were blown up; and on the 26th of August, four hundred officers and men were blown into the air, and their limbs scattered to a distance.

The working parties underground, with the guards which attended them, were sometimes inundated with water; many men were buried alive in the cavities by explosions; and a number of veterans of the Queen's, who had triumphed at Blenheim, Ramilies, and Oudenarde, lost their lives in these subterraneous attacks. The siege was prosecuted with vigour, and some of the works having been demolished by the batteries, the garrison hoisted a white flag on the 31st of August, and agreed to surrender.

The possession of Tournay, a rich and populous city, was rendered more valuable by the acquisition of a province in the French Netherlands, remarkable for the fertility of its soil; it was also important in a military point of view, as it covered Spanish Flanders; and the British commander, pursuing his career of conquest, resolved to undertake the siege of Mons, the capital of the province of Hainault.

As the allied army traversed the country in the direction of Mons, it was brought into contact with the forces of the King of France, under the command of Marshals Villars and Boufflers, who took up a position near the village of Malplaquet, where they threw up intrenchments and constructed defences, until their camp resembled a fortified citadel.

On the morning of the eventful 11th of September, 1709, as the first dawn of light appeared, the Queen's Regiment assembled under arms, and the chaplain performed divine service; it afterwards took its post in brigade with the regiments of Lalo (Twenty-First), and Primrose (Twenty-Fourth), under Brigadier-General Lalo; Ingoldsby's (Eighteenth) was numbered in this brigade, but did not arrive from Tournay in time to take its post in line. When a thick fog, which concealed both armies from each other, cleared, the batteries opened their fire, and the troops moved to the attack with a firm and steady pace; treble intrenchments, studded with cannon and bristling with bayonets, were before them; but their previous successes under their favourite chief, led them to indulge in anticipations of victory, and to view the formidable works they had to storm, without dismay.

The Queen's was commanded on this occasion by Lieutenant-Colonel Louis de Ramsey, an officer of distinguished merit, who had served with the regiment several years, and had given repeated proofs of his valour and ability. They were engaged in the attack of the enemy's intrenchments, in the woods of Taisniere, and when the French were driven from their works, a sharp fire of musketry was kept up among the trees. Several French brigades, fluctuating through the marshy grounds and the thickest parts of the wood, became mingled together in considerable disorder; the British, dashing forward among the trees, kept up a sharp fire, and the conflict was maintained among the thick foliage with varied success.

The commanding officer of the Eighth, Lieutenant-Colonel de Ramsey, was killed; and their colonel, Lieutenant-General Webb, was dangerously wounded. The shout of victory was alternately raised by both parties, and the woods re-echoed the din of battle. The British gained ground; the Dutch, under the Prince of Orange, and the Germans, under Prince Eugene of Savoy, were victorious at their points of attack; and the French were overpowered and forced to retreat with the loss of sixteen pieces of cannon, twenty colours, twenty-six standards, and an immense number of officers and men.

After this victory, the Queen's formed part of the covering army during the siege of Mons, and on the surrender of this fortress, it returned to its former winter station at Ghent, from whence several officers and non-commissioned officers were sent to England to procure recruits.

1710. Leaving Ghent on the 14th of April, the regiment once more took the field, and was engaged in the movements by which the French lines were forced at Pont-à-Vendin, on the 21st of April. The Queen's were also engaged in covering the siege of Douay, and in the movements by which the relief of this fortress was prevented. After the surrender of Douay, on the 27th of June, the siege of Bethune was undertaken. The Queen's formed part of the army encamped at Villers-Brulin, and a detachment was employed in draining the inundations near the town. Bethune surrendered in August; the French Army kept behind a series of intrenchments, to avoid a general engagement, and the allies invested Aire and St. Venant, which were both captured before the army retired into winter quarters. Thus, four additional fortresses were wrested from the French monarch.

1711. Numerous and well-appointed armies, headed by experienced generals, had proved ineffectual against the British commander and his warlike bands; and, before the campaign of 1711, the French had prepared a line of intrenchments to cover their country, so strong, that Marshal Villars vauntingly styled it Marlborough's *ne, plus ultra*; but the English general, by a series of movements, which evinced the most consummate skill, passed these stupendous works at Arleux, and besieged Bouchain, a fortified town of Hainault, situate on the Scheldt. The Eighth was formed in brigade with the regiments of Erie, Sybourg, and Pocock (afterwards disbanded), and took part in these services. The siege of Bouchain proved a most difficult undertaking; but by extraordinary efforts of skill, valour, and perseverance, this fortress was reduced.

1712. The French monarch saw his generals overmatched, his fortresses and provinces captured, and a victorious army ready to penetrate into the heart of his kingdom; and soon after the Queen's (Eighth) Regiment had taken the field to serve the campaign of 1712, under the Duke of Ormond, a suspension of arms was proclaimed, which was followed by a treaty of peace. The regiment retired from the frontiers of France, and after encamping a short time near Ghent, went into quarters in that city.

During this war the pikes had been laid aside, and every soldier was armed with a musket, bayonet, and sword; about the same period the grenadier companies ceased to carry hand-grenades.

1713. When the treaty of Utrecht was signed, the British regiments were withdrawn from Flanders excepting the Queen's and Steamers (Eighth and Eighteenth), which were selected to garrison the citadel of Ghent, until the barrier treaty was concluded.

1714. Previous to this period, the Duke of Marlborough, not coinciding in political views with Queen Anne's new ministry, had been removed from all his appointments dependent on the British crown, and he was residing on the Continent. In July, while the Eighth and Eighteenth Regiments were in garrison in the citadel of Ghent, information was received that His Grace would pass that city on a named day; and such was the attachment of the officers of the two regiments to this distinguished commander, who had so often led them to battle and to victory, that they could not forego the gratification of meeting him on the road, and showing that respect which was due to his talents and virtues, although they were almost certain to incur the displeasure of Queen Anne, and of the government in England, by so doing.

They were accompanied by the magistrates and other civil authorities of Ghent, and a handsome breakfast was prepared at a village on the road. Captain Parker, of the Eighteenth Foot, who was one of the officers, observes in his *Memoirs*:—

> He (the Duke of Marlborough) and his duchess came up to us on horseback; they stopped and talked to us about half an hour, seeming very well pleased with the compliment we had paid them.
> The duchess stated, in a letter published in the duke's *Memoirs*:—
> "I was so much surprised and touched with their kindness, that I could not speak to the officers without a good deal of concern."

Towards the end of July, His Grace embarked at Ostend for England, and on approaching the coast near Dover, on the evening of the 1st of August, the vessel was hailed by a messenger from the postmaster-general, who conveyed the tidings of the Queen's death, and of the quiet accession of King George I.

Section 7—At Home, 1714-1742.

Soon after this event, the Queen's was ordered to return to England, and having landed on the 23rd of August, it was directed by the regency (the king not having arrived from Hanover) to march to Berwick.

1715. The accession of the house of Hanover to the throne being followed by a short period of tranquillity, the regiment was sent to Ireland, in the month of April, and reduced to a peace establishment.

Lieutenant-General Webb having incurred the displeasure of King George I. and of the government, was required to dispose of the colonelcy of the regiment, and was succeeded by Colonel Henry Morrison, by commission, dated the 5th of August, 1715.

While the regiment was in Ireland, an insurrection was organised in England, by the partisans of the house of Stuart; at the same time, the Earl of Mar summoned the Scottish Highland clans to arms, and proclaimed the Pretender King of Great Britain. The Queen's was ordered to embark for Scotland, to aid in suppressing the rebellion, (the establishment consisted of ten companies of fifty men each.— *MS. Records, R.U.S.I.*); and on arriving at Glasgow, towards the end of October it was stationed at that city a few days.

In the early part of November, it marched for Stirling, and on the 11th of that month, it joined the army commanded by the Duke of Argyle. On the following day, the king's forces advanced towards Dunblane, to oppose the rebel army in its design to pass the Firth, and penetrate southward; and during the night the two armies occupied positions within a few miles of each other. The Queen's was on the right of the second brigade, commanded by Brigadier-General the Earl of Forfar.

On the morning of Sunday, the 13th of November, the troops stood to their arms: they had passed a very cold night in the open air; and looked with anxious glance for the enemy. At length the rebel army of ten thousand men was seen approaching in order of battle; and the royal forces, not four thousand strong, formed line. When the formation of the rebels, and the direction of their march, were discovered, it was found necessary to change front, and to alter the disposition of the Royal Army. This was delayed too long, and as the Queen's and several other corps, were in the act of performing a difficult evolution, they were charged by an immense body of Highlanders, the *élite* of the insurgent host.

An elevation of the ground had concealed the Highlanders from the view of the troops until the instant when the assault was made: the soldiers had no time to level their muskets before they were charged by the clans with sword and target; and the Queen's, being thus attacked, at a critical moment, and in the act of changing front, when the advantages of discipline and experience were of little avail, it was unable to oppose effectual resistance to the very superior numbers by whom it was assailed. The ranks were instantly broken, and all formation and order were lost; the soldiers and Highlanders became a confused crowd of combatants, struggling with desperation for the mastery; and a series of single combats followed, in which individual acts of gallantry were performed: in some places a veteran of the Queen's was seen contending manfully against four or five mountaineers.

The Earl of Forfar was at the head of the regiment; he evinced signal valour and intrepidity, and was wounded and taken prisoner. Lieutenant-Colonel Hanmer was surrounded; he held several opponents at bay for a short time, but was overpowered and killed. Ensign Justine Holdman, a young officer of great promise, was conspicuous for personal bravery, and was mortally wounded and taken prisoner. The soldiers were unable to withstand the very superior numbers of their opponents; ten officers and a hundred men of the Queen's had fallen, when the remainder, being favoured by a very gallant charge of the dragoons, on the left of the line, fell back to re-form their ranks.

The left wing was separated from the remainder of the army, and retired beyond Dunblane to gain possession of the passes leading to Stirling. In the meantime, the right wing of the Royal Army had overpowered the left wing of the rebel host; and thus, one wing of each army was triumphant, and one wing defeated. The fighting ceased; both armies remained in the field until night, and afterwards retired.

The loss of the regiment on this trying occasion was very severe:— one field-officer, two captains, four lieutenants, three ensigns, four sergeants, and ninety-seven men, were killed; one captain and thirteen men wounded; Ensigns Holdman and Glenkennedy, and ten men, were taken prisoners. Ensign Holdman died of his wounds while in the enemy's custody.

★★★★★★

A letter from General Wright, dated 14th November, 1715, gives one other name. He says:—"General Webb's regiment, now Morrison's (the King's), was one of the unfortunate regiments on the left that was not formed, and suffered most. Major Hanmer is killed, and young Hellary and many other officers are wounded."—*MS. Records, R.U.S.I.*

★★★★★★

Brigadier-General the Earl of Forfar, who commanded the brigade of which the Queen's formed part, and was at the head of the regiment when it was attacked, was severely wounded and taken prisoner; when the Highlanders found they could not carry him off, they inflicted seven wounds and left him for dead; he was afterwards found lying among the killed, and survived several days.

1716. After the Battle of Dunblane, the regiment encamped near Stirling for several weeks, during which time reinforcements joined the army; and in January the Duke of Argyle advanced towards Perth. (During this year the establishment of the regiment was ten companies of sixty-one men.—*MS. Records, R.U.S.I.*)

The Pretender and the Earl of Mar, being unable to oppose effectual resistance, withdrew from their army privately, and escaped to France, and the Highlanders dispersed.

After the suppression of this rebellion, the Queen's was stationed a short time at Glasgow: and King George I was graciously pleased to reward its good conduct on all occasions with the distinguished title of "The King's Regiment of Foot."

On obtaining the distinguished title of the King's Regiment, the facing was changed from yellow to blue, and the regiment was authorised to bear the White Horse as a regimental badge, with the motto "*Nic aspera terrent.*"

******

The White Horse, on a red field, was the armorial bearing of ancient Saxony, or Westphalia, and has for many centuries been borne by the illustrious House of Brunswick. Historians state that Henry the Proud, Duke of Bavaria (father of Henry the Lion, Duke of Bavaria and Saxony,) married in 1126, Gertrude, daughter and heiress of the Emperor Lothaire the Second, by his consort, the Empress Richenza, who was the daughter and heiress of the last Count of Nordheim, and, in right of her mother, heiress of Eckbert the Second, Margrave of Saxony and Thuringia, and Prince of Brunswick; and that in consequence of this marriage with the lineal descendant of Wittekend, the last Saxon king, Henry the Proud assumed the armorial bearing of that sovereign. The banner of Wittekend bore a black horse, which, on his conversion to Christianity by Charlemagne, was altered to whiter as the emblem of the pure faith he had embraced.

In the year 1700, a medal was struck at Hanover, to commemorate the accession to the electorate of George Lewis, Duke of Hanover, afterwards King George the First. This medal bears on one side the head of the Elector and on the reverse the White Horse, with the circumscription "*Nec aspera terrent.*"

After the accession of the House of Hanover to the imperial crown of Great Britain and Ireland, the White Horse was introduced as a royal badge in the standards and colours of certain regiments of cavalry and infantry.

******

1717. When the rebellion in Scotland was suppressed, the commotions in England subsided, and a reduction of ten thousand men was made in the strength of the army, at which time the King's Regiment was ordered to proceed to Ireland, where it arrived in May, to replace a newly-raised corps, which was directed to be disbanded. (During this year the establishment of the regiment was ten companies of fifty-five men each.)

1720. In October of this year Brigadier-General Morrison died, and was succeeded in the colonelcy by Brigadier-General Sir Charles Hotham, Baronet, from the Thirty-Sixth Regiment.

1721. This year Sir Charles Hotham was removed to the Royal Dragoons, and was succeeded by Colonel John Pocock, from the Thirty-Sixth Regiment, by a commission dated the 21st of April, 1721.

1722. After a short repose, the hopes of the partisans of the Pretender began to revive, and some intimations of a conspiracy having been received, the King's Regiment was ordered to return to England. It landed near Chester, from whence it proceeded, in May, 1721, to Berwick; but returning towards the south in the early part of 1722, it was directed to pitch its tents on Salisbury plain, where several regiments of cavalry and infantry were encamped. The king visited the camp, and reviewed the several regiments, on the 30th of August, and was pleased to declare his royal approbation of the excellent order in which they appeared.

In September, the regiment struck its tents and marched to Worcester, from whence it was removed to Bristol, and, the designs of the conspirators having been frustrated, it embarked for Ireland during the winter.

1727. Gibraltar had been taken from the Spaniards in the reign of Queen Anne, and ceded to Great Britain by the treaty of Utrecht; and the King of Spain was so intent on regaining possession of this important fortress, that he assembled an immense force, and commenced the siege in the early part of this year without first making a declaration of war. Several corps were sent to reinforce the garrison, and the King's Regiment, having proceeded to England, was augmented to twelve companies of sixty-three men each, and held in readiness to embark.

While this siege was in progress, His Majesty, being immersed by treaties in continental politics, was on the verge of being involved in war with the Emperor of Germany; and the King's Regiment was placed under the command of General the Earl of Orkney, and held in readiness to proceed to Holland; but preliminary articles for a general pacification were signed at Paris in May, and in the autumn the regiment returned to Ireland.

1732, 1738, 1739. Major-General Pocock, after commanding the regiment eleven years, died on the 25th of April, 1732; and King George II. conferred the colonelcy on Major-General Charles Lenoe, from the Thirty-Sixth Foot. This officer commanded the regiment six years, and died in 1738; and the colonelcy remained vacant until the summer of 1739, when it was conferred on Colonel Richard Onslow, from the Thirty-Ninth Regiment. (On 1st February, 1731-2, Major George Keightley succeeded to the lieutenant-colonelcy of the regiment. This officer received his first commission of ensign on 2nd May, 1708.)

In this year the British monarch became involved in another war with Spain, and the King's Regiment was withdrawn from Ireland and placed on the British establishment. It arrived in England in the autumn of 1739; at the same time, it was augmented to seventy men per company.

1740, 1741, 1742. An expedition was fitted out, in 1740, to attack the Spanish settlements in the West Indies; but the King's was detained on home service. The decease of Charles VI., emperor of Germany, in the autumn of this year, was followed by war between the Archduchess Maria Theresa and the Elector of Bavaria. France took part with the Elector, and the British monarch took part with the House of Austria, and sent, in the summer of 1742, an army to Flanders, under Field-Marshal the Earl of Stair.

Section 8.—Abroad, 1742-1745.

The King's did not form part of the first embarkation; but it proceeded to Flanders during the winter, and, after landing in Ostend, was placed in cantonments.

In a series of coloured prints representing the costume of the British Army, published at this period, the uniform of the King's Regiment is three-cornered cocked hats, bound with white lace, and ornamented with a black cockade; scarlet coats, the cuffs, facing, and turn-backs of royal blue, and ornamented with white lace; scarlet waistcoats, reaching below the hips; blue breeches, and white linen gaiters reaching above the knee.

1743. From Flanders, the regiment marched, in the early part of this year, through Brabant, the principality of Liege, and province of Limburg, to Lower Germany, and was engaged in operations on the River Maine; while encamped near Aschaffenburg, King George II and his Royal Highness the Duke of Cumberland joined the army.

On the 20th of June, the British, Hanoverians, and Austrians, under His Majesty's command, marched in the direction of Hauau, where they expected to be joined by a body of Hanoverian and Hessian troops, in British pay. On arriving near Dettingen, a French force was discovered in position to oppose the march; and the British formed in order of battle, the King's Regiment having its post in the front line. The action was commenced by the cavalry; the infantry was speedily engaged, and the King's had an opportunity of signalising itself under the eye of its sovereign. Its commanding officer, Lieutenant-Colonel Keightley, and the second in command, Major Barry, were both wounded, and the command devolved on Captain Gray.

The regiment forced the French corps opposed to it to fall back, and continued gaining ground until the fortune of the day was decided in favour of the British. The French were forced to re-pass the Maine with precipitation, and with the loss of many officers and men killed, wounded, and taken prisoners, besides a number of standards, colours, and kettledrums, which remained in possession of the victorious allied army.

The regiment had one sergeant and five private soldiers killed on this occasion; Major Barry died two days after the battle; Lieutenant-Colonel Keightley and Lieutenant Robinson recovered of their wounds; two sergeants and twenty-eight private soldiers were also wounded, and several of them died within a few days after the battle.

After passing the night on the field, the army resumed its march, and the regiment was subsequently encamped several weeks near Hanau; and Captain Gray was rewarded for his gallant conduct with the majority of the regiment.

From Hanau, the regiment marched towards Mayence, and, having crossed the Rhine, was employed in operations in West Germany. In the autumn, the army returned to Mayence, from whence it marched, by divisions, for Brabant and Flanders, for winter quarters; the King's forming part of the seventh division, under Major-General Howard.

1744. Having passed the winter among the Flemish peasantry, the regiment took the field, and served the campaign of 1744, under Field-Marshal Wade; but no engagement occurred.

1745. In April, Major-General Onslow was removed to the first troop of Horse Grenadier Guards; and the colonelcy of the King's was conferred on Colonel Edward Wolfe, from the First Regiment of Marines.

The regiment formed part of the army assembled at Brussels, under His Royal Highness the Duke of Cumberland, and afterwards advanced to the relief of Tournay, which fortress was besieged by an immense force, commanded by the French monarch in person. The covering army took up a position near the village of Fontenoy, where it was attacked by the allies on the 11th of May, 1745. The British infantry evinced on this occasion the most astonishing intrepidity and firmness, and the soldiers of the King's had an opportunity of proving that the same valour and constancy inspired their breasts, as were so nobly displayed by their predecessors, under the great Duke of Marlborough. The French lines were forced, their entrenchments were carried; and a thirst for glory, with the most sanguine expectations of gaining a complete victory, urged the soldiers to deeds of heroism; but the Dutch failed at their point of attack, and this, with other circumstances, rendered the brilliant success of the British infantry unavailing. A retreat was ordered, and the army proceeded to Aeth.

The King's Regiment had sixteen private men killed; Lieutenant-Colonel Keightley, Major Gray, Captains Dallons, Loftus, and Ekins, Lieutenants Cook and Thompson, two sergeants, and eighty-one private men wounded; one sergeant and thirty men missing.

From Aeth the regiment proceeded to the plains of Lessines, and after taking part in several movements, it was encamped near Brussels.

SECTION 9.—AT HOME, 1745-1746.

In the meantime, Charles Edward, eldest son of the Pretender, had arrived in Scotland; and being joined by a number of the Highland clans, he obtained possession of Edinburgh, and penetrated into England. The King's was immediately ordered to return home: it formed part of the army assembled at Newcastle, under Field-Marshal Wade; and was employed in several movements designed to cover Yorkshire: being formed in brigade with the Second Battalion of the Royals (First), and the regiments of Blakeney (Twenty-Seventh), and Munro (Thirty-Seventh). On the flight of the insurgent clans from England, the regiment returned to Newcastle, where it arrived on the 24th of December, and afterwards marched to Edinburgh, and was placed under the orders of Lieutenant-General Hawley, the Commander of the Forces in North Britain

1746. The insurgents, having obtained a reinforcement, and a supply of ammunition and artillery, besieged Stirling castle. (In 1746, the total strength of the regiment, all ranks included, was nine hundred and seventy-seven men.—*MS. Records, R.U.S.I.*) Lieutenant-General Hawley advanced to raise the siege, and an encampment was formed near the village of Falkirk. During the forenoon of the 17th of January, the rebel army was discovered advancing towards some high grounds on Falkirk-moor; the King's regiments immediately stood to their arms, and after a short pause, they advanced towards the moor to confront the Highland host. After traversing the rugged grounds between themselves and their opponents, they formed in two lines on the moor, the King's being on the left of the first line, next the cavalry on that flank.

A little before four o'clock in the afternoon, the first line advanced to attack the clans; at this moment a heavy storm of wind and rain beat in the faces of the soldiers, and nearly blinded them: at the same time it beat upon the backs of the Highlanders and caused them but little annoyance. The soldiers could not see to take aim, more than half the muskets would not give fire, and the powder became wet and useless: but the Highlanders, having their backs to the wind, were enabled to keep up a heavy fire of musketry. Being thus blinded and confounded by the pelting storm, the soldiers became disheartened: several corps faced about and retreated, in some confusion, while others maintained their ground. At night both parties withdrew from the field of battle; and the King's troops proceeded to Edinburgh.

His Royal Highness the Duke of Cumberland arrived in Scotland to command the army: and on the 31st of January, the troops were again in motion towards the enemy, who instantly raised the siege of Stirling castle and made a precipitate retreat. The King's was engaged in the operations of the army until the Battle of Culloden, on the 16th of April; on which occasion it was posted on the left of the second line, under Major-General Huske. After a sharp cannonade had been kept up a short time, several select clans rushed forward and attacked the left of the King's forces. The Fourth Foot sustained the brunt of this attack with signal gallantry: the King's moved forward in support of the Fourth; and a furious struggle ensued, in which the Highlanders were overpowered, and driven from the field, with commander was, however, determined to carry this post: he ordered forward fresh brigades; and the village was lost and won several times. The Duke of Cumberland highly commended the British regiments in his despatch: and stated that:

> They rallied and charged into the village four or five times each: the French but once, as they could not be rallied; but were always replaced by fresh troops.

The Irish brigade in the French service was nearly annihilated; also the brigades of Navarre, La Marque, Monaco, Royal des Vaisseaux, and others.

This protracted contest tried the fortitude and endurance of the British soldiers; but their innate qualities were conspicuous; and the French infantry gave way so fast that cavalry was posted on their flanks and rear, to drive them to the charge with their swords. For some time, the fortune of the day was in favour of the allies; but five Dutch squadrons giving way, produced some confusion, and the enemy broke the centre of the Allied Army. The British cavalry performed astonishing feats of valour and heroism; but were unable to retrieve the fortune of the day, and a retreat was ordered. Thus, ended a battle in which the British acquired great honour. The French lost seven standards, eight pair of colours, and about ten thousand men killed, wounded, and prisoners.

The loss of the King's on this occasion, was Captain Magott, and nine men killed; Lieutenant-Colonel Martin, Major La Fausille, Captain Catherwood, Lieutenant Conway, Ensigns Wilson, Webb, and Hamilton, three sergeants, one drummer, and eighty-five men wounded; twenty-five men prisoners of war and missing.

After withdrawing from the field of battle, the army continued its retreat to Maestricht, where it arrived on the same evening. The King's was subsequently employed in various parts of the provinces of Limburg and North Brabant. (At this time the establishment, all ranks included, was nine hundred and seventy-seven men, while at Gibraltar the establishment was eight hundred and fifteen.—*MS. Records, R.U.S.I.*)

1748. Having passed the winter among the Dutch peasantry, and received a body of recruits from England, the regiment again took the field, in the spring of 1748, and was employed in several operations: but no general engagement occurred.

Section 11—At Home, 1748-1750.

Hostilities were terminated by a treaty of peace, which was concluded at Aix-la-Chapelle, and during the winter the regiment returned to England.

1749. On its arrival from Holland, the establishment of the regiment was reduced. (On 27th April, 1749, Major(?) John Lafausille succeeded to the lieutenant-colonelcy of the regiment.)

Section 12—Abroad, 1750-1752.

1750. The King's was ordered to proceed to Gibraltar, in which fortress it was stationed during the three succeeding years.

1751. In the Royal Warrant, dated the 1st of July, 1751, the regiment is designated. The Eighth, or the King's Regiment: its regimental costume was scarlet, faced and turned up with blue; scarlet waistcoats, blue breeches; and cocked hats. Its first colour was directed to be the great union; and the regimental colour to be of blue silk, with the union in the upper canton. The regimental distinctions were:—

In the centre of the colour the White Horse on a red ground

within the garter, and crown over it: in the three corners of the second colour, the King's cypher and crown. On the grenadier caps, the White Horse, as on the colours; the White Horse and motto, 'Nec aspera terrent.' on the flap. The same device of the White Horse within the garter, on the drums and bells of arms, rank of the regiment underneath.

SECTION 13.—AT HOME, 1752-1760.

1752. In 1752, the regiment was again stationed in Great Britain, where it remained several years.

1755. When the seven years' war commenced, in 1755, the regiment was stationed in England. The first act of aggression was committed by the French in North America, and Europe soon became the theatre of war.

1756-1757. In 1756, the regiment was augmented to twenty companies, and divided into two battalions. Both battalions were encamped, during the summer of 1757, near Dorchester, under the command of Lieutenant-General Sir John Mordaunt, and were held in readiness to repel a threatened invasion by the French; but the formidable preparations in England, and other causes, deterred the enemy from making the attempt. (In the mouth of May of that year two companies were detached and were engaged in quelling a riot at Frome, in Somersetshire.—*MS. Records, R.U.S.I.*)

From Dorchester, both battalions were removed to the Isle of Wight, and, embarking on board of transports, formed part of the land force under Sir John Mordaunt, which, being accompanied by a division of the Royal Navy, under Admiral Sir Edward Hawke, was designed to make a descent on the coast of France. Aix, a small island on the western coast of France, between the isle of Oleron and the continent, twelve miles north-west of Rochfort, was captured; and an attack on Rochfort was contemplated; but unfavourable weather and other circumstances rendered this design impracticable, and the troops returned to England. (The number of men engaged in this expedition was seven hundred.—*MS. Records, R.U.S.I.*)

1758. In 1758, the second battalion was constituted a regiment, and numbered the Sixty-Third Foot; the command of this corps was conferred on Colonel David Watson, who had held, for several years, the appointment of quartermaster-general in North Britain; the lieutenant-colonelcy was conferred on Major Peter Desbrisay, from the Fiftieth Foot, and the majority on Captain John Trollop of the Eighth, who was wounded at Roucoux, in 1746. Lieutenant-Colonel La Fausille, of the King's, who was wounded at Val, in 1747, was promoted to the colonelcy of the Sixty-Sixth Regiment. (He was succeeded in the Lieutenant-Colonelcy of "the King's" by John Mompesson, who, on 24th August, 1758, was transferred from the Fiftieth, in which regiment the date of his commission was 16th December, 1755.)

1759. Lieutenant-General Edward Wolfe died in March, 1759; the colonelcy remained vacant until October following, when it was conferred on Major-General the Honourable John Barrington, from the Fortieth Foot, who had, a few months before, signalised himself in the West Indies, particularly in the capture of Guadaloupe.

1760. In the meantime a British Army had proceeded to Germany, to aid in rescuing the electorate of Hanover from the power of the French; and the King's, commanded by Lieutenant-Colonel John Mompesson, having been selected to reinforce the troops on the continent, embarked for Germany in May, 1760.

Section 14.—Abroad, 1760-1763.

The regiment landed at Bremen in June, and on the 20th of that month, it joined the camp of the Allied Army, commanded by Prince Ferdinand of Brunswick, near the banks of the Eder, in the vicinity of Fritzlar, in the principality of Lower Hesse.

The regiment took part in the movements and skirmishes of the main army, previous to the Battle of Warbourg, on the 31st of July, on which occasion the grenadier company was sharply engaged, and highly distinguished itself; but the French were driven from their position with severe loss, before the main body of the British infantry arrived at the scene of conflict. The grenadier company had one sergeant and two private soldiers killed; Captain Wilkenson and thirteen private men wounded, and one man missing.

The French having been driven through Warbourg, and chased across the River Dymel, where a number of men were drowned in their haste to escape, the King's was subsequently encamped behind the Dymel; and while in this position, the grenadier company was detached, with several corps of cavalry and infantry, across the river, and engaged, during the night of the 5th of September, in surprising a body of French in the town of Zierenberg. After some sharp fighting in the streets, about forty French officers and three hundred soldiers were made prisoners, and the allies returned to their camp at Warbourg. The grenadier company of the King's was subsequently detached to the Lower Rhine, and was engaged, on the 16th of October, in an attack on the French troops at the convent of Campen, near Rhineberg. It formed part of the grenadier battalion, under Lord George Lennox, and had Lieutenant Morrison wounded, also several private soldiers killed and wounded.

In December, the regiment went into cantonments, in villages near the River Weser.

1761. From its village cantonments the regiment was withdrawn in February, and proceeding through a deep snow into Hesse Cassel, was engaged in several operations. The French were forced to surrender several fortified towns and extensive magazines, and the allies returned in March to their former quarters.

In June, the regiment again took the field; it was formed in brigade with the Twentieth, Twenty-Fifth, and Fiftieth Regiments, under Major-General Townshend, in the division commanded by Lieutenant-General Conway; the grenadier company was in the division under the Marquis of Granby. On the 15th of July, the French attacked the Marquis of Granby's division at Kirch-Denkern, and were repulsed. They renewed the attack on the following day; the King's was posted on the high grounds between Illingen and Hohenover, and a detachment stationed in front had a slight skirmish with the enemy, and had one private soldier killed and one taken prisoner. The French were repulsed, and the grenadier battalion, of which the company of the King's formed part, took the regiment of Rougé (formerly Belsunce) prisoners, together with its cannon and colours.

The regiment was subsequently employed in numerous operations in the bishopric of Paderborn, and on the River Weser, and took part in several skirmishes. In November, it was engaged at Eimbeck, in the electorate of Hanover; it was subsequently encamped on the banks of the Have, near Eimbeck, and in December marched into cantonments in the bishopric of Osnaburgh.

1762. During the campaign of 1762, the King's was formed in brigade with the Twentieth and Fiftieth Regiments, under Major-General Mompesson, and it took part in the surprise and discomfiture of the French Army at Groebenstein, on the 24th of June, on which occasion it formed part of the centre column, under Prince Ferdinand of Brunswick. It crossed the Dymel at four o'clock in the morning, and, after a long march, gained the front of the French camp, and opened a sharp fire. The enemy made a precipitate retreat to Cassel, and one division was surrounded and made prisoners in the woods of Wilhelmsthal. (The casualties of Barrington's regiment (the King's) was one non-commissioned officer wounded.—*London Gazette 20th June,* 1762.)

This success was followed by other advantages, and the King's Regiment was actively engaged in numerous operations, and in several skirmishes. The campaign concluded with the siege and capture of Cassel. This event was followed by a suspension of arms, and a treaty of peace was afterwards concluded at Fontainebleau.

Section 15.—At Home, 1763-1768.

1763. The regiment commenced its march from Germany in January, and proceeding through Holland to Williamstadt, embarked for England; at the same time its numbers were reduced to a peace establishment. From England, the regiment proceeded to Scotland, where it was stationed two years.

1764. Major-General the Honourable John Barrington died at Paris on the 2nd of April, 1764; and King George III. conferred the colonelcy of the regiment on Major-General John Stanwix, from the Forty-Ninth Regiment.

1765. Leaving Scotland in the spring, the regiment returned to England, where it remained three years.

1766. In 1766, the Eighth lost their colonel, Lieutenant-General John Stanwix. This distinguished officer embarked from Dublin in the *Eagle*, with his lady, and only daughter, and four servants; the ship was lost at sea, and they all perished. He was succeeded by Major-General Daniel Webb, from the Forty-Eighth Foot.

******

In 1766, the regiment was reviewed in Hyde Park by His Majesty King George the Third. In 1767-8, it was quartered at Dover Castle, under orders for Canada. Its strength was thirty-two officers, twenty-seven sergeants, four hundred and seven effective rank and file; sick, fifteen; wanting to complete, nineteen. Establishment, five hundred.—*MS. Records, R.U.S.I.*

******

Section 16.—Abroad, 1768-1785.

1768. After five years of home service, the King's Regiment embarked, in May, for North America, to relieve the Fifteenth. It proceeded to Canada, and was stationed at Quebec, Montreal, &c. (On 23rd November, 1768, Major Dudley Auckland was promoted to the lieutenant-colonelcy of the regiment.)

By the Royal Warrant, of the 19th December, 1768, containing regulations for the colours, clothing, &c., of the marching regiments of foot, it was directed that:

> The VIII, or King's Regiment, should bear in the centre of their colours the White Horse, on a red ground, within the garter, and crown over it. In the three corners of the second colour, the King's cypher and crown.
> On the grenadier caps, the King's crest; also, the White Horse, as in the colours.
> The same device of the White Horse within the garter, on the drums and bells of arms. Rank of the regiment underneath.

1771. On the 20th of October, Lieutenant General Webb was removed to the Fourteenth Dragoons, and His Majesty conferred the command of the Eighth Foot on Major-General Bigoe Armstrong, from colonel-commandant of a battalion of the Sixtieth Regiment.

******

On 29th October, 1772, Major John Caldwell was transferred from the Seventh Regiment (or Royal Fusiliers), and promoted to be lieutenant-colonel in the King's Regiment.

******

1773. After passing several years at Quebec, Montreal, St. John's, Chambly, &c., the regiment was removed up the country to the large lakes. One division landed at the extremity of Lake Ontario, and occupied the forts and town of Niagara, near the celebrated water-falls of that name. Another portion of the regiment proceeded to Detroit, a town on the west side of the river, between Lake Erie and Lake St. Clair, and the remainder of the regiment occupied several small posts on the borders of the large lakes, &c.

1774. While stationed in these remote posts, the King's witnessed the grounds in the vicinity of their quarters changed, by the woodman's axe and the farmer's plough, from almost impenetrable forests, to scenes of rural industry and comfort; the bears and wolves receding to the more remote regions; while rude cottages rising up on every side as if by enchantment, marked the extent of the infant settlements.

In the meantime, a misunderstanding between the British Government and the colonists of the other settlements in North America, on the subject of taxation, was followed by hostilities in 1775, and a number of states united in a confederacy, and, eventually, declared themselves independent of the mother country.

1775. Hostilities commenced at Boston, and the Battle of Bunker's Hill proved the stern valour of British soldiers, Canada being left almost without troops, the confederated states sent a body of men to invade that province. The Seventh and Twenty-Sixth Regiments occupied several posts, which were not prepared to withstand a siege, and a great part of the two regiments was made prisoners at St. John's and Chambly. Lieutenant-General Carleton vacated Montreal and retired with the remainder of the two regiments to Quebec, where he was besieged by the Americans during the winter.

While this was taking place in the lower province, the King's were unmolested at the forts up the country, where its services were limited to the affording of protection to the settlers.

1776. (On 11th November, 1776, Major Mason Bolton was transferred from the Ninth Foot, and promoted to the lieutenant-colonelcy of the King's.)

After the severe frosts of a Canadian winter were abated, part of the regiment descended from the upper lakes to take part in the expulsion of the insurgent Americans from Canada: and soon afterwards, some British ships, forcing their way through the ice, arrived with reinforcements at Quebec, and the Americans raised the siege: this took place in the early part of May, 1776. (Beatson has erroneously stated, in his *Naval and Military Memoirs*, that the Eighth proceeded to Canada in the spring of 1776, with Major-General Burgoyne.)

About this period, Captain George Foster of the King's who had descended from the upper lakes with a detachment of the regiment, undertook a most gallant enterprise against about four hundred Americans, who were stationed at a fort, on the River St. Lawrence, above Montreal, called Cedars, situated within a mile of the Cascade, at a place naturally strong—the land stretching so far into the river as to render the east and west points inaccessible. Captain Forster commanded at the post of Oswegatchie, and five days after the siege of Quebec was raised, he left this post with two lieutenants and thirty-eight men of the King's, ten Canadian volunteers, and a hundred and twenty Indians.

Arriving at the village of St. Regis, he convened a council of warrior chiefs, who refused to accompany the expedition, but permitted their young men to go: a number of Canadians also agreed to engage in the enterprise. Thus reinforced, the captain embarked with his party on the 17th of May; and, sailing down the St. Lawrence, landed at ten o'clock at night at Point-du-Diable, six miles above the Cedars. On the 18th, he proceeded under the cover of a thick wood, to within a mile of the fort; from whence he sent forward a few private soldiers of the King's, the Canadian volunteers, and a hundred Indians, who were directed to move secretly through the trees, and take post as near the fort as possible. At the same time a hundred Indians were despatched towards the falls at the entrance of the Cascade, to cut off the communication of the garrison with the Island of Montreal. This body fell in with a detachment of the garrison returning with provisions from the Cascade; and the American soldiers escaped to the fort with the loss of one man.

The garrison was summoned, and the commandant, Major Butterfield, requested four hours' consideration; but Captain Forster observing that should hostilities commence, and any of the Indians be killed, he could not answer for the consequences, the major agreed to surrender on condition of being allowed to retire to Montreal This was refused; a redoubt was constructed, and the fort was attacked on the morning of the 19th of May; at mid-day the garrison surrendered, and the commandant, and three hundred and ninety officers and soldiers, became prisoners of war.

On the 20th of May, information was received of the advance of a party of American soldiers from Montreal towards the fort; and Captain Forster sent forward a party to take possession of the woods, on both sides of the road along which the Americans were obliged to pass. As they advanced through the wood, the American soldiers were suddenly enveloped in a sharp fire of musketry; they fought until one Indian was killed and three wounded, and afterwards surrendered. The warriors were so enraged at the loss of their companions that when they arrived at the vicinity of the fort they halted for the purpose of putting their prisoners to death; but Captain Forster, by his most spirited and decisive conduct, prevented the savage butchery taking place, although he hazarded the loss of himself and all his party, by his determined proceeding on this occasion.

The prisoners were lodged in the fort, where a small garrison was left; and Captain Forster advanced with the remainder of his party to Vaudreuil, six miles from the Cedars. Having ascertained that a body of Americans, under Colonel Arnold, had taken post at La Chine, he advanced to dislodge them; but on learning that his opponents were six hundred strong, and would be treble that number on the following day, he returned to Vaudreuil; his small party consisting only of thirty men of the King's, besides Canadians and Indians. On the 27th of May, Colonel Arnold proceeded up the river with seven hundred men in boats; and Captain Forster formed his party into three divisions, and posted them on three points of land that stretched a little way into the river.

The enemy's flotilla approached the left point, but was repulsed by the fire of the Indians; the Americans next attempted to effect a landing at the central point; but were driven back by the fire of the thirty men of the King's, who opposed the landing of seven hundred opponents with the most distinguished gallantry. On proceeding to the third point, the American soldiers were repulsed by the Canadian volunteers, and they returned to St. Ann's, on the Island of Montreal, dispirited and exhausted.

Captain Forster being much incommoded with his American prisoners, who were more numerous than his own party, delivered them up, on condition that they should not serve against the British Government until exchanged; but the American congress violated the cartel, on the pretence that the prisoners had been ill-treated; this was, however, fully proved to be a false and frivolous excuse to evade the conditions of the agreement. (See a letter on this subject in Steadman's *History of the American War*, vol. i, in which the conduct of Captain George Forster, of the Eighth Foot, is fully justified by one of the American officers.)

While Captain Forster and the gallant officers and men of the King's with him, were thus signalising themselves in so extraordinary a manner. General Sir Guy Carleton, K.B., was advancing up the St. Lawrence towards Montreal. The Americans were repulsed at Trois Rivières, and they vacated Montreal A naval force was established on Lake Champlain; the American vessels were attacked and overpowered, and Canada was freed from the presence of the enemy. The King's were subsequently re-established at their former posts at Niagara, Detroit, &c., where they passed the winter.

1777. This year, when Lieutenant-General Burgoyne commenced his unfortunate expedition from Canada, by the lower lakes, with the view of penetrating to Albany, the protection of a portion of the Canadian frontiers was confided to the King's; the regiment also furnished a detachment of one hundred men, to engage in an expedition up the Mohawk River, under the command of Colonel Barry St. Leger, of the Thirty-Fourth Foot, as a diversion in favour of the main army. Part of the force employed on this service consisted of Indians.

Having crossed Lake Ontario to Oswego, the detachment proceeded by Wood Creek, to the Mohawk River; and, in the beginning of August, besieged Fort Stanwix, a square log fort, with four bastions and a stockaded covered way, situate on a rising ground at the upper end of the Mohawk River. A body of American militia advanced to relieve the garrison, and Colonel St. Leger placed a detachment in ambush. As the Americans marched incautiously through a woody part of the country, they were suddenly assailed by a heavy fire of musketry from behind trees and bushes; and the savages, rushing from their concealment, made a dreadful slaughter with their spears and tomahawks.

More than half the American party was cut off, and the remainder escaped. While this was taking place, the *commandant* of the fort made a sally with his garrison, and plundered the Indian camp. In prosecuting the siege, the artillery proved too light to make any impression on the works; and the Indians having lost thirty of their principal warriors, their friendship began to abate. They had engaged in the enterprise in the hope of plunder, and their expectations not being likely to be realised, many of them withdrew; and, when information arrived of the advance of a body of Americans, under Major-General Arnold, their discontent had arisen to such a height, that some doubt was entertained whether they would not turn their arms against the British troops.

Under these circumstances the siege was raised, and the detachment retired to Montreal, from whence it proceeded, by the lower lakes, to Ticonderoga, for the purpose of joining the troops under Lieutenant-General Burgoyne. This did not, however, take place; General Burgoyne, after encountering numerous difficulties, was surrounded by an American force of so very superior numbers, that he capitulated.

1778-1785. The King's remained in Canada during the succeeding seven years. The long residence of the soldiers in the country, united with their knowledge of the roads, and of the localities of the frontiers, rendered their services particularly valuable to the government.

★★★★★★

On 1st November, 1780, Major Alexander Dundas was transferred from the Thirty-Fourth Regiment and promoted to the lieutenant-colonelcy of the King's Regiment, which he held until 18th September, 1783, when he retired from the regiment, and was succeeded by Major Arent Schuyler de Peister, who was promoted to be colonel by brevet on 12th October, 1793, and resigned his commission 22nd April, 1794.

******

In 1782, the American war was terminated by Great Britain acknowledging the independence of the United States.

Section 17.—At Home, 1785-1794.

1785-1793. On the arrival of the 60th Regiment in Canada in the summer of 1785, the King's returned to England, where it arrived in September. It remained in South Britain until 1791, when it proceeded to Ireland. (In 1786-7, the regiment was quartered in Plymouth, in 1790-91-92, in Jersey, and in 1793 in Ireland.—*MS. Records, R.U.S.I.*)

It was stationed in Ireland when the republican party in France added to their enormities the beheading of their sovereign, which was followed by another war, and a British force was sent to Flanders in the summer of 1793. In the same year, the flank companies of the King's were formed, with those of several other corps, into Grenadier and Light Infantry battalions, and were employed, under Lieutenant-General Sir Charles Grey, at the capture of the islands of Martinique and Guadaloupe.

******

During the operations in Guadaloupe between 19th June, and 2nd July, 1794, the casualties among the officers of the King's were killed Captain Armstrong and Lieutenant Booth.—*Extract from Despatch of General Sir Charles Grey, K.B., dated Guadaloupe, 8th July, 1794.*

******

Section 18.—Abroad, 1794-1795.

1794. The establishment of the Eighth was augmented; a second lieutenant-colonel was added; and in the summer of 1794, the regiment was destined to proceed to the Continent.

******

On 3rd March, 1794, Major Edward Dawson was promoted to the lieutenant-colonelcy of the regiment; on the augmentation of the establishment, Major Gordon Drummond was transferred from the Twenty-Third Foot, and on 22nd April, 1794, promoted to be second lieutenant-colonel in the King's Regiment. He was promoted to the rank of major-general on 1st January, 1805, and to that of lieutenant-general on 4th June,

1811; but he continued to be borne on the establishment of the regiment as a lieutenant-colonel until 1814.—For summary of services of this officer *vide* Appendix No. 2.

★★★★★★

It left Ireland in April; embarked from England in June, and after landing at Ostend, was stationed a short period at that fortress, with a detachment at Nieuport.

When the superior numbers of the enemy rendered it impossible to preserve Flanders, Ostend was evacuated, and the King's, having embarked from the fortress and sailed to Holland, joined the army commanded by His Royal Highness the Duke of York, and was formed in brigade with the Twenty-Seventh, Twenty-Eighth, and Fifty-Seventh Regiments, commanded by Major-General de Burgh, afterwards Earl of Clanricarde. Nieuport was besieged and captured by the French, and the garrison became prisoners of war.

On the 30th of July, the colonelcy of the King's Regiment was conferred on Major-General Ralph Dundas, from the lieutenant-colonelcy of the Eleventh Dragoons, in succession to General Armstrong, deceased.

The regiment was engaged in the operations of the army, and for a short period it formed part of the garrison of Nimeguen. This fortress was besieged by the French; and on the 4th of November, a detachment was engaged in a sortie for the purpose of destroying the enemy's works. The attack was made with the most distinguished gallantry, and the French were driven from their works at the point of the bayonet.

The King's had three men killed on this occasion; Captain Bland, and nine private soldiers, wounded.

Having been withdrawn from Nimeguen before the surrender of that fortress, the regiment was formed in brigade with the Thirty-Seventh, Forty-Fourth, Fifty-Seventh, and Eighty-Eighth Regiments, under Major-General de Burgh, and was stationed near the Waal, to defend the passage of that river.

1795. The waters of the Waal having become frozen so as to bear an army with its *matériel*, the regiments retired in January, 1795, through a country covered with ice and snow; and the sufferings of the soldiers (which they bore with exemplary fortitude), were of the most distressing and calamitous description. The superior numbers of the enemy, with the severity of the weather, and the defection of the Dutch people, having rendered the evacuation of Holland indispensable, the

British troops returned to Germany, and were quartered a short time in the duchy of Bremen.

After halting a short period in comfortable quarters, the King's proceeded to Bremen-Lee, where it embarked in transports, and arrived in England in May.

Section 19.—At Home, 1795-1799.

In the autumn of this year, the Eighth, or King's Regiment, was embarked for the West Indies, with the expedition under Major-General Sir Ralph Abercromby, and was present at the capture of St. Lucie, and at the suppression of the rebellion in Grenada.

******

The regiment embarked in November (strength eight hundred and twelve effective and two hundred and five non-effective non-commissioned officers and privates), but immediately after the commencement of the voyage, the fleet encountered a terrific storm. The transports were dispersed, many were wrecked, and many driven back; only four companies of the King's Regiment reached the West Indies. The remaining six companies were driven back and disembarked. On 1st March, 1796, these six companies were at Newport, in April at Basingstoke, and in July, in Scotland, where in October, they were rejoined by the four companies from the West Indies.

No mention is made of the King's Regiment in Sir R. Abercromby's despatches detailing the operations which resulted in the capitulation of St. Lucie, on 25th May, nor are any casualties reported between 28th April, and 5th May. I do not know on what authority Mr. Cannon states that the regiment took part in these operations.—A. C. R.

The regiment landed at Grenada on 24th of March, 1796, and was present at the capture of Port Royal in that island.

The causalities during the operations between 9th, and 19th June, 1796, as reported in Major-General Oliver Nichols' despatch, dated 21st June, were:—Killed, one rank and file; wounded, five rank and file.

******

1796, 1797, 1798. The war with the republican government of France was continued, and, eventually. Great Britain became involved in hostilities with the court of Spain. In 1798, a British force, commanded by Lieutenant-General the Honourable Charles Stuart, captured from the Spaniards Minorca, the second of the Balearic Islands, situate in the Mediterranean, near the coast of Spain.

★★★★★★

On 4th May, 1798, Major George Airey was transferred from the Sixty-Eighth Regiment, and promoted by purchase to be a lieutenant-colonel in the King's. He was promoted to the rank of major-general on 4th June, 1811, but he continued to be borne on the establishment of the King's Regiment as a lieutenant-colonel until 1814.—For summary of services of this officer *vide* Appendix No. 2.

★★★★★★

SECTION 20.—ABROAD, 1799-1803.

1799. On the 6th of May the King's embarked for that island, where it was stationed during the succeeding twelve months.

1800. In May, 1800, a body of British troops landed on the Island of Minorca from England; and the arrival, in June, of Lieutenant-General Sir Ralph Abercromby, accompanied by Major-Generals Hutchinson and Moore, occasioned the most lively anticipations of being called upon to engage in some important enterprise. Several corps immediately embarked; but the King's was left for the defence of the island.

After about a month's absence, the fleet returned to await the arrival of fresh instructions from England: and on the 12th of August, the King's was inspected at Fort George by the Commander of the Forces, who was so well pleased with its efficient, clean, and healthy appearance, and with the excellent state of discipline which prevailed in the corps, that, a few days afterwards, the regiment was removed from the list of corps to be kept in garrison, to that of the corps held in readiness to embark at a moment's notice. At the same time the regiment was formed in brigade with the Second and Ninety-Second Regiments, commanded by Brigadier-General Doyle.

On the 28th of August, the regiment embarked on board His Majesty's ship *Diadem*, mustering six hundred and ten effective rank and file, and sailed with the expedition against Cadiz; but a contagious disease carrying off great numbers of the inhabitants, the enterprise was abandoned for fear of infection, and the fleet sailed to Gibraltar.

Egypt was, at this period, occupied by an army of French veterans, who were emboldened by conquest, and inured to the climate; Bonaparte had styled them the "Army of the East;" and this ambitious leader had meditated the subjugation of Asia by their means.

While at Gibraltar, the King's was selected to form part of an expedition under Sir Ralph Abercromby, designed to effect the expulsion of the French from Egypt. From Gibraltar the fleet proceeded to Malta; and the health of the soldiers, which had been impaired by being so long at sea, was speedily restored by the abundance of fresh provision which the island afforded. (The regiment was four hundred and ninety strong; it was attached to the second brigade—Major-General Cradock's. The fleet left Minorca and sailed for Malta on 20th December.—*MS. Records, R.U.S.I.*)

In December, the expedition sailed to Marmorice, in Asiatic Turkey, and the fleet anchored in a magnificent basin of water, capable of containing five hundred ships of the line. This bay was surrounded by mountains of irregular shape, the sides of which were adorned with trees of various kinds; and the town appeared on the sides of a marble rock.

1801. At this picturesque spot the troops were landed and exercised; a plan of co-operation was arranged with the Turks; and no attention was omitted, that superior knowledge and the most active zeal could suggest, for the advantage of every person, and everything connected with this enterprise. The King's, commanded by Colonel Gordon Drummond, was formed in brigade with the Thirteenth, Eighteenth, and Ninetieth Regiments, under the orders of Major-General Cradock.

From Marmorice the fleet sailed in February, and on the 2nd of March, anchored in Aboukir Bay, a few miles from the city of Alexandria, the ancient capital of Egypt. Boisterous weather occasioned the landing to be delayed until the morning of the 8th of March, when the flower of a brave army moved in boats towards the shore, exposed to a shower of shot, shells, grape, and musketry, from the French troops which had assembled to oppose the landing.

The moment they arrived at the beach, the British leaped out of the boats, and, rushing forward in the face of dangers and difficulties of a most formidable character, they forced the enemy from his position, and captured several pieces of cannon and a number of horses. Sir Ralph Abercromby thanked the troops, in general orders, for their gallant conduct, which was marked equally for ardent bravery, and by coolness, regularity, and order."

After this victory, the army advanced several miles on the road to Alexandria. The French were discovered in position on an advantageous ridge, with their right to the canal of Alexandria, and their left towards the sea; and on the morning of the 13th of March, the British advanced in two lines, by the left, in order to turn the enemy's right flank, the brigade of which the King's formed part being at the head of the first line. On passing through the wood of date trees, in front of Mandora tower, the French descended from the heights to attack the leading brigades of both lines. (The Ninetieth Regiment formed the advance-guard of the right column; the Ninety-Second Regiment formed the advance-guard of the left column.)

The King's, with the remainder of their brigade, formed to confront their opponents in gallant style; and some severe fighting took place, in which British valour was conspicuous, and the regiment had an opportunity of signalizing itself. The French were driven back with severe loss, and the British stood triumphant on the scene of conflict Sir Ralph Abercromby expressed his approbation of the conduct of the troops, in general orders, in the following terms:—

> The commander-in-chief has great satisfaction in thanking the troops for their soldier-like and intrepid conduct in the action of yesterday. He feels it particularly incumbent upon him to express his most perfect satisfaction of the steady and gallant behaviour of Major-General Cradock's brigade (Eighth, Thirteenth, Eighteenth, and Ninetieth Regiments), and he desires that Major-General Cradock will assure them that their meritorious conduct commands his admiration.

The King's lost, on this occasion, one sergeant and ten rank and file killed; Major Duke, Captains McMurdo and Fortye, Lieutenants Church, O'Brien, and Eason, eight sergeants, and fifty-seven rank and file wounded; total, eighty-two killed and wounded. Lieutenant O'Brien died of his wounds.

Having received a reinforcement from the interior, the French issued from their fortified position in front of Alexandria, and made a resolute attack on the British troops, on the 21st of March. The post occupied by the King's was assailed by the French, who were speedily repulsed and driven back; but the attack on the right was more obstinate. British valour, however, prevailed; but the splendour of the victory was clouded by the loss of the brave Sir Ralph Abercromby, who was wounded in the action, and died a few days afterwards. The loss of the King's was limited to one man killed and two wounded.

✶✶✶✶✶✶

The King's was attached to the second brigade, which consisted of the Eighth, Thirteenth, Eighteenth, and Ninetieth Regiments. On 30th March, when encamped four miles west of Alexandria, the numbers given in the states were twenty-four officers, five hundred and thirty-two non-commissioned officers and privates; of these there were three hundred and sixty-one non-commissioned officers and privates present and fit for duty.—*MS. Records R.U.S.I.*

✶✶✶✶✶✶

Soon after this victory, a body of British and Turks marched to the city of Rosetta, situated near the mouth of one of the great channels of the River Nile. The enemy withdrew from the city; but Fort St. Julian held out, and, while the siege was in progress, the King's traversed the country to Rosetta, where it arrived on the 19th of April, the day on which the fort surrendered.

From the city of Rosetta, a place celebrated for the beauty of its environs, being completely embosomed in a grove of date, banana, sycamore, orange, lemon, pomegranate, and palm trees, the King's advanced up the Nile, through a rich country, abounding in rice, wheat, barley, and other necessaries and luxuries of life, and on the 7th of May the French were driven from the post of El-Aft. The enemy occupied a formidable position at Rahmanie, to prevent the advance of the British troops up the country; but this post was forced, and the French retired through the desert towards Cairo. The loss of the King's on this occasion was limited to two private soldiers wounded.

Continuing their route along the banks of the Nile, the British troops arrived on the 1st of June, within sight of the Pyramids, and on the 8th, pitched their tents within a few miles of these stupendous structures.

From the Pyramids the army advanced to Cairo, the metropolis of modern Egypt, and the French surrendered this city after a few days' siege.

This conquest added fresh lustre to the British arms, and the troops retired down the Nile to the vicinity of Alexandria, and this important city was surrendered in the beginning of September.

The valour and patient endurance under trials, difficulties, and privations of an extraordinary character, evinced by the British troops in Egypt, excited the most lively feelings of gratitude and exultation in Great Britain; and King George III. conferred on the King's, and the other corps engaged in those services, the honour of bearing on their colours and appointments the "Sphynx," with the word "Egypt," as a mark of His Majesty's royal approbation of their conduct.

1802. The successful termination of this splendid enterprise was followed by a treaty of peace. While negotiations were pending, the King's was withdrawn from Egypt. The treaty was concluded in 1802, and the regiment proceeded to Gibraltar.

★★★★★★

On 26th October, 1802, Lieutenant Scholey died of a fever, stated to have carried off about one-third of the population of Gibraltar. On 28th. October the deaths among the troops (Royal Artillery, Second, Eighth, Tenth, Thirteenth, Fifty-Fourth, and De Rolles Regiment) are stated to have been thirty daily. On account of the weak state of the garrison, as a precaution against attack, the guards watching the Spanish lines were ordered to load every evening at sunset, and the matches at the principal battery were kept lighted.

★★★★★★

1803. This peace was, however, of short duration. The treacherous conduct of Napoleon Bonaparte, First Consul of France, occasioned the renewal of hostilities in 1803, and the Eighth was withdrawn from Gibraltar, and landed at Portsmouth in August.

Section 21.—At Home, 1803-1805.

Bonaparte assembled an army for the invasion of England, and preparations were made on a most stupendous scale to repel the enemy; all ranks and conditions of men evincing the most steady and determined resolution to support the government, and to maintain their liberties against the power of the enemy.

1804. This year a second battalion was added to The King's Regiment, and was formed of men raised in the West Riding of Yorkshire, for limited service, under the Additional Force Act, passed in July of that year. This battalion was placed on the establishment of the army, on the 25th of December, 1804.

★★★★★★

(*a*.) On 27th August, 1804, the King's and other regiments were reviewed by His Royal Highness the Duke of York, at a camp near Eastbourne.—*Mil. Extracts, Folio III., R.U.S.I.*

(*b*.) On 22nd November, 1804, Major Daniel Hoghton was promoted to be lieutenant-colonel in the regiment, and posted to this battalion.

★★★★★★

About the period when the second battalion was embodied, Spain united in hostilities against Great Britain with Bonaparte, whom the French had elevated to the dignity of Emperor.

1805. A treaty of concert between Great Britain and Russia, for putting a stop to the encroachments of France, and to effect the re-establishment of peace and of the balance of power in Europe was signed in April. Austria afterwards joined the alliance, and while preparations for carrying these resolutions into effect were in progress, the first battalion of the King's embarked at Portsmouth, on the 17th of May. (In the beginning of 1805 the first battalion was at Colchester, and the second at Doncaster.—*MS. Records, R.U.S.I.*) Several circumstances concurred in preventing the battalion being engaged in any important enterprise at this period, and it landed at Cork on the 7th of August.

It was, however, not destined to remain long in Ireland. The victory of Trafalgar, gained by the British fleet under Viscount Nelson, over the French and Spanish squadrons, gave Great Britain a more decided superiority at sea than formerly; at the same time Russia and Austria were in arms against France; and on the 29th of October, the first battalion embarked for the Continent.

Section 22.—Abroad, 1805-1806.

In November the battalion landed at Cuxhaven, a port belonging to the city of Hamburgh, and situated at the mouth of the River Elbe. From Cuxhaven, the King's advanced up the country, and formed part of the force under Lieutenant-General Lord Cathcart, designed to cooperate with the Austrians and Russians. The occupation of the electorate of Hanover, which had recently been overrun by the French, was one object of the expedition: but after the defeat of the Russians and Austrians at Austerlitz, the preponderance of French power was established on the Continent, and a treaty was concluded at Vienna, in which it was stipulated that Hanover should be occupied by the Prussians; the British troops were consequently withdrawn. The King's marched to Bremen-Lee, where it embarked on the 11th of February, 1806, and landed on the 26th of that month at Ramsgate. (In 1806 the first battalion was quartered in Hastings.—*M.S. Records, R.U.S.I.*)

Section 23.—At Home, 1806-1808.

1806. In March, 1806, the first battalion proceeded to Liverpool, and embarked for Ireland.

1807. After remaining in Ireland six months, the first battalion embarked from Dublin on the 23rd, and landed at Liverpool on the 27th of July. At the same time, it was selected to form part of an expedition under Lieutenant-General Lord Cathcart, against the capital of Denmark, for the purpose of preventing the navy of that kingdom being employed by Napoleon against Great Britain.

The battalion embarked for this service from Hull, in the early part of August, (it was attached to Major-General McFarlane's Brigade of the left division.—*MS. Records , R.U.S.I.*); and the Danish Government not acceding to the proposed conditions, the army landed on the island of Zealand, and invested Copenhagen, the King's disembarking on the 16th of August, at the village of Wisbeck, situated about halfway between Elsineur and Copenhagen. After a short siege, the city surrendered, and the fleet was given up on the 7th of September. This undertaking having been accomplished, Copenhagen was evacuated; the King's embarked on the 14th of October, and landed at Portsmouth in November.

Section 24.—Abroad, 1808-1815.

1808. The first battalion remained in England until January, 1808, when it embarked from Portsmouth for North America, and landed at Halifax, in Nova Scotia, in April following. It was withdrawn from Nova Scotia in November, and sailing to the West Indies, formed part of an expedition, under Lieutenant-General Beckwith, against Martinique, the largest of the Caribbee islands, which was, at this period, in possession of the French.

1809. The expedition assembled at Carlisle Bay, Barbadoes; and the King's, commanded by Major Bryce Maxwell, with the Thirteenth, and four companies of the First West India Regiment, constituted the second brigade, under Brigadier-General Colville. Leaving Carlisle Bay on the 29th of January, the troops arrived before Martinique on the following day, and landed in two divisions; the King's disembarking at Bay Robert, and advancing towards Morne Bruno and the heights of Surrey. Frequent skirmishes occurred during the march, and on the 2nd of February, the French made a resolute stand on the heights of Surrey.

A sharp action ensued, in which British valour was most conspicuously displayed, and the French were driven from their position with considerable loss. The commanding officer of the King's, Major Maxwell, and four men, were killed, and thirteen men wounded.

Batteries were subsequently erected, and the siege of Fort Bourbon was commenced with such vigour, that the garrison surrendered on the 24th of February. Among the trophies captured on this occasion, were three eagles. This valuable island having been thus captured, Lieutenant-General Beckwith congratulated the troops, in general orders, on their brilliant success, and stated in his public despatch—

> Having had the command of such an army, will constitute the pride of my future life. To these brave troops, conducted by generals of experience, their king and country owe the sovereignty of this important colony; and I trust, by a comparison with the force that defended it, and the time in which it has fallen, the present reduction of Martinique will not be deemed eclipsed by any former expedition. (Among the casualties between 6th and 15th March, Ensign Foote, of the King's, is reported wounded.—*MS. Records, R.U.S.I.*)

On the embarkation of the troops from Martinique, Lieutenant-General Beckwith addressed to them the following order:—

> At the close of this short but brilliant campaign, and at the moment in which the army is on the point of separation, the commander of the forces is led by every feeling which can actuate the human heart, but in language feeble indeed when compared with the occasion, to renew, for the last time, his expressions of thanks and affectionate respect to the generals and the field-officers, and others of the staff, and to the officers, non-commissioned officers, and soldiers composing the army, for the eminent services they have rendered their king and country, in the course of the late operations, which have terminated in a manner splendid and honourable to all concerned. The commander of the forces desires to express his obligations to Lieutenant-General Sir George Prevost, for his general exertions, and to the fine and efficient corps led by him from North America, now embarking.

The royal authority was subsequently given for the regiment to bear on its colours the word "Martinique," as a testimony of its conduct at the capture of that valuable island.

Leaving the West Indies, the battalion returned to Nova Scotia, and landed at Halifax on the 17th of April. (On 29th April, 1809, Major R. Young was promoted to be a lieutenant-colonel in the regiment, and on 4th June, 1811, he was succeeded by Major Peter Thomas Roberton.)

1810. At this period a misunderstanding existed between Great

Britain and the United States. The decrees of Napoleon, which were designed to effect the destruction of British commerce, had been followed by regulations which the Americans deemed injurious to their trade; at the same time they complained of the practice of pressing British seamen who were found on board of American ships, and hostilities appeared to be on the eve of taking place. The first battalion of the King's embarked from Nova Scotia in May, 1810, for Canada, and landed at Quebec on the 28th of that month.

★★★★★★

At the same time the second battalion was ordered to return from Jersey to Portsmouth, where it landed on the 21st June; and in August six companies embarked for Nova Scotia and New Brunswick, where they arrived in October.

★★★★★★

1812. The first battalion remained at Quebec until the summer of 1812, when, the Americans having declared war, it was removed up the country to Montreal The Americans appear to have considered the conquest of Canada as an enterprise of easy accomplishment. A body of troops, under General Hull, crossed the river above Detroit, and commenced hostilities; but was driven back and forced to surrender. Another attack made by the Niagara frontier was repulsed; and Major-General Dearborn's design against Montreal was frustrated. The Americans were also defeated on several other occasions; but their favourite project of the conquest of Canada was not abandoned.

A detachment of the King's was removed to Chambly in August, where it was encamped, and in the autumn the battalion proceeded to Upper Canada. It presented a most superb appearance, producing a thousand officers and soldiers on parade, and was admired for its conduct and discipline.

1813. During the winter, the Americans availed themselves of the frozen state of the River St. Lawrence, to make nocturnal depredations on British subjects who resided beyond the immediate support and protection of a regular military post. To put a stop to these proceedings, and to facilitate the passage of stores up the river, four hundred and eighty regulars and militia, of which force a company of the King's, under Captain James Hardy Eustace, mustering one hundred and twenty men, formed part, were despatched, under Major Macdonald, of the Glengarry Light Infantry Fencibles, from Prescott, (the first frontier post of Upper Canada,) against the American troops at Ogdenberg, a village of the United States, situate at the confluence of the Oswegatchie with the St. Lawrence.

Crossing the St. Lawrence on the ice, the troops advanced on the morning of the 13th of February, 1813, through deep snow, in two columns, towards Ogdenberg. As they approached this post, the enemy's batteries opened a heavy cannonade; but the British, pushing rapidly forward, under a heavy fire of artillery and musketry posted on an eminence near the shore, soon gained the right bank of the river. The company of the King's turned the enemy's right in gallant style, and rushing upon the Americans with the bayonet, drove them through the village with severe loss; some escaping across the Black River into the fort,—others seeking for safety in the woods,—and many of them taking refuge in houses, from whence they were driven by the fire of the British artillery.

Having gained the high ground on the brink of the Black River, the British troops halted a few moments to recover their breath, being nearly exhausted. The enemy refusing to surrender, his eastern battery was carried, and, by it, another was silenced. The company of the King's, with the Highland militia, led by Captain Eustace, of the King's, rushed into the fort, which was carried with the bayonet.

Eleven pieces of cannon were captured, with the enemy's marine, commissariat, and ordnance stores; four officers and seventy men were made prisoners; two armed schooners, two large gun-boats, and the two barracks were destroyed; and the British troops afterwards returned to Prescott.

The conduct of Captain Eustace, the subalterns, and the non-commissioned officers and soldiers of the King's Regiment, was commended in the public despatches. *The King's had the honour of capturing two stand of American colours, which General Sir George Prevost sent to England to he laid at the feet of his Royal Highness the Prince Regent.*

The loss of the regiment on this occasion was one sergeant killed; Ensign J. G. Powell and twelve private soldiers wounded.

In March, the battalion received orders to proceed to Kingston, with five companies detached to Fort George. Two companies (the grenadiers under Captain Neal Mc Neal, and the third company commanded by Captain James Hardy Eustace, mustering one hundred and seventy rank and file,) being on their route to Fort George, halted at York (now called the city of Toronto), the capital of Upper Canada, where a small force was stationed, under Major-General Sir Roger Hall Sheaffe. On the morning of the 27th of April, an American fleet, with a land force under Major-General Dearborn, appeared on the lake off York harbour; and the troops, to oppose this armament, consisted of only about six hundred men, including militia and dockmen, with a few Indians.

Eight hundred Americans, under Major-General Pike, effected a landing, and were speedily followed by additional brigades. The two companies of the King's, a company of the Royal Newfoundland Regiment, and a few militia, confronted the American brigades in the woods near the lake, and a severe contest ensued. The bush is the natural fortress and element of the American riflemen, and they rushed forward in crowds to envelope and annihilate the few Britons who dared to oppose their advance; but the stem valour of the English soldiers was not to be overcome at once. and a determined resistance was opposed for some time. Captain Neal Mc Neal, of the King's, fell mortally wounded, in the act of encouraging his men, and the soldiers suffered severely from an excess of daring. Volunteer D. Mc Lean, one sergeant-major, three sergeants, and forty rank and file were killed; volunteer H. P. Hill, three sergeants, and thirty-six rank and file were wounded.

At length they fell back; they rallied several times, and were encouraged by the presence and example of Major-General Sir Roger Sheaffe; but further resistance proved unavailing against the very superior and increasing numbers of the enemy. The contest had lasted several hours, when it was found necessary to retire to the batteries, where another resolute stand was made; but the accidental explosion of a portable magazine dismounted the guns, and the soldiers had become so reduced in numbers, that a retreat was resolved upon. The stores, &c., were set on fire, and a train was laid to the magazine; the Americans, rushing forward, arrived at the arsenal the moment the magazine exploded, and Major-General Pike and a number of men were blown into the air. On withdrawing from York, the detachment met the light company of the King's Regiment, which covered the retrograde movement; but no interruption was experienced from the enemy.

The two companies of the regiment were one hundred and ninety-three strong, out of which they lost, on this occasion, nearly one hundred officers and men, killed, wounded, and prisoners.

Five companies of the regiment, commanded by Brevet-Lieutenant-Colonel James Ogilvie, were stationed at Fort George. The morning of the 27th of May, was particularly foggy, and on the mist clearing, an American fleet was seen standing towards the shore of the lake, accompanied by about a hundred boats, crowded with soldiers.

Against this powerful armament, the commandant, Brigadier-General John Vincent, had only a very small force to oppose, and the piquets were withdrawn from the coast. The soldiers and Indians, at Two Mile Creek, opposed the enemy as long as possible; but the fire from the American fleet so completely enfiladed and scoured the plains, that it became impossible to approach the beach. Between three and four thousand Americans landed, with several pieces of artillery, and advanced in three columns.

The British light troops were speedily forced back; but they were gallantly sustained by the companies of the King's, commanded by Major Ogilvie, and a most sanguinary combat was maintained. Brigadier-General Vincent observed in his despatch:

> Nothing could exceed the ardour and gallantry of the troops, who showed the most marked devotion in the service of their king and country, and appeared regardless of the consequence of the unequal contest. Being on the spot, and seeing that the force under my command was opposed by tenfold numbers, who were rapidly advancing under cover of their shipping and batteries, from which our positions were immediately seen, and exposed to a tremendous fire of shot and shells, I decided on retiring.

The guns of Fort George were spiked, the ammunition destroyed, and the troops withdrew across the country in a line parallel to the Niagara River, to the position near the Beaver Dams, beyond Queenstown Mountain. Two companies of the King's (the light company and one battalion company) joined during the night, and the whole afterwards withdrew to the head of the lake.

Lieutenant James Drummie, of the King's, and many men were killed; Major Edward Cotton, Lieutenants Mortimer, Mc Mahon, and Noel were wounded; Lieutenant Lloyd and Ensign Nicholson were severely wounded and taken prisoners; the loss of men in killed, wounded, and prisoners, was eleven sergeants, four drummers, and one hundred and eighty-one rank and file.

While the American fleet was employed in the enterprise against Fort George, five companies of the King's, commanded by Major Thomas Evans (later Major-General) were engaged to an attack on the American post at Sackett's Harbour; the corps employed on this service being commanded by Colonel Edward Baynes; and the right wing of the expedition, by Colonel Robert Young, of the King's. The boats assembled at Kingston, at ten o'clock on the night of the 28th of

May; and, proceeding across Lake Ontario in the night, a landing was effected on the following morning, under a heavy fire, at Horse Island. A causeway, connecting the island with the main land, was forced with distinguished gallantry; and Major Evans, at the head of several officers and men of the King's and other corps, dashed through an expanse of water, and captured an American six-pounder.

The enemy occupied a thick wood; the British gun-boats fired into the wood; but the American soldiers, being secure behind large trees, were only to be dislodged by the bayonet. The spirited advance of a section produced the flight of hundreds; and on the British soldiers skirting the wood, and plunging fearlessly among the trees, the Americans fled in crowds to their block-house and forts; at the same time, their store-houses in the vicinity of the fort were set on fire. As no further object could be accomplished from the want of artillery, the troops withdrew to the boats and re-embarked; and several wounded officers and soldiers fell into the hands of the enemy.

The commander of the expedition stated in his despatch:—

The two divisions were ably commanded by Colonel Young, of the King's Regiment, and Major Drummond, of the Hundred and Fourth. The detachment of the King's, under Major Evans, nobly sustained the high and established character of that distinguished corps.

The King's had five private soldiers killed in this enterprise; Lieutenant Nutall afterwards died of his wounds; Captains Blackmare and Tythe, Ensign Greig, and seven rank and file were wounded, and taken prisoners; Major Evans, Lieutenant Lowry, three sergeants, and sixty rank and file were wounded.

In the meantime, the five companies of the regiment under Major Ogilvie, which had retired from Fort George, had taken post on Burlington heights, at the head of Lake Ontario, where about sixteen hundred men were assembled under Brigadier-General Vincent. Three thousand five hundred Americans, with a field train, and two hundred and fifty dragoons, advanced against the British detachment, and drove the piquets from Stoney Creek.

The light companies of the King's and Forty-Ninth Regiments, commanded by Lieutenant-Colonel Harvey, moved forward, on the 5th of June, to reconnoitre, and having ascertained the position of the enemy's camp, the five companies of the King's, under Major Ogilvie, and the Forty-Ninth Regiment (mustering together only seven hundred and four bayonets) advanced at eleven at night against the enemy's post, at Stoney Creek, where nearly four thousand opponents were assembled.

After traversing seven miles of difficult road with great secrecy, the enemy's camp was surprised; the British dashed among their opponents with undaunted bravery, routed the very superior numbers of the Americans, with great slaughter, and made Brigadier-Generals Chandler and Winder (first and second in command), with upwards of one hundred officers and men, prisoners: also captured three guns, one brass howitzer, and three tumbrils. Brigadier-General Vincent observed in his report of this brilliant enterprise:—

> Major Ogilvie led on in the most gallant manner, the five companies of the King's Regiment; and whilst one half of that highly disciplined and distinguished corps supported the Forty-Ninth Regiment, the other part moved to the right and attacked the enemy's left flank, which decided our midnight contest.

The Americans, though driven from the camp, hovered in crowds in the neighbouring woods, and being four times more numerous than the British, the latter withdrew. The Americans, being reinforced, took post at Forty-Mile Creek.

The loss of the King's at the surprise of the American camp at Stoney Creek was—Lieutenant Hooker, two sergeants, and seven rank and file killed; Major Ogilvie, Captains Munday and Goldrick, Lieutenants Weyland and Boyd, four sergeants, and fifty-one rank and file wounded; thirteen rank and file missing.

Early in June, the five companies of the regiment which had been engaged at Sackett's Harbour embarked from Kingston, with some artillery, on board the squadron, under Commodore Sir James Yeo, to reinforce the British troops at Fort George. Major Evans, though still suffering from his wounds, was carried on board and placed in command. News of the evacuation of Fort George having been obtained, Sir James Yeo received directions to land the men as near York town as possible; but the fleet being detained by contrary winds. Major Evans and Lieutenant Finch travelled by land to York, which the Americans had evacuated, and hearing of the gallant affair at Stoney Creek, Major Evans returned to the fleet, and induced Sir James Yeo to attack the American camp at Forty-Mile Creek; at the same time, Lieutenant Finch proceeded by land to apprise Brigadier-General Vincent of the approach of the shipping and troops.

A combined movement was arranged, in which the light company of the King's was employed; and the Americans, being thus menaced by water and land, fled from their post with precipitation; the British pressed upon them, captured several boats, and obtained possession of a great part of the camp equipage and baggage of the American Army.

Being thus weakened and confounded by the daring enterprises of a comparatively small number of British soldiers, the American commander, Major-General Dearborn, withdrew his detachments from Fort Erie, &c., and concentrated his forces at Fort George; and the British made a forward movement from the head of Lake Ontario, to support the light infantry and Indians in circumscribing the enemy, so as to compel him to maintain his army from his own resources.

Five hundred and seventy Americans, commanded by Lieutenant-Colonel Boestler, advanced to disperse a few British troops, which were collecting at Beaver Dams for the purpose of procuring provisions. The Americans being attacked while on the march, on the 24th of June, by the Indian warriors under Captain Kerr, retired to an open piece of ground, and sent to their main army for succours; but a detachment of the Forty-Ninth, under Lieutenant Fitzgibbon, with the light company of the King's, flank companies of the Hundred and Fourth, and a few Canadian cavalry, arriving at the scene of conflict, the Americans surrendered, delivering up their arms, artillery, and a stand of colours of the Fourteenth United States Regiment.

The King's continued actively employed during the remainder of the campaign.

★★★★★★

On 8th July, a party of the King's, detached from Chippawa, after a skirmish in which the Americans lost twenty killed and ten prisoners, recovered some stores, buried near Fort George, when the fort was evacuated on 27th May. On 11th July, a detachment of the King's, under Lieutenant Barstow, formed part of a force commanded by Lieutenant-Colonel Bisshopp, which attacked the naval establishment of Black Rock. The batteries were carried, and the barracks, block houses, and one schooner burned; the casualties of the detachment were three privates killed and six wounded.—*Mil. Extracts, Folio III, 106-152, R.U.S.I.*

★★★★★★

The Americans sustained several severe repulses, and two of their divisions were forced to quit the Canadas. Fort George was captured by the British in December; and also Fort Niagara.

Two thousand Americans assembled at Black Rock and Buffalo, to check the further progress of the British; and a detachment of the King's Regiment, commanded by Lieutenant-Colonel Ogilvie, formed part of the force under Major-General Riall, which crossed the Niagara River on the night of the 29th of December, and attacked the enemy soon after daybreak on the following morning. The impetuosity and steady resolution of the British, overpowered the resistance of their more numerous antagonists, who fled from their batteries to the town of Buffalo, where another stand was made; but the Americans were again routed, and they abandoned the village in dismay, leaving three guns behind them.

Two schooners and a sloop were destroyed; and the town of Buffalo and village of Black Rock were burnt, as a measure of retaliation for the acts of plunder and conflagration committed by the Americans in their invasion of Upper Canada. The King's had seven men killed on this service; and Lieutenant-Colonel Ogilvie, Lieutenant Young, and fourteen rank and file wounded. After Lieutenant-Colonel Ogilvie was wounded, the command of the detachment devolved on Captain Robinson. Lieutenant-General Drummond thanked the troops in general orders for their exertions, and:

> Expressed his admiration of the valuable qualities which they had displayed in the course of that short but severe service, in which they have cheerfully borne the absence of almost every comfort, and the rigours of a climate for which they were far from being prepared.

******

Extract from Report of Major-General Riall to Lieutenant-General Drummond:—"I must particularly mention the steadiness and bravery of the King's Regiment and Eighty-Ninth Light Infantry, led by Lieutenant-Colonel Ogilvie, of the King's. After Lieutenant-Colonel Ogilvie was wounded, the command of the regiment devolved on Captain Robinson, who by a very judicious movement to the right with three battalion companies, made a considerable impression on the left of the enemy's position."

The strength of the King's was two hundred and forty rank and file.

******

1814. On the decease of General Ralph Dundas, the colonelcy was conferred on General Edmund Stevens, from the Sixty-Fifth Regiment, by commission dated the 8th of February, 1814.

Lieutenant-Colonel Ogilvie not having recovered of his wounds, and Major Cotton having died from severe exertions, Major Evans was ordered from Quebec to the Niagara frontier, to rejoin the first battalion, which was labouring under depression from fever and ague, contracted by severe service and exposure to inclement weather. The health of the men soon improved by care and attention; and they were employed in throwing up a breastwork on the banks of the Chippawa. The battalion was subsequently embarked for Kingston; but on arriving at York, Colonel Young was directed to proceed to Kingston to assume the command at that station, and the battalion was ordered back to the Niagara frontier. The men afflicted with ague, all solicited to be allowed to accompany the battalion, to confront the enemies of their king and country. The King's landed at Fort George on the 4th of July, and advanced, by a forced march, upon Chippawa.

The United States continued to prosecute their designs upon Canada, notwithstanding their failures and heavy losses; and on the 3rd of July, an American Army (estimated at six thousand men) commanded by Major-General Brown, traversed the Niagara at the ferry opposite Black Rock, and afterwards took post near that river; Major-General Riall advanced from the lines of Chippawa, and being joined by the King's, he ventured to attack the very superior numbers of the enemy, on the afternoon of the 5th of July. The British bands, mustering only fifteen hundred men, besides a few Canadians and Indians, moved to the attack in three columns, the King's Regiment being in advance; but, after some sharp fighting, it was found impracticable to force the enemy's position with so great a disparity of numbers, and a large body of American riflemen joining their army during the action, a retrograde movement was ordered.

★★★★★★

The troops engaged in this affair were First Royal Scots, five hundred; First Battalion Eighth, the King's, four hundred and eighty; Hundredth Regiment, four hundred and fifty; one troop of Nineteenth Light Dragoons, in all about one thousand five hundred regulars, besides three hundred Indians and some militia. The casualties were six officers and one hundred and forty-two non-commissioned officers and privates killed; twenty-six officers and two hundred and ninety-five non-commissioned officers and privates wounded: one lieutenant and forty-two rank and file missing.—(Extracted from Major-General Riall's Report to Lieutenant-General Drummond, dated Chippawa, 6th July.)

******

The King's covered the retreat upon Chippawa, and all the officers and men of the regiment were commended for their conduct Major Evans was reported to have signalised himself on this occasion, and his conduct was spoken of in terms of commendation. Lieutenant Greig, of the King's, Staff-Adjutant to Colonel Pearson, was mentioned in the public despatches of General Fisher, for his zeal and conduct at the storming of Oswego, on the 6th of May, 1814; also by Major-General Riall, in the action of the 5th of July, 1814, on the Plains of Chippawa; and in general orders after the action of the 25th of July, 1814, at Lundy's Lane, for the capture of Colonel Stainton, of the United States Army.

The regiment had three men killed; Lieutenant Boyde, one sergeant, and twenty-two rank and file wounded.

On the 7th of July, the British retired upon Fort George, covered by the King's Regiment; the Americans followed with caution, and encamped within three miles of the British lines. During the night of the 12th of July, Major Evans with the light company of the King's, under Captain Henry Sadlier, advanced with great secrecy towards a cottage situated between the two armies, in the expectation of being able to seize some American officers of distinction.

Arriving at the cottage, the King's were informed that the enemy was in force betwixt themselves and their camp, and they were speedily assailed by a volley of musketry from the road along which they had advanced. The night being dark, Major Evans succeeded by a stratagem, in bringing two parties of Americans into collision; he then directed the light company to retrograde through the wood, and gain, if possible. No. 1 redoubt on the Niagara River.

Major Evans, having on a round hat with a brown coat over his uniform, was enabled to pass through the American troops without detection. This force of the enemy proved to be three hundred volunteers, under the American General Swift, who was killed in the rencounter; and their object appears to have been to carry off Major-General Riall, and his staff, who occupied an isolated cottage; but the design was thus happily frustrated. The King's had four men killed, and two missing; but the Americans sustained a much greater loss.

On the 13th of July, while the Americans were firing minute guns for General Swift, the British troops withdrew to Twenty-Mile Creek, covered by the King's Regiment; and, in a few days afterwards, they were reinforced by the One Hundred and Third Regiment, and some artillery. The Americans withdrew from their position, and were followed by the British on the 23rd of July. Two days afterwards a sharp action was fought at Lundy's Lane, near the falls of Niagara. The Americans attacked the leading British brigade, and a retrograde movement was commenced, when Lieutenant-General Drummond arrived with a small reinforcement, (including a detachment of the King's, under Captain Francis Campbell,) drawn from Fort George and Mississaga, and renewed the contest.

The Americans repeatedly attempted to force the British centre to gain the crest of the position, but were repulsed. The detachment of the King's, under Captain Campbell, was engaged at this point, and highly distinguished itself Captain Campbell's horse was killed under him, and his detachment suffered a heavy loss; but the ground was maintained with sanguinary perseverance. About nine in the evening, an intermission of firing took place.

The Americans renewed the attack with fresh troops; a fierce combat of artillery and musketry followed in the dark, and the ground was contested with the most determined bravery. The headquarter division of the King's, commanded by Major Evans, arrived at the scene of conflict; and being guided by the blaze of musketry and cannon flashing continually in the dark, penetrated into the fight. The Americans charged up the hill; bayoneted the British gunners in the act of loading, and gained possession of the guns; but the British troops in the centre, where the detachment of the King's, under Captain Campbell, was fighting, drove back the Americans and retook the guns. The storm of battle still raged along the heights; the muzzles of the British and American artillery were within a few yards of each other, and the combatants were so mingled in close fight., that, in limbering up the guns, an American six-pounder was put by mistake on a British limber, and a British six-pounder on an American limber.

The enemy's efforts to carry the hill were continued until about midnight, when he had suffered so severely from the superior steadiness and discipline of His Majesty's troops, that he gave up the contest, and retreated with great precipitation to his camp, beyond the Chippawa. On the following day he abandoned his camp, threw the greatest part of his baggage, camp equipage, and provisions, into the rapids, and having set fire to Street's mills, and destroyed the bridge at Chippawa, continued his retreat, in great disorder, towards Fort Erie. (Lieutenant-General Drummond's despatch.)

The gallant conduct of the detachment of the King's under Captain Campbell, was commended in the public despatches; and the headquarter companies, under Major Evans, were declared to have behaved with equal gallantry and firmness. Captain Robinson of the regiment (provincial lieutenant-colonel) commanded an incorporated militia battalion, highly distinguished himself, and was wounded.

******

The Lieutenant-General cannot refrain from expressing in the strongest manner his admiration of the gallantry and steadiness of ——, and of the detachment of the King's Regiment, under Captain Campbell, by whom the brunt of the action was for a considerable time sustained, and whose loss has been severe.— (Extracted from District Order of Lieutenant-General Drummond, dated Headquarters, Falls of Niagara, 26th July, 1814.)

******

The regiment had twelve rank and file killed; Lieutenant Noell, Ensigns Swayne and Macdonald, three sergeants, and fifty-four rank and file wounded; one quartermaster and twelve rank and file missing. (On 28ih July, 1814, Brevet Lieutenant-Colonel James Ogilvie was promoted to be a Lieutenant-Colonel in the regiment.)

Following the American Army in its retrograde movement, the British arrived at Fort Erie and commenced the siege of that place. The King's was employed in this service, and on the 12th of August, Major Evans, being in command of the piquet of this and De Watteville's Regiment, repulsed a sortie of the garrison. Lieutenant-General Drummond having been brought to the spot by the firing, thanked the piquet for its conduct.

On the 15th of August, the King's and De Watteville's Regiments were engaged, under Lieutenant-Colonel Fischer, in the attack of the American post at Snake Hill; at the same time another portion of the works of the fort was stormed by detachments selected for that service.

The flank companies, under Major Evans, advanced for the purpose of turning the position between Snake Hill and the lake; and the battalion companies followed in support. After a circuitous route in the dark, exposed to heavy rains, the troops approached the works; but found it impossible to advance by the narrow road parallel with the lake, from the enemy's cannon completely sweeping it, and they entered the water, wading along the edge of the lake waist deep, over rocks and stones. On arriving at the abattis, it was found impossible to penetrate it; the enemy kept up a tremendous fire, and the troops were forced to abandon the advantages they had gained, and to retire. The King's had Lieutenant Noell, one sergeant, and fifteen rank and file killed; Lieutenant Young and fourteen rank and file wounded; one Sergeant and fifteen rank and file missing.

During the afternoon of the 17th of September, when the King's, commanded by Lieutenant-Colonel Ogilvie, was on duty, the Americans sallied from their works and attacked the British posts with overwhelming numbers. The King's suffered severely on this occasion, and the enemy gained some advantage, but was eventually driven back with great loss.

★★★★★★

Extract from District Order by Lieutenant-General Drummond, dated Camp before Fort Erie, 18th September, 1814:— "The attack on the right, favoured by the weather (the rain was falling in torrents) was partially successful. No. 2 Battery, defended by the King's and by De Watteville's regiments was carried, both corps suffering such severe loss in killed and wounded as afforded incontestable proof that the battery was not gained without a vigorous resistance. It was afterwards recovered, and the enemy driven out of our entrenchments by three companies of the Sixth and seven companies of the Eighty-Second, under Major Proctor. The blockhouse on the right was well defended by a detachment of the King's stationed in it."

★★★★★★

Lieutenant-Colonel Ogilvie was thanked by Lieutenant-General Drummond, for his conduct on this occasion. The regiment had Lieutenant Barstow, one sergeant, and twelve rank and file killed; Lieutenant Lowry and twelve rank and file wounded; Captain Bradbridge, Lieutenant McNair, Ensign Matthewson, eight sergeants, and sixty-three rank and file missing.

On the 21st of September, the British troops withdrew from before the fort, to proceed into quarters of refreshment; and the Eighth, or King's Regiment, being reduced to a skeleton by its severe losses on numerous occasions, was ordered to retire to Montreal.

The distinguished gallantry displayed by the regiment while serving on the Niagara frontier, was subsequently rewarded with the royal authority to bear on its colours the word "Niagara," as a distinguished mark of favour and approbation.

Section 25.—At Home, 1815-1818.

1815. A treaty of peace having been concluded with the Americans, the first battalion embarked from Quebec in June, and arrived at Portsmouth in July.

In the month of December of this year, all men fit for service belonging to the second battalion were transferred to the first, and the establishment of the King's Regiment was reduced to a single battalion consisting of one thousand and seventy-seven non-commissioned officers and privates.

1816, 1817, 1818. The regiment embarked at Portsea, in February, 1816, for Ireland, in which country it remained nearly two years, and embarked at Cork, in January, 1818, for Malta.

Section 26.—Abroad, 1818-1824.

While at Malta the establishment was reduced to seven hundred and seven non-commissioned officers and private soldiers.

1819, 1820. From Malta the regiment was removed to the Ionian Islands, in January, 1819, and landed at Corfu on the 19th of that month.

******

During the years 1817, 1818, and 1819, the records of the regiment were stained by various discreditable incidents, attributable to the misconduct and mismanagement of the commanding officer, Lieutenant-Colonel Peter T. Roberton, who at Corfu, on 21st May, 1819, was tried by a general court-martial, convicted, and cashiered. He was succeeded by Lieutenant-Colonel J. Duffy, transferred from half-pay list, whose commission in the regiment was dated 9th September, 1819.

******

A detachment of three companies, under the command of Brevet-Major Robinson, embarked for Santa Maura, to reinforce the garrison, the inhabitants having assembled in arms, and threatened the town: this detachment, in conjunction with detachments of the Twenty-Eighth and Thirty-Second Regiments, under the command of Lieutenant-Colonel Sir Frederick Stovin, was successfully engaged in an attack on the position of the rebels, on the 4th of October, 1819.

1821. In consequence of an insurrectionary spirit having shown itself in Zante, and the adjoining islands, the regiment was employed, in conjunction with the Ninetieth Light Infantry, in disarming the population: for the performance of this duty it received the approbation of His Majesty King George IV, which was signified through the commander-in-chief to Major-General Sir Frederick Adam, the Lord High Commissioner of the Ionian Islands.

1824. The regiment embarked from Cephalonia in June, and arrived at Portsmouth on the 3rd of August following.

SECTION 27—AT HOME, 1824-1830.

1825. On the 13th of September, the colonelcy was conferred on Lieutenant-General Sir Henry Bayly, G.C.H., in succession to General Stevens, deceased.

1826. In March, the regiment embarked from Plymouth for Scotland, and arrived at Glasgow towards the end of the same month.

1827-1830. After remaining ten months in Scotland, the regiment embarked for Ireland, and landed at Belfast in January, 1827.

★★★★★★

On 20th March, 1828, Lieutenant-Colonel the Honourable George Cathcart was transferred from half-pay to the Lieutenant-Colonelcy of the King's Regiment (to carry rank, 15th August, 1826).—For summary of services of officer, *vide* Appendix No. 2.)

★★★★★★

It remained in Ireland until 1830.

SECTION 28.—ABROAD, 1830-1841.

1830. In the summer of this year the six service companies embarked for Nova Scotia, and landed at Halifax in July, at the same time four depot companies embarked for England, and landed at Liverpool.

1833. From Nova Scotia, the service companies were removed in May; they landed at Bermuda in June, and remained at that island until the end of July, when they were removed to Jamaica.

1835. The four depot companies embarked for Ireland in the summer of 1835, and landed at Cork on the 30th of June. (On 2nd October, 1835, Major Thomas Gerard Ball was promoted to the lieutenant-colonelcy of the regiment.—For summary of his services, *vide*

Appendix No. 2.)

1838. In August, the depot companies were removed from Ireland, to the island of Guernsey.

1839. After remaining in Jamaica nearly six years, the service companies were ordered to return to Nova Scotia. They embarked from Jamaica in April, and arrived at Halifax in May.

1840. On the night of the 17th of June, the depot companies, under Major Malet, were employed in extinguishing a fire which had broken out in a Spanish vessel in the harbour.

1841. The depot was ordered to Ireland in the autumn of this year, and previously to its embarkation, a record was made in the annals of the Royal Court of Guernsey, at the recommendation of the bailiff and principal law officers, expressive of the high esteem they entertained for the corps on of its excellent conduct and discipline during the three years it had been stationed in the island, and also in commemoration of its services on the occasion of the fire above alluded to. An authenticated copy of this record was forwarded through the Governor, Major-General Sir James Douglas, to Major Malet, the commanding officer.

On the 2nd of December, the service companies embarked from Halifax, for Ireland: they landed at Cork on the 27th of December, and were joined by the depot companies.

SECTION 29.—AT HOME, 184-1846.

1842. In the spring of 1842, the regiment proceeded to Dublin. (On 25th October, 1842, Major Charles St. Lo Malet was promoted to the lieutenant-colonelcy of the regiment.—For summary of his services *vide* Appendix No. 2.)

1843. On the 22nd of March, the regiment was reviewed by the Lord Lieutenant in the square of the Royal Barracks. On that occasion there were present on parade twenty-eight officers and five hundred and seventy-three non-commissioned officers and privates, the total strength at the time being thirty-nine officers and eight hundred and forty-nine non-commissioned officers and privates.

On the 7th of April, four companies under the command of Major Hartley, and one company under Captain Chearnley, embarked at Dublin in the steamers *Ballinasloe* and *Britannia*, and disembarked at Liverpool on the following day. On the 10th, Headquarters and the remaining five companies under Lieutenant-Colonel Malet and Captain Longfield, embarked in the same two steamers, and disembarked at Liverpool on the 11th

After disembarkation the regiment was distributed as follows:—

At Salford Barracks, Manchester, Headquarters and I Company, under Lieutenant-Colonel C. St. Lo Malet.
At Preston, E and H Companies, under Major Hartley.
At Stockport, Grenadiers and B Companies, under Major Kenyon.
At Wigan, A and C Companies, under Captain J. Longfield.
At Ashton-under-Lyne, the Light Company, under Captain Chearnley.
At Oldham, F Company, under Captain Ogilvy.
At Staleybridge, D Company, under Captain Liston.

On the 7th of July, the three detachments quartered at Stockport, Preston, and Wigan were withdrawn, and the six companies composing these detachments rejoined Headquarters at Manchester.

On the 7th of October, the regiment was inspected by Major-General Sir William Warre, C.B., Commanding the Northern District, and while on parade received orders to relieve the Headquarters and detachments of the Sixty-Fifth Regiment. These orders were carried out on the two following days, and when completed the regiment was thus distributed:—

At Bolton, Headquarters, Grenadier and I Companies, under Colonel C. St. Lo Malet.
At Burnley, A and B Companies, under Major Kenyon.
At Blackburn, C and E Companies, under Captain Longfield.
At Bury, Light and D Companies, under Major Hartley.
At Colne, H Company, under Captain Greathed.
At Rochdale, F Company, under Captain Ogilvy.

On the 10th of November, F Company was withdrawn from Rochdale to reinforce the Bury detachment.

On the 10th of November, Grenadier and I Companies from Bolton, and F and Light Companies from Bury, exchanged quarters.

1844. Between the 21st of May, and 1st of June, during the election of Members of Parliament for South Lancashire, the troops were withdrawn from Bolton and Bury, the Headquarter companies being billeted at Over Hutton and the adjacent villages, and the Bury detachment at and around Accrington.

On the 8th of July, the Bury detachment was relieved by the Sixty-

Seventh Regiment, one of the companies rejoining Headquarters at Bolton, and the remainder of the detachment being distributed between Burnley and Blackburn.

Between the 17th and 25th of September, during the election of Members of Parliament for North Lancashire, the Burnley and Blackburn detachments were withdrawn from their barracks, and billeted in villages adjacent to these towns.

In October the old colours of the regiment were deposited in Salisbury Cathedral.

Between the 3rd and 9th of December, Headquarters were removed from Bolton to Chester, and the regiment was distributed in the following quarters:—

> Chester, Headquarters, C and D Companies, under Major Hartley.
> Stockport, A and E Companies, under Captains Holmes and Lumley.
> Preston, B and H Companies, under Lieutenant Hinde and Captain Greathed.
> Wigan, Grenadiers Company, under Captain Roper.
> Liverpool, Light Company, under Captain Chearnley.
> Blackburn, F Company, under Captain Holder.
> Isle of Man, I Company, under Lieutenant Young.

Between the 26th and 30th of December, the Headquarters were removed from Chester to Weedon, all detachments were relieved and the regiment, after having been broken up for twenty-one months, was concentrated in that place.

1845. In January of this year, a drum-major's cane and embroidered belt was presented to the regiment by its Colonel, General Sir Henry Bayly, G.C.H.

On the 29th of May, Lieutenant-General Sir Thomas Arbuthnot, K.C.B., Commanding the North-West, North-East, and Midland Districts, made his half-yearly inspection, when out of a total strength of thirty-nine officers and eight hundred and thirty non-commissioned officers and privates, there were present on parade thirty-one officers and seven hundred non-commissioned officers and privates.

On the 13th of June, five companies under Major Hartley, and on the following day the remaining five companies and Headquarters under Lieutenant-Colonel C. St. Lo Malet were moved from Weedon to Portsmouth. F and I Companies, under Captain Alfred Malet, were detached on the 14th, to occupy Fort Cumberland, but these companies rejoined Headquarters on the 26th of July. On the 10th of October, Major-General the Honourable Sir Hercules Pakenham, K.C.B., Commanding the South-western District, made his half-yearly inspection. There were present on parade thirty-one officers and six hundred and eighty-nine non-commissioned officers and privates, out of a total strength of thirty-nine officers and eight hundred and forty-three non-commissioned officers and privates.

On the 15th of December, Lieutenant-Colonel Charles St. Lo Malet retired on half-pay unattached, and was succeeded in the lieutenant-colonelcy of the regiment by Major Henry Winchcombe Hartley.

1846. On the 18th of March, the regiment received orders to hold itself in readiness to embark for India immediately, and by a War Office letter, dated 16th of March, its establishment was augmented to fifty-two officers and one thousand and seventy-nine non-commissioned officers and privates. The number of companies, including one left at the depot, was ten.

******

The detail of the establishment authorised by this letter consisted of ten companies, one colonel, two lieutenant-colonels, two majors, ten captains, twenty-two lieutenants, eight ensigns, one paymaster, one adjutant, one quartermaster, one surgeon, three assistant surgeons. Total officers, fifty-two. One sergeant-major, one quartermaster sergeant, one paymaster sergeant, one armourer sergeant, one schoolmaster sergeant, one hospital sergeant, one orderly room clerk, ten colour-sergeants, forty-one sergeants, fifty corporals, one drum major, twenty drummers, nine hundred and fifty privates. Total non-commissioned officers and privates, one thousand and seventy-nine. Total of all ranks, one thousand one hundred and thirty-one.

******

On the 24th of April, General Sir Gordon Drummond, G.C.B., was appointed Colonel of the regiment in succession to General Sir Henry Bayly, deceased.

On the 25th of April, A and C Companies, under command of Major Greathed, embarked for Bombay on board the *Duke of Cornwall*.

On the 27th, the Grenadiers and F Companies, under command of Captain Holder, embarked on board the *Mary*.

On the 28th, D and H Companies under the command of Major Holmes, embarked on board the *John Fleming*.

On the 29th, B and I Companies under the command of Captain Stephenson Brown embarked on board the *Duke of Portland*.

On the 30th, the Headquarters, with E and Light Companies, under command of Lieutenant-Colonel Longfield, embarked on board the *Anne Armstrong*; the total strength embarked in the five ships was thirty-four officers and eight hundred and seventy-six non-commissioned officers and privates.

Captain Lumley was left in charge of the depot (strength three officers and sixty-nine non-commissioned officers and privates), which as soon as the Headquarters of the regiment embarked, was sent to Chatham.

Section 30.—Abroad, 1846-1860.

The five ships arrived at Bombay in the following order:—

1st August, *Duke of Portland*; sailed, 29th April; at sea ninety-four days.

1st August, *Duke of Cornwall*; sailed, 25th April; at sea ninety-eight days.

3rd August, *Mary*; sailed 27th April; at sea ninety-eight days.

13th August, *John Henry*; sailed 28th April; at sea one hundred and seven days.

29th August, *Anne Armstrong*; sailed 30th April; at sea one hundred and twenty-one days. Average length of passage, one hundred and three and three-fifths days.

The troops from each ship a few days after landing were ordered to march to Poona. Headquarters with the troops landed from the *Anne Armstrong* left Bombay on the 5th, and reached Poona on 12th September, on which day the whole regiment was concentrated at that station. A month and twelve days therefore elapsed from the day the first division of the regiment landed at Bombay until the day Headquarters and the last marched into Poona.

1847. On 5th January, Major-General Roderick McNeill, commanding at Poona, made his half-yearly inspection of the regiment. There was present on parade twenty-six officers and seven hundred and thirty-eight non-commissioned officers and privates out of a total strength of forty-six officers and nine hundred and forty-one non-commissioned officers and privates.

1848. On 17th January, a wing of the regiment, consisting of C, D, F, H and I Companies, under the command of Major Edward Harris

Greathed, left Poona and marched to Bombay, where it was quartered in the Colaba barracks.

On 29th September, this wing, under Major Greathed, embarked on board the Honourable East India Company's steamer *Ajdaha*, and on 4th October landed at Kurrachee in Scinde.

The Headquarter wing, consisting of the Grenadier, A, B, and light Companies, under the command of Lieutenant-Colonel Longfield, leaving a depot of invalids under Lieutenant Dowse, marched from Poona in three divisions on 29th and 30th September, and 1st October. On 6th October, these three divisions were reunited at Panwell, whence they were conveyed in boats to Bombay, where, on account of unfavourable weather, they were ordered to disembark, and were detained until the 10th. On that day Headquarters, with the Grenadier and B Company under Colonel Longfield, embarked on board Honourable East India Company's steamer *Atalanta*, and Major Holmes with the Light Company under Captain Marsden, embarked on board the Steam Navigation Company's steamer *Dwarka*. These two vessels arrived at Kurrachee on the 14th.

The day after these companies landed. Captain Marsden, a most energetic and vigorous young man, in the prime of his strength, died of constipation and inflammation of the bowels after less than three days' illness. (This year the regiment lost two other of its captains. Captain Holder, who died on the 29th May, and Captain Stephenson Brown, who died on the 15th of November.)

"A" Company under Captain Daniell embarked on board Honourable East India Company's steamer *Victoria* on the 13th, and landed at Kurrachee on the 18th, and on the 22nd December Lieutenant Dowse, having left the invalided men at Bombay for conveyance to England, rejoined the regiment with the women and children of the Poona depot (strength, one officer, twenty-one non-commissioned officers and privates, ninety women, and one hundred and thirty children).

1849. On the 4th January, Brigadier Douglas made his half-yearly inspection. (Present on parade: thirty-four officers, eight hundred and ninety-nine non-commissioned officers and privates; total strength, forty-nine officers, one thousand one hundred and thirty-four non-commissioned officers and privates.)

On the 21st January, a wing consisting of A, B, D, F, and H Companies, under the command of Major Greathed, left Kurrachee under orders to march to Hyderabad, but at Wattajee, the second halting-place, the orders were countermanded and the wing returned to Kurrachee.

Orders for detaching a wing to Hyderabad having, however, been again issued early in the following month, Major Greathed with A, B, D, F, and I Companies marched from Kurrachee on the 12th, and arrived at Hyderabad on the 22nd February.

On the 3rd of August Major Francis Sanderson Holmes died at Kurrachee of fever.

1850. Brigadier-General A. Manson, C.B., commanding in Scinde, made his half-yearly inspection on the 25th March. (Present on parade: nineteen officers, four hundred and sixty-one non-commissioned officers and privates; total strength, fifty officers, one thousand and twenty-nine non-commissioned officers and privates.)

On the 11th November, the Grenadier, C, H, and Light Companies with the Headquarters, under the command of Lieutenant-Colonel John Longfield, embarked at Kurrachee in country craft. On the 14th they arrived at Cutch Mandavie, on the 18th they marched from Mandavie, and on the 12th December they arrived at Camp Deesa, and were there stationed. The left wing, under Major J. C. Brooke, embarked in river steamers at Hyderabad on 11th November, was transhipped on board country craft at Kurrachee, disembarked at Cutch Mandavie on the 20th, and rejoined Headquarters at Deesa on 19th December.

1851. On the 13th March, Brigadier G. I. Wilson made his half-yearly inspection. (Present on parade: twenty-seven officers, seven hundred and ninety-four non-commissioned officers and privates; total strength, fifty-one officers, one thousand and fifty-one non-commissioned officers and privates.)

1852. On the 15th March, Brigadier G. I. Wilson made his half-yearly inspection. (Present on parade: twenty-seven officers, six hundred and ninety-one non-commissioned officers and privates; total strength, fifty officers, one thousand and twenty-one non-commissioned officers and privates.

1853. On the 19th February, Major-General H. Somerset, C.B., commanding the Northern Division, made his half-yearly inspection. (Present on parade: twenty-nine officers, seven hundred and nine non-commissioned officers and privates; total strength, fifty officers, nine hundred and eighty-nine non-commissioned officers and privates.)

By a War Office letter, dated 18th April, the establishment was increased by two captains, and diminished by two lieutenants and four ensigns. Though two additional captains were authorised, the total strength of non-commissioned officers and privates (one thousand and seventy-nine) remained unchanged, but there was a decrease in the establishment of officers from fifty-two to forty-eight.

On the 24th of May, Lieutenant Bagenell, who had two days before been mortally wounded by a tiger, died; the same tiger also killed one of the natives belonging to the party.

★★★★★★

During the time the regiment was quartered at Deesa many tigers were killed by the officers—one of them, killed by Lieutenant Alfred Ingleby Garnet, on the 11th of February, 1853, was an enormous animal. It weighed four hundred and fifty-two pounds, which is a most exceptionally heavy weight.

★★★★★★

On the 14th June, Lieutenant-General Lord Frederick Fitzclarence, commanding the Bombay Army, communicated to the regiment the following extract from a letter received from Viscount Hardinge:—

> The report on the Eighth Foot is perfectly satisfactory in all respects, and the regiment seems in admirable order in every particular. The General Commanding-in-Chief has not failed to observe the very creditable fact of Ensign Bayly having passed his examination in no less than five of the native languages, a circumstance which will doubtless lead to his employment now that certain staff appointments are proposed to be opened to Her Majesty's officers.

Orders having been received for the removal of the regiment from the Bombay to the Bengal Presidency on 1st December, the Headquarters, with the Grenadier, A, B and light Companies under command of Lieutenant-Colonel Hartley marched from Deesa and were followed on the 4th, by the left wing, consisting of C, D, F, H, and I, under command of Major Edward Harris Greathed, on the occasion of the regiment leaving the Bombay Presidency, His Excellency Lieutenant-General the Right Honourable Lord Frederick Fitzclarence, G.C.B., commanding the Bombay Army, published a very complimentary General Order (No. 75, dated 24th November, 1853). It contained the following passages:—

> The testimony of his (Lord Frederick's) predecessors in command, and of the several general officers to whose care the regiment has been confided, combine to depict a state of discipline and interior economy almost faultless, and a rare combination

of every quality most to be desired in a body of British infantry..... His Lordship is stating a simple and undeniable truth when he declares that the absence of crime amongst the non-commissioned officers and privates of the regiment, and their exemplary conduct under all circumstances which have come before him in the most authentic shape have, from time to time, elicited his unfeigned applause, and established a claim to his lasting admiration.

1854. On 20th January, the Headquarter wing, and on the 24th the left wing arrived at Agra, the Headquarters arriving on the fifty-first and the left wing on fifty-second day after leaving Deesa. The distance between stations is four hundred and sixty-three miles. The average rate of progress, halts included, was, therefore, nine miles per day. (The distance is divided into forty-two marches; there were, therefore, ten days of rest, and the average length of each day's march was eleven miles.)

On 6th March, Major-General the Honourable George Anson, commanding the Meerut Division, made his half-yearly inspection. (Present on parade: thirty-one officers, and seven hundred and eighty-four non-commissioned officers and privates; total strength forty-nine officers, nine hundred and ninety-three officers and privates.)

On 27th July, a General Order, No. 39, was published, authorising the formation of the regiment in ten service companies, to take effect from 1st September.

On 26th November, the following extract from a letter of the Deputy Adjutant-General of the Army, dated Horse Guards, 4th September, 1854, was communicated to the regiment by the Adjutant-General of Her Majesty's Forces in India:—

> The report on the Eighth Foot is very satisfactory. The remarks made by the political agents in Rajpootana, Sir Henry Lawrence and Sir Richmond Shakespear, on the arrangements of the regiment for the transit of baggage on the march from Deesa to the Bengal Presidency, without calling for assistance from the native states, is highly creditable to Lieutenant-Colonel Hartley and the commissariat arrangements of the regiment. (The commissariat arrangements were made and superintended by Quartermaster J. Ross—a very efficient officer.)

On the 10th of October, lieutenant-General John Duffy, C.B. and K.C., from the Twenty-Eighth Foot, was gazetted to the colonelcy of the King's Regiment, vice General Sir Gordon Drummond, G.C.B., deceased. (For services of this officer, *vide* Appendix No. 2.)

1855. On the 24th of January, Captain Hext died. On the 18th of March, Lieutenant-General Sir Roderick MacNiel was gazetted Colonel of the King's Regiment, vice General John Duffy, deceased. (For services of Lieutenant-General MacNiel, *vide* Appendix No. 2.)

On the 22nd of March, Brigadier-General H. F. Salter, C.B., made his half-yearly inspection. (On parade: twenty-seven officers, seven hundred and thirty-two non-commissioned officers and privates; total strength forty-eight officers, nine hundred and seventy-seven non-commissioned officers and privates.)

On the 24th of November, the regiment, under the command of Lieutenant-Colonel Edward Harris Greathed (strength eighteen officers and eight hundred and twenty-two non-commissioned officers and privates), marched from Agra *en route* to Jullundur.

On the 8th of December, the copy of a letter from the Adjutant-General of Her Majesty's Forces in India (1096/27, of the 30th of March) was communicated to the regiment, which contained the following passage:—

> You will especially notice His Excellency's (Sir William Gomm's) gratification on observing that during a period of upwards of seven months there are recorded only sixty cases of minor punishments in the general's summary.

On the 20th of December, in passing through Umballa, the regiment was inspected by Brigadier-General M. C. Johnstone, commanding the division. There were present on parade seventeen officers and eight hundred and forty-six non-commissioned officers and privates.

On the 30th of December, the regiment arrived at Jullundur, having marched three hundred and sixty miles in thirty-seven days, halts included. This gives an average of nearly ten miles per day. (The distance is divided into thirty-two marches; there were, therefore, six days of halt, and the average length of each day's march was eleven and a quarter miles.)

1856. On the 10th of March, Brigadier S. H. Franks, C.B., commanding the Jullundur Brigade, made his half-yearly inspection. (Present on parade: twenty-two officers, six hundred and eighty-five non-commissioned officers and privates; total strength, forty-five officers, eight hundred and fifty-five non-commissioned officers and privates.)

On the 3rd of November, Brigadier M. C. Johnstone, commanding the Sirhind Division, made his half-yearly inspection. (Present on parade: fifteen officers, seven hundred and eleven non-commissioned officers and privates; total strength, forty-four officers, nine hundred and forty-one non-commissioned officer and privates.)

1857. On the 28th of March, the half-yearly inspection of the regiment was again made by Brigadier M. C. Johnstone. The numbers present on this occasion and total strength have not been recorded.

In the month of May, when the mutiny of the *Sepoy* Army in Bengal broke out, the Thirty-Sixth and Sixty-First Native Infantry, the Sixth Native Cavalry, one European and one native troop of Horse Artillery were quartered with the regiment at Jullundur. Two marches to the south was the fort of Phillour, commanding the bridge of boats which at that point connected the Punjab with the North West Provinces. It contained a magazine, siege train, and stores, protected by guards of the Third Native Infantry, which regiment was in the adjacent cantonment.

Immediately after the Meerut outbreak, orders were despatched from Simla by the commander-in-chief, directing the officer commanding at Jullundur to secure Phillour. But before the order reached the station. Colonel H. W. Hartley, of the King's, who commanded during Brigadier Johnstone's temporary absence, had taken measures for the purpose on his own responsibility. (This statement is made on the authority of Lieutenant-General Sir Henry Norman, who, after correspondence on the subject with Colonel Hartley, is satisfied that it is correct). The Meerut outbreak took place on the 10th, and the news reached him by electric telegraph on the 12th. The same night he detached Brevet-Major R. S. Baynes with Lieutenant Longfield, Lieutenant W. Webb, one hundred and sixty-two men of his own regiment and two guns, and on the morning of 13th May, these troops obtained possession of the fort without bloodshed.

This important success, which secured valuable material for the siege of Delhi, was not obtained too soon, for, as became known afterwards, the fort was to have been seized next day, on behalf of the mutineers, by the Third Native Infantry. Major Baynes and his party remained at Phillour.

As May advanced, the state of the native troops in Jullundur, who had unfortunately been left in possession of their arms, began to cause uneasiness. The King's Regiment was therefore kept ready in its lines, and a captain and subaltern with one hundred of its men, mounted guard in those of the artillery, where the women and children of the station were assembled for safety. On the night of the 7th June the native troops, numbering over two thousand two hundred men, broke into revolt. The strength of the King's Regiment on that day, as shown by the morning state, was twenty-three officers and seven hundred and thirty-five non-commissioned officers and privates (of whom thirty-two were in hospital).

The outbreak at Jullundur, like many others throughout India, was immediately preceded by a great incendiary fire. On the alarm being given, about 11 p.m., the detachment of the King's, which was on duty in the artillery lines under Captain J. M. Bannatyne, stood to its arms. Continuous firing in the native infantry lines having broken out a little later, the main body of the regiment got under arms also, but, as previously arranged, it waited for orders on its own parade, which was three-quarters of a mile from that of the artillery. Meanwhile the detachment in the artillery lines proceeded at once to guard the guns and protect the gunners while harnessing the horses.

The guns were then placed in position with the men of the detachment on either flank; and the women and children, as well as the wounded officers of the mutinous regiments, who soon began to drop in, were sent to the gunsheds behind. The brigadier joined soon after and sent for the main body of the King's. The regiment started at once under Colonel H. W. Hartley, leaving Captain W. Bayly and Lieutenant Stebbing with a detachment and two guns to protect the lines. It lost its way in a sandstorm, and before it reached the artillery lines the Sixth Cavalry and Thirty-Sixth Native Infantry had attacked the guns. Disconcerted in their advance by the sandstorm, these mutineers however had been easily repulsed by a round of grape and musketry, which cost them about a dozen men and horses, and when the King's arrived they had disappeared in the darkness.

Notwithstanding the reinforcement brought by the regiment, the brigadier remained in front of the gunsheds till morning. It was then found that all the native troops at the station, except a few artillerymen, had marched off in the night towards Delhi. Soon after 7 a.m., Brigadier Johnstone moved in pursuit with a detachment of seven officers and three hundred and nineteen non-commissioned officers and privates of the King's under Colonel J. Longfield, six guns, and some irregular cavalry which had arrived at Jullundur a few hours before. When he reached the Sutlej, he found that the mutineers, reinforced by the Third Native Infantry from Phillour, had nearly all crossed in spite of the opposition of an irregular force from Loodianah. He decided that further pursuit would be hopeless, but he directed Colonel

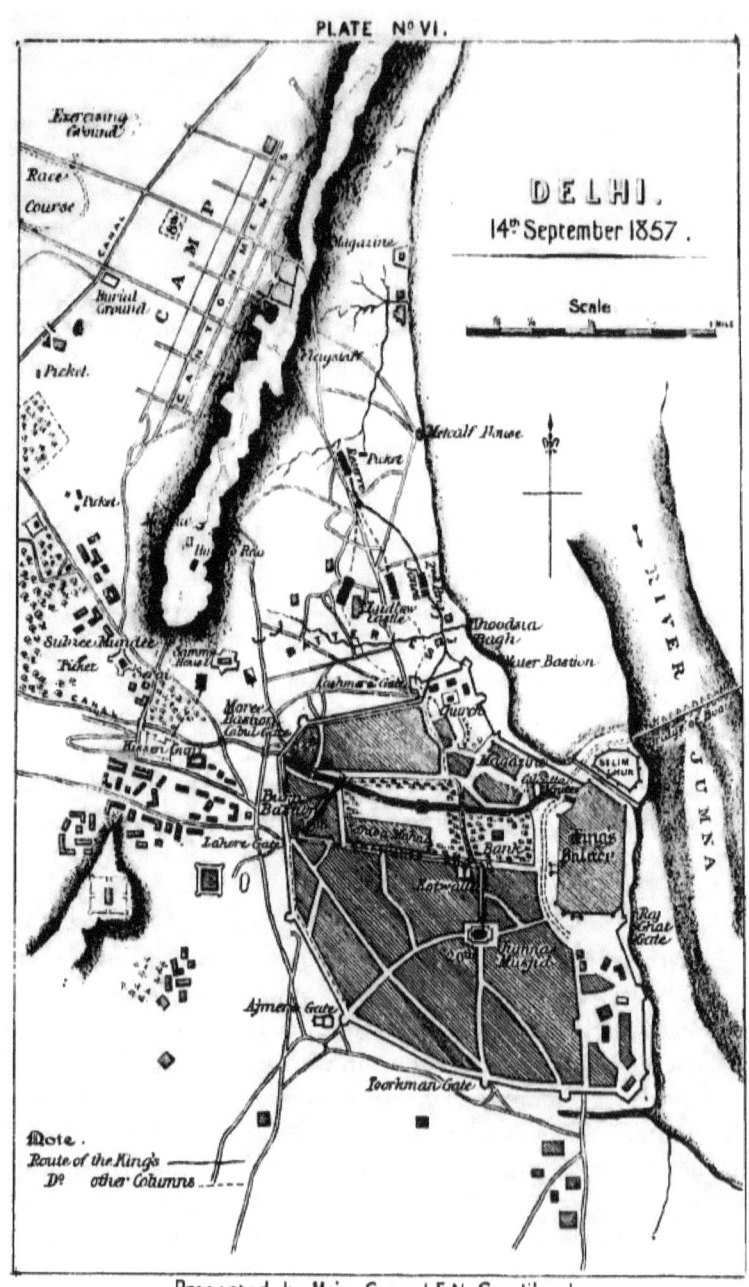

Presented by Major General E.N. Sandilands.

Longfield's detachment to go on to Umballa.

On the 14th June, the regiment received orders to proceed to reinforce the army under Sir Harry Barnard, then engaged in the siege of Delhi. It started the same night under Colonel Hartley, with two guns. Captain A. T. Welsh, Lieutenant Stebbing, and one hundred and twenty men were left at Jullundur under Lieutenant-Colonel Greathed. The sick soldiers and families were sent to Lahore in charge of Lieutenant T. Aldridge. At Phillour, the regiment received in charge some material for the army at Delhi, and left a detachment to garrison the fort under Captain J. Hinde who relieved Brevet-Major E. S. Baynes. On the 21st it reached Umballa, where Colonel Longfield's detachment rejoined. Two companies (F and H) under Captain Tupper were left there, and on the 28th, the regiment joined the army before Delhi, and was attached to the Third Brigade. The heat of the weather and forced marching had tried the regiment severely. The casualties on the march were Quartermaster Ross and eight men, who died from sunstroke or fever.

The strength of the regiment on arrival was twenty-one officers and three hundred and forty-one non-commissioned officers and privates. These numbers did not vary much throughout the siege, for the reinforcements occasionally received from Umballa were counterbalanced by the sick and wounded men who from time to time returned to that station. Sir Harry Barnard's army consisted of about nine hundred reliable cavalry, and three thousand nine hundred infantry, with twenty-eight field and sixteen siege guns. His camp lay on the north of the ridge running south-west from the Jumna, which at a distance varying from a mile to half a mile commanded the north-west front of the defences of Delhi. The piquets and batteries occupied this ridge, but the weakness of the British as yet precluded any serious attempt to lay siege to the place.

At this period the rebel force in Delhi it is supposed may have consisted of about nine thousand *sepoys* with their corps; there were also many furlough men, and a large number of armed customs guards, jail guards, and the like.

★★★★★★

This force was composed of the following corps:—Headquarters of the Sappers and Miners, No. 5 and No. 6 Horse Field Batteries; No. 2 and No. 3 Companies of Seventh Battalion Native Artillery; Third and Sixth Light Cavalry; a large part of the Fourth Irregular Cavalry; a few of the First Bombay Lancers; the Third, Ninth, Eleventh, Fifteenth, Twentieth, Thirtieth,

Thirty-Sixth, Thirty-Eighth, Fifty-Fourth, Sixtieth, Sixty-First, and Seventy-Fourth Native Infantry; also detachments of Forty-Fourth and Sixty-Seventh; a large part of the Forty-Fifth, and many deserters from the Fifth Native Infantry. (*This enumeration is given from information furnished by Lieutenant-General Sir H. Norman.*)

******

Besides these there must be reckoned a multitude of Mussulman insurgents. The total number of armed men available for the defence of the city may be roughly estimated at thirty thousand. (This is Lieutenant-General Sir H. Norman's estimate.) The artillery at the disposal of the rebels consisted of sixty field pieces, and there were one hundred and fourteen guns on the walls. The defences were in good order, and consisted of a rampart with berm and dry ditch, and with bastions at irregular intervals. Those facing the British position extended to three-quarters of a mile—equal to about an eighth of the whole *enceinte*—and were flanked by three bastions, the "Water," "Cashmere," and "Moree." The distance or length of "front" between the salients of the Water and Cashmere bastions was a quarter of a mile, and that between the Cashmere and Moree half a mile.

The place contained ample supplies of small arms, guns, and ammunition. Hardly a day passed without an attempt by the garrison to force the British position or destroy its communications. Although not so resolutely executed as skilfully planned, these attempts inflicted losses that made it difficult to keep up even the semblance of a siege. The situation was at its worst when the King's brought its scanty numbers to Sir Harry Barnard's aid, but the stream of reinforcements from the Punjab which was to enable the British to assume the offensive now set in.

The brigade to which the regiment belonged occupied the left of the position on the slope of the ridge near the Jumna. It was composed of a wing of the Sixty-First and the Fourth Sikh Infantry, and was commanded by Brigadier Jones, C.B., of the former regiment. Colonel H. W. Hartley was now, for medical reasons, ordered to resign the command of the regiment, which devolved on Colonel J. Longfield. Colonel Hartley was appointed to command the Umballa Brigade, but was afterwards transferred to Jullundur, where he died on the 25th June, 1858. Colonel Longfield soon obtained command of the Second Brigade, when Lieutenant-Colonel E. H. Greathed, who had rejoined on the march from Jullundur, succeeded to the temporary command of the regiment.

Soon after arrival the white linen or cotton clothing worn by the officers and men of the regiment was dyed the *Khakee* or mud colour used by the Sikhs. This colour was found to be much less conspicuous than white, especially on night duty, and the example was soon followed by other European regiments in camp.

Early in July the regiment began to suffer from cholera, which was prevalent in camp. On the 5th, Sir Harry Barnard died, and was temporarily succeeded by General Reid.

On the 8th the regiment formed part of a force sent under Brigadier Longfield to blow up the canal bridge at Bussee, nine miles to the right rear of the camp, which was used by the rebels in their efforts to interrupt the communication with Umballa.

On the 9t,h the regiment commanded by Lieutenant-Colonel Greathed, with other troops, was sent under Brigadier Chamberlain to dislodge a large rebel force which had occupied some gardens beyond the extreme right of the British position. These gardens were thickly wooded and enclosed, and they contained some houses which had been converted into defensive posts. The King's was on the right of the line, but the nature of the ground was such that no regular formation could be long preserved, and the troops eventually fought in groups.

After a severe contest, lasting several hours, the enemy was forced to retire on Delhi through the suburb of Kissen Gunj; but being reinforced from the town they rallied, again advanced, and surrounded a *serai* which had been occupied by the regiment, and by detached parties of the Sixty-First, and of several of the Punjab corps. As the ammunition of these troops was beginning to run short, and as the enemy had effected a lodgement close under the walls, and had begun to pierce openings for firing into the *serai*, it became necessary to evacuate the place.

Lieutenant Greathed, (brother of Lieut.-Colonel Greathed), Bengal Engineers, with a small party, volunteered to hold the gate of the *serai* next the town, whilst Colonel Greathed and the main body retired by another gate on the side of the camp. Colonel Greathed met with no serious opposition, but when Lieutenant Greathed and his party prepared to follow they found a considerable number of rebels barring their way out of the *serai*, and had to force a passage by a determined charge through the gateway. No. 2041, Private John Brown, greatly distinguished himself by his gallantry in this charge, and was in consequence promoted to the rank of corporal

During this day's fighting the loss sustained by the regiment was eleven men killed. Captain Daniell, Ensign Mounsteven, and twenty-one men wounded. Ensign Mounsteven died of his wound on the following day, and Captain Daniell was completely disabled for the rest of the campaign. Lieutenant and Adjutant Walker had his horse shot. The strength shown in the morning state was three hundred and twenty-three non-commissioned officers and privates, of whom twenty-seven were in the hospital.

Brigadier A. Wilson of the Bengal Artillery was now appointed to command the army, and Colonel Baird Smith became chief engineer. Under the direction of these officers the batteries were improved and better armed, but the supply of men and material at their disposal was not yet sufficient for a vigorous prosecution of the siege.

On the 14th July, the enemy attacked the right of the position with numerous forces. On that day one hundred and thirty men of the regiment under Captains A. C. Robertson and J. M. Bannatyne were on piquet at the fortified post of the Subzee Mundee *serai*, which covered the extreme right of the ridge. The Sammy House, another fortified post in the immediate vicinity, being seriously threatened by the enemy, forty men of the piquet under Lieutenant Grierson were detached to its aid. Several attacks subsequently made on it by strong columns of rebel infantry, supported by field artillery and a heavy fire from the guns on the ramparts of the city, were repulsed.

The Subzee Mundee piquet also was itself attacked by other large bodies of rebels, who, taking advantage of ruined buildings and enclosures, established themselves close to the walls on three sides of the post, and for several hours kept up an incessant but nearly harmless fire. Except a few marksmen posted at loopholes, the men of the piquet were kept under cover ready to repel the enemy had they come to close quarters. No assault was attempted, and the only casualty of the piquet was one man wounded. About 3 p.m., Brigadier Showers brought out a brigade and drove the enemy into the town. His loss was fifteen officers and one hundred and sixty-five men killed or wounded. Among the officers severely wounded was lieutenant-Colonel Neville Chamberlain, Adjutant-General of the Army. The main body of the regiment under Colonel Greathed was kept in reserve at the flagstaff tower on the ridge and was not engaged.

On the 17th July, the Third Brigade changed camp to the parade ground of the old cantonment. Cholera still continued, and the regiment had about eighty men on the sick list, but the change of camp had a beneficial effect

On the 18th July, the regiment commanded by Captain A. C. Robertson, together with the Sixtieth Rifles, a Goorkha Battalion, and the Fourth Sikh Infantry, was employed under Brigadier Jones of the Sixtieth in repelling a sortie on the British right. The enemy having occupied a ruined village in rear of the Subzee Mundee piquet, Captain W. Bayly with the light company of the regiment was sent round it, whilst Lieutenant Souter with the grenadiers led the attack in front. The enemy was thus driven out and fell back on Delhi. The force advanced as far as the enclosures below Ghosipore and then withdrew, being covered in its retreat by the companies of Captains G. E. Baynes and J. M. Bannatyne, which alternately relieved each other in extended order.

The regiment was again engaged on the 23rd, under the command of Major Brooke as part of a force which under Lieutenant-Colonel Greathed repulsed a sortie on the British left. The enemy having taken possession of some houses in front of the Cashmere Gate the regiment with other troops advanced in line without firing, and carried them by assault. The rebels retired into the town and a fire of grape from the walls immediately opened, under which the troops fell back on the ridge. In this action Lieutenant Pogson was slightly wounded.

The losses sustained by the regiment in action between 10th and 31st July, were twelve men killed, one officer and thirty-three men wounded. The deaths from disease in July were fifty.

Throughout August the increasing strength of the British was gradually making the prospects of the siege more hopeful. The duties were now very severe, and the regiment was almost constantly on outpost. But when off duty the men had rest, for the defence of the position was generally left to the piquets which were strengthened, and so strongly posted that although frequently attacked they rarely required support.

Lieutenant Sandilands was severely wounded by the splinter of a shell whilst on piquet on 10th August.

Before daybreak on 12th August, a detachment of the brigade consisting of one hundred men of the King's with one hundred of the Sixty-First, commanded by Captain A. C. Robertson, was sent with other troops under Brigadier Showers to attack a large body of rebels which had taken up a position at Ludlow Castle, threatening the Metcalfe piquet. The enemy lost four of his guns and retreated into

Delhi. The force had one hundred and thirteen men killed or wounded, of whom only four belonged to the King's. The brigadier being wounded, Lieutenant-Colonel Greathed was sent to take command and bring the troops back to camp. Captain Robertson's detachment, supported by the First Bengal Fusiliers, covered the retreat.

On the 14th, Brigadier Nicholson brought from the Punjab an important reinforcement consisting of about one thousand British, six hundred and fifty Native Infantry, two hundred Native Cavalry, and six field guns.

About the end of August, six officers and fully half of the men with the regiment were on the sick list, and Captains A. C. Robertson and W. Bayly and Lieutenant Grierson were invalided to Umballa, Lieutenant Grierson died at Umballa on the 4th September; Captain Robertson rejoined in January, and Captain Bayly in February 1858.

On the 4th September, twenty-five siege guns and the last of the available reinforcements from the Punjab joined the army; with these came the detachments of the King's from Jullundur and Phillour, in all about two hundred men, with Lieutenants Beere and Stebbing. The strength of the army, reckoning recruits and new levies, was about nine thousand eight hundred and sixty-six men; of these about four thousand were British. There was also at the disposal of General Wilson the Cashmere and Jheend contingents, numbering about two thousand five hundred men. (This is Lieutenant-General Sir H. Norman's estimate of the effective force at the disposal of General Wilson on 11th September). The strength of the King's at this time was fourteen officers and three hundred and eight non-commissioned officers and privates.

The time for a decisive effort was come; trenches were at once opened, and on the 7th Lieutenant-Colonel Greathed with six hundred and fifty men of various regiments seized Ludlow Castle and the Khoodsia Bagh—the latter a walled garden within two hundred yards of the walls. The batteries were now pushed forward to breaching distance, and on the evening of the 13th September two of the three breaches were examined and reported practicable.

The three breaches were within a distance of four hundred yards in the most northern front of the fortification. One was in the left face of the Water Bastion, another in the right face of the Cashmere Bastion, and the third in the curtain connecting these bastions. Looking from the breaching batteries towards the town, the Water Bastion breach was on the left, the Cashmere Bastion breach on the right, and the curtain breach intermediate between the two.

The breach in the curtain was, as the event proved, the most practicable of the three, but its practicability had not been ascertained, and its approaches were flanked by the fire of the bastions. The two bastion breaches were therefore selected for attack, and a simultaneous effort was to be made to force a way through the Cashmere Gate, which was close to the left flank of the Cashmere Bastion in the curtain between it and the Moree Bastion.

At 11 p.m. the same night orders for the assault were issued.

******

During the months of July and August, in spite of frequent defeats and heavy losses, the strength of the insurgent forces had been constantly increasing. Besides the daily arrival of armed adherents, singly and in small parties, attracted to Delhi from all the neighbouring provinces, the regular troops had been reinforced on 1st and 2nd July by the Rohilcund Brigade, consisting of the Sixth company Eighth Battalion Artillery, No. 15 Horse Battery, two six-pounder guns with Native Artillery from Shabjehanpore, the Eighth Irregular Cavalry, and the Eighteenth, Twenty-Eighth, Twenty-Ninth, and Sixty-Eighth Native Infantry; and subsequently to this before 1st August, by the Jhansi troops, consisting of half of No. 18 Field Battery, a wing of Twelfth Native Infantry and the Fourteenth Irregular Cavalry; by the Neemuch Brigade, consisting of a native troop of Horse Artillery, a wing of First Light Cavalry, Seventy-Second Native Infantry, Seventh Infantry Gwalior Contingent, and the cavalry and infantry of the Kotah Contingent.

This completes the muster-roll of regularly drilled troops, hut no data exist for even a tolerably exact approximate estimate of the total number of armed men available for the defence of the city on the 14th of September. (The detail of reinforcements received after 1st of July is copied from a memorandum furnished by Sir Henry Norman. *Vide* in connection with these details estimate given earlier, of the number of troops and armed men in the city at the end of June.)

******

The army paraded at 3 a.m. on the 14th September. The infantry was in five columns. The *first*, commanded by Brigadier Nicholson, and led by the First Bengal Fusiliers was to storm the Cashmere Bastion; the *second*, commanded by Brigadier Jones, Sixty-First Regiment, and led by the King's Regiment, was to storm the Water Bastion; the *third*, commanded by Brigadier Campbell, Fifty-Second Light Infantry, and led by his own regiment, was to enter by the Cashmere Gate after it had been blown in by a party of Sappers; the *fourth*, commanded by Major Reid and led by the Sixtieth Rifles, was to pass through the suburb of Kissen Gunj, and threaten the defences on the west of the city; the *fifth*, under Brigadier Longfield of the King's, was to act as a reserve. The cavalry was to afford a general support, preserve the communications and protect the camp. The first and second columns were provided with ladders.

The King's, leaving out camp guards and sick, had two hundred and eighty men available, who were told off in four companies as follows, *viz*.:—

No. 1. (Storming party carrying ladders). Captain G. E Baynes, Lieutenants Pogson and Metge, and seventy-five R and F.

No. 2. Brevet-Major R S. Baynes, Lieutenants J. V. Webb and McGrigor, and sixty-eight R. and F.

No. 3. Captain J. M. Bannatyne, Lieutenants Beere and Stebbing, and sixty-eight R and F.

No. 4. Lieutenant E. N. Sandilands, Lieutenant Bayly, Lieutenant W. Webb, and sixty-nine R. and F.

The field and staff officers present were Major Brooke, Lieutenant and Adjutant Walker, Surgeon Annesley, Assistant Surgeons Yates and Biddle.

When formed the columns proceeded to their posts to await the signal for the assault, which was to be the explosion at the Cashmere Gate. The post of the second column was in the vicinity of the left flank breaching battery, but as the storming party had to proceed first to the gorge near the Metcalfe Piquet to receive the ladders from the Engineers, the rest of the column waited for it in the Khoodsia Bagh, immediately behind the battery. Here Colonel Greathed, who had been on duty all night in charge of the left attack, joined and took command of the regiment.

A heavy artillery fire from the British batteries was going on, and had to some extent silenced the guns on the bastions. The rebels, however, still kept up a fire of musketry from the ramparts, and had sent guns across the Jumna to enfilade the British batteries and outflank the assaulting columns during their advance. The outwork of Selim Ghur, covering the palace at the north-east angle of the city, also maintained a constant cannonade on the Khoodsia Bagh and the British battery in front of it. Although under cover the regiment had Major Brooke (severely) and several men wounded.

After half an hour's delay, during which the usual morning ration of rum was issued, the column, having been joined by the storming party, moved to the front and took up a position on the right, but slightly in rear of the battery. (The statement in Sir John Kaye's history, that a double dram was issued is incorrect, so far, at least, as the King's were concerned.) There it nearly faced the unexamined breach in the curtain, and had the breach in the Water Bastion, which it was intended to assail, a little further off on its left front. It is obvious that the column, on its way to the bastion, would have the breach in the curtain on its tight front, but the dense smoke obscured the view.

The column was now within one hundred and sixty yards of the walls and was ordered to lie down. A small temple and a mud enclosure with prickly pears gave some welcome shelter, for the spot was exposed to the fire converging from many points on the adjacent battery. The guns were still in action and the gunners looked tired and jaded, for they had been on duty all night—many of them for several days and nights consecutively. The head of the first column could be seen a little to the right, its men also lying down. The detachment of the Sixtieth Rifles, intended to cover the advance of both columns, was extended in front, under such shelter as was available, but had not yet begun filing.

Day now broke, and soon a movement at the head of the first column was perceptible. The roar of so many guns prevented the second column hearing the signal, but it was evident that the time for action was come. The artillery fire on the British side immediately ceased, and was replaced by the musketry of the covering party. The fire of the enemy broke out with renewed vigour, as the assaulting columns rushed through the smoke across the glacis.

The Second Column was in the following order:—

Storming party of the King's with ladders.
Support of seventy-five men, Second Fusiliers.
Remainder of the King's in three companies.
Remainder of Second Fusiliers.
Fourth Sikh Infantry.

The storming party was guided by Lieutenants Greathed and Hovenden of the Bengal Engineers, and made straight, as directed, for the breach in the Water Bastion. But the supporting party of the Second Fusiliers, which was not encumbered with ladders, pressing eagerly forward on the right of the storming party, soon came in full view of the easy breach in the curtain. The temptation it presented was too strong to be resisted, or perhaps in the confusion and smoke it was mistaken for the breech in the bastion. In any case, the seventy-five men of the Second Fusiliers, closely followed by the rest of the column, leaving the stormers of the King's to pursue their course alone, rushed to the counterscarp of the curtain, slid into its ditch, swarmed up its breach and won the rampart.

The three companies of the King's thus led to the wrong breach by the support which they had been ordered to follow, had Brevet-Major R. S. Baynes, Lieutenants Beere and Walker severely wounded, and about fifty of their men fell on the glacis or in the ditch. Lieutenant Sandilands also received a severe wound—his second within five weeks—whilst securing a gun still in action on the ramparts. Drum-Major Byrne was wounded while sounding the advance on the top of the breach. The defenders retreated to the cover of some buildings from which they continued their fire.

Meanwhile the storming party of the King's advanced alone to the breach in the Water Bastion. What occurred is thus described in a letter, written by Captain G. E. Baynes, who commanded the party, dated 16th September, (two days after the assault):—

> Off we went at a trot up the glacis (the distance was about one hundred and fifty yards). It was now broad daylight. I looked at the wall and saw it crammed with *sepoys*. The wall in perfect order except just at the breach which was twelve feet wide. I hope I may never see again a carnage like that which followed. A nine-pounder played upon us with grape from the bastion, and a fearful fire of musketry from the walls—steady, rapid file firing—unchecked by the fire of a covering party, so not a shot was returned.

★★★★★★

Note: Two hundred of the Sixtieth Rifles were told off as stated in the text, to cover the advance of the columns. When the main body of the Second Column diverged to the right, and instead of the Water Bastion attacked the curtain, its covering party would naturally incline in the same direction, and direct its fire on the ramparts adjoining the curtain breach.

★★★★★★

You may easily imagine the consequence to a party advancing steadily and slowly in face of such a fire. The men were knocked over by sixes and sevens. Young Greathed was one of the first wounded. Metge also fell, and ladder after ladder went down. When I got within thirty yards of the edge of the ditch, I looked round, and out of eighteen ladders I saw only three left. I ran on to the edge to see what sort of place was before us, and called out to the ladder bearers to hurry on. I don't know what occurred after this as I fell to the ground and remained insensible for a few minutes. (Captain Baynes was at this time in a feeble state of health, and had insisted on leading the storming party, notwithstanding the advice of the medical officer, who wished to place him on the sick list.)

When I recovered, I saw no one standing near me, but two grenadiers were lying down a short distance off. I was too much exhausted to move, besides to lie still was the best thing to do. The fire from the walls continued as heavy as ever. I knew that threequarters of the storming party were knocked over, and I looked in vain for the strong supports that were to follow us. We were evidently left to shift for ourselves.

Suddenly the fire from the walls ceased. I got up and with the few men left went into the ditch, and into the bastion. In it we found some artillerymen who had got in through the Cashmere Gate and breach. (Captain Baynes has stated in another letter that Mr. Harvey Greathed, B.C.S., Chief Political Officer with the Army, brother of Colonel Greathed, was one of the first to enter the bastion after its capture.)

In the ditch I found eight of our men killed, and Pogson wounded by grape, lying all together. It was Pogson who brought up the ladders after I fell—poor fellow!—Nothing could exceed his coolness. (Lieutenant Pogson had his leg amputated and died a few days afterwards. He had been previously slightly wounded on the 23rd.)

Metge also behaved admirably. As soon as we saw we had no covering party we knew it was a desperate affair, but not a man flinched. When I got into the bastion I could only muster twenty-five men and one sergeant. As the storming party consisted of five officers (including Engineers) and seventy-five men, this would make our loss in killed and wounded four officers and fifty men.

After mustering his party Captain Baynes had to be carried to the rear himself, being unable to stand from excessive exhaustion. Colour-Sergeant Walker, who had greatly distinguished himself, now took command of the twenty-five men left. He was unable to find his own regiment, which had pushed on with the second column immediately after entry.

✶✶✶✶✶✶

In vol. ii, of the first edition of his *History of the Indian Mutiny*, Colonel Malleson erroneously states that this colour-sergeant was in command of the party when it entered the bastion. This mistake has been pointed out to him, and he promised to correct it in the subsequent editions.

✶✶✶✶✶✶

A party of the Fifty-Second drew near a little later, but the sergeant and his men were detained in the bastion by Major Brind of the artillery, and employed for some days in working the guns which were immediately directed against the outwork of Selim Ghur—still held by the rebels. The colour-sergeant subsequently received the medal for distinguished conduct in the field.

The mistake, or whatever it was, that made the support separate from the storming party and lead the rest of the column to the curtain breach, produced fortunate results. Nothing could have more effectually paralysed the defence than this movement, which forced the place at a vital point, turned the defenders' positions in the adjoining bastions, and fell on their line of retreat. It is impossible to say with precision what influence it had in securing the success of the first and third columns. But when it is remembered that one of them had to storm a large bastion held by superior numbers, and that the other had to force its way at a re-entering angle of the works through a gateway which was still susceptible of defence, although the gate itself had been destroyed, the effect may safely be assumed to have been considerable.

To the storming party of the King's struggling to make its way alone into the Water Bastion, it probably brought more effectual aid than direct support would have given it. On the other hand, the intrepid advance of the storming party, by distracting the attention of the defenders, and drawing a large share of the fire from the walls, no doubt diminished the losses sustained by the main body, and contributed to the success of its attack. Thus, the lives of the brave men who fell in the attempt to escalade the Water Bastion were not uselessly sacrificed.

Only Colonel Greathed and six officers of the regiment, *viz.*, Captain J. M. Bannatyne, Lieutenants J. V. Webb, A. R. Bayly, McGrigor, and Stebbing, and Lieutenant W. Webb, now remained unhurt, but Lieutenant Walker, who had managed with a little help to scramble up the breach, and Lieutenant Sandilands, accompanied it for some hours notwithstanding their wounds. The rank and file of the regiment now numbered only about one hundred and fifty.

As the interior wall of the curtain was high and uninjured, the column had to file to the right under the enemy's fire, and descend by a ramp near the Cashmere Bastion into the open space in rear of that work and the Cashmere Gate. There they had to pass through some of the men of the first and third columns who were streaming rapidly into the place. The column was quickly extricated from the confusion, and led by the King's, started at a rapid pace along the rear of the ramparts towards the Moree Bastion. Amongst other casualties during the advance a promising young officer of the regiment. Lieutenant W. Webb, was mortally wounded. The defenders of the Moree were still firing on the British cavalry and reserves outside the walls, but they fled from the work on the approach of the column, and only a few were bayoneted.

The next point reached was the Cabul Gate, which was easily secured, but the wide street (occupying both sides of the canal) which leads thence into the city, was still commanded by the enemy who, from the further end, raked it with round shot and musketry. Up to this point an impetuous advance had carried everything before it, but now it was necessary to pause. The risk to a detached body of losing itself amongst the intricacies of a large city had been foreseen, and the second column had directions to halt at the Cabul Gate and await orders. Part of the column however, in its eagerness, went a quarter of a mile beyond the gate, along the road in rear of the ramparts, and got near the Burn, or Lahore Bastion, on the west of the city.

This work might probably have been carried, for as yet it was not held in force, but before the attempt could be made, the brigadier had stopped the advance, and ordered such troops as had passed the Cabul Gate to return there without delay. This order does not seem to have been understood by all, for Lieutenants Bayly, Stebbing, and McGrigor, with a few men of the regiment, and some of the officers and men of other corps who had advanced furthest, remained at the point near the Lahore Bastion where it reached them. There they were exposed to a heavy fire, for the enemy, seeing them halt, plied them with musketry from a screen at the bastion, and from the house-tops in its vicinity, as well as with grape from a field-piece in the lane. They captured this gun by a rush, and, although they were unable to keep it, they continued to hold their ground, sheltering themselves as best they could.

Meanwhile, the remainder of the column had been concentrated at the Cabul Gate. The cessation of the advance encouraged the enemy, and his fire became so heavy that orders were given by the brigadier to place the regiments under cover in the adjacent houses. This had been partly done when Brigadier Nicholson and the first column having followed a different route, arrived at the Cabul Gate also. He soon after proceeded with his own column, now greatly reduced in numbers, to the advanced point near the Lahore Bastion, still held by the few officers and men of the second column.

On reaching it General Nicholson found that the bastion was strongly held by the rebels, and that the fieldpiece already referred to commanded the narrow lane up which his advance would have to be made. He succeeded in recapturing this gun, and spiked it; but another gun, higher up the lane, immediately opened, pouring a destructive fire through his necessarily compact ranks. Notwithstanding severe losses, he tried to push on, but the troops hesitated. Nicholson commanded and entreated by turns but to no purpose.

In the midst of his efforts he was struck down himself, and his men gave way at once. Nicholson was carried a few steps when he said "let me walk." Lieutenant Bayly of the King's tried to support him, but he had to be carried, and the retreat was continued in disorder, the *sepoys* doubling down the lane in pursuit. As the party fell back on the Cabul Gate, there was some risk that the second column might be affected by the disaster, but discipline prevailed and the enemy was repulsed. When General Nicholson was carried to the rear, his regiments joined the second column under Brigadier Jones.

As the day advanced the Lahore Bastion opened with shot and shell, and the troops at the Cabul Gate were thus placed between two fires. Being without artillery, and without orders or any information as to what had happened in other parts of the city, Brigadier Jones left Colonel Greathed in command, and went to report the state of affairs to General Wilson.

Colonel Greathed now proceeded to reconnoitre, and occupy the line of the canal. Retaining his hold on the Cabul Gate as a point of appui, he thus sought to join hands with the columns in other parts of the city, whose whereabouts could only as yet be conjectured from the sound of firing. Some of the large houses on either side of the canal were taken possession of, a regiment or strong piquet being placed in those that overlooked the streets and lanes in the vicinity. With the command obtained from the roofs, and with the aid of some guns which soon arrived, the enemy's fire was controlled.

On the brigadier's return he found the orders he brought from General Wilson anticipated by the measures taken by Colonel Greathed, and it only remained to perfect the communications and provide for the comfort and security of the troops.

The regiment occupied a large two-storeyed house about two hundred yards from the Cabul Gate, and on the north bank of the canal. The soldiers found in it a large number of women and children—apparently of a superior class. These poor people were treated with respect and kindness, and sent under escort to the British camp. The position covered a great part of the city lying north of the canal, although it was not yet connected with that of the third and fifth columns, the latter of which, after acting as a reserve during the assault, had now entered the city. As all the most important defensible buildings, however, were in the parts still held by the rebels, a portion of the siege train was brought in during the night. The fourth column having failed to force its way through the suburb of Kissen Gunj, was now available for service within the walls.

The casualties of the regiment during the day had been eight officers out of fourteen, and one hundred men out of two hundred and eighty, killed or wounded. A telegram was sent to the depot at Umballa requesting that every available officer there should be directed to join the regiment.

On the 15th, a force of about two thousand rebels attacked the posts held by the King's and the Fourth Sikh Infantry, but was repulsed. The streets and lanes near the canal having been further reconnoitred by Colonel Greathed, a detachment of the regiment under Lieutenant J. V. Webb was sent to prolong the left of the position, by occupying a post in the direction of the third and fifth columns, which with General Wilson's headquarters were located near the church. Another small detachment, under Lieutenant Stebbing, was placed in the Moree Bastion. Some of the troops fell this day into a trap laid for them by the enemy in the form of large supplies of liquor, and it has been asserted that excesses occurred, but the first and second columns escaped this danger, except in a solitary instance, in connection with which Lieutenant J. V. Webb and Sergeant Thorn of the King's rendered good service.

On the 16th, the troops near the church breached and stormed the magazine, and on the following day they took the house of the Delhi Bank. During these days the first and second columns remained chiefly on the defensive, but a slight advance was made by the Seventy-Fifth, which occupied a post two hundred yards to the south of the canal. Some efforts were also made by the Engineers, under Colonel Greathed's direction, to gain ground by sapping through houses, but as no working parties were supplied, it does not seem that General Wilson had as yet fully determined on this mode of attack.

Colonel Greathed however found a narrow lane, leading from the advanced post of the Seventy-Fifth above mentioned, into the broad street known as the Chandnee Chowk—one of the main arteries of Delhi. Starting from the Lahore Gate, the course of this street was nearly parallel to that of the street and canal occupied by the British, and the distance from one to the other might be about a quarter of a mile. Colonel Greathed suggested that a small body of troops advancing unperceived along the connecting lane, might take the enemy so far by surprise, that once in the Chandnee Chowk, it could secure the Lahore Gate, and thus get in rear of the Lahore Bastion, without being exposed to its fire.

General Wilson approved of this plan being put in execution by Colonel Greathed himself, the King's, the Seventy-Fifth, and the First Bengal Fusiliers, in all about three hundred men, with two guns, being detailed for the duty. The attempt was accordingly made on the 18th; the Seventy-Fifth led, the King's were in support, the remainder in reserve. The following extract from Sir John Kaye's history of the Sepoy War correctly states what happened, *up to a certain point*:—

> The force made good its way without difficulty to the narrow street leading into the Chandnee Chowk, but the enemy were posted in force behind a gate at the end of it, which was unexpectedly flung open, for we thought our movements were unknown, and a six-pounder gun was brought to bear on our advancing detachments. On this Colonel Greathed ordered up a gun under Lieutenant Harrington, and directed the Seventy-Fifth to charge under cover of the smoke when the gun should

be fired. But the Seventy-Fifth did not charge.

The circumstances resembled those which had foiled Nicholson—a closely packed body of men confronted by grapeshot and musketry in a place like a shooting gallery—and Colonel Greathed instantly ordered up his own regiment which was in rear, under Captain J. M. Bannatyne. The King's, accompanied by the Seventy-Fifth, rushed at the gateway and occupied it at once.

★★★★★★

Sir John Kaye's assertion that when the King's were ordered to the front "they also refused to charge," is a grave misstatement which he would no doubt have hastened to correct had he lived long enough. When his attention was drawn to the matter by a letter from Lieut.-Colonel J. M. Bannatyne, which was concurred in and forwarded by Major-Gen. Sir Edward Greathed, he was on his deathbed and could only reply that he was "too ill for controversy." Sir John's whole statement of the circumstances following the extract given in the text is unfair to the troops and misleading in every way.

★★★★★★

Colonel Greathed and the officers were of course in front, but a private of the King's, Peter Murphy, was at the gateway as soon as any of them. Lieutenant Briscoe of the Seventy-Fifth was killed during the charge.

But Colonel Greathed now found himself confronted by difficulties that were insurmountable. As a surprise the attack had failed, and the houses on both sides of the Chandnee Chowk were filled with *sepoys* who commanded the entrance at the gateway with a concentrated fire from the windows. As both ends of the Chowk were also in the enemy's possession, the advance to the Lahore Gate would have had to be effected, not only against desperate numerical odds, but under fire from front, rear and flanks. Colonel Greathed quickly saw that his intentions had been frustrated by the vigilance of the enemy, and he therefore gave the order to retire without attempting to enter the Chowk. The retreat was executed in perfect order and without loss, for the enemy, strong as he was, did not venture to enter the lane.

Working parties, directed by Engineers, were now placed under Colonel Greathed's orders to cut through the deserted houses and lanes south of the canal. So successful was this work that in about twenty-four hours, that is to say on the evening of the 19th, a way had been made, without attracting the enemy's attention, to a point immediately in rear of the Lahore (or Burn) Bastion. There it was discovered by Captain Gordon of the Seventy-Fifth that the bastion was almost deserted. He immediately took possession of it with his men, and the position was made secure soon after by the arrival of Brigadier Jones with a force consisting of the King's, under Captain J. M. Bannatyne, and other corps. This success, gained without loss, was the crowning event of the siege.

When Brigadier Jones' force, of which a part including the King's had spent the night in the bastion, advanced to the Lahore Gate at daybreak on the 20th, it found that the enemy had disappeared from that part of the city. The brigadier was now ordered to divide his force and proceed with one part along the ramparts towards the Ajmere Gate at the south-west angle of the walls detaching the remainder up the Chandnee Chowk to occupy the Jumma Musjid which was about a mile distant. This celebrated building, standing in an elevated position, overlooked the parts of the city still held by the rebels, and it was believed that its occupation by the British would speedily bring the struggle to a close.

The King's, still commanded by Captain J. M. Bannatyne, and the 1st Bengal Fusiliers under a subaltern, two guns with two eight-inch mortars and some sappers, formed the detachment, which was placed under the command of Major Brind of the Bengal Artillery. (Lieutenants W. R. Ximenes and F. B. McCrea, who had rejoined from sick leave on the 18th, were with the regiment during the occupation of the Lahore Bastion and the Jumma Musjid.) As they proceeded, the appearance of the city was striking. Not a soul was to be seen, but from the firing heard in the direction of the palace it was evident that part of the enemy's forces still held their ground there.

At the Kotwallee the detachment halted to admit of a view being had from its roof. No signs of the enemy being visible it then proceeded cautiously to the Jumma Musjid, which was found deserted except by a few *fakirs*. As the firing at the palace continued, the Musjid was rapidly prepared for defence, and. the King's and other troops were allotted to stations.

But in little more than an hour the cessation of firing, and the loud cheering, seemed to indicate that the fight was over. And so, in truth it proved, for the king had fled, and the city had at last fallen into the hands of the British. Communications throughout were soon established, guards and detachments posted, and the various brigades were allotted to districts. The King's remained at the Jumma Musjid, where Captain Hinde and Lieutenant Horace Ximenes from Umballa and the detachments from the various posts in the city, joined the Headquarters of the regiment.

Thus, ended the siege of Delhi.

★★★★★★

The total killed, wounded, and missing during the siege (all ranks included) is stated by Lieutenant-General Sir H. Norman in his narrative of the Delhi campaign to have been—

From the 30th of May to the 8th of September, the day on which the batteries were opened	2,163
From the 8th to the 14th of September	327
During assault on the 14th of September	1,187
From the 14rh of September until final capture of the city on the 20th of September	177
Total casualties from the 30th May to the 20th of September	3,854

The casualties of the King's Regiment during that period (30th of May to the 20th of September) was: Killed, three officers, five sergeants, thirty-six rank and file, total forty-four; wounded, seven officers, nine sergeants, one hundred and twenty rank and file, total one hundred and thirty-six; total casualties, all ranks included, one hundred and eighty.

★★★★★★

The men of the King's had behaved throughout with admirable steadiness and good order. Their constancy in the wearying duties of the siege, their valour in the assault, and their soldierlike discipline during the operations in the city, did honour to them as soldiers: their chivalrous humanity to the women and children found in the city did honour to them as men.

On the 21st, a movable column was ordered to proceed down country through the "Doab," between the Ganges and Jumna, to clear it of rebel forces, and to re-open communication with Cawnpore. Lieutenant-Colonel Greathed was appointed to command it, with Captain J. M. Bannatyne of the King's as Brigade-Major. The column was composed of the Ninth Lancers, squadrons of First, Second, and Fifth Punjab Cavalry, squadron of Hodson's Horse, two troops horse artillery, one field battery, two five and a half inch mortars, two hundred Sikh sappers, the King's (under Captain J. Hinde), and Seventy-Fifth Regiment, Second and Fourth Regiments of Punjab Infantry, in all about two thousand eight hundred men, with sixteen pieces of artillery; of this force only about nine hundred were British.

The column crossed the Jumna on the 24th, and marched to Ghazee-oo-deen Nuggur. The regiment now mustered only two hundred and twelve non-commissioned officers and privates, of whom fifty-eight were on the sick list from fever on the day it left Delhi. The men were much weakened by the labour of the siege and the polluted air of the city, but from this time their health steadily improved.

On the 27th, the column reached Secunderabad, where it was ascertained that a body of three or four thousand rebels, with six or eight guns, was at Bulandshahr, the next halting place. The column started at three o'clock next morning, and soon after dawn the enemy was found strongly posted in the village and surrounding enclosures. The extent and thickness of these enclosures prevented any attempt to turn the position. Colonel Greathed's artillery supported by the King's and Seventy-Fifth was brought into action at once, and several determined flank attacks made by the rebel *sowars* were frustrated by his cavalry. In one of these the rebel Fourteenth Irregulars were severely handled by the Punjab Corps. The enemy's artillery being silenced. Colonel Greathed's infantry threw itself on the main body, drove it from its positions and routed it with considerable slaughter.

The enemy fled towards Rohilcund, suffering severely from Colonel Greathed's cavalry, which pursued them for many miles. Two guns, with a quantity of ammunition and stores, were captured, and the fort of Malaghur, abandoned by the rebels, was occupied the same day. The King's, under Captain Hinde, was on the right of the line during the attack on the enemy's position and engaged in driving his left out of some gardens. Lieutenant Edgeworth was severely wounded whilst leading part of the regiment up to a loopholed stone wall held by the enemy. The column had ten officers and sixty men killed or wounded, of whom only the officer above named and four privates belonged to the regiment.

The column halted for some days to send its wounded to Meerut, to demolish the fort of Malaghur, and to await the arrival of a Belooch Battalion from Delhi which was to garrison Bulandshahr. It resumed its march on the 3rd October, and on the 5th reached Alighur, a town held by about two thousand rebels under a Moulvee. In effecting his retreat, the Moulvee lost three hundred men and some guns. At Akrabad on the 6th, another small rebel force was broken up, and two ringleaders in the late disturbances were killed, with about one hundred of their followers.

At Byjygurh, reached on the 8th October, Colonel Greathed received an appeal for aid from the authorities at Agra, who expected that the fort in which all the Europeans of the station and district were collected would shortly be attacked by a large body of rebels from Dholpore and Gwalior. He determined to diverge from his route far enough to judge for himself of the position of affairs, and to be then guided by circumstances. With this view he sent forward Major Ouvry with the Ninth Lancers, the squadrons of First, Second, and Fifth Punjab Cavalry, and two troops horse artillery to make a reconnaissance towards Agra, and to co-operate with the garrison there in securing the bridge of boats.

Purposing to follow as fast as he could without harassing the infantry, he marched on the 9th to Hatrass, and would have completed the distance to Agra in two marches more.

But at Hatrass such urgent demands for immediate help awaited him that he decided on a forced march of thirty miles in order to reach Agra next morning. He arranged that the European infantry should be carried on elephants, camels, and carts, and the force started at 6 p.m. About midnight, Major Ouvry's cavalry was overtaken in camp at Saidabad, and soon after the whole column pushed on under Colonel Greathed. The bridge of boats was reached early in the morning (10th), and it was found that Agra was as yet undisturbed by any hostile force.

Here Colonel Greathed was met by Colonel Fraser, the Civil Commissioner, and Colonel Cotton, the officer commanding the troops, both of whom were senior to him in military rank. They represented that five or six thousand rebels with twelve guns, some of which were fitted for siege purposes, were rapidly approaching; but that the garrison had a patrol on the Karee Nuddee, a stream thirteen miles south of Agra, which must be crossed by troops advancing from that direction, and that none had as yet done so. They urged that as the fort was full of women and children, was short of gunners, and garrisoned by only one weak regiment of Europeans, Colonel Greathed should delay long enough to meet the advancing enemy. To this Colonel Greathed assented. The column immediately crossed the river, and proceeded past the fort towards the cantonment which lay to the south of it, on the probable line of the enemy's advance.

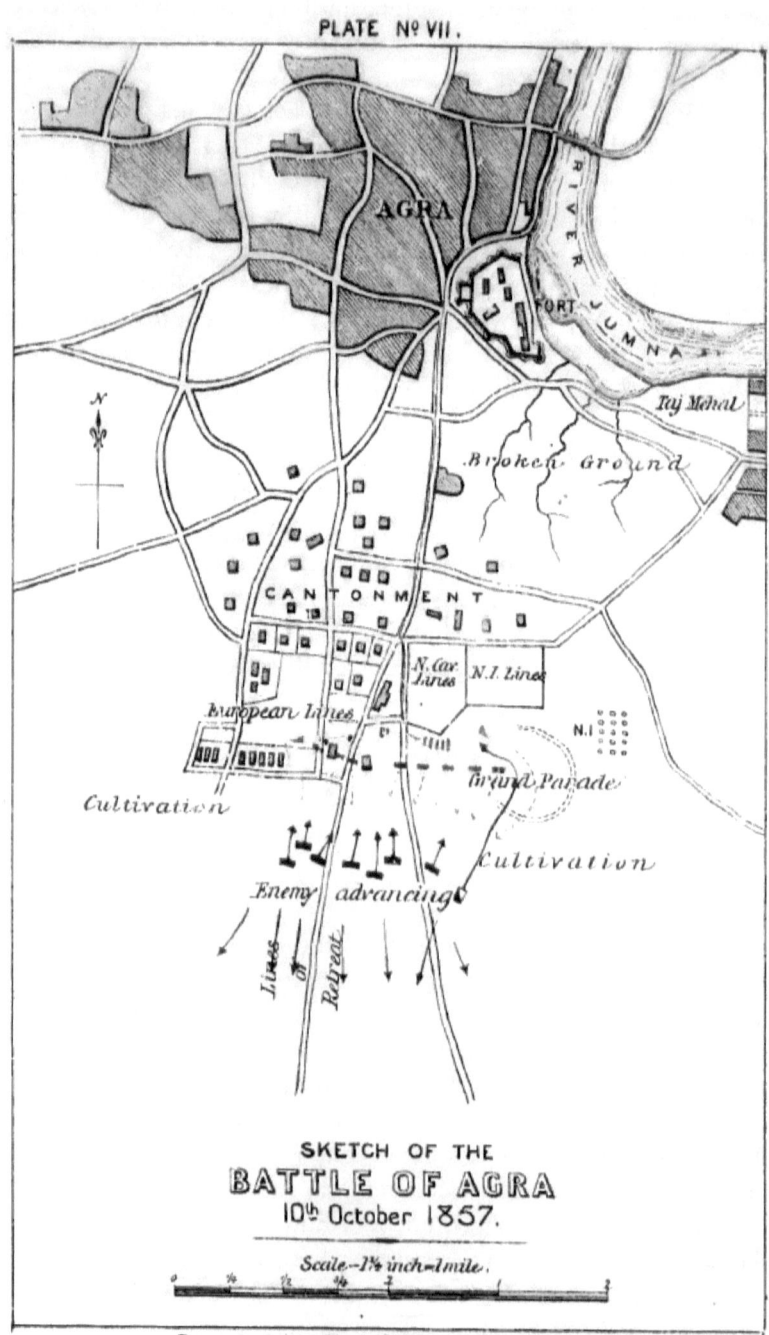

✶✶✶✶✶✶

The following description of the appearance of the regiment at this time is borrowed from Mr. Raikes' *Notes on the Agra Revolt*, quoted in Malleson's history:

"We went this morning to see Colonel Greathed's column cross the bridge. The Queen's Eighth, passed within three yards of us. 'Those dreadful looking men must be Afghans,' said a lady to me, as they slowly and wearily marched by. I did not discover they were Englishmen till I saw a short clay pipe in the mouth of nearly the last man. My heart bled to see these jaded, miserable objects, and to think of all they must have suffered since May last to reduce fine Englishmen to such worn, sundried skeletons."

Fortunately, courage, discipline, and the power of endurance had not disappeared with good looks, as was proved within two hours after these remarks were made.

✶✶✶✶✶✶

The brigade parade ground at Agra is fully a mile long by about half a mile wide, and together with the European lines occupies the whole south front of the Agra cantonment. A better place for manoeuvring troops could not be found. The force took up a position in a line facing south on this ground, having about six hundred yards between it and the crops in front. As forty-four miles had been marched in the preceding twenty-eight hours, and as a bridge of boats had been crossed, the tents could not be expected for some hours.

Under these circumstances Colonel Greathed ordered the men to pile arms as they stood in line, but to remain accoutred and ready to fall in. The guns were parked, facing south, and ready for use, between the European and Sikh Infantry, but the horses were not unharnessed, and the cavalry did not remove their saddles. Colonel Greathed directed two small parties of Sikhs to be thrown out in front as a precaution, but as the men were ready for action, he directed the posting of the general piquets to be delayed until the tents arrived. It is believed that the advance of these parties unmasked the enemy who, instead of being beyond the Karee Nuddee as represented, actually lay concealed by the crops within a thousand yards, and thus was brought on the action which is about to be described.

At the first gun Colonel Greathed's men stood to their arms. His artillery soon opened in reply, and a few minutes' observation sufficed to show the enemy's dispositions. Their line was parallel to that of his force, but rather to its right front, and their guns were opposite his right, on or near the high-road from Agra to Gwalior. Colonel Greathed's knowledge of the ground (for the regiment had recently occupied the station), suggested a way by which the enemy's left might be turned and their guns captured.

He accordingly moved the King's with the Fourth Punjabis to the right in prolongation of his line, and extended them, with supports, on the road leading from the native parade ground to the European barracks, directing them, as soon as the order to advance should reach them, to clear some compounds in their front which were being rapidly occupied by the enemy's infantry. A nine-pounder battery belonging to the Agra garrison was ordered to move forward by a lane abreast of these regiments. He then took three squadrons of Punjab Cavalry to the European barracks, still further to the right, and showed their commander how to turn the enemy's left and fall on their guns.

The order for a general advance of the line having been given, the King's and the Punjab Corps performed their task without much difficulty or loss. The advance of these regiments and the battery enabled the three squadrons to execute their flank movement with such effect that the enemy's left was routed, and several of their guns and standards captured. Meanwhile, the advance of the remainder of the British line had been checked by the enemy's cavalry which succeeded in turning its left. The rebel *sowars* galloped along the rear, captured a gun, and cut down the gunners, but the Ninth Lancers speedily fell on them, recovered the gun, and drove them back in confusion.

The advance was then resumed, and the enemy defeated on both flanks, made no further stand, although he continued to fire as long as any guns were left in his hands. The pursuit continued for three miles to a village on the Gwalior road, where Colonel Greathed's right halted to enable the left to come up.

Near this village, the King's had distinguished itself under Captain Hinde in taking an eighteen-pounder gun, a service which was specially noticed in despatches.

Colonel Greathed's troops were now joined by the Third Bengal European regiment from the Agra garrison, and by Colonel Cotton, who as senior officer assumed command and continued the pursuit. The cavalry and horse artillery clung to the enemy till they reached the Karee Nuddee, thirteen miles from Agra, but the exhausted infantry were halted half-way, at a place where the rebel camp was found standing. The rout was now complete, and the country was covered with fugitives. The enemy lost the whole of their guns, ammunition, tents, and baggage.

★★★★★★

The rebel force numbered from six thousand to eight thousand men. It consisted of the Mhow mutineers, part of the Neemuch mutineers, a body of fugitive *sepoys* from Delhi, Holkar's revolted regiments, and some troops from Gwalior. Their artillery, all of which was captured, consisted of one eighteen-pounder, one twelve-pounder, one ten-pounder, three nine-pounders, two eight-pounders, two seven-pounders, and two six-pounders; in all twelve guns. Their loss in killed was about five hundred men.—*Colonel Norman's Narrative.*

★★★★★★

The victorious column returned to Agra about dusk. The cavalry and artillery had covered sixty-four, and the infantry fifty-four miles of road in less than thirty-six hours, besides manoeuvring during the action. The loss was five officers and sixty-seven men killed or wounded, of whom only two men belonged to the regiment.

The column halted for three days, and the sick and wounded were sent into the fort. On the 14th, it returned to the left bank of the Jumna, where it was joined by convalescents from Delhi. Lieutenant Sandilands, scarcely yet recovered from his wound, Lieutenant Longfield and one hundred and thirty-six men, joined the regiment, and raised its strength to about three hundred and fifty.

The march to Cawnpore was resumed on the 15th, and on the 18th, Brigadier Hope Grant, on his way from Delhi to join Sir Colin Campbell, overtook the column and, as senior officer, assumed command. Mynpooree was reached on the 19th, and some guns were found, but the *rajah* and *sepoys* had fled. Passing Futtehghur (which was held by the enemy) at a distance of twenty miles, the column had a brush with a small force on the 23rd, took two guns, and killed about one hundred and fifty men.

★★★★★★

On the 28th October, the establishment of the regiment was augmented by the addition of a Second Battalion. The news of this augmentation reached the First Battalion on 12th December, while encamped at Cawnpore. The officers of the First Battalion, promoted and posted to the Second, were Captain John Hinde to be major; Lieutenants Daniel Beere, Erskine Nimmo

Sandilands, George Corry, John V. Webb, William R. Ximenes, to be captains.—*Vide* Part 2.

******

On the 26th October, the force reached Cawnpore, where detachments of the Fifth, Fifty-Third, Sixty-Fourth, Seventy-Eighth, and Madras Fusiliers, in all about one thousand men, held an entrenchment protecting the bridge of boats over the Ganges. The Ninety-Third were to arrive next morning, and to be followed by other reinforcements from Calcutta. Sir Colin Campbell too was daily expected. Pending his arrival, Brigadier Grant took command of the troops, and Colonel Guy of the Fifth Fusiliers, as next senior officer, superseded Colonel Greathed in command of the infantry of the Delhi column.

Cawnpore was then a place of terrible interest, as it must ever be. The wretched entrenchments so long and so gallantly held by Sir Hugh Wheeler and his unfortunate companions were just as they had left them, and the house where the poor women were slaughtered still bore ample testimony to the atrocities that accompanied the deed.

The state of affairs at this time was critical. Bithoor, Futtehghur, and other places on the right bank of the Ganges were held either by foes, or by those who waited for some disaster to the British arms to declare their hostility; whilst across the river, the whole of Oude was in rebellion. At Lucknow, Havelock's and Outram's attempt to relieve the garrison had resulted in their being shut up with it.

The overwhelming force of the besiegers, the prevalence of disease in their own ranks, and the presence of the helpless crowd of women and children in the Residency had not only extinguished all hope of escape by their own efforts, but had made it doubtful if they could hold out long enough to be relieved by the efforts of others. At Cawnpore, from which place alone relief could come, the troops seemed to have enough on their hands already. The well-disciplined, well-armed Gwalior contingent, now a rebel force, eight thousand to ten thousand strong, with four batteries and siege guns, was at hand preparing to attack and seize the bridge of boats.

The one chance of being yet able to save the Lucknow garrison lay in the speedy arrival of reinforcements from Calcutta. These, at first weak and few, were now increasing in strength, and arriving more frequently; and it was hoped that before many more days had passed, a sufficient number of fighting men would be available at once to hold the bridge, and to make a hasty dash at Lucknow. In this hope, and that no time might be lost, Sir Colin Campbell, on his way from Calcutta, sent orders to Brigadier Grant to enter Oude and move slowly forward.

Taking with him the Delhi column, and as many troops as could be spared from Cawnpore, in all about four thousand men, the brigadier crossed the Ganges and encamped three miles beyond it on the 30th October. Further reinforcements as soon as they reached Cawnpore were to be sent after him. The infantry was now divided into wings of three battalions. The right, to which the King's belonged, was commanded by Colonel Greathed, and the left by Colonel the Honourable Adrian Hope. Owing to the numerical weakness of the King's and Seventy-Fifth, these regiments were linked together for field service as a single battalion under the senior officer.

The force moved on the 31st to Buseerat Gunj, and on the 1st November, to Bunnee. The latter was within one march of the Alumbagh, a fortified enclosure near Lucknow, which was held by about seven hundred men, of whom some had been left by Havelock and Outram when they advanced to the Residency, and some had been afterwards detached from Cawnpore.

It was now intended to wait for Sir Colin Campbell and the remainder of the reinforcements, but the ground at Bunnee being unsuitable, the camp was moved on the 3rd three miles forward to the village of Marigunj. Starting at 7 a.m., the force had just reached the new ground, when the advanced guard began firing, and an action ensued which resulted in the enemy's retreat to Lucknow, with the loss of about one hundred men and one gun. The British lost one officer and twenty men, of whom none belonged to the regiment. On the 5th November provisions were thrown into the Alumbagh, but the regiment was not engaged in this duty.

Reinforcements from Cawnpore came in daily. On the 9th the camp was moved forward half a mile, and on the same day the commander-in-chief arrived. Continuous firing in and around the Residency of Lucknow could now be distinctly heard. On the 10th the Oude field force was divided into brigades. The infantry actually present formed two brigades which were numbered the Third and Fourth, and it was intended that the Lucknow garrison, when relieved, should form two more, to be numbered the First and Second. The King's and Seventy-Fifth linked together were posted to the Third Brigade, of which Colonel Greathed was Brigadier, and Captain J. M. Bannatyne, Brigade Major. Brigadier-General Hope Grant commanded the division.

On the 12th, the division meeting with little opposition from the enemy, moved to the Alumbagh, and the garrison there was relieved

PLATE No VIII.

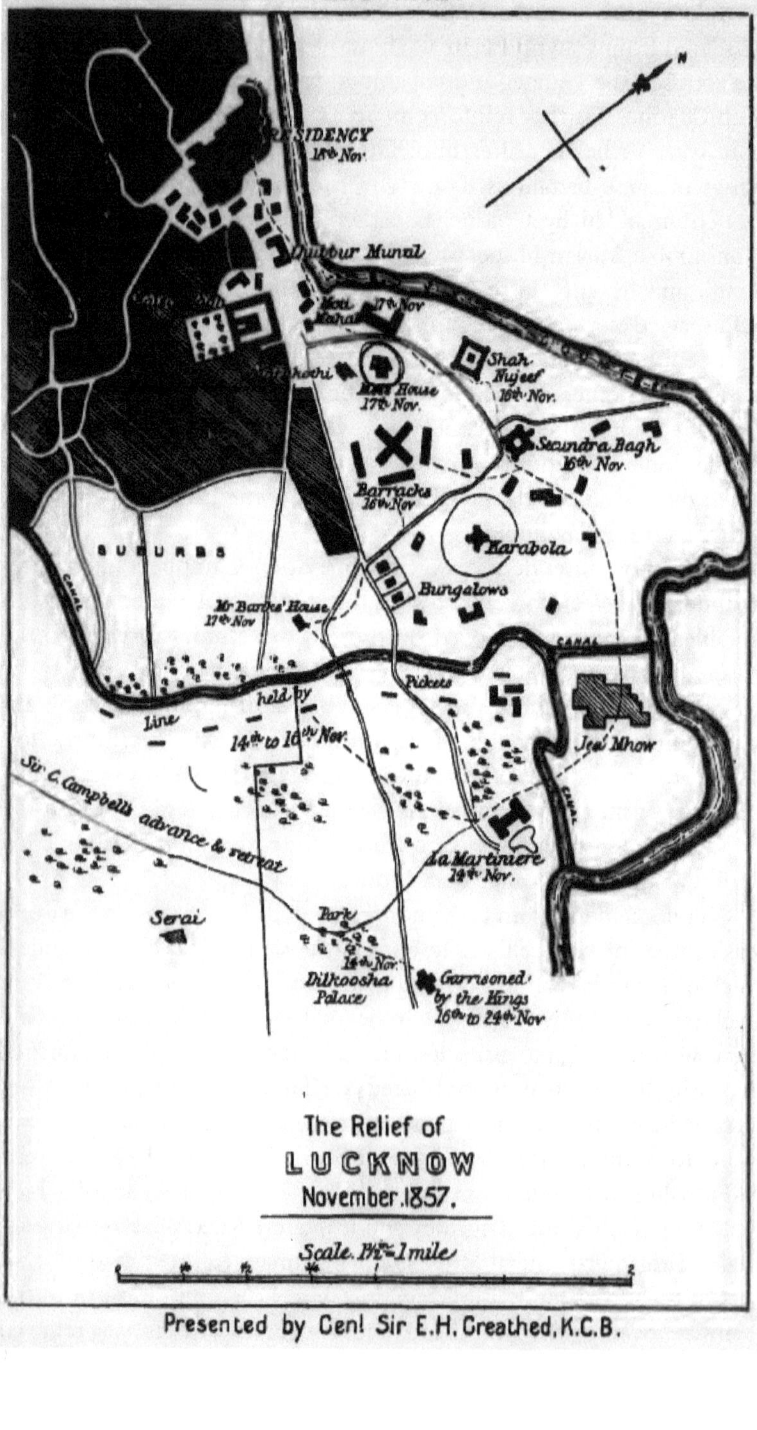

The Relief of
LUCKNOW
November 1857.

Scale ¼ = 1 mile

Presented by Genl Sir E.H. Greathed, K.C.B.

by the Seventy-Fifth and a detachment of the Ferozepore regiment. As no other corps was linked to the King's in place of the Seventy-Fifth, the regiment once more took its place as a separate battalion. All sick and convalescent soldiers, and the whole of the tents, knapsacks, and bedding were sent into the Alumbagh.

The last of the expected reinforcements having joined on the 13th, another brigade of infantry was formed, which was numbered the Fifth. The field force now consisted of the Cavalry Brigade numbering nine hundred men, the Third, Fourth, and Fifth Brigades numbering three thousand eight hundred infantry, twenty-six field guns, and a siege train. The operations for the relief of the Residency at once began.

The force started at 7 a.m., on the 14th, proceeding round the outskirts of Lucknow to the right or eastward. The enemy, deceived no doubt by a reconnaissance made on the preceding day in another direction, did not at first show himself, but on the advanced guard reaching the Dilkoosha Park he was found strongly posted. Brigadier Greathed led the attack with the King's, under Captain Hinde, and the other regiments of his brigade, which advanced in line under a smart but ill-directed fire. A skirmish ensued, and resulted in the occupation of the Dilkoosha and Martinière buildings with the parks and enclosures surrounding them.

On the 15th, the force halted in these positions, and to deceive the enemy as to his further route. Sir Colin Campbell poured a heavy fire of shot and shell into the part of the city and suburbs which lay directly between him and the Residency. At 9.30 p.m. Brigadier Greathed's brigade (including the King's), relieved all the troops on the advanced posts and piquets covering the British position, and was directed to retain them after the departure of the other brigades on the following day, and until the receipt of orders from the commander-in-chief. The brigade was then to form the rear guard under the guidance of the staff officer who should bring the orders.

On the 16th, the commander-in-chief moved to his right, crossed the canal which covers the east of Lucknow, and, avoiding the district shelled on the preceding day, forced his way at an unexpected point through the suburbs, and stormed the Secundra Bagh, and Shah Nujeef Mosque. While inflicting a severe loss on the rebels, he thus established himself in Lucknow, at no great distance from the Residency, with his right resting on the Goomtee.

In the meantime, Brigadier Greathed with his brigade retained the posts at the Dilkoosha and Martinière. On the arrival of the staff officer, the King's was left with some cavalry and five guns, under Brigadier Little, to hold the Dilkoosha; and the rest of the brigade closed to its right, and was led into Lucknow. The duty which now fell on the regiment and the troops with it was not attended with difficulty. The post was frequently threatened and on one occasion nearly surrounded, but no serious attack was attempted.

On entering Lucknow Colonel Greathed with the remaining regiments of his brigade was posted near the Secundra Bagh, a position which he retained throughout the operations. On the 17th, the barracks and mess house were taken by the commander-in-chief, and on the 18th, the Residency was reached. The force being too weak to attempt more than the rescue of the garrison, the rest of Lucknow was allowed to remain in the enemy's possession.

It was found impossible to complete the evacuation of the place before the 22nd, when all the women, children, sick and wounded, having been got out and sent to Dilkoosha, Sir Colin Campbell fell back on that place and the Martinière, abandoning for the time the posts he had taken in Lucknow. The retreat began at midnight, and was so cleverly managed without attracting the enemy's attention that his fire on the Residency, and the other posts, continued after the last brigade had quitted the place. As in the advance, so during the retreat, the rear guard was composed of Colonel Greathed's brigade. On its arrival at the Dilkoosha it was rejoined by the King's.

Throughout the 23rd the force remained at the Martinière and Dilkoosha, and on the 24th, the arrangements being complete. General Grant's division, without molestation from the enemy, escorted the non-combatants, sick and wounded, to the Alumbagh. Owing to deficiency of transport. General Outram's division, composed of the Lucknow garrison, had to wait at Dilkoosha till next day. Some of General Grant's transport having been sent back for its use, it then followed to the Alumbagh, where it was intended it should remain to watch Lucknow.

On the 25th, the King's was detached along the Cawnpore road to protect the sappers engaged in repairing the bridge at Bunnee. The wounded men from Lucknow and some prisoners proceeded under its escort. A number of ladies from Lucknow now became guests of the mess of the King's.

On the 27th, the commander-in-chief marched with General Grant's division, and the whole of the women, children, non-combatants, and an immense train, towards Cawnpore. About 2 p.m., heavy firing at that station was heard, and Sir Colin Campbell pushed on to within twenty-seven miles of the bridge, when on account of the convoy, he had to halt for the night. On the 28th, the tents and baggage of the troops were left in charge of the Fifth Brigade, whilst the convoy, escorted by the remainder of the force, proceeded. The sound of firing continued until the troops halted for the night at the Ganges, opposite Cawnpore.

It was then found that the Gwalior contingent had at last attacked the British troops under General Windham, and driven them into the entrenchment. In another day it would no doubt have destroyed the bridge which was already under fire, and have thus seriously compromised the safety of the convoy. The regiment was sent to occupy the bridge through the night

On the 29th, the Fourth Brigade was sent across the Ganges to support General Windham, who had been again attacked, and the King's was also sent forward to occupy and protect the ground selected for the camp of the convoy on the Cawnpore side. The remainder of the Third and the Fifth Brigade (which had rejoined in the night) were left on the Oude side. At 3 p.m. the Gwalior contingent having been pushed back, the convoy began crossing. The delays consequent on the nature of the convoy, and the state of the bridge, were such that the operation lasted twenty-seven hours. The convoy and troops encamped on the plain near the barracks, the left of the position being then covered by the King's. Although prevented from firing on the bridge during the passage of the convoy, the enemy still occupied positions from which his guns could reach the entrenchment as well as the camp; but no notice was taken of this, as it was desired to avoid bringing on an action till the convoy had proceeded down country.

Next day, however, the fire became so heavy, that many officers and men in camp were killed or wounded, and at 11 a.m., Brigadier Greathed with his brigade and some guns was sent out to force the enemy further back. Having done this, he occupied the line of the canal which divided the part of the station held by the commander-in-chief from that in possession of the enemy. The brigade remained in this position for six days, the King's and the other regiments belonging to it being constantly on duty under fire.

A sixth brigade of infantry was now formed of the Cawnpore troops.

On the 3rd December, five hundred sick and wounded soldiers and the whole of the families from Lucknow started for Calcutta under escort of the Thirty-Fourth Regiment. Throughout the 4th and 5th, the commander-in-chief remained at Cawnpore holding the Gwalior contingent in check, but fighting as little as possible. On the latter date, the enemy forced on an action, but was repulsed by Brigadier Greathed; the regiments chiefly engaged being the King's and Second Punjab Infantry. A twenty-four-pounder howitzer, which had opened fire at seven hundred yards, was compelled to limber up and retire by the effectual fire kept up by two officers of the regiment with Enfield rifles, which were loaded and handed to them by the soldiers as fast as they could use them.

******

As the regiment generally was still armed with the smooth-bore musket, and as only a few Enfield rifles per company had been issued, this incident, shewing the superiority of the new weapon, had much interest for the soldiers.

******

The mutineer gunners used cotton bales like sap rollers; by passing the bales in front of them they protected themselves while withdrawing their guns from exposed positions. The strength of the army was now about six thousand five hundred men, including one thousand men just arrived from Calcutta.

On the 6th December, the families being then well on their way, the commander-in-chief suddenly fell on the Gwalior rebels, drove them headlong out of Cawnpore, chased them for thirteen miles, captured their camp, large stores of ammunition, with seventeen guns, and scattered them in every direction. The regiment under Captain Hinde's command being still at the outposts was engaged during the earlier part of the action in covering the advance of the Thirty-Eighth and Rifle Brigade, but when the pursuit began it was left with its brigade to hold the line of the canal, and to prevent any part of the enemy's forces breaking through. The regiment had Lieutenant Vincent killed, and several men killed and wounded.

On the 7th, the brigade rejoined the commander-in-chief at a point two miles north of Cawnpore. The Gwalior contingent being disposed of, it was determined before returning to Oude, where Sir James Outram still maintained his position, to clear the rebels out of Futtehghur and the country north of Cawnpore—between the Ganges and Jumna. With this view the Fourth and Sixth Brigades were detached with cavalry and guns to Bithoor and Calpee respectively. At the former place Brigadier-General Grant defeated a large body of rebels and captured fifteen guns.

On the 24th, the commander-in-chief, leaving a garrison at Cawnpore, proceeded northwards by the Trunk road; the force at Calpee was ordered to move in the same direction along the Jumna, whilst that at Bithoor was to stand fast. Sir Colin Campbell had with him about four thousand men; and the brigade, to which the regiment was attached, formed part of the force. Brigadier Greathed had been appointed Adjutant-General, Queen's troops, Bombay, but was directed to retain his command in the field till the close of the campaign.

On the 28th, communication was opened with a column end convoy commanded by Brigadier Seaton, which had reached Mynpooree from Delhi, after defeating the rebels in several engagements. About the same time the Fourth Brigade rejoined from Bithoor.

On the 30th, the Third Brigade (including the King's), was detached with cavalry and guns under Brigadier Greathed, to destroy a village on the Ganges, a few miles to the right of the line of march. The work was done without meeting the enemy, who retreated into Oude, and the brigade rejoined the army, which by that time had advanced one march further northward.

1858. On the 1st January, Futtehghur being a march distant, the Fourth Brigade, with sappers, was sent to repair a bridge five miles in advance, where on the following day it was attacked by the enemy. The commander-in-chief at once advanced in support, and an action ensued at Khuda Gunj, in which the rebels were defeated, and lost seven guns, with a considerable number of men. The regiment, which was commanded by Captain Hinde, lost seven men, of whom five were killed, and one wounded by a round shot, which passed obliquely through the line.

This shot was fired from a six-pounder from a distance of about five hundred yards. The gun was soon afterwards destroyed by an eight-inch howitzer belonging to the Naval Brigade laid by Lieutenant Vaughan, R.N. The first shot he fired broke the wheel of the carriage, the second dismounted the gun, the third blew up the tumbril. This action closed the campaign, as the enemy retreated into Oude, leaving the country between the Ganges and Jumna in the possession of the commander-in-chief.

The fort of Futtehghur, a large earthwork, much out of repair, containing warlike stores, and a gun-carriage manufactory, was taken possession of on the 3rd, and the King's was specially selected by the commander-in-chief to form its garrison. On the same day, Colonel

Seaton's Column and the Sixth Brigade joined the army. Captain A. C. Robertson, who had been invalided from Delhi, now rejoined the regiment, having accompanied Colonel Seaton's column as Deputy Assistant Quartermaster-General. A few days later he was appointed Assistant Adjutant-General of General Windham's division, and on that division being broken up, he became Deputy Judge Advocate of Sir Hope Grant's division, with which he served till the end of the war. Colonel Greathed was now directed to take up his appointment in Bombay.

On the 9th January, the regiment was relieved in the fort, and was complimented by the commander-in-chief on its good order and discipline. On the 17th, Colonel Longfield, who had been detained on duty at Delhi, was appointed brigadier of that station.

The Third Brigade was broken up on the 23rd January. Next day the King's, which was to go into cantonments, set out, with two guns, on its return to Agra. The regiment was in splendid training, ready and fit for anything; its discipline was perfect, and all its departments in the highest order. Its commissariat arrangements were so excellent that the men, throughout the campaign, had never been without rations. In drawing the rations, the plan adopted was this: immediately on arriving at the camping ground, the supplies for the next day were drawn from the commissary and placed under charge of the quartermaster, by whom they were carried and issued when required.

Thus, the men of the King's often had their breakfasts and dinners cooked and ready to serve out while the men of other corps were waiting for their rations. But efficient as it was in all other respects, the numerical strength of the regiment had fallen too low for it to be of service in the field, now that many strong corps from England were on their way up country to meet the commander-in-chief, on his return to Cawnpore.

The regiment arrived at Mynpooree on the 27th, and at that station was joined a few days later by a draft from England, consisting of Captain Whiteside, Lieutenant Corfield. Lieutenants Whelan and Moynihan, and one hundred and thirty-five non-commissioned officers and privates. Captain Hinde, having been promoted into the Second Battalion, left the raiment here, and was succeeded in command by Captain J. M. Bannatyne. The march was resumed on the 4th February, and Agra was reached on the 9th. After a few days in the fort, the regiment once more took up its quarters in the barracks it had occupied during 1854-55. It was there joined, on 27th February, by convalescents from Umballa, and Captain W. Bayly, who arrived with them, took command as senior officer.

On the 12th April, the Mean Meer depot, with the women and children, rejoined Headquarters.

On the 2nd and 11th March, on the 17th May, and on the 21st and 26th June, detachments of the regiment were engaged in expeditions against bands of mutineers, who infested the villages in the neighbourhood of the cantonment. The detachment which left Agra on the 11th March, was commanded by Captain Corry. It consisted of Lieutenants Moynihan and Whelan, and two hundred and eight non-commissioned officers and privates, and formed part of a flying column, commanded by Brigadier Showers. The enemy occupied an entrenched village, situated among the ravines of the Chumbul.

From this position the mutineers were quickly driven by two companies of the King's, which attacked in skirmishing order. The mutineers were pursued for four miles, and lost about one hundred men. On the 26th, the column returned to cantonments; there were no casualties among the men of the detachment of the King's. None of the other detachments were engaged, the mutineers having retired at their approach; but the party which left cantonments on the 21st June lost two privates by sunstroke.

On the 25th June, Colonel Henry Winchcombe Hartley died of consumption, at Jullundur, where he held the appointment of brigadier. His services and death were commemorated by a very handsome monument, erected by his friends in the parish church of Malvern. Major and Brevet Lieutenant-Colonel Edward Harris Greathed was gazetted to the vacant lieutenant-colonelcy, and Colonel John Longfield succeeded to the command of the battalion. (For services of these officers, *vide* Appendix No. 2.).

On the 7th July, five recruits joined from England, and on the 19th July, the regiment (strength eleven officers and seven hundred and thirty-two non-commissioned officers and privates), under command of Brevet Lieutenant-Colonel Brook, marched from Agra, *en route* for Futtehghur, where it arrived on the 28th, having on the 26th detached Captain McCrea's company to occupy Meerum-ke-Serai. This detachment did not rejoin until 1st November.

On the 3rd September, a draft from England, under the command of Lieutenant Reginald Whitting, joined Headquarters. It had left Calcutta on the 25th of March, with drafts of Tenth and Thirteenth Regiments. These three drafts (strength about one hundred and twenty non-commissioned officers and privates) were directed to escort a large ammunition train proceeding from Raneegunj, *en route* to Cawnpore. In consequence of a threatened attack of several thousand rebels, and ten guns, led by Koer Singh, the escort was halted at Sasseram, and attached to Brigadier Corfield's field force, to which Lieutenant Whitting was appointed Staff-Adjutant.

The draft of the King's took part in various operations carried on by Lieutenant-General Sir Edward Lugard, K.C.B., against Koer Singh, in the jungles of Jugdespoor. One of these was the attack and capture of Perroo, on the 11th of May. In June Colonel Turner, C.B., succeeded Brigadier-General Corfield in the command of the Sasseram column; from that time until the 12th of August, the draft was incessantly engaged in the arduous and harassing duty of keeping open communications on the line of the Grand Trunk Road, and while thus employed it took part in many skirmishes with the rebels.

On the 12th, having received orders to join the Headquarters of the regiment, the draft commenced its march to Futtehghur, where it arrived on 3rd September, in most pitiable plight. It had lost nearly half its original number from casualties in the field, and from deaths from cholera and other diseases: the survivors had no kits; many of them had not even boots to their feet.

In the month of October, the commander-in-chief organised and set in motion several moveable columns for the subjugation of Oude, where, after the capture of Lucknow, the chief force of the rebels was concentrated.

The King's Regiment was directed to form part of one of these columns, which was commanded by Brigadier-General Hale, C.B.

On the 18th of October, the regiment (strength about five hundred and fifty non-commissioned officers and privates), under the command of Captain Whiteside, left its cantonments, crossed the Ganges, and joined this column; Captain Forster Longfield was appointed to act as its Brigade Quartermaster.

******

Ensign J. E. Whitting, of the Indian Army, brother of Lieutenant Whitting, was attached to the regiment and marched with it. Afterwards he was appointed ensign in the Thirty-Seventh. A detachment of one hundred and fifty men, chiefly consisting of sick and married soldiers, was kept at Futtehghur, under command of Lieutenant Stebbing. The Sixty-Fourth Regiment had also arrived to hold the fort and station during the absence of the King's.

******

Early in the morning of 24th October, Brigadier-General Hale reached Sandee, a fort strongly situated on the River Ghurra, and held by a numerous body of rebels. In order to enable the infantry and guns to cross the river, it was found necessary to construct a bridge. This work, owing to a hot fire from the fort, was attended with considerable difficulty. Three companies of the King's were sent across to clear the walls, and for several hours the fort was shelled by a battery of eight-inch mortars. The enemy then evacuated the place, and succeeded in effecting their escape. The column having marched into, and taken possession of the fort, its defences were blown up and effectually destroyed.

After the capture of Sandee a combined movement was made on Rooya, by the columns of Brigadier Hale and Brigadier Barker, and on the 28th, these two columns arrived before it. Rooya was a fort of great natural strength; its massive mud walls were surrounded on three sides by trees and dense jungle; on the fourth by a broad marshy *jheel* (or lake). It is the fort which, in the month of April, had cost the British Army the loss of Colonel Adrian Hope; but its defenders did not feel sufficient confidence in its strength to await a second attack: as the troops approached, dense volumes of smoke were observed issuing from the place, and it was found that it had been set on fire and abandoned by the rebels.

On the 2nd of November, the right wing of the regiment, consisting of B, C, and D Companies, under the command of Captain J. Whiteside, was detached from the column of Brigadier Hale, and ordered to join the column of Brigadier Barker: Lieutenant Reginald Whitting was appointed to act as Adjutant of this wing.

On the 8th of November, Brigadier Barker's column advanced on Goosagunj, and after making several long marches, and razing to the ground several strong forts, on the 20th of November, it crossed the Goomtee, and encamped at Neemsah. A large rebel force which was entrenched near this place, was dispersed by the cavalry, and Brigadier Barker's column, marching from fourteen to twenty miles a day in pursuit of these fugitives, followed them up to Misreegunj, Mincheta, and Kyrabad. On the 3rd of December, it made a long, forced march to Bishwah, where it joined the column of Brigadier Troop. Here the scouts, having reported that the rebels were in great force, and that their picquets were only two miles off, an entrenched camp was formed for the protection of the sick and of the baggage.

On the 5th of December, it was reported to the general that a large body of the rebels had doubled back in rear of the column. Colonel Leith Hay, with the 93rd Highlanders, was ordered to remain in charge of the entrenched camp, and the remainder of the force, without tents or baggage, made a rapid march to Baree, where the column arrived on the 7th of December. Here it halted until the 14th, when Brigadier Barker, leaving the wing of the King's and other troops to guard communications, marched with the remainder of his force to Sandala and the Seetapoor district

1859. The detached wing of the King's remained at Baree until the 12th of January. Meanwhile Brigadier Hale's column, to which the Headquarter Companies were attached after the capture of Rooya, had taken up a position near Hurdui, where it had remained in reserve.

On the 12th of January, the Headquarter Companies, which were then commanded by Captain Meade, received an order to leave Hurdui, and to return by forced marches to Futtehghur, where they arrived on the 16th. The same day that Headquarters left Hurdui (12th of January), the detached wing under Captain Whiteside was ordered to march from Baree to Hurdui, where it arrived on the 16th, and remained until the 28th, during which time Lieutenant Reginald Whitting acted as Field Quartermaster to Brigadier Hale's column.

On the 28th, the wing was ordered to proceed to Futtehghur as escort to a siege train: it arrived there on the 2nd of February, and rejoined the Headquarters of the regiment.

The return of this detachment terminated the field services of the regiment.

******

A memorial cross, designed by H. S. Leifchild, to commemorate the services and death of the officers, non-commissioned officers, and private soldiers, lost by the regiment during the campaigns of 1857-68, was erected on the Grand Parade at Portsmouth in 1862, by the officers of the King's. In 1877, this monument was remoted to the grounds of the Royal Hospital, Chelsea, where it now stands. Subsequently, (in 1879), a monumental slab was also placed in the wall of the cemetery, near the Cashmere Gate of Delhi, in memory of the officers and soldiers who fell during the siege and of whom, some were buried there, and some in the cantonment cemetery.—*Vide* Appendix No. 5.

******

The officers specially mentioned in despatches as having distinguished themselves in the various actions of the campaign were: Colonel John Longfield, mentioned on one occasion, the capture of Delhi; Colonel Edward Harris Greathed, on five occasions, *viz.*, the capture of Delhi, the actions at Bulandshahr, Agra, and Cawnpore, and the relief of Lucknow; Captain John Hinde on four occasions, *viz.*, actions at Bulandshahr, Agra, and Cawnpore, and relief of Lucknow; Captain Alexander Cuningham Robertson on one occasion, attack by Brigadier Showers on post at Ludlow Castle on the 12th of August, 1857; Captain George Edward Baynes on one occasion, the assault of Delhi; Captain John Millar Bannatyne on six occasions, *viz.*, Mutiny at Jullundur, capture of Delhi, actions at Bulandshahr, Agra, and Cawnpore, and the relief of Lucknow. These officers all received promotion for distinguished service in the field, and three of them were also gazetted Companions of the Bath, Colonel Greathed on the 1st, Colonel Longfield on the 21st of January, and Captain Hinde on the 16th November, 1858; Colonels Longfield and Greathed were further rewarded by Good Service pensions.

On the 22nd of January, Brevet Lieutenant-Colonel A. Cuningham Robertson (who on being promoted to a regimental majority had resigned the appointment of Deputy Judge Advocate) rejoined Headquarters, and assumed temporary command of the regiment, which he continued to hold until the 10th of September, of the following year.

On the 12th of November, the station was visited by the Governor-General Lord Canning and the Commander-in-Chief Lord Clyde, and Their Excellencies remained at Futtehghur until the 17th. On the 16th the regiment was reviewed by the commander-in-chief, and in the evening the officers gave a ball in the Mess House in honour of Lady Canning.

On the 2nd of December, in pursuance of orders to proceed to Calcutta for embarkation, the Headquarters and five companies, commanded by Brevet Lieutenant-Colonel A. Cuningham Robertson, marched out of Futtehghur, and were followed on the 24th by the remaining five companies, under Captain Meade. Headquarters arrived at Cawnpore on the 11th of December, and the left wing on the 1st of January, 1860.

1860. From Cawnpore to Allahabad the regiment was moved by rail in four detachments, which left Cawnpore respectively on the 7th, 8th, 9th, and 10th of January. From Allahabad to Calcutta two detachments were moved by bullock train, where they arrived on the 31st of

January and 1st February. The other two detachments were embarked at Allahabad in river steamers, and arrived together at Calcutta on the 13th of February. The strength of the regiment on leaving Cawnpore was seventeen officers and five hundred and sixty-six non-commissioned officers and privates.

On the 19th of February, two hundred and sixty-four non-commissioned officers and privates volunteered for various corps, most of them for the Second Battalion Sixtieth Rifles and Eighty-Seventh Regiment, both of which were then under orders for active service in China.

On the 5th of April, a detachment of the regiment, under the command of Captain Meade, embarked in the freight ship *Monica*, and commenced its homeward voyage. On the 14th and 19th two other detachments, under the command of Captain Forster Longfield and Lieutenant Tarte, embarked in the *Lady Clarendon* and *Sevilla*, and finally, on the 5th of May, Headquarters and the remaining companies, under the command of Brevet Lieutenant-Colonel Alexander Cuningham Robertson, embarked in the *Clara*.

Thus, terminated fourteen years of Indian service. The four freight ships carried home twenty-one officers and five hundred and nine non-commissioned officers and privates. Among the officers who embarked at Calcutta, only two, Brevet Lieutenant-Colonel Robertson and Quartermaster Keating, were with the colours when the regiment left Portsmouth in April, 1846.

The following farewell order was published by His Excellency the Governor-General of India.

Camp, Roopur, 6th April, 1860.

His Excellency the Governor-General considers it due to Her Majesty's Eighth, the King's Regiment of Foot, to take leave publicly of the regiment on its departure to England, and to offer to its officers and men the acknowledgments of the Government of India for their services in this country.

The King's Regiment embarked for India in April, 1846, and after serving for some years in the Presidency of Bombay, was transferred to the Bengal Presidency in December, 1853.

The regiment was at Jullundur in 1857, when the mutiny of the Bengal Army broke out, and did essential service at that station in resisting and punishing the mutineers.

It joined the army before Delhi soon afterwards, and served

with much distinction at the siege and capture of that fortress. It bore a conspicuous part in the complete repulse given to the forces of the mutineers in their persevering sorties on the 14th, 18th, and 23rd of July, 1857, and in the glorious struggle within the city, which lasted for six days after it was stormed, the King's Regiment was among the foremost in exhibiting the irresistible effect of the valour and endurance of British soldiers.

The regiment formed part of the pursuing column, under Brigadier Greathed, C.B., and was present at the actions of Bulandshahr, Allyghur, and Agra. It subsequently served with the force under His Excellency the Commander-in-Chief in the relief of the garrison of Lucknow, and at Cawnpore, and was afterwards employed in the final conquest of the province of Oudh, and exhibited its characteristic bravery in the capture of the town and fort of Sandee.

The Governor-General begs to assure the King's Regiment of the very high sense entertained by him of its services and soldierly conduct, whether in quarters or in the field, and the interest which he will always feel in its future welfare.

(Signed) R J. H. Birch,
Major-General, Secretary to the
Government of India
with the Governor-General,

On the homeward voyage the Headquarters' ship called at Simon's Bay (1st-6th of July), and at St. Helena (20th of July), at which island the whole of the men were landed and marched up to the tomb of the Emperor Napoleon.

Section 31.—At Home, 1860-1866.

The *Clara* anchored at Spithead late in the afternoon of the 3rd of September, and on the forenoon of the 5th, Headquarters landed at Gosport.

★★★★★★

The troops embarked on board

The *Monica* 5th April; disembarked 10th August; length of voyage   127 days

The *Lady Clarendon* 4th April; disembarked 27th August; length of voyage   185 "

The *Sevilla* 19th April; disembarked 20th August;

length of voyage 123 "
The *Clara* (H.Q.) 5th May; disembarked 6th September;
length of voyage 123 days
During the voyage there were 5 deaths on board the *Lady Clarendon*, and 11 on board the *Clara*. The strength shown by the disembarkation returns was—

From the *Monica*	2 officers,		50 n.c.. officers and privates		
Lady Clarendon	3	"	138	"	"
Sevilla	3	"	14	"	"
Clara	13	"	291	"	"
Totals	21	"	493	"	"

******

On the 10th, Colonel Frederick Paul Haines, C.B., joined and assumed command of the battalion. (For services of this officer, *vide* Appendix No. 2.) He had been transferred from half-pay and appointed lieutenant-colonel in the King's on the 28th of October, 1859, in succession to Colonel John Longfield, who retired on half-pay, and who was promoted to the rank of major-general on the 3rd of August, 1860.

1861. The battalion remained at Gosport until the 8th of August of the following year: on that day it was moved by rail to Aldershot, and quartered in G and H lines, South Camp (strength, twenty-two officers and eight hundred and sixty-six non-commissioned officers and privates).

In September, the battalion formed part of a flying column, commanded by Brigadier-General Brook Taylor, which was encamped at Woolmer from the 6th to the 10th.

1862. On the 2nd of September, Colonel Haines, having been appointed Deputy Adjutant-General for Ireland, retired on half-pay, and was succeeded in the command of the battalion by Colonel John Hinde, C.B., who was transferred from the Second Battalion. The senior major, James Johnston, was gazetted to the vacant Lieutenant-colonelcy, and succeeded Colonel Hinde in the command of the Second Battalion. (For services of this officer, *vide* Appendix No. 2.)

On the 2nd of September, Headquarters and six companies were moved by rail to Sheffield: detachments of two companies each were on the same day moved to Weedon and Bradford.

1863. On October 9th, Major William Bayly, who had enlisted as a drummer boy on the 25th of November, 1807, after a service of fifty-six years in the regiment, retired on full-pay with the rank of lieutenant-colonel.

******

Lieutenant-Colonel Bayly died at Hastings on the 16th December, 1874. His only son received the commission of ensign in the regiment on the 2nd of April, 1847, and served in it until 1860, when he exchanged to the Eighty-Eighth, and was afterwards transferred to the Bengal Staff Corps: at the time of his father's death he had attained the rank of lieutenant-colonel. Before retiring Lieutenant-Colonel Bayly presented his portrait to the officers of the regiment.

******

On the 3rd of September, a general order was issued authorising the words "Delhi" and "Lucknow" to be borne on the colours of the regiment.

1864. On the night of the 12th of March, owing to the bursting of a reservoir, a destructive inundation occurred. Many houses were swept away by the torrent, and about two hundred and fifty people perished. The lower storey of some of the quarters occupied by the married soldiers was flooded, and in one room during the confusion, caused by the first rush of the water, two young children of Colour-Sergeant Fold were drowned. The battalion received the thanks of the Corporation for the services rendered during this calamity, and a dinner was given to the non-commissioned officers and soldiers.

******

The following details respecting the destruction of property caused by this inundation have been obtained from the Chief Constable of Sheffield. There were one hundred and forty-three manufactories, workshops, warehouses, dwelling houses, shops, bridges, and buildings of various kinds totally destroyed, four hundred and eighty-six were partially destroyed or seriously damaged, five thousand and eighteen were flooded. The amount of compensation paid, as assessed by a Parliamentary Commission, was—

	£	s.	d.
For loss of life	9,080	7	11
For bodily injuries	4,993	4	6
For property destroyed or damaged	262,844	19	3

Total amount of compensation paid 276,918 11 7

The number of claimants among whom this sum was distributed was seven thousand and seventy-seven.

******

On the 22nd of July, the battalion was moved by rail to Manchester, and quartered in Salford Barracks; the Weedon and Bradford detachments rejoined, and two companies were sent to Chester.

1865. On the 2nd of February, the depot from Templemore joined Headquarters. (Strength, six officers and one hundred and seven non-commissioned officers and privates.)

On the 16th of March, the battalion was moved to Liverpool by rail, and embarked by wings on board the *Windsor* and *Iron Duke*: on the 17th, the battalion disembarked at Kingston, and marched to the Curragh Camp under the command of Colonel Hinde.

On the 20th of July, a detachment of six companies, under command of Major Baynes, was moved by rail to Dublin and quartered in Ship-Street Barracks; and on the 26th, Headquarters and the remaining six companies, under command of Colonel Hinde, were also moved to Dublin and quartered in Richmond Barracks. On the 18th of August, Major Baynes's detachment rejoined Headquarters at Richmond Barracks. On the 18th of December, the battalion left Richmond and took up its quarters in the Royal Barracks, sending a detachment of four companies under Major Baynes to occupy the Linen Hall Barracks.

This detachment was ordered to act as a support to an outlying picquet posted at Mountjoy Prison. On the 21st, a fire broke out in a store room belonging to the recruiting department under the rooms occupied by the detachment, but by great exertions of the officers and men, this fire was extinguished in a very short time. A communication was received from the deputy adjutant-general, dated 23rd December, directing Major Baynes and all belonging to the detachment to be informed that Sir Hugh Rose, the General Commanding the Forces, was much pleased with the zealous and efficient efforts of the detachment, and had expressed his approbation of their soldier-like conduct. On the 29th of December, this detachment was relieved by the Sixtieth Rifles, and rejoined Headquarters at the Royal Barracks.

During the winter very great excitement and apprehension was caused in Dublin by the seditious proceedings of the Fenians. Many persons belonging to that treasonable association were tried, convicted, and confined in the Dublin prisons; and it was known to the authorities that a large body of men, well provided with arms and trained to organised action, were at the disposal of a secret council, which was on the watch for a favourable opportunity to attempt a forcible rescue of these prisoners.

The precautions necessary to guard against the success of such an attempt imposed very severe and harassing duties on the Dublin garrison, which, besides the King's Regiment, consisted of the Fifth Dragoon Guards, Tenth Hussars, First Battalions of Twenty-Fourth and Sixtieth Rifles, and the Sixty-First Regiment. Strong picquets were posted in the different prisons; the streets were patrolled during the night, and the troops were kept in constant readiness to turn out at a moment's notice.

Ceaseless and persevering efforts were also made by Fenian agents to obtain the sympathy and assistance of the Irish soldiers serving in the ranks of the regiments quartered in Dublin and other Irish stations. These efforts failed to produce any serious disaffection; but in individual instances they were sometimes successful, and they caused great anxiety both to officers commanding corps and to the Headquarter military authorities. Several non-commissioned officers and soldiers were convicted of treasonable connection with Fenian plots and outrages; but there is no proof that any soldier of the King's Regiment was guilty of a species of misconduct which is not only disgraceful to the individual, but brings suspicion and discredit on the corps to which the offender, belongs.

1866. On the 9th of March, the battalion (strength twenty-five officers and seven hundred and seven non-commissioned officers and men), under the command of Colonel John Hinde, C.B., was moved from Dublin to Kingston, and embarked on Her Majesty's steam transport *Tamar*, which on the following day commenced its voyage to Malta.

SECTION 32.—ABROAD, 1866-1879.

The *Tamar*, after a voyage of nine days, arrived at Malta on the 19th of March: the battalion landed on the following day, and was encamped on the St. Clements Glacis, Cottonera District: it was posted to the Second Brigade, commanded by Major-General M. R Atherley.

On the 28th of March, the battalion left camp; Headquarters and four companies were quartered at Isola Grate Barracks, four companies at Polverista, and two at San Francisco di Paolo.

The Second Battalion had been stationed at Malta since October, 1863; the two battalions of the King's, therefore, now met for the first time, and continued to be quartered together until the 24th of February, 1868, when the Second Battalion embarked for England.

On the 15th June, Colonel John Hinde retired on full-pay with the rank of Major-General, and was succeeded in command of the battalion by Brevet Lieutenant-Colonel Henry George Woods, the senior major who was at that time doing duty with the Second Battalion. (For services of this officer, *vide* Appendix 2.). Lieutenant-Colonel Woods joined and assumed command of the First Battalion on the 4th of July.

1867. On the 3rd of July, the battalion changed its quarters, and was attached to the First Brigade commanded by Major-General Ridley. Headquarters and six companies moved into Lower St. Elmo Barracks, one company into Marsamucetto, and one company into St. James Cavalier Barracks. On the 24th August, the band and two companies, under command of Captain Wheely, were detached from Lower St. Elmo Barracks, and encamped on the glacis of Fort Manoel. On the 12th September, the camp of this detachment was removed to the parade ground at Floriana, and on the 4th of November, the encampment was broken up, and the detachment rejoined Headquarters at Lower St. Elmo Barracks.

1868. In April of this year, a detachment of two companies, which was afterwards increased to four under Major Colman, was sent to occupy Fort Manoel. On the 4th of May, a general order was published increasing the establishment of the battalion, and fixing its strength at forty-five officers and nine hundred and ninety-four non-commissioned officers and privates, and on the 7th of May, a notification was received that it would proceed to India by the overland route, and would probably embark in October. On the 10th day of that month at 7 a.m., the embarkation on board Her Majesty's troop ship *Serapis* was eifected in two detachments. Headquarters and six companies embarking from Lower St. Elmo, and four companies from Fort Manoel.

Next day at 8 a.m., the *Serapis* left Malta, and at 2 p.m. on the 14th ,anchored at Alexandria: next day the baggage was landed and forwarded by train to Suez; and on the evening of the 16th, the men disembarked, and were moved by rail to Suez in two detachments. The first, under command of Major Colman, consisted of four companies, with the whole of the women and families. The second, under command of Lieutenant-Colonel Woods, consisted of Headquarters, six companies, and various drafts proceeding to join their corps in India.

The journey across the desert occupied sixteen hours, and at 8 a.m. on the 17th, the battalion arrived at Suez, and reembarked in Her Majesty's troop ship *Jumna*. At 6 a.m. on the following morning, the

Jumna left Suez, and at 2 p.m. on the 23rd, she arrived at Aden. On the 25th, after a delay of two days, caused by a defect in the coaling arrangements, the voyage was resumed, and at 7 a.m. on the 2nd of November, the *Jumna* anchored at Bombay. Next day the battalion disembarked, and was moved to Poona by two special trains: it arrived on the morning of the 5th, and was quartered in the Wanourie and Ghoopoorie Barracks, five companies and Headquarters occupying the former, and five companies the latter barracks.

On the 7th, the battalion was inspected by Brigadier-General Raines, C.B., when its strength on parade was thirty-six officers and six hundred and sixty-one non-commissioned officers and privates. On the 16th of November, a detachment of four companies, commanded by Major Colman, left Poona, and, after a march of eight days, arrived on the 23rd at Sattara, where it took up military districts and sub-districts, and in each sub-district there was established, under the command of a colonel, a brigade depot, consisting of the depot companies of two battalions of the Line, and the permanent staff of two battalions of militia: all the local corps of Rifle Volunteers were also placed under the command of the colonel of the brigade depot.

The two battalions of the King's and the Second Royal Lancashire Militia (which it was ordered should be augmented by a second battalion) were assigned to the thirteenth or Liverpool sub-district.

✶✶✶✶✶✶

The annexed extract of a letter from the Right Honourable Thomas Townshend, Secretary at War to His Grace the Duke of Rutland, Lord Lieutenant of the county of Leicester, dated Whitehall, 19th July, 1782, shows that a proposal was at that time under consideration for connecting the King's Regiment with the county of Leicester:—"A plan having been laid before the King for giving county names to the several regiments of infantry in His Majesty's Service, and the commanding officer of the Eighth Regiment having expressed his wish that his corps should be attached to the county of Leicester and bear its name, I have His Majesty's command to signify the same to you." (*Vide* p. 117, vol. vi, of *Unpublished Regimental Records* belonging to the Library of Royal United Service Institution.)

✶✶✶✶✶✶

Colonel J. C. H. Jones was appointed to the command of the Brigade Depots of both the thirteenth and fourteenth sub-districts; Warrington was fixed upon as the Headquarters of the two sub-districts, and arrangements were made for the construction at that place of barracks for the accommodation of the Depot companies of the two battalions of the King's, of the permanent staff of the Second Royal Lancashire Militia (for an abstract of the services of the Second Royal Lancashire Militia, *vide* Appendix No. 6), and of the depot companies of the line, and the permanent staff of the militia corps belonging to the fourteenth sub-district. These barracks were not completed until April, 1878, and until that time no soldier of the King's was quartered in the subdistrict, and no real connection was established between the locality and the regiment.

On the 31st August, in consequence of a threatened outbreak of cholera, two companies were withdrawn from barracks and encamped on the parade ground, where they remained until the 4th of October. About this time the deputy surgeon-general inspected the regiment, and, finding it in a very sickly condition, recommended that it should be sent to a hill station. This recommendation having been approved, a depot was formed, consisting of five officers and two hundred and fifty-five non-commissioned officers and privates, chiefly weak and sickly men; these, together with the women and children, were placed under the command of Major Longfield, and ordered to proceed to Chakrata. The remainder of the battalion, consisting of six hundred non-commissioned officers and privates, all in splendid condition, were directed to join a camp of exercise formed near Roorkee, under the command of Major-General the Honourable F. Thesiger, C.B.

In compliance with these orders, the battalion under command of Colonel Woods marched from Cawnpore on the 24th of October, and arrived at Camp Bhugwanpoor (five miles from Roorkee) on the 27th November, having marched four hundred and twenty-seven miles in thirty-five days.

On 2nd December, Colonel Woods was appointed to command the Second Brigade of the troops in camp, and from this date until 16th March Major Webb was in temporary command of the battalion.

The Depot, left at Cawnpore under Major Longfield, was moved by rail to Saharunpoor on the 22nd of November, and from thence marched to Chakrata, where it arrived on the 5th of December, having marched ninety-three miles in fourteen days.

1874. On the 16th of March, the battalion left the Camp of Exercise and arrived at Kalsee on the 23rd. Here, the right half-battalion, under Major Webb, halted; the left half-battalion, under Colonel Woods, continued its march, and arrived at Chakrata on the 25th, where it was rejoined by the right half-battalion on the 29th.

On the 7th of November, Captain Charles Dudley Ryder Madden died of typhoid fever, at Cork, while in command of the Depot: he had served sixteen years in the battalion, and was much respected and beloved by all ranks. A tablet to his memory was erected by his brother officers in St. Patrick's Cathedral, Dublin.

1875. On the 15th, 16th, and 17th of November, the battalion marched from Chakrata in three divisions; on the 26th, the three divisions were re-united and encamped together at Saharunpoor.

On the 28th, two companies with the women and children, forming a depot under the command of Captain C. F. Malet, were moved by rail to Meean Meer, from whence they marched to Peshawur, where they arrived on the 10th of January, 1876.

The remaining six companies (strength, ten officers and six hundred and fifty non-commissioned officers and privates), under Colonel Woods, marched from Saharunpoor on the 29th, and arrived at Delhi on the 10th of December, where they encamped outside the Cabul Gate; on the following day, having been posted to the First Brigade of the Third Infantry Division, they marched to Bussai and joined the Standing Camp. Colonel Woods was appointed to the Umpire Staff, and the temporary command of the battalion devolved on Major Cochrane.

The distance from Chakrata to Saharunpoor is seventy-four miles, and from Saharunpoor to Delhi one hundred and ten miles. The former march was accomplished in nine, the latter in twelve days.

1876. On the 3rd of January, the battalion marched to the Khootub for experimental ball practice. Subsequently it took part in the attack of a position supposed to be occupied by an enemy, and returned to the Standing Camp on the 6th.

On the 7th, the Third Division shifted its camp to Badlee-ke-Sarai, four and a-half miles from Delhi on the Alipore road. On the 12th, the battalion, together with the whole of troops in the Camp of Exercise, was reviewed by His Royal Highness the Prince of Wales.

On the 18th, the battalion left the Camp of Exercise and, under command of Major Cochrane, commenced a march of five hundred and eighty-five miles. (Colonel Woods had received fifteen months' leave of absence.) Proceeding *via* Umballa, Meean Meer, and Rawul Pindee, it reached Peshawur on the 17th of March, the sixtieth day after leaving Delhi.

On the 16th of April, a wing of the regiment (strength, eleven officers and four hundred non-commissioned officers and privates), under Major Longfield, was attached to a moveable column commanded by Major Cochrane. The column encamped at Mattuni, about sixteen miles from Peshawur, in the direction of Fort Mackeson; after remaining in camp for about a week two of the companies of Major Longfield's detachment were sent back to Peshawur and the other two directed to occupy Fort Mackeson, but a few days afterwards these companies were also ordered to rejoin Headquarters at Peshawur.

On the 18th of April, a detachment of convalescents and recruits, under command of Captain Stuart, was sent to the hill station of Cherat, where it remained until the 23rd of December.

On the 4th of August, for sanitary reasons, another detachment, consisting of three officers and two hundred non-commissioned officers and privates, under the command of Captain Roberts, was sent to Nowshera, where it remained until the 16th of November.

On the 28th of September, cholera, which had been raging in the town for some time previously, made its appearance in cantonments. Small cholera camps were therefore formed at various points in the district, which were occupied by detachments of the battalion. It was found that in proportion to the number of cases which occurred in these camps and in cantonments there were more recoveries in the camps than in the cantonments. The loss sustained during the outbreak was: Sub-Lieutenant Hervey, Sergeant-Major Snowden, and sixteen non-commissioned officers and privates.

******

In a General Order dated Quartermaster-General's Office, Peshawur, 17th April, 1877, Major F. Longfield, Captain J. S. Wheely, Surgeon-Major Owen Owen, and Surgeon J. A. Smith received the acknowledgments of the Military Department of the Government of India for the excellent arrangements made by them during the outbreak.

******

1877. On January 1st, there was a parade of all the troops in garrison in review order, on the occasion of a proclamation being read announcing that Her Majesty had assumed the title of Empress of India. A *feu de joie* of one hundred and one guns was fired by the artillery, and three rounds by the infantry: each non-commissioned officer and soldier received a gratuity of one day's pay, and a silver medal was presented to one soldier of each corps selected by its commanding officer. No. 1449, Private W. Lynch, of D Company, was the soldier of the King's Regiment selected for this distinction.

On the 14th of February, the battalion was relieved by the Fourth Battalion Rifle Brigade, and commenced its march to Nowshera, where it arrived on the following day.

On the 23rd, G Company, under the command of Brevet Lieutenant-Colonel W. D. Martin, was detached to garrison the fort at Attock.

On the 4th of March, Colonel Woods rejoined from leave and resumed command of the battalion.

On the 5th and 6th of March, the annual inspection of the battalion was made by Brigadier-General Ross, commanding the Peshawur district. (Present on parade: sixteen officers, six hundred and fifty-eight non-commissioned officers and privates.)

On the 30th of June, ninety-six non-commissioned officers and privates desirous of remaining in India were transferred to various corps.

During the month of July, Martini-Henry rifles were served out to the men of the battalion in lieu of Sniders, which had been in use exactly ten years.

On the 19th November, the battalion commenced its march to Meean Meer *en route* to Bombay and Aden. (Strength, eighteen officers, six hundred and thirty-eight non-commissioned officers and privates, thirty-one women and forty-six children.)

★★★★★★

On the 22nd November, Captain Charles Malet died at Pachmari, where he held the appointment of Station Staff Officer: his father, Captain Alfred Augustus Malet, formerly served in the regiment, and his uncle, Lieutenant-Colonel Charles S. Malet, commanded the King's from 25th October, 1842, to 16th December, 1845. He was buried at Pachmari, where a monument was erected to his memory by the officers of the regiment and the men of his company.

★★★★★★

On the 26th, it was at Rawul Pindi, and on the 29th, at Camp Mundra, it met the Second Battalion, under Colonel F. Barry Drew, on its way to Rawul Pindi: the officers of the two battalions dined together; on the following day the battalions exchanged camp equipage and transport, and on 1st December the First Battalion continued its march to Meean Meer, where it arrived on the 15th of December, and remained until the 22nd: on that day the left wing was despatched by rail to Deolalee Depot, where it arrived on the 28th: Headquarters and the right wing left Meean Meer on the 23rd, and arrived at Deolalee Depot on the 30th.

1878. On the 1st and 2nd of January, the battalion left Deolalee in two divisions, which respectively embarked from Bombay on board Her Majesty's troop ship *Serapis*, on the 2nd and 3rd; strength, fifteen officers, five hundred and seventy-one non-commissioned officers and privates, and seven women. The *Serapis* left Bombay 10.30 a.m. on the 3rd, and arrived at Aden about 6 a.m. on the 11th. The same day the battalion disembarked. The Headquarters, with A, C, E, and G Companies, were quartered at the Crater Camp; B, D, and F, under Major Longfield, at the Isthmus; and H Company, under Captain Egerton, at Steamer Point.

The annual inspection was made on the 15th, 16th, 18th, and 19th of March, by Brigadier-General F. A. E. Loch, C.B., Commanding at Aden. On the 16th of July, His Excellency the Commander-in-Chief of the Bombay Army published a general order, in which it was stated that in the musketry season of 1877-78, (the first in which the Martini-Henry rifle was used), out of ten battalions serving in the Presidency, the First Battalion of the King's was the first in order of merit.

The figure of merit was 119.04, and was 14.76 points above that of any other battalion. C, or Captain Louis's Company, with a figure of merit of 123.08, was the best shooting company in the Presidency, and Private James Ball, who belonged to that company, was the best shot in the Presidency; his score was 188 points.

On the 31st of October, preparatory to the embarkation of the battalion for England, sixty-seven men were transferred to the Second Battalion, and seven men were allowed to volunteer for other corps. On the 20th of December, the Headquarter Companies left the Crater position and were encamped at Steamer Point.

On the 28th, the battalion, under command of Colonel H. G. Woods, embarked in Her Majesty's troop ship *Malabar*; strength, fifteen officers and five hundred and seven non-commissioned officers and privates.

The *Malabar* left Aden on the 28th of December, arrived at Suez on 4th January, at Port Said on 5th January, at Malta on 10th January, and at Portsmouth on the 22nd of January, 1879, having completed a tour of foreign service of twelve years and ten months, of which two years and seven months were spent at Malta, and the remainder in the East Indies.

The following statement shows the variations which took place in the strength of the non-commissioned officers and privates of the battalion during the ten years of its service in India:—

Strength of non-commissioned officers and privates on arrival in India 2nd November, 1868		734
Add increase—		
Joined from England	622	
Headquarter recruits	11	
Transfers received from other corps	159	
		792
Total		1526
Deduct decrease—		
Died	156	
Gazetted to commissions	2	
Sent to England	547	
Discharged in India	34	
Transfers given to other troops	276	
		1015
Strength on returning to England 22nd January, 1879		511

Out of the five hundred and eleven who disembarked, there were only two hundred and one who had landed with the battalion at Bombay in November, 1868.

Section 33.—Home Service, 1879.

1879. At 8.30 a.m. on the 23rd of January, the battalion disembarked at Portsmouth, and was moved by special train *via* London to Warley Barracks, in Essex.

On 30th January, it was inspected by Major-General Radcliffe, C.B., Commanding Eastern District. (Strength on parade: nineteen officers, five hundred and seventy-six non-commissioned officers and privates.) Total strength, twenty-five officers and seven hundred and twenty-three non-commissioned officers and privates.

The regiment paraded in a heavy snowstorm, and with deep snow on the ground. The men wore white helmets and great coats over their belts, and the white helmets, the use of which was to protect the men from the fierce rays of the Indian sun to which they had been so recently exposed, contrasted strangely with the great coats which they now required to protect them from the snowy blasts and icy rigours of an English winter.

On the 12th of February, Colonel H. G. Woods was granted a pension of one hundred pounds a year for meritorious service.

On the 29th of March, a detachment, consisting of one captain, one subaltern, and seventy-three non-commissioned officers and privates was sent to Purfleet.

On the 5th of August, Major-General Radcliffe, C.B., made his annual inspection of the battalion: its total strength was twenty-five officers and five hundred and seventeen non-commissioned officers and privates, and there were present on parade thirteen officers and two hundred and seventy-nine non-commissioned officers and privates.

On the 24th of September, ninety-eight non-commissioned officers and privates were transferred to the Second Battalion, and under the command of Brevet-Major C. B. Brown, embarked at Portsmouth in Her Majesty's Indian troop ship *Jumna* for service in Afghanistan.

1880. The promotion of Colonel Henry George Woods to the rank of Major-General, (on 30th January), appeared in the *Gazette* of 24th February, and on the 26th, he issued a farewell order taking leave of the battalion, which he had commanded for thirteen years.

******

In this order Colonel Woods said: "From the old soldiers the young ones may learn with what order and cheerfulness the men of the regiment made long marches and endured hot seasons in India. How the officers shared in all the sports and all the troubles of the soldiers, and how the King's has everywhere been distinguished by the spirit of good comradeship which has always prevailed in it."

******

He was succeeded by the senior Major, Brevet Lieutenant-Colonel Edward Tanner, who being then serving in India with the Second Battalion, Major Whitting assumed the temporary command. (For Lieutenant-Colonel Tanner's services, *vide* Appendix No. 2.)

Between the months of February, and June, the battalion was called upon to furnish volunteers for corps serving in South Africa against the Zulus. Sixty-one non-commissioned officers and privates were transferred to the Ninety-First Regiment, three officers and fifty-three non-commissioned officers and privates to the Twenty-Fourth Regiment, and one man to the Fourth Regiment, making in all three officers and one hundred and fifteen non-commissioned officers and privates.

On the 2nd of July, the battalion was inspected by Major-General W. P. Radcliffe, C.B. (strength twenty-three officers and five hundred and eleven non-commissioned officers, drummers, and privates; present on parade, fourteen officers and three hundred and forty non-commissioned officers, drummers, and privates).

On the 19th of August, Lieutenant-Colonel Edward Tanner joined on promotion, and took over command of the battalion from Major Whitting.

During this month a Horse Guards' letter, dated 10th August, was communicated to the regiment, authorising a piece of red cloth to be placed under the helmet plate as a means of perpetuating the distinction that was indicated by the red ball tuft which was lost when the chaco was superseded by the helmet.

On the 2nd of October, a draft, consisting of one captain, one subaltern, two sergeants, two corporals, and one hundred and twenty privates left Warley to join the Second Battalion in India.

During the seasons 1869-1880, the ball practice of the battalion was carried out at Colchester, each company being detached in succession to complete its course of musketry instruction.

On the 4th of December, the Purfleet detachment rejoined Headquarters, and on the 7th of December, the battalion, (strength twelve officers and four hundred and ninety-six non-commissioned officers, drummers, and privates, with forty-four women and fifty-five children), under command of Lieutenant-Colonel Edward Tanner, left Warley at 9 a.m., and was conveyed by special train to Manchester, where it was quartered in Salford barracks.

On the last day of the year, D Company under the command of Captain Sinkins was detached to Chester.

Section 34.—Recapitulation.

The King's Regiment was raised in June, 1685. During the one hundred and ninety-five and a half years that have elapsed between that date and January, 1881, the First Battalion has served abroad one hundred years, and in the field against an enemy the whole or a part of thirty-seven years. It has been present at twenty-four battles, sixteen sieges, and forty-three minor engagements and skirmishes. The aggregate of the recorded casualties sustained by the battalion is killed, twenty-five officers and three hundred and twenty non-commissioned officers, drummers, and privates; wounded, missing, and prisoners, seventy officers, and nine hundred and sixteen non-commissioned officers, drummers, and privates. Total casualties, ninety-five officers and one thousand two hundred and thirty-six non-commissioned officers, drummers, and privates. But in many of the engagements no record has been preserved of the losses sustained by the regiment, and in others only the names of a few of the officers killed and wounded have been recorded.

The following is a summary of the field services of the battalion and of the casualties recorded during each period:

	Officers.		Non-commissioned Officers, Drummers, and Privates.	
	Killed.	Wounded.	Killed.	Wounded, missing, and prisoners.
1690–91— Service in Ireland: one battle; four sieges; no record of casualties	—	—	—	—
1702–12— Service in Germany and the Low Countries: eight battles; ten sieges; record of casualties extremely imperfect. A few names of officers mentioned; loss of rank and file only once stated	3	5	5	33
1715–16— Rebellion in Scotland: one battle.	7	3	97	24
1745–46— Rebellion in Scotland: two battles; casualties of rank and file not recorded	—	1	—	—
1743–45, 1746–48, 1760–62— Service in the Low Countries and Germany: eight battles; one minor engagement	1	21	39	332
1776–77— Service in North America: three minor engagements; no casualties recorded	—	—	—	—
1798–06— West Indies and Low Countries: three minor engagements	2	1	4	14
1801— Expedition to Egypt: one battle; three minor engagements	1	5	12	69
1809–1815— Service in North America: one battle; one siege; fifteen minor engagements	7	26	117	307
1857–58— Indian Mutiny: two battles; one siege; eighteen minor engagements	4	8	46	137
Total casualties	25	70	320	916

Part 2: Services of the Second Battalion

Section 1.—At Home, 1756-1758.

1756. This year the King's Regiment was augmented to twenty companies, and divided into two battalions. Both battalions continued to serve together until 1758, when the second was constituted a separate regiment, and numbered the Sixty-Third Foot.

Section 2.—At Home, 1804-1810.

1804. In that year the establishment of the regiment was again augmented by the addition of a second battalion. It was formed of men raised in the West Riding of Yorkshire, for limited service, under the Additional Force Act passed in July of that year, and was placed on the establishment of the army on the 25th of December, 1804. Major Daniel Hoghton, who had been promoted to be Lieutenant-Colonel in the regiment on the 22nd of November, was posted to the command of this battalion.

******

In the beginning of 1805, the battalion was quartered at Doncaster; the strength at this time was forty officers, twenty sergeants, and eighty rank and file.—Unpublished volumes of MS. notes, *R.U.S.I.*

******

1806. In the month of March, the battalion marched from York to Scotland: it returned to England in December.

1809. (In May, the battalion was quartered at Pevensey: strength, twenty three officers, twenty-two sergeants, four hundred rank and file.—*Volume of MS. Military Notes, R.U.S.I.*) In June, it embarked at Portsmouth for the island of Jersey, but before the vessels left the port, was ordered to disembark, and its flank companies were selected to form part of an expedition under General the Earl of Chatham destined to make an attack on Holland. These companies embarked from Portsmouth on the 16th of July.

******

The effective strength of the battalion at this time was five hundred and forty-two; of this number four hundred were embarked. They were attached to the Fourth Brigade (Major-General Picton's) of General Frazer's division, which formed the left wing of the force.—MS. *Volume of Regimental Records, R.U.S.I.*

******

The army landed on the Dutch island of Walcheren, situated at the mouth of the Scheldt, and captured Flushing; but some delay occurring in the execution of the design of proceeding up the Scheldt and attacking Antwerp, the enemy had time to assemble an immense body of troops at this point, and an epidemic having broken out, about the same time, among the British troops, the design was abandoned.

The flank companies returned to Portsmouth in September, and in December the battalion proceeded to Jersey. (During 1809, a bounty of sixteen guineas was offered for recruits, by Captain Smith.—*MS. Volume of Regimental Records, R. U.S.I.*

1810. In the month of June, it was ordered to return to Portsmouth, where it landed on the 21st of that month.

Section 2.—Abroad, 1810-1815.

1810. In the month of August, six companies embarked at Portsmouth for New Brunswick and Nova Scotia; they arrived there in October.

1814. In the month of February, of this year, these six companies having been provided with snow shoes, commenced their march across the ice from St. John's and St. Andrew's, New Brunswick, for Quebec, under Brevet Lieutenant-Colonel Evans, who had been detached from the First Battalion, and sent from Upper Canada to assume command of them. With him were also sent two hundred and eighty seamen for service on the Canadian lakes. This long and painful winter march through regions of snow and ice, exposed to violent storms, and during the most intense frost, was accomplished with little loss, and the condition of the troops on their arrival at Quebec in March, was such as to call forth the approbation of the commander-in-chief in Canada.

These six companies formed part of an invading force under the command of Sir George Prevost, which, crossing the frontier line of the United States, appeared before the town of Plattsburg on the 6th September. During the four following days preparations were made to storm the enemy's fortified position on the Saranac, and, on the 11th, a combined attack on it was made by the British Naval and Military forces.

The American position was defended by three redoubts and two strongly fortified block houses. There was also a flotilla, consisting of fourteen vessels and gunboats, moored in the Bay.

The troops advanced in two columns, one of which, under General Robinson, was directed to ford the Saranac and attack the works in front, while the other, led by General Brisbane, was to make a circuit and assault them in the rear. At the same time the British squadron on Lake Champlain, consisting of eight vessels and gunboats, under the command of Captain Downie, attacked the American flotilla. This attack failed: after a very obstinate and bloody engagement the British squadron was overpowered and completely defeated. The troops were then ordered to desist from the attack, the enterprise was abandoned, and the force recrossed the Canadian frontier.

The King's had a few men wounded on this expedition, but the exact number is not recorded.

SECTION 3.—AT HOME, 1815 (AUGUST TO DECEMBER).

1815. A treaty of peace having been concluded with the United States, both battalions of the King's were ordered to return to England, and they both embarked at Quebec in June.

The six companies of the Second Battalion landed at Portsmouth in August.

In the month of December, all men of the Second Battalion, fit for service, were transferred to the First, and on the 24th day of that month, the establishment of the regiment was reduced to a single battalion, consisting of one thousand and seventy-seven non-commissioned officers and privates. (For the history of the regiment from this date until 1867, *vide* Part 1.)

SECTION 3.—AT HOME, 1857-1858.

1857. This year in consequence of large reinforcements being sent to India to assist in the suppression of the Great *Sepoy* Mutiny, it became necessary to augment the strength of the army, and the establishment of the King's, and of many other regiments, was increased by the addition of second battalions.

On the 28th of October, the officers were gazetted. Colonel Thomas Maitland Wilson (for services of this officer, *vide* Appendix No. 2), was transferred from the half-pay of the Ninety-Sixth and appointed to the command of the battalion, and the following officers of the First Battalion received a step of promotion, and were posted to the new battalion:—

Captain John Hinde to be Major; Lieutenants Daniel Beere, Erskine Nimmo Sandilands, George Cony, John Vere Webb, and William E. Ximenes, to be Captains; the other officers were transferred from half-pay and from other regiments. (For names of these officers, *vide* Succession List, Appendix No. 1).

The establishment fixed for the battalion was eight companies, three field officers, eight captains, ten lieutenants, six ensigns, five staff, thirty-eight sergeants, seventeen drummers, six hundred and forty rank and file: total strength, thirty-two officers, six hundred and ninety-five non-commissioned officers and privates. Buttevant was assigned as the Headquarters of the battalion, the formation of which was immediately commenced, and was completed during the winter.

1858. On the 23rd of March, the battalion left Buttevant and was moved to Kinsale with a detachment at Charles Fort. On the 1st of April, the establishment of the battalion was augmented to twelve companies, the number of captains being increased to twelve, of lieutenants to fourteen, of ensigns to ten, of staff to six, of sergeants to fifty-four, drummers to twenty-eight, and rank and file to nine hundred and fifty, making a total strength of forty-five officers and one thousand and twenty-nine non-commissioned officers and privates.

On the 1st and 2nd of July, the battalion left Kinsale, and was moved in two divisions to the Curragh Camp.

On the 20th of August, the battalion received orders to form a depot of two companies, and to hold the remaining ten companies in readiness for embarkation for foreign service. On the 7th of September, the service companies were moved from Dublin to Kingstown, and embarked for Gibraltar on board the hired steam transport *Iwia* (strength, twenty-eight officers and seven hundred and seventy-three non-commissioned officers and privates). The depot (strength, five officers and ninety-two non-commissioned officers and privates), under the command of Brevet-Major Bannatyne, on the embarkation of the service companies, was moved to Templemore.

Section 4.—Abroad, 1858-1868.

1858. The service companies landed at Gibraltar on the 13th of September, being on the seventh day after leaving Kingstown.

1859. On the 1st of April, the establishment of sergeants was increased from fifty-four to fifty-six.

1860. On the 3rd of July, a sergeant instructor of musketry was added to the establishment.

1861. On the 20th of June, one assistant surgeon was added to the establishment. On the 27th of September, Colonel Thomas Maitland Wilson retired on half pay, and was succeeded in the command of the battalion by the senior Brevet Lieutenant-Colonel, John Hinde, who was then at Gibraltar doing duty with it. (For services of Lieutenant-Colonel Hinde, *vide* Appendix No. 2.)

1862. On the 5th of April, the establishment of rank and file was reduced from nine hundred and fifty to nine hundred. On the 1st of July, Colonel F. Paul Haines retired on half pay; Lieutenant-Colonel John Hinde was transferred from the Second to the First Battalion, and the senior major, James Johnston, was promoted to be Lieutenant-Colonel, and succeeded to the command of the Second Battalion. (For services of this officer, *vide* Appendix No. 2.)

1863. On the 1st of April, the establishment of rank and file suffered a further reduction of one hundred men, being reduced from nine hundred to eight hundred. On the 25th of September, the battalion embarked on board Her Majesty's ship *Orontes*, and on the 1st October, the seventh day after leaving Gibraltar, it disembarked at Malta and occupied Verdala barracks.

1865. On the 25th of April, the battalion left Verdala. Headquarters and four companies were quartered in Fort Manoel, and six companies in the Lazarette.

On the 15th of June, two companies, under Captain Moynihan, V.C., were moved from the Lazarette to Pembroke Barracks, Saint George's Bay; and on the 25th of June, Brevet Lieutenant-Colonel Woods with the other four companies were also moved from the Lazarette to Pembroke Barracks.

On the 29th of December, Lieutenant-Colonel James Johnston died at Fort Manoel. He was buried in the garrison cemetery, and a marble monument was afterwards placed there by his brother officers to mark his grave and commemorate his services and death. The senior major of the regiment, Brevet Colonel A. Cuningham Robertson, then doing duty with the First Battalion, succeeded to the command of the

Second Battalion. (For services of this officer, *vide* Appendix No. 2.)

1866. On the 1st of April, the establishment was augmented by one sergeant cook. On the 1st of May, Colonel A. C. Robertson joined from England and took over the command of the battalion from Brevet Lieutenant-Colonel Woods, who had been in temporary command from date of Colonel Johnston's death. On the 11th of October, Headquarters were transferred to Pembroke Camp, the four companies in Fort Manoel still remaining there under the command of Major Meade.

1867. On the 30th of March, the battalion changed its quarters from Pembroke Camp Barracks and Fort Manoel to Floriana Barracks, relieving the First Battalion of the Sixtieth Rifles. On the 1st of April, a detachment of sixty privates was transferred to the First Battalion, and on that date the establishment of rank and file was reduced from eight hundred to six hundred and twenty men. On the 14th May, Captain Moynihan, V.C., died of fever.

In July the breech-loading Snider rifle was issued to the battalion, and on the 11th and 12th of November, it was inspected by Major-General W. J. Ridley (strength, thirty-four officers, six hundred and forty-six non-commissioned officers and privates). This year, during the absence on leave of Colonel A. C. Robertson, the battalion was temporarily commanded from the 30th of June to the 29th of August, by Major Meade, and from the 30th of August, to the 14th of October, by Captain Cusack.

Section 5.—At Home, 1868-1877

1868. On the 24th of February, the battalion embarked on board Her Majesty's troop-ship *Himalaya*, Captain Shute Piers, R.N. (strength, thirty-four officers and six hundred and forty-six officers and privates). At 1 a.m. on the morning of the 29th, the *Himalaya* anchored at Gibraltar, where the ship remained until ten in the evening.

On the 5th of March, it arrived at Portsmouth, completing the voyage on the eleventh day after leaving Malta. On the following morning the troops disembarked and were moved by rail to the North Camp Station, Aldershot. The battalion was quartered in A, B, and E lines, South Camp. Here it was joined by the depot under Captain Cochrane, which had arrived in camp on the 14th of February, (strength, five officers and seventy-one non-commissioned officers and privates).

On the 7th of March, the strength of the battalion was forty-one officers and six hundred and eight-five non-commissioned officers and privates, and the establishment was reduced, from the 6th inclusive, to ten companies, the strength being fixed at three field officers, ten captains, twelve lieutenants, eight ensigns, five staff, and forty sergeants, forty corporals, twenty-one drummers, and five hundred and sixty privates; total, thirty-eight officers and six hundred and sixty-one non-commissioned officers and privates. Major-General Renny made his half-yearly inspections on the 1st of May, and 5th of October. At the former inspection the strength was forty officers and five hundred and twelve non-commissioned officers and privates; at the latter thirty-eight officers and six hundred and fifty-seven non-commissioned officers and privates.

1869. On the 1st of April, the establishment of privates was reduced from five hundred and sixty to five hundred and twenty, and on the 7th of April, the battalion, under the command of Colonel A. Cuningham Robertson, was moved by rail from Farnborough Station to Portsmouth, where it embarked on board Her Majesty's ship *Urgent*, and was conveyed to Liverpool. The *Urgent* arrived on the 9th, and on the 10th, the troops disembarked: Headquarters and four companies were moved to Bury, and six companies, under Major Drew, detached to Ashton-under-Lyne.

Major-General Sir John Garvock, K.C.B., commanding northern district, made his half-yearly inspections at Bury, on the 19th of May, and on the 29th of September. At the former inspection the strength was thirty-seven officers and five hundred and eighty-three non-commissioned officers and privates, and at the latter thirty-eight officers and six hundred and twenty-five non-commissioned officers and privates.

1870. On the 28th of February, two companies, under Captain Reginald Whitting, were detached to Burnley, and on the 1st of March, the two depot companies of the First Battalion, under the command of Captain Longfield, having been attached to the Second Battalion, arrived at Bury and joined Headquarters. Strength, two officers, fifty-six non-commissioned officers and privates.

On the 1st of April, the establishment of privates was reduced from five hundred and twenty to four hundred and sixty.

On the 25th of April, H Company rejoined Headquarters from Ashton-under-Lyne. On the 14th of May, the battalion was inspected at Bury, by Major-General Sir John Garvock, K.C.B. Strength, thirty-seven officers, five hundred and fifty-six non-commissioned officers and privates.

From the 29th of June, to the 24th of September, the Headquarter companies at Bury, and from the 11th of June, to the 10th of September, the five companies detached at Ashton-under-Lyne were under canvas, and the barracks at these places were handed over to the Engineer Department, for painting and repairs. On the 15th of August, the establishment of privates was increased from four hundred and sixty to six hundred and sixty.

On the 18th of October, the Headquarter companies, depot of the First Battalion, and the Ashton-under-Lyne detachment, marched into Manchester, and were quartered in Salford Barracks, relieving the Hundredth Regiment; two days afterwards the Burnley detachment rejoined Headquarters.

1871. On the 1st of February, the establishment of privates was reduced from six hundred and sixty to five hundred and sixty.

On the 5th of June, the battalion was inspected by Major-General Sir John Garvock, K.C.B., and on the 7th of October, by Major-General G. S. Carey, C.B. (Strength, at first inspection, thirty-five officers and seven hundred and eleven non-commissioned officers and privates; at the second, thirty-two officers and six hundred and seventeen non-commissioned officers and privates.) On the 31st of July, a draft of sixty men were transferred to the First Battalion.

1872. On the 1st of April, the battalion was inspected by Major-General Carey, C.B. (Strength, thirty-three officers, six hundred and thirty-eight non-commissioned officers and privates.)

On the 1st of May, the rank of ensign was abolished, and the establishment of the battalion was ordered to be three field officers, ten captains, sixteen lieutenants, one paymaster, one adjutant, one quartermaster (total, thirty-two officers); one sergeant-major, one quartermaster-sergeant, one bandmaster, one drum-major, one paymaster-sergeant, one armourer-sergeant, one orderly-room clerk, ten colour-sergeants, one sergeant pioneer, one sergeant cook, one sergeant instructor of musketry, twenty-eight sergeants, eighteen drummers, forty corporals, four hundred and eighty privates (total, five hundred and eighty-six non-commissioned officers and privates).

On the 17th of July, the battalion and attached depot, under command of Colonel A. C. Robertson (strength of battalion, thirty-one officers, five hundred and eighty-four non-commissioned officers and privates), were moved by rail to Fulwood Barracks, Preston, where the battalion relieved the First Battalion of the Twelfth Regiment.

On the 2nd of July, the depot of the Fifty-Fifth Regiment arrived at Preston, and was attached to the battalion. (Strength, two officers, and thirty-eight non-commissioned officers and privates.) On the

22nd of July, the battalion was inspected by Major-General D. Lysons, C.B. (Strength, thirty-two officers and five hundred and eighty-six non-commissioned officers and privates.)

On the 4th of November, the depot of the Fifty-Fifth left Preston, and was struck off the strength, and on the 19th, the depot of the Fortieth arrived from the Curragh, and was attached to the battalion. (Strength, two officers, one hundred and forty non-commissioned officers and privates.)

1873. On the 31st of July, the battalion was inspected by Major-General Lysons, C.B.: its strength was thirty officers and five hundred and ninety-nine non-commissioned officers and privates.

On the 11th August, one company, commanded by Captain Williams, and on the 13th of August, Headquarters and seven companies, under command of Colonel A. Cuningham Robertson, were moved by rail from Preston to Rugeley, and encamped at Lower Cliffe, Cannock Chase. Here they were joined by Lieutenant Jocelyn, and a detachment of twenty-eight men, which, some time before, had been sent to Aldershot, to take charge of the camp equipment of the battalion, and to be trained to perform transport duties.

Exclusive of this detachment, the strength of the eight companies, encamped at Cannock Chase, was twenty-four officers and four hundred and thirty-five non-commissioned officers and privates. The battalion was attached to the First Brigade, commanded by Colonel Bell, C.B., and formed part of the Second Division, commanded by Major-General Sir John Douglas, K.C.B. On the 25th August, the camp of the division was moved from Lower Cliffe to Brindley Heath, and on the 6th of September, from Brindley Heath to the Beeches, near High Oak. On the 11th of September, the whole of the field force, under the command of Major-General Lysons, C.B., was reviewed by Lieutenant-General the Honourable Sir James Lindsay, K.C.M.G.

On the following day, (the 12th), the encampment was broken up, and the eight companies (leaving behind Lieutenant Jocelyn and the transport detachment) under command of Colonel A, Cuningham Robertson, were moved by rail from Rugeley to Birkenhead. Here they were joined by the other two companies and by the depot of the First Battalion, left at Preston, under command of Major F. Barry Drew, and the battalion and depot embarked on board Her Majesty's troopship *Tamar*. (Strength, twenty-three officers and six hundred and three non-commissioned officers and privates.) Next day, (the 13th), the battalion and depot disembarked at Kingstown, and were moved by rail to the Curragh Camp, where they were quartered in I lines.

On the 30th September, the battalion, and the attached depot, were moved by rail to Cork, under the command of Colonel A. Cuningham Robertson, where they relieved the Second Battalion of the Seventh Regiment.

On the 6th of October, A and H Companies, under command of Captain R Whitting, were detached to Youghal.

1874. On the 2nd of June, Major Tanner and seven companies were detached to Fort Carlisle, where for the remainder of the summer all the men, not required for other duties, were employed as a working party under the Engineer Department.

On the 2nd of July, Major-General Sir R. D. Kelly, KC.B., inspected the Headquarters of the regiment at Cork, and on the 4th and 6th, its detachments at Fort Carlisle and Youghal.

During the month of November, Martini-Henry rifles were issued to the men of the battalion, and the Snider rifles were returned into store.

1875. On the 24th of March, Colonel Alexander Cuningham Robertson retired on half-pay.

******

Immediately after retiring on half-pay, Colonel A. C. Robertson appointed lieutenant-colonel of the Second Battalion Second Royal Lancashire Militia, the regiment which, in the reorganisation of the military forces in 1873, had been brigaded with the King's (*vide* Part 1). He resigned this commission in September, 1876, having, on the death of Colonel J. C. U. Jones, been selected for the command of the thirteenth and fourteenth sub-districts, which he held until relieved by Colonel Dalyell, in February, 1878, four months after his promotion to the rank of major-general.

******

Brevet Lieutenant-Colonel Wm. F. Adam Colman, the senior major, was gazetted to the vacant lieutenant-colonelcy; he was attached to the First Battalion, and without joining the Second on the 12th of May, he retired on full-pay, and was succeeded by the senior major, John Vere Wm. Henry Webb; he also was attached to the First Battalion, but he was at home on leave, and in the month of July he joined the Second, and assumed command of it. (For services of Lieutenant-Colonels Colman and Webb, *vide* Appendix No. 2.)

On the 20th of April, the Fort Carlisle and Youghal detachments rejoined Headquarters, and the battalion, under the command of Brevet Lieutenant-Colonel F. Barry Drew (strength twenty-three officers and five hundred and seventy non-commissioned officers and privates) was moved by rail to Fermoy, where it was quartered in the new barracks, relieving the Thirty-Third Regiment.

On the 12th of May, a new valise equipment was issued to the battalion in lieu of knapsacks; and on the 20th the battalion (strength twenty officers and five hundred and one non-commissioned officers and privates), under the command of Brevet Lieutenant-Colonel F. Barry Drew, was moved by rail from Fermoy to the Curragh, and encamped in rear of D square. On the 20th of September, at conclusion of the drill season, the battalion (strength seventeen officers and four hundred and forty-one non-commissioned officers and privates) returned to Fermoy and re-occupied its old quarters, detaching K Company, under Captain Dixon, to Mitchelstown. On the 18th and 19th of October, the battalion was inspected by Major-General Sir R. D. Kelly, KC.B.

1876. On the 1st of April, the establishment of rank and file was augmented from five hundred and twenty to eight hundred and twenty. On the 12th of April, G and I Companies were detached to Waterford, relieving two companies of the One Hundredth Regiment; and on the 8th of May, Brevet Lieutenant-Colonel F. Barry Drew, with A, C, and D Companies, was detached to Cork.

On the 29th of May, the Headquarters of the battalion and attached depot of the First Battalion from Fermoy, under Lieutenant-Colonel J. V. Webb, together with the detachments from Cork, Waterford, and Mitchelstown were simultaneously moved to Queenstown, and embarked on board Her Majesty's ship *Simoom*, which conveyed the troops to Portsmouth, where they arrived on the 31st. The same day the battalion disembarked and was moved by rail to Aldershot, where it was attached to the Second Infantry Brigade, and encamped on Rushmoor Hill (strength twenty-nine officers and six hundred and ninety-six non-commissioned officers and privates). On the 28th of June, it was inspected by Major-General R. S. Shipley, C.B.; and on the 3rd of July, the encampment on Rushmoor Hill was broken up, and the battalion quartered in the east block of the Permanent Infantry Barracks.

1877. On the 7th of March, Lieutenant-Colonel John Vere W. H. Webb retired on full-pay, and was succeeded in command of the battalion by the senior major. Brevet Lieutenant-Colonel Francis Barry Drew, who had done duty with it from the 15th of September, 1868, the date of his exchange from half pay into the King's Regiment. (For services of this officer, *vide* Appendix No. 2.)

On the 22nd of June, the battalion was inspected by Major-General R. S. Shipley. On the 9th of July, it marched, under command of Colonel F. Barry Drew, from Aldershot to Chobham, where it encamped. Next morning it marched to Windsor Great Park, and, with the rest of the Aldershot Army Corps, was reviewed by Her Majesty the Queen. In the evening it marched back to the camp at Chobham, and on the following day, (the 11th), returned to Aldershot and reoccupied its former quarters. (Strength, twenty-three officers and six hundred and ninety non-commissioned officers and privates.)

On the 21st of September, the Headquarters of the battalion and its eight service companies (strength, nineteen officers and nine hundred and twenty non-commissioned officers and privates), under command of Lieutenant-Colonel Francis Barry Drew, was moved by rail from Aldershot to Portsmouth, and embarked on board Her Majesty's troop ship *Euphrates* for conveyance to Bombay.

On the embarkation of the battalion, its two depot companies, together with the two depot companies of the First Battalion, were attached to the Eighty-Sixth Regiment, commanded by Lieutenant-Colonel Adams. They remained at Aldershot until the 1st of November, when the two depots (strength, eight officers and two hundred and forty-five non-commissioned officers and privates) were moved by rail to Portsmouth and quartered on Portsdown Hill in the detached forts of Widley and Southwick. Both depots were under the command of Brevet-Major Butler, and Lieutenant H. Granger was appointed to act as the depot-adjutant and quartermaster.

In the month of April, 1878, the Warrington Barracks having been completed, the depots received orders to occupy them. On the 17th, under command of Captain Williams, they were moved by rail from Cosham and Porchester Stations to Warrington, and took possession of their new quarters. (Strength, absentees included, seven officers and two hundred and seventy-one non-commissioned officers and privates.) Thus, after the lapse of five years, those provisions of the Army Reorganisation Scheme of 1873, which referred to the King's Regiment, were at length fully carried out.

★★★★★★

Vide Part 1. Colonel G. F. De Berry was at this time in command of the Thirteenth and Fourteenth Brigade Depots. Lieutenant Henry Thos. Granger was appointed adjutant of both these brigade depots. On the return of the First Battalion from foreign service on 22nd January, 1879, Major Forster Longfield was detached to command the four depot companies of the two battalions.

✶✶✶✶✶✶

SECTION 5.—ABROAD, 1877-(1ST JANUARY, 1881. THE SECOND BATTALION IS STILL SERVING IN THE EAST INDIES.)

The *Euphrates* left Portsmouth on Sunday, the 23rd of September, arrived at Malta on the 2nd of October, left the following day, passed through the Suez Canal on the 8th, 9th, and 10th, and arrived at Bombay on the 25th.

Next day the troops disembarked, and were moved by rail in two divisions to Meean Meer, where the First Division arrived on the 4th, and the Second on the 6th of November. After a halt of six days, during which camp equipage was served out, the battalion (strength, nineteen officers and nine hundred non-commissioned officers and privates) under the command of Lieutenant-Colonel Francis Barry Drew, commenced its march to Rawul Pindi. At the village of Mundra it met the First Battalion, under Colonel H. Woods, on its way to Bombay. The two battalions encamped together, and after a day's halt, during which they exchanged camp equipage, both resumed their march on the 1st of December.

On the 3rd the Second Battalion arrived at Rawul Pindi, and was quartered in the Church lines.

1878. In the month of August of this year certain information was received by the Government of India that a Russian mission had been cordially welcomed at Cabul, and that the policy of the Ameer Shere Ali was guided by influences which were considered hostile and even dangerous to British interests. It was therefore resolved to send an envoy to the Court of Cabul for the purpose of counteracting these influences, and, if possible, establishing more satisfactory relations.

His Excellency General Sir Neville Chamberlain was selected as the representative of the viceroy, and on the 30th of August, a native agent, the Nawab Gholam Hussein Khan, left Peshawur to deliver a letter to the *ameer* announcing Sir Neville Chamberlain's appointment, and requiring the *ameer* to make the requisite arrangements for his safe conduct and honourable reception. The *ameer* evaded replying to this letter, and on the 21st of September, when Major Cavagnari, one of the officers attached to the mission, presented himself at the frontier post of Ali Musjid and demanded a safe conduct, this request was absolutely refused, and he was informed that if the envoy attempted to advance further, he would be resisted by force.

This discourteous and unfriendly refusal was treated as an act of hostility, and on the 30th of October, an ultimatum was addressed to the *ameer*, informing him that unless a suitable apology were made for the insult offered to the envoy, and certain other specified conditions were complied with before the 20th of November, he would be treated as a declared enemy of the British Government.

In the meantime, troops were assembled, and active preparations made for undertaking such military operations as might be necessary to enforce compliance with these demands.

On the 8th of October orders were received to hold the battalion in readiness for active service, and on the 15th, twenty-seven officers and eight hundred and three non-commissioned officers and privates, under the command of Lieutenant-Colonel F. Barry Drew, commenced their march from Rawul Pindi to join a force assembling at Kohat under the command of Major-General Fred. Roberts, C.B. and V.C.

An unusually sickly autumn had much impaired the strength of the men, most of whom were very young. Fever was prevalent among them, and they suffered much from the intense heat in the day time, and from the crowded state of the bell tents, to each of which sixteen men were allotted. The road from Rawul Pindi to Kohat crosses a sandy plain, without shade and without water, and the long wearisome marches were a severe trial to the young soldiers, but they were excited with the idea of seeing active service, and though physically in bad condition their spirit was excellent.

The River Indus was crossed at Kooshalghur on the 22nd, by a bridge of boats, and two more marches brought the battalion to Kohat, where it was attached to the First Infantry Brigade, commanded by Brigadier-General Cobbe. Here twenty days were spent in collecting carriage and making various arrangements. Advantage was taken of this halt to weed out from the ranks all sick and weakly men; these were placed under the command of Captain Lewis, and ordered to remain at Kohat.

On the 13th of November, when the troops again moved forward, the strength of the battalion was twenty-six officers and six hundred and fifty-six non-commissioned officers and privates. Thull, on the left bank of the Kurrum River, was reached on the 18th. Here the force halted to await the reply of the Ameer of Cabul to the ultimatum of the viceroy. The 20th, which was the latest day allowed, passed without any answer being received from the *ameer*, and early on the following morning the force under the command of Major-General

PEIWAR KOTAL FROM BRITISH CAMP.

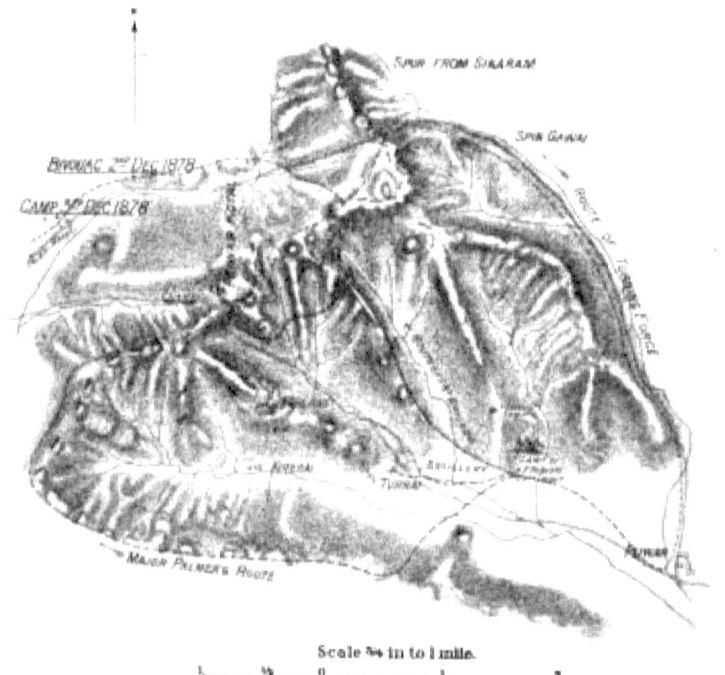

Scale ¾ in to 1 mile.

SKETCH PLAN OF
THE PEIWAR KOTAL.
ACTION 2 DEC. 1878.

PRESENTED BY COL. BARRY DREW, C.B.

Roberts crossed the river. The battalion had been ordered to leave another detachment at Thull, consisting of about seventy sickly and convalescent men, under Lieutenant Schletter, and when it crossed the river there were with the colours only twenty-five officers and five hundred and fifty-nine non-commissioned officers and privates, being two hundred and forty-four men less than the number which had marched out of Rawul Pindi thirty-seven days before.

The fort of Kapigunj, opposite Thull, had been evacuated before the troops crossed, and during the next four marches the enemy offered no opposition. Following a road on the right bank of the river, and traversing the Darwaza defile, the brigade reached Kurrum on the 25th. Mahomed Azim's fort, at that place, had been abandoned the previous day on the approach of our cavalry; but it was ascertained that the enemy had resolved to make a stand at the Peiwar Kotal, and that reinforcements from Cabul were on their way to assist in the defence of the position. On the 27th, orders were issued for an advance next morning in light marching order. It was directed that each battalion should consist of four hundred rank and file, and that the quantity of baggage should be reduced as much as possible. (Three officers were told off to a small tent measuring eight feet by seven, and for two officers' baggage only a single mule was allowed.)

About one hundred and twenty non-commissioned officers and privates were left at Kurrum under command of the musketry instructor. Lieutenant Ruck. Major G. Cochrane was also left here as commandant of the fort

The troops were ordered to parade at 2 a.m., but it was six o'clock before the battalion marched off the ground where the camp had stood. As the men had a long day's march before them, they were obliged to parade without great coats, and as lightly clothed as possible, so for three long dark hours they suffered severely from the bitter cold of the night air. After a march of twenty-two miles, about 1 p.m. the troops reached the edge of the plain at the foot of the Kotal.

During the remainder of the afternoon a reconnaissance in force was pushed up the south-western flank of the Peiwar. There was some hot skirmishing in front, but the battalion, being in reserve, was not engaged. It was ascertained that the enemy had taken up a strong position to defend the pass, and that they were provided with guns, which were judiciously placed. At nightfall the troops were withdrawn, and the camp was pitched just out of range, the King's occupying the front, and giving the advanced picquets during the night. Next morning the camp was shifted a little further to the rear, and out of sight of the enemy.

The next three days (29th and 30th November, and 1st December) were spent in reconnoitring the country in the front and on both flanks, and in bringing up from the rear three guns of G III Royal Artillery, two guns of F.A. Royal Horse Artillery and the Twelfth Bengal Cavalry.

The enemy's position faced the east, and was about four miles in extent. It lay along the summit of a lofty precipitous mountain ridge mostly covered with dense pine forests. Its left, or northern extremity, rested on the Spin Gawai Kotal; its right, or southern, on some commanding heights about a mile south of the Peiwar Kotal. The position was most easily accessible on the Spin Gawai Kotal flank. On that side the approach was through a comparatively open valley, and the ascent, excepting near the summit, was not steep.

The Afghan force defending this position consisted of about three thousand five hundred infantry, including three regiments which arrived from Kushi on the afternoon of the 1st of December; there was also a large force of Jagis Ghilzais, and other tribes whose numbers could not be ascertained. The artillery consisted of two twenty-four-pounder bronze howitzers and sixteen guns of smaller calibre, mostly seven-pounders and six-pounders. Seven of these were rifled muzzle-loading mountain guns.

At 10 p.m. on the night of the 1st of December, Major-General Roberts left camp to assail the Spin Gawai with a portion of his force, consisting of four guns F.A. Royal Horse Artillery, No. 1 Mountain Battery, a wing of the Seventy-second Highlanders, Second and Twenty-Ninth Punjab Native Infantry, Fifth Goorkhas, and Twenty-Third Pioneers, in all five hundred and fifteen British and one thousand seven hundred and forty-eight natives; total, all ranks included, two thousand two hundred and sixty-three. (These numbers are taken from General Roberts' dispatch.)

Brigadier Cobbe was left in camp with the remainder of the force, consisting of two guns F.A. Royal Horse Artillery, three guns G Battery Third Brigade Royal Artillery, Twelfth Bengal Cavalry, Second Battalion of the Eighth, the King's Regiment, Fifth Punjab Native Infantry, in all five hundred and fifty-nine British and five hundred and eighty Natives, all ranks included (total one thousand one hundred and thirty-nine).

★★★★★★

In General Roberts' dispatch three hundred and forty-eight is given as the strength of the rank and file of the King's Regiment; this is a mistake. On 2nd December, the strength of the battalion was eighteen officers and four hundred and thirty-six non-commissioned officers, drummers, and privates. To correct this error eighty-eight has been added to the total strengths given in the dispatch.

******

He received general instructions to open fire upon the enemy about 6 a.m., to get his troops into position in front of the Peiwar Kotal about half-past eight, and to storm the pass as soon as the troops defending it showed symptoms of being shaken by the development of the flank attack.

The guns, under Major Parry, escorted by one hundred men of the King's, under Captain Dawson, came into action about 6.15 a.m. They opened fire on a gun placed on a crag (called by the soldiers the "crow's nest") about one thousand seven hundred yards to their left front, which commanded the lower part of the pass, and about an hour later (about 7 a.m.) the fire of some of the guns was directed towards the more distant batteries which defended the summit of the pass, and which were about two thousand six hundred yards distant. To this fire the enemy's batteries replied vigorously; for the next three hours a well sustained cannonade was kept up by the artillery on both sides, with the result that before eleven o'clock two of the enemy's guns, situated to the left of the pass, were silenced.

The infantry took up a favourable position to the right of the guns, and slightly in advance of them, the King's Regiment, under Colonel F. Barry Drew, and the Fifth Punjab Infantry, under Major Macqueen. The brigade was concealed by trees and jungle, and was sheltered from fire by a spur running down from a range of hills on the right. About eight o'clock the infantry was ordered to take ground to the front, and a ridge, about three hundred and fifty yards nearer the enemy, was secured by two companies of the King's, under Brevet Lieutenant-Colonel Tanner, and the Fifth Punjab Infantry, under Major Macqueen.

Without halting here the infantry, keeping the regular road to the summit on their left flank and not far from the extremity of the line, continued steadily to advance from ridge to ridge, the soldiers being kept well under cover, until between 11 and 12 noon they reached a position not more than one thousand four hundred yards from the top of the pass. Here they were exposed to a cross-fire of artillery; in front from a battery of six guns placed near the summit of the pass; on the left flank from the gun on the detached crag called by the soldiers "the crow's nest"; they were also exposed to a cross-fire of musketry from the Afghan riflemen, who occupied the ridges in front and on the right flank of the line.

From this position the regiment kept up a sharp musketry fire for upwards of two hours, during which time, although the trees and rocks afforded excellent cover, a good many casualties occurred. It was here that Brigadier Cobbe was wounded in the thigh by a musket bullet, and obliged to resign the command of the brigade to Colonel F. Barry Drew, who was succeeded in the command of the battalion by Brevet Lieutenant-Colonel Tanner; two sergeants and several privates belonging to the King's were also wounded about this time, but the only man killed was Drum-Major Owen Cuningham.

The Fifth Punjab Infantry were now detached to the right to re-inforce the troops who, under the personal command of the Major-General, were operating against the left flank and rear of the Afghan position. At intervals the fire of the guns which accompanied these troops was distinctly heard beyond the hills on the right. After this there only remained five weak companies of the King's to continue the direct attack. (Two companies under Captain Dawson were with the guns, and one company under Lieutenant Balfour had been left in reserve to hold a position on the right of the line of attack.)

The next advance was up a precipitous ascent; it was very difficult and laborious. Arrived at the summit of this ridge, the little band of King's men found themselves within eight hundred yards of the battery defending the pass, and although the Afghan artillerymen continued to serve their guns with great gallantry for a considerable time, the guns Were at last silenced by the withering fire of the Martini-Henry rifles. The Afghans then brought up horses and endeavoured to withdraw the guns, but they were compelled to relinquish the attempt.

About 2 p.m., it was evident the enemy were thoroughly shaken. The guns under Major Parry were therefore ordered to move forward and take up a new position, and the two companies of the King's, under Captain Dawson, which formed their escort, to ascend the pass by the road; leaving the duty of protecting the guns to the Twelfth Bengal Cavalry.

The ridge occupied by the five advanced companies of the King's was separated from the road leading to the pass by two deep ravines with precipitous sides. While crossing these, and up to the time they reached the road, a dropping fire was kept up on these companies. But, once on the road, all resistance ceased. Under shelter of the shoulder of a projecting hill the regiment was rapidly formed for a final rush up the steep, rugged road leading to the summit of the pass, which Colonel Barry Drew, the acting brigadier, was the first to reach.

Here not a single Afghan was to be seen. Our enemies had evidently fled with the greatest precipitation, for they had left behind them their guns, their camp equipage, and a large quantity of ammunition and miscellaneous stores.

The Twelfth Bengal Cavalry, under Colonel Hugh Gough, C.B. and V.C, was immediately pushed forward in pursuit. Several additional guns were captured which had been abandoned on the road, but every Afghan had escaped to the mountains, where they could not be followed. Meanwhile, strong picquets were thrown out by the King's, and at 9 p.m. the tents having arrived, the battalion encamped alone on the ground it had won, and there passed the night.

******

A correspondent of the *Lahore Civil and Military Gazette* thus describes the impression made on him by the conduct and appearance of the men of the regiment. "The reputation of our young soldiers was bravely sustained by the King's at the Battle of the Peiwar; the average age of the men is about twenty-two; but on this day, in resolute courage, in cheerful endurance and contempt of fatigue, they nobly sustained the honour of the British Army. I saw them in the evening, after a day of toil and combat in skirmishing order, advancing with cheery, reckless enthusiasm, but, at the same time, with as much regularity, order, and precision as if they had been on parade; indeed, one of their officers said to me, 'the men moved better than ever they did on a field day.'" The same correspondent says: "The cold that night on the Peiwar was intense; although I had three *posteens* over me, the spoil of the enemy, I could not get warm."

******

The strength of the battalion on the morning of the 2nd was eighteen officers and four hundred and thirty-six non-commissioned officers and privates.

******

The officers with the colours during the day were Colonel F. Barry Drew (afterwards in command of brigade), Lieutenant-Colonel E. Tanner, Captains J. Dawson, E. Jervis, S. N. Roberts, Lieutenants J. M. Taylor, W. L. Brereton, L. S. Mellor, H. A. Fletcher, A. C. G. Banning, J. H. Balfour, O. D. C. Grattan, Sub-lieutenants C. G. Robertson, L. C. Dundas, H. J. Evans,

J. B. Edwards, Lieutenant and Adjutant Fred J. Whalley, Quartermaster P. Spencer. Lieutenant G. V. Turner was attached as orderly officer to the staff of General Thelwall, C.B., commanding Second Brigade, and Lieutenant E. L. Maisey was attached in the same capacity to the staff of Brigadier-General Cobbe, commanding First Brigade. Surgeon-Major J. G. Gibsone was in medical charge of the regiment.

★★★★★★

The casualties during the day were: killed, Drum-Major Owen Cuningham; wounded, two sergeants and five privates; total casualties, eighty.

★★★★★★

The men wounded were Sergeant James Howard (dangerously; right arm amputated), Colour-Sergeant William Innes (severely). Private J. Burgess (severely), Lance-Corporal J. S. Savage, Privates L. Jones, R. Jones, C. Delaney.

★★★★★★

The corps belonging to the Second Brigade bivouacked without tents at various points between the Spin Gawai Kotal and the village of Zarbadast Kila. About 9 o'clock on the night of the action Major-General Roberts had received from Lieutenant-Colonel Drew a report informing him that the King's Regiment were encamped on the Peiwar Kotal. Next morning communications were established between the two brigades and Headquarters, and four companies of the King's were detailed by the major-general for the duty of holding the position they had taken. The men of these companies instantly began to construct log-huts, for which abundant materials were found from the forests which grew thick on the hills.

1879. For five days, from the 5th, to the 10th of January, the work of hutting was interrupted, and the men were day and night kept constantly on the alert by large bodies of Mongols and Jagis, who threatened to attack the post, but who dispersed without venturing to do so. On the 19th, the huts were completed, and the men took possession of them; these huts were eight thousand four hundred and fifty feet above the sea level.

The cold at night was extreme, and on one occasion six degrees below Fahrenheit's zero was registered. During February and March, the snow lay on the ground to a depth which varied from three to five feet; and in the ravines and hollow parts of the road leading up to the pass there were in many places drifts fifteen feet in depth. Notwithstanding the severity of the weather, the state of health of the battalion was excellent. During December, 1878, and January and February, 1879, the daily average of sick was only one *per cent.*; four men died from pneumonia.

On the 14th of February, the left half battalion, under Major George Cochrane, after furnishing detachments at Kurrum, Hazar Pir, and Thull, was concentrated at Kohat.

On the 24th of March, His Excellency General Sir Paul Frederick Haines, G.C.B., the commander-in-chief, arrived at the station, and, after inspecting the battalion, addressed the men in the following terms:—

> Soldiers of the King's Regiment: Now that I have seen the ground you have come over and taken, I think you have done wonders, and that you have performed deeds that any men should be proud of.
>
> The two happiest years of my life were spent in the command of the First Battalion of the King's Regiment, and I look upon you as its brother; consequently, I feel that all my sympathies must now be with the Second Battalion of the King's.

On the 10th of April, a native follower having been murdered within half a mile of the camp, the murderers (some twenty in number) were pursued by Captain Cope, Lieutenant and Adjutant Whalley, and Lieutenant Dundas, and five soldiers. After an eight miles' chase, they were overtaken; five of them were killed on the spot, and several others wounded. The major-general published a divisional order thanking the party for this service.

On the 26th April, C Company, under Lieutenant Taylor, which had been detached at Kohat, rejoined Headquarters, and F Company, under Lieutenant Orme, was detached to Kurrum. On the 29th of April, G Company, under Captain Jervis, rejoined Headquarters from Kohat, and A Company, under Captain Cope, was detached to Kurrum.

On the 27th of May, peace was signed at Gundamuck.

On the 30th June, A Company, under Captain Cope, and F Company, under Lieutenant Orme, rejoined Headquarters from Kurrum: and B Company, under Lieutenant Schletter, and H Company, under Captain Short, were detached to replace them. On the 14th of July, Sir Louis Cavagnari, the British Envoy, passed through the camp with his suite *en route* to Cabul. On the 29th of August, B Company, under Brevet-Major Lewis, and H Company, under Lieutenant Schletter, rejoined Headquarters from Kurrum.

On the 3rd of September, the British Embassy at Cabul was treacherously attacked by the troops of the *amir*, and the envoy, the officers of his suite, and the whole of his escort (with the exception of one or two *sowars*, who managed to escape), after a heroic defence, were barbarously massacred.

Immediately on the receipt of this news the regiment received orders to hold itself in readiness for active service; all officers on leave were ordered to rejoin, and the necessary preparations were made to enable it to take the field on a moment's notice. On the 16th of September, Lieutenant Fletcher and fifty non-commissioned officers and privates were detached to Turi: and on the 25th, G and H Companies, under the command of Captain Jervis, were moved from the Peiwar Kotal to Ali Kheyl. Headquarters with A, B, C, and F Companies remained at the Peiwar Kotal under the command of Brevet Lieutenant-Colonel Tanner, who rejoined from leave on that day.

An order had been given to transfer the Headquarters of the regiment to Ali Kheyl, but it was cancelled; and the quartermaster and sergeant-major, who had accompanied Captain Jervis' detachment, returned to the Peiwar Kotal on the 2nd October. On the same day Lieutenant Fletcher's detachment from Turi, and D and E Companies under Lieutenants Ruck and Mellor, from Kurrum, rejoined Headquarters.

At daybreak on the morning of the 14th, just as the bugles finished sounding the reveille, the camp at Ali Kheyl, the Headquarters of Major-General Gordon, was attacked by several thousand Afghans. The first onset was directed against a picquet of the Twenty-Ninth Bengal Infantry, which held a barricade that protected the approaches to the left flank of the camp. Under cover of the darkness and of broken ground in front of the barricade a large body of the enemy established themselves within a hundred yards of the picquet. As soon as they were discovered the *sepoys* of the Twenty-Ninth, leaving the protection of the barricade, dashed forward to meet them with the bayonet. The hill men (many of whom were only armed with knives and hatchets) gave way, and making for the valley in the rear of the camp, found shelter behind eminences on the reverse slopes of the hills.

Meanwhile another party had opened fire against the right front of the position; but the rifles of the detachment of the King's commanded by Captain Jervis, soon compelled them to retire from the lower ridges to a great plateau, where a large portion of the Cabul field force had encamped previous to its advance, and where the huts and stone breastworks, which had been at that time constructed by our soldiers, afforded excellent cover. From this shelter they were dislodged by the *sepoys* of the Twenty-Ninth, who, coming from the right, drove them into the open, where the guns of C-IV Royal Artillery, stationed on a ridge behind the camp, had time to drop a few shells amongst them: and finally a mixed squadron of Native cavalry, which had been sent out by the road, suddenly appearing on the left, lance and sabre completed the discomfiture of the assailants on this part of the field about nine o'clock.

The attack on the left flank took a somewhat longer time to develop. The enemy's plan was evidently to wait until the troops on the right were drawn off in pursuit, and then to advance by a *nullah* that runs a certain length between the plateau in front and the ridge behind the camp, and to make a dash up the steep side of the ridge at the guns on its summit. This attack was met and repulsed by the Eleventh Native Infantry, who drove the enemy to the furthest point of the plateau, which extends five or six hundred yards beyond the left of the camp. A detachment of Ghoorkhas was ordered to descend the *nullah*, and, wheeling to the right round the base of the plateau, to cut off their retreat; but the Ghoorkhas did not arrive in time to prevent the hill men crossing the river and occupying a village on the opposite bank. Soon afterwards the firing ceased; twenty dead bodies were brought into camp, and the total loss of the enemy was estimated at about one hundred and twenty. On our side one *sowar* and four *sepoys* were wounded; there were no casualties among the soldiers of the detachment of the King's.

The attack was not repeated, but bodies of hill men for several days afterwards continued to infest the vicinity of the camp, and the soldiers were harassed by night alarms. After the 19th of October, when the determined attack which had been simultaneously made on the Shutar Gardan post was finally repulsed, these alarms entirely ceased, and the troops at Ali Kheyl and the Peiwar were not again molested during the winter.

On the 6th of November, the Ali Kheyl detachment was withdrawn, and G and H Companies, under Captain Jervis and Lieutenant Grattan, rejoined Headquarters at the Peiwar.

On the 11th November, G Company, under Captain Jervis, was detached first at Kurrum and afterwards at Budesh Kheyl, and on the 26th of November, H Company, under Lieutenant Grattan, was detached to Kurrum; the same day a draft of ninety-eight rank and file, under Brevet-Major C. B. Brown, arrived from England.

On the 13th of November, Colonel Charles Edward Grogan, who

on the 13th of September, had exchanged (from the 14th Foot) with Colonel F. Barry Drew, joined and took over from Brevet Lieutenant-Colonel Tanner the command of the battalion. (For services of this officer, *vide* Appendix No. 2.)

This month G Company, under Lieutenant George Villiers Turner (strength forty rank and file) was attached to the force under General Tytler during its operations in the Zymukt Valley. This company was present at the capture of Zowa; on the 5th of January it rejoined Headquarters. During this service there were no casualties from wounds among the men of the company; but they suffered so severely from cold that five of them died of pneumonia.

1880. On the 8th of January, Brigadier-General Watson, C.B. and V.C., inspected the battalion.

During the months of January and February, the weather was very severe. For several weeks snow, upwards of four feet in depth, covered the ground, and the cold at night was intense, Fahrenheit's thermometer in February constantly registering twenty degrees below the freezing point.

Four men died of pneumonia brought on by exposure, but the soldiers were very well and warmly clothed, and the supply of wood was plentiful, so that their health did not suffer much. Throughout the winter the average percentage of sick was about one *per cent.*, the chief diseases being pneumonia and colds.

On the 16th of March, C and F Companies, under Captains Blake Humfrey and Dawson, were detached to Kurrum, and H Company, under Lieutenant Grattan, rejoined Headquarters.

On the 29th of April, Brevet Lieutenant-Colonel Tanner, having been promoted to the vacancy caused by the promotion of Colonel Woods, was struck off the strength, and ordered to return to England to assume command of the first battalion. (For services of this officer, *vide* Appendix No. 2; *vide* also Part 1.)

On the 28th of April, C and F Companies, under Captains Blake Humfrey and Dawson, rejoined Headquarters from Kurrum, and A Company, under Captain Cope, was detached to replace them; but on the 12th of May, in consequence of a rising of the Waziri tribe being considered imminent, A Company was relieved by a detachment of the Eighty-Fifth King's Light Infantry, and under the command of Captain Cope, marched to Thull to reinforce the troops at that place.

On the 12th of June, D Company under Lieutenant Taylor was moved to Kurrum to relieve the detachment of the Eighty-Fifth, and on the 14th, E Company under Captain Roberts was moved to Thull to relieve A Company, which rejoined Headquarters.

On the 9th July, G Company under Lieutenant Schletter was moved to Kurrum and relieved D Company, which rejoined Headquarters; and on the 3rd August, C Company under Captain Blake Humfrey relieved G Company, which rejoined Headquarters.

On the 11th of August, Colonel C. E. Grogan was appointed to the command of the Lower Kurrum Brigade, with the rank of Brigadier-General, and Major W. Bannatyne succeeded to the temporary command of the battalion.

On the 28th August E Company under Captain Roberts was moved from Thull, and C Company under Captain Blake Humfrey from Kurrum to reinforce the post of Shalozan, Captain Dawson with F Company being detached from Headquarters to replace C Company at Kurrum. On the 3rd of September, H Company with Headquarters moved from the Peiwar Kotal to Shalozan, and were joined by the two companies detached at that post.

The Sirdar Abdur-Rahmann Khan having been recognised by the Indian Government as Ameer of Cabul, in accordance with arrangements made with His Highness, on the 9th September, the British troops were withdrawn from the Peiwar Kotal. A, B, and G Companies joined Headquarters at Shalozan, and D Company was detached to reinforce the troops at Kurrum. On the 5th October, Headquarters and six companies under the command of Major Bannatyne moved from Shalozan to Kurrum, and were there rejoined by D and F Companies.

At this time C-IV Royal Artillery and the 13th Bengal Lancers were also quartered at Kurrum: these troops, together with the King's Regiment, were placed under command of Major J. C. Auchinleck, R.A., and Lieutenant and Adjutant Whalley was appointed to act as his staff officer. On the 15th this column commenced its march towards Thull, and on the 21st it recrossed the frontier and arrived there.

The strength of the battalion on that day was one field officer, three captains, nine subalterns, two staff, thirty-eight sergeants, seventeen drummers, and seven hundred and fifty-five rank and file (total fifteen officers and eight hundred and ten non-commissioned officers, drummers, and privates). Of the fifteen officers there were only four (Lieutenant and Adjutant Whalley, and Lieutenants Brereton, Evans, and Edwards) who were with the colours when the battalion crossed the frontier on the 21st of November, 1878, and who had done duty with it throughout the two campaigns. During the twenty-three months' field service, fifty-one non-commissioned officers and privates died, and eighteen officers and two hundred and forty-five non-commissioned officers and privates were either invalided or transferred.

The names of Lieutenant-Colonel F. Barry Drew, Brevet Lieutenant-Colonel E. Tanner, and Captain E. Jervis, were mentioned in despatches. Lieutenant-Colonel Drew on 29th of July, 1879, and Brevet Lieutenant-Colonel Tanner on 1st of March, 1881, were gazetted Companions of the Bath, and on the latter date Captain Jervis was promoted to a Brevet Majority. A war medal was granted to every officer, non-commissioned officer, and private who served with the colours during any part of the campaigns of 1878-79-80: and a clasp to those who were present at the forcing of the Peiwar Kotal.

The Lower Kurrum Brigade having been broken up. Colonel Grogan rejoined on the 22nd, and resumed command of the battalion, which received orders to relieve the Sixty-Eighth Light Infantry at Meean Meer. Rawul Pindi was reached on the 6th November. Here the depot rejoined Headquarters, and the battalion continuing its march, arrived at Meean Meer on the 29th. The strength shown in the marching-in state was three field officers, four captains, thirteen subalterns, two staff, thirty-eight sergeants, seventeen drummers, and eight hundred and one rank and file (total twenty-two officers and eight hundred and fifty-six non-commissioned officers, drummers, and privates).

D Company under Lieutenant Taylor was detached to occupy Fort Lahore.

On the 6th of December a draft of two sergeants and one hundred and twenty-two rank and file arrived from the First Battalion.

Section 6—Recapitulation.

The establishment of the King's Regiment has consisted of two battalions during three different periods, forming an aggregate of thirty-six years. Out of this aggregate period the Second Battalion has served abroad eighteen years, and in the field against an enemy the whole or part of four years.

In 1809, the flank companies were selected to form part of the Walcheren Expedition, and in 1814, the battalion formed part of the force which invaded the United States, and was present at the Battle of Plattsburg. In 1878-79-80, during the Afghan War, the battalion was attached to the Kurrum Valley Force: it was present at the Battle of the Peiwar Kotal, and a detachment at the repulse of the attack on Ali Kheyl.

The loss sustained by the battalion in 1809, and 1814, has not been recorded; during the Afghan War the casualties were one non-commissioned officer killed, seven non-commissioned officers and privates wounded.

POSTSCRIPT

1881. About five o'clock in the evening of 14th January, a bag, containing an explosive substance, was introduced through an aperture in the south wall of Salford Barracks, from which a grating had been wrenched, into a shed where the rations are served out, and fired by means of a slow match. The explosion did not injure any of the soldiers, and the damage done to the boundary wall of the barracks was slight; but the shed was completely wrecked, and a woman and child who happened to be passing in the street outside received severe wounds, from the effects of which the child died. The perpetrators of this outrage were not discovered, but were believed to be agents of the Fenians, or of some other organisation of disaffected Irishmen.

During the months of January, February, and March, the country in the vicinity of Manchester was in a very disturbed state, in consequence of strikes and riots among the colliers. Major-General Cameron was detached from Aldershot on special service to take command of the troops, and established his Headquarters in Salford Barracks. By his order a detachment of the regiment, under Captain Egerton, was sent to Chowbent to assist the civil power in preserving order. This service was performed successfully without a collision between the rioters and the soldiers.

Another detachment of two companies, under Captains Stuart and Jocelyn, were sent to Wigan from the depot at Warrington, and were equally successful in performing the duties required of them without being obliged to use their arms against the rioters.

On the 1st June a general order was published, announcing that the queen had been graciously pleased to sanction the words "Peiwar Kotal" and "Afghanistan, 1878-80," being borne on the colours of the regiment in commemoration of its gallant behaviour during the Afghan campaign.

On 1st July the regimental constitution of the Line and Militia was reorganised, and sixty-nine territorial regiments were formed, each consisting of two battalions of the line and two battalions of militia. (In some regiments the fourth battalion was not formed, and in a few there were one or more additional battalions of militia.)

In accordance with the provisions of this reorganisation the two battalions of the Eighth, the King's, and the two battalions of the Second Royal Lancashire Militia, were united, and formed into a single territorial regiment (numbered the Eighth), having its headquarters at Warrington, and bearing the name of The King's (Liverpool Regiment).

A state showing the establishment of the regiment as thus reconstituted, is given on the following page.

Establishment of the King's (Liverpool) Regiment, 1st August, 1881.	Line Battalions.		Militia Battalions.		Depôt.
	I. Home.	II. Abroad.	III.	IV.	
Number of companies	8	8	8	6	4
Lieutenant-colonels	2	2	1	1	1
Majors	3	4	2	1	1
Captains	5	4	8	6	1
Lieutenants	12	16	12	9	2
Adjutant	1	1	1	..	..
Quartermaster	1	1	1	1	..
Total officers	24	28	25	18	5
Serjeant-major	1	1	1	1	1
Quartermaster-serjeant	1	1	1	1	1
Bandmaster	1	1	..	..	..
Serjeant drummer	1	1	1	1	..
Paymaster-serjeant	1	1	1	1	1
Armourer-serjeant	1	1	..	..	..
Orderly room serjeant	1	1	1	1	1
Hospital serjeant	..	1	..	..	..
Colour-serjeants	8	8	..	..	4
Serjeant pioneer	1	1	..	..	..
Serjeant cook	1	..	..	..	..
Serjeant instructor of musketry	1	1	1	1	..
Serjeants	24	32	*32	†24	4
Total warrant officers and serjeants	42	50	38	30	12
Drummers	16	16	8	6	2
Corporals	40	40	32	24	10
Privates	440	780	800	600	40
Total rank and file	480	820	832	624	50
Total all ranks	562	914	903	678	69

* 3rd Battalion .... { 16 Serjeants, Permanent Staff.
16 do. Militia.

† 4th Battalion .... { 12 Serjeants, Permanent Staff.
12 do. Militia.

Appendix 1

Succession List of all the Colonels of the King's Regiment and of all Lieutenant-Colonels, Majors, Captains, Captain-Lieutenants, Lieutenants, Ensigns, Sub-Lieutenants, Second Lieutenants, Adjutants, Musketry Instructors, Paymasters, Quartermasters, Surgeons, Assistant-Surgeons, and Chaplains who have served in the regiment from 1754, to 1st August, 1881, extracted from the series of Army Lists belonging to the Royal United Service Institution, (the name of any officer who entered the regiment after 1st January, and left it before 31st December of the same year, will most probably not be found in this list), together with such other officers as are elsewhere recorded to have served in any of these ranks previous to 1754. The records from which the names of officers who served in the regiment previous to 1754, were compiled are:—

1. From the first edition of the regimental records, edited by Mr. Cannon.

2. From five MS. Army Lists for the years 1702, 1709, 1736, 1743, 1752. The lists for 1736, and 1743, exhibit in a column of remarks the dates of all vacancies and the names of the officers who succeeded to them up to 1854, the year from which the present series of annual Army Lists commences; the list of officers who served in the regiment subsequent to the year 1736, may therefore be considered as complete. Mr. Thomas Cave Brown Cave, of the War Office, was good enough to give me extracts from these five lists.

3. From a printed Army List of the year 1740, belonging to the library of the Royal United Service Institution; this list is believed to be unique. No copy of it exists either at the War Office or in the British Museum.

N.B.—Column A contains the names of the officers; the small numerals which follow some of the names in this column refer to corresponding numbers in the series of biographical notices and abstracts of war services given in Appendix No. 2.

The letters in Column B indicate the mode of succession to each regimental rank; the letter A. stands for "by *Appointment*;" P. for "by *Promotion*;" E. for "by *Exchange*;" T. for "by *Transfer*;" H. P. for "from *Half Pay*." The numerals which in some instances follow the letters P., B., or T. in this column, and also in Column D, denote the number of the corps into or from which the officer was promoted, exchanged, or was transferred. The letter S. denotes "*Serving*" in the rank at the date given in Column C or E.

Column C gives the date of succession to each regimental rank.

The letters in Column D indicate the cause of each officer's removal from the list. The letter P. stands for "*Promoted*;" R. for "*Retires*" or "*Resigns*;" H. P. for retires on "*Half Pay*" F. P. for retires on "*Full Pay*;" E. for "*Exchanges*;" T. for "*Transferred*;" D. for "*Death*" from accident or disease; K, for "*Killed*" in action: W. for death from "*Wounds*" received in action; C. M. for dismissed or cashiered by sentence of "*Court Martial*."

Column E gives the date of each officer's removal from the list.

A blank space in Columns B, C, D, or E, indicates "not *ascertained*."

The letter 𝕽 is prefixed to the names of seven officers who have served in the regiment continuously and in every rank in succession from Ensign to Lieutenant-Colonel. These officers are Lieutenant-Colonels John Longfield, Edward Harris Greathed, John Hinde, James Johnston, John Vere, William Henry Webb, Edward Tanner, and Forster Longfield.

******

Since the printing of Appendices Nos. 1 and 2 was completed, two other officers have been added to this list, Lieutenant-Colonel R. Whitting promoted on 7th March, and Lieutenant Colonel E. Williams on 10th June, 1882; two old and distinguished officers have died, General Sir E. H. Greathed, K.C.B., on 19th November, and General T. G. Ball on 18th December, 1881; General J. Longfield, C.B., has been appointed Colonel of the Regiment (19th December, 1881), and Lieutenant-Colonel G. H. Cochrane has succeeded to the command of the Second Battalion (7th March, 1882).

******

COLONELS.

A	B	C	D	E
Robert Lord Ferrars[1]	A	19 June 1685	R	1686
James, Duke of Berwick[2]	A	1 Nov. 86		88
John Beaumont[3]	A	31 Dec. 88	R	95
John Richmond Webb[4]	A	26 Dec. 95	R	1715
Henry Morrison[5]	*	5 Aug. 1715	D	20
Sir Charles Hotham, Bart.[6]	T 36	3 Dec. 20	T (SD) †	21
John Pocock[7]	T 36	21 April 21	D	25 April 32
Charles Lenoe[8]	T 36	8 May 32	D	Dec. 38
Richard Onslow[9]	T 39	6 June 39	T (HGG) ‡	April 45
Edward Wolfe[10]	T 44	25 April 45	D	Mar. 59
The Hon. J. Barrington[11]	T 40	24 Oct. 59	D	2 April 64
John Stanwix[12]	T 60	11 April 64	D	66
§Daniel Webb[13]	T 48	18 Dec. 66	(T 14 Lt.D)	22 Oct. 72
Bigoe Armstrong[14]	T 83	20 Oct. 71	D	24 July 94
Ralph Dundas[15]	A	30 July 94	D	7 Feb. 1814
Edmund Stevens[16]	A	8 Feb. 1814	D	12 Sept. 25
Sir Henry Bayly, G.C.H.[17]	A	13 Sept. 25	D	23 April 46
Sir Gordon Drummond, G.C.B.[18]	T 49	24 April 46	D	9 Oct. 54
John Duffy[19]	T 28	10 Oct. 54	D	17 Mar. 55
Sir Roderick Macneil, K.C.B.[20]	A	18 Mar. 55	T 78	3 June 60
Eaton Monins[21]	A	3 June 60	D	16 June 61
¶Thos. Gerard Ball[22]	T 46	17 June 61	S	

* Purchased appointment.
† Royal Dragoons.
‡ Horse Grenadier Guards.
§ In the Succession List of Colonels given in the Army Lists, the date of General D. Webb's appointment to the Fourteenth Light Dragoons is 22nd October, 1772. The date of the appointment to the King's of his successor, General Bigoe Armstrong, is 20th October, 1771. I am unable to explain why the two dates do not correspond.—(A. C. R.)

¶ General T. Gerard Ball held the appointment of Colonel on 1st August, 1881.

LIEUTENANT-COLONELS.

A	B	C	D	E
John Beaumont[3]	A	19 June 1685	D	Sept. 1688
Ramsay[23]	A	88	*	* *
* * *	*	* *	*	* *
Richard Sutton[24] (A*)		10 Dec. 1702		25 Mar. 1708
Lewis de Ramsey[25] (B) ..	P	25 Mar. 08	K	11 Sept. 09
* * *	*	* *	*	* *
George Keightly[26] (C, D)		1 Feb. 32		1 May 45
Edmund Martin[27]	P	1 May 45	D	26 April 49
John Lafausille[28] (E, F)	P	27 April 49	P 63	24 Aug. 58
John Mompesson[29]	T	24 Aug. 58		23 Nov. 68
Dudley Auckland[30] ..	P	23 Nov. 68		27 Oct. 72
John Caldwell[31]	T	27 Oct. 72		11 Nov. 76
Mason Bolton[32]	T	11 Nov. 76		1 Nov. 80
Alexander Dundas[33] ..	T	1 Nov. 80		13 Sept. 83
Arent Schuyler De Peister[34] ..	P	13 Sept. 83		3 April 94
Edward Dawson[35]	P	3 April 94		1 Mar. 96
Gordon Drummond[18] ..	T	22 April 94	HP	8 Feb. 1814
George Airey[36]	T	4 May 98		1814-15
Daniel Hoghton[37] (2 B.)	T	22 Nov. 1804	D	5 June 11
Robert Young[38]	P	27 April 09		4 June 14
Peter Thomas Roberton (2 B.) .	P	6 June 11	†	9 Sept. 19
James Ogilvie[39]	P	28 July 14	R	25 Feb. 16
John Duffy[19]	T	9 Sept. 19	HP	20 Mar. 28
Hon. George Cathcart[40] ..	T 57	20 Mar. 28	E	25 Sept. 35
Sir W. P. De Bathe, Bt.[41] ..	E	25 Sept. 35	R	2 Oct. 35
Thomas Gerald Ball[22] ..	P	2 Oct. 35	HP	25 Oct. 42
Charles St. Lo Malet[42] ..	P	25 Oct. 42	HP	16 Dec. 45
Richard Henry Winchcombe Hartley[43]	P	16 Dec. 45	D	25 June 58
※ John Longfield[44] ..	P	3 April 46	HP	May 60
Thomas Maitland Wilson[45] (2 B.)	HP	21 Oct. 57	HP	27 Sept. 61
※ Edward Harris Greathed[46] ..	P	26 June 58	HP	28 Oct. 59
Frederick Paul Haines[47] ..	HP	28 Oct. 59	HP	1 July 62
※ John Hinde[48]	P	27 Sept. 61	FP	15 June 66
※ James Johnston[49] (2 B.) ..	P	1 July 62	D	29 Dec. 65

* The letters A, B, C, D, and E denote that the names to which they are affixed appear in the MS. War Office Army Lists: A, 1702; B, 1709; C, 1736; D, 1743; E, 1752. The letter F denotes the order of succession in the printed Army List of 1754, after which year the annual series of printed A Lists is consecutive.

† Cashiered.

A	B	C		D	E	
LIEUTENANT-COLONELS—*continued.*						
Alexander Cuningham Robertson[50] (2 B.)	P	30 Dec.	1865	HP	24 Mar.	1875
Henry George Woods[51] ..	P	15 June	66	P	30 Jan.	80
W. F. A. Colman[52]	P	24 Mar.	75	FP	12 May	75
※ John Vere W. H. Webb[53] (2 B.)	P	12 May	75	FP	7 Mar.	77
Francis Barry Drew[54] (2 B.) ..	P	7 Mar.	77	E14	13 Sept.	79
Charles Edward Grogan[55] (2 B)	E 14	13 Sept.	79	S‖		
※ Edward Tanner[56]	P	30 Jan.	80	S‖		
George H. Cochrane[57]	P	1 July	81	S‖		
※ Forster Longfield[58]	P	,,	,,	S‖		

‖ These Officers were serving in this rank on 1st January, 1881.

MAJORS.

A	B	C		D	E	
John Innes	A	20 June	1685			
Lewis de Ramsey[23] (A*)		10 Dec.	1702	P	25 Mar.	1708
Frederick Cornwallis[59]				K	13 Aug.	04
* * * *	*	*	*	*	*	*
Anthony Columbere (B)	P	23 Mar.	08			
* * * *	*	*	*	*	*	*
George Keightly			08	P	1 Feb.	31
Hanmer[50]	S		15	K	13 Nov.	15
James Beschefer (D)	P	10 Dec.	31	PT	6 Dec.	39
Edmund Martin[27] (D)	P	6 Dec.	39	PT	7 Feb.	43
James Barry[61] (C, D)	P	7 Feb.	41	W	29 June	43
John Grey[62] (C, D)	P	14 July	43	PT	17 Feb.	45
John Lafausille[28] (C)	P	17 Feb.	45	P	27 April	49
Arthur Loftus[63] (E)	P	27 Apr.	49	D	26 Aug.	53
Nehemiah Donnellan (E, F)	P	27 Aug.	53		Sept.	56
John Cook[64] (2 B.)	P	25 Aug.	56	T 63	28 Feb.	61
Henry Boisragon		28 Feb.	61		19 April	65
William Hunter		19 April	65		29 June	67
Dudley Ackland[20]		24 June	67	P	23 Nov.	68
John Corrance	P	23 Nov.	68		4 Mar.	76
Hon. Lewis Duffe	P	4 Mar.	76		6 May	77
Arent Schuyler De Peister[24]	P	6 May	77	P	13 Sept.	83
Richard Ber Lernoult	P	13 Sept.	83		27 Jan.	86
William Potts	P	27 Jan.	86		18 Oct.	86
Andrew Parke	P	18 Oct.	86	R	31 Aug.	93
Edward Dawson[35]	P 51	31 Aug.	93	P	3 April	94
Thomas Armstrong[65]	P	3 April	94	K	June	94
George Armstrong		27 Nov.	94	D	19 Oct.	96
Durell Saumarez[66]	P		94	K		94
Thomas Bland[67]	P	17 Dec.	94	R	4 Jan	97
Archibald Campbell	Π P	20 Oct.	96		8 Oct.	1803
Robert Young[36]	P	4 Jan.	97	P	27 April	09
Alexander Duke[68]	P	10 July	99	R		04
Bryce Maxwell[69]	P	8 Oct.	1803	K	2 Feb.	09
Peter Thomas Roberton	P	23 Oct.	04	P	6 June	11
Thomas Fortye[70]	P	24 Oct.	04	T	18 April	05
Samuel Huskisson	T	4 July	05		4 June	07
James Ogilvie[39]	P	4 June	07	P	28 July	14
Edward Cotton[71]	P	3 Feb.	09	PT	21 Oct.	13
Francis Battersby	P	11 May	09	PT	3 Sept.	12
Thomas Buck	P	6 June	11		20 June	20
Thomas Evans[72]	P	3 Sept.	12	T 70	14 Mar.	16
James Mundy[73] (2 B.)	P	21 Oct.	13		25 Feb.	16
John Blackmore[74] (2 B.)	P	29 Sept.	14		"	16
Hon. Gerard De Courcy	T	14 Mar.	16	R	24 June	24
Robert Melville Browne	T	20 June	20	PT	11 July	26
Thomas Gerard Ball[22]	P	24 June	24	P	2 Oct.	35
John Styles Powell	P	11 July	26	D	22 Jan.	37

MAJORS—continued.

A	B	C		D	E	
Simcoe Baynes[75]	P	2 Oct.	1835	PT	26 Oct.	1841
Charles Barker Turner[76]	T	3 Feb.	37	T	9 Jan.	38
Charles St. Lo Malet[42]	P	10 Jan.	38	P	25 Oct.	42
Richard H. Winchcombe Hartley[43]	P	26 Oct.	41	P	16 Dec.	45
Thomas Kenyon	P	25 Oct.	42	R	19 Nov.	44
¶ John Longfield[44]	P	19 Nov.	44	P	3 April	46
Henry Welladvice Roper	P	16 Dec.	45	R	28 April	46
¶ Edward Harris Greathed[46]	P	3 April	46	P	26 June	58
Francis Saunderson Holmes	P	28 April	46	D	3 Aug.	49
F. Douglas Lumley	P	4 Aug.	49	E 31	11 Dec.	49
James Croft Brooke[77]	E 31	11 Dec.	49	H P	15 Oct.	61
¶ John Hinde[45] (2 B.)	P	21 Oct.	57	P	27 Sept.	61
John Butler Wheatstone[78] (2 B.)	P T 45	17 Nov.	57	F P	24 Aug.	58
¶ James Johnston[49] (2 B.)	P	26 June	58	P	1 July	62
Alex. Cuningham Robertson[50]	P	24 Aug.	58	P	30 Dec.	65
William Bayly[79]	P	27 Sept.	61	F P	9 Oct.	63
Henry George Woods[81] (2 B.)	H P	15 Oct.	61	P	15 June	66
Edwin Gream Daniell[80]	P	1 July	62	H P	28 Jan.	63
Thos. De Courcy Hamilton[81] (2 B.)	H P	23 Jan.	63	P 64	20 May	68
George Edward Baynes[82]	P	9 Oct.	63	PT	2 Nov.	66
De Vic Tupper[83]	P	30 Dec.	65	H P	22 May	66
William F. Adams Colman[52]	H P	22 May	66	P	24 Mar.	75
Richard R. Meade[84] (2 B.)	P	15 June	66	H P	2 Sept.	68
¶ John Vere W. H. Webb[53]	P	2 Nov.	66	P	12 May	75
Fred. Bradford McCrea[85] (2 B.)	P	20 May	68	R	24 Mar.	69
Francis Barry Drew[54] (2 B.)	H P	2 Sept.	68	P	7 Mar.	77
¶ Edward Tanner[56] (2 B.)	P	24 Mar.	69	P	30 Jan.	80
George H. Cochrane[57] (2 B.)	P	24 Mar.	75	P	1 July	81
¶ Forster Longfield[58]	P	12 May	75	P	1 July	81
Reginald Whitting[86]	P	7 Mar.	77	S‡		
William Bannatyne[87] (2 B.)	P	30 Jan.	80	S‡		
Edward Williams	P	1 July	81	S‡		
Thomas Gorges Crawley	P	,,	,,	S‡		
William W. Egerton (2 B.)	P	,,	,,	S‡		
Bennett F. Handy[88]	P	,,	,,	S‡		
Francis James Stuart	P	,,	,,	S‡		
Nash Short[89] (2 B.)	P	,,	,,	S‡		
John James Hamilton	P	,,	,,	S‡		

‡ These Officers were serving in this rank on 1st August, 1881.

CAPTAINS.

A	B	C	D	E
Rowland Okeover	A	20 June 1685		
Charles Chudd	A	,, ,,		
Thomas Paston	A	,, ,,	*	Sept. 1688
William Cooke	A	,, ,,	*	,, ,,
Simon Packe	A	,, ,,		,, ,,
Walter Burdet	A	,, ,,		
Thomas Orme	A	,, ,,	*	,, ,,
Sir John Reresby	A	87		
John Porte	S	88	*	,, ,,
Barnes	P	88		
Fielding	P	88		
Southern	P	88		
Mackarty	P	88		
Fletcher	P	88		
* * * *	*	* * *	*	* *
Ralph Congreve (A)†		22 Feb. 92		
Peter Hammers (A, B)		25 April 94		
Anthony Columbier (A, B)		12 Mar. 91	P	23 Mar. 1708
Burluce Webb (A, B)		1 Jan. 1704		
John Farcey (A, B)		2 April 04		
William Congreve (A, B)		30 May 1696		
Francis Napper (A)		25 April 94		
John Balfoure (B)		4 May 1707		
Leonard Lloyd[90] (A, B)		10 Dec. 02		
Fielding (A)				
Rater (A)				
Benjamin Cuttle (B)		25 Mar. 05		
Arthur Usher (B)		17 May 06		
James Beschefer (B)		24 April 06	P	10 Dec. 1731
Edmond de Fisher (B)				
* * * *	*	* * *	*	* *
Edmund Martin[27] (D)		17 Mar. 18	P	6 Dec. 39
John Sprunger (D)		29 June 19	R	20 June 39
James Barry[61] (D)	P	7 Jan. 20	P	7 Feb. 40
George Banastre (C, D)	P	23 Oct. 24	T	15 June 43
John Grey[62] (C, D)	P	10 Dec. 31	P	14 July 43
John Dallons[91] (C, D)	P	31 Aug. 33	D	16 Feb. 46
Edward Cornwallis (D)		3 April 34	PT	13 May 42
Peter Guerin (C, D)	PT	20 June 39	D	16 Feb. 46
Thomas Launder (C, D)	P	12 Jan. 40	D	,, ,,
William Hele (C, D)	T	7 Feb. 40	D	,, ,,
Peter Ribton (C, D)	P	13 May 42	R	4 Oct. 43
Francis Mercer (C)	HP	25 June 44	PT	29 Nov. 45
Philip Jennings (C)	PT	26 June 44	E	4 June 46
Malcolm Hamilton (C, D)	P	15 June 43	D	17 Feb. 46
John Lafausille[28] (C, D)	P	14 July 43	P	17 Feb. 46
Arthur Loftus[63] (C)	P	4 Oct. 43	P	27 April 49
Richard Miggot[92] (C)	T	17 Feb. 45	K	2 July 47

* Dismissed by sentence of court-martial.

A	B	C		D	E	
CAPTAINS—continued.						
Nehemiah Donellan (C, E)*	P	17 Feb.	1746	P	27 Aug.	1753
Charles Desclouseaux (F)	P	,,	,,	T	26 Feb.	55
William Catherwood[93]	P	,,	,,	E	16 Jan.	52
Henry Rogers	P	,,	,,	D	25 Sept.	49
John Cook[64] (E, F)	P	17 Feb.	46	P	25 Aug.	56
†John Ekins[94]	P	29 Nov.	45	D	15 Aug.	50
Elliot Lawrence	E	4 June	46	R	5 Mar.	47
John Trollop[95] (F	P	5 Mar.	47	P 63	30 April	58
Richard Knight		25 June	47	R		
Purcell Kempe (F)	HP	25 Sept.	49	PT		
Jacob Conway[96] (E)	P	16 Aug.	50	D	21 April	52
William Arnott (F)	E	16 June	52	P 55		
Henry Boisragon (F)	P 23	22 April	52	P	28 Feb.	61
Francis Wilkinson[97] (F)	P	27 Aug.	53	R		
John Corrance	P	26 Feb.	55	P	23 Nov.	68
Thomas Spencer Wilson	P	16 Oct.	55			
James Webb[98]	P	2 Nov.	55		22 Nov.	75
James Dundas (2 B.)	HP	25 Aug.	56	R	May	62
Robert Cleiland (2 B.)	T 2	26 Aug.	56	T 63	26 Aug.	56‡
Obadiah Bourne (2 B.)	T 2	27 Aug.	56		5 May	69
Joseph Fish (2 B.)	P	28 Aug.	56	T 63	28 Aug.	56‡
John Blomer (2 B.)	T 57	29 Aug.	56	T 63	29 Aug.	56‡
Henry Rogers (2 B.)	T 17	30 Aug.	56	T 63	30 Aug.	56‡
John Ellis (2 B.)	P	31 Aug.	56	T 63	31 Aug.	56‡
Charles Hamilton[99] (2 B.)	P	1 Sept.	56	T 63	1 Sept.	56‡
Charles Gilman (2 B.)	T 25	2 Sept.	56	T 63	2 Sept.	56‡
William Wade (2 B.)	T 3DG	3 Sept.	56	T 63	3 Sept.	56‡
Henry Lee	P	28 Feb.	61		18 Dec.	66
Hon. Lewis Duffe		17 Dec.	61	P	4 Mar.	76
Robert Bridges		12 May	62		15 July	67
Massenden Johnston		18 Dec.	66		27 Mar.	70
Richard Ber-Lernoult		15 July	67	P	13 Sept.	83
A. Schuyler De Peister[34]	P	23 Nov.	68	P	6 May	77
George Steele	T	5 May	69		5 Nov.	76
Theophilus Dame	P	27 Mar.	70		12 Oct.	71
George Forster[100]	P	25 Dec.	70	P 21	5 Nov.	76
Henry Hatton	P	12 Oct.	71		8 Mar.	78
William Potts		25 May	72	P	27 Jan.	86
Kenny Powell		15 Aug.	75		11 May	78
Andrew Parke		22 Nov.	75	P	18 Oct.	86
John Mompesson		16 Mar.	76		26 Oct.	85
Robert Clements	P	29 Mar.	76		14 Sept.	85
Francis Le Maistre	T	5 Nov.	76		8 Aug.	88
Samuel Willoe	P	6 May	77			93

† J. Ekins, misprinted Atkins in *Records*.
‡ Dates of Commissions in 63rd Regiment.

CAPTAINS—continued.

A	B	C	D	E
Robert Mathews		7 May 1777		22 Sept. 1783
Stephen Watts	T	8 Mar. 78		12 Dec. 81
Henry Bird	P	11 May 78		84
Thomas Bennet	P	13 Sept. 83		17 Feb. 90
W. Osb-Hamilton	T	22 Sept. 83		84
Thomas Armstrong[65]		14 Sept. 85	P	3 April 94
John Delgarno	P	26 Oct. 85		31 July 92
George Clowes	P	27 Jan. 86		31 Mar. 90
Daniel Mercer	P	18 Oct. 86		93
Thomas Pepyat	P	8 Aug. 88		93
George Armstrong	P	17 Feb. 90	P	27 Nov. 94
Durell Saumarez[66]	P	31 Mar. 90	P	94
Gonville Bromhead	T	31 July 92		93
Thomas Bland[67]		31 July 92	P	17 Dec. 94
Alexr. Duke[68]	P	31 Mar. 93	P	10 July 99
Thos. St. George Armstrong	P	31 Mar. 93	R	18 Aug. 95
Robert Young[39]	P	29 June 93	P	4 Jan. 97
Robt. Pollard	P	8 Aug. 93	D	97
Bryce Maxwell[69]	P	26 Oct. 93	P	8 Oct. 1803
Bryce MacMurdo[101]	P	3 April 94		03
James Booth[102]	P	94	K	12 June 1794
*George A. Armstrong	P	27 Nov. 94	PT	1 July 95
Peter Thomas Roberton	T 38	25 Aug. 94	P	23 Oct. 1804
John Armstrong	P	1 July 95	D	19 Oct. 1796
Richard Oliver	T	19 Aug. 95		1802
George Bowles	T	1 Sept. 95		05
Marcus McCausland	P	18 Nov. 95	D	20 Dec. 1796
Thomas Fortye[70]	P	27 Nov. 94	P	1804
Ralph Peter Dundas	P	17 Nov. 94		02
Robert Smyth		26 Jan. 96		00
Francis Battersby	P	10 April 1801		02
Stephen Pendergast	T	29 Oct. 02		27 Mar. 06
Edward Cotton[71]	P	18 Nov. 02	P	3 Feb. 09
James Ogilvie[39]		13 May 02	P	4 June 07
Francis Battersby	T	25 May 03	P	11 May 09
Thomas Buck	P	16 June 03	P	6 June 11
Septimus Walp. Loane	P	25 June 03	D	11
Thomas Evans[72]	P	19 Nov. 03	P	3 Sept. 12
John Charles Smith	T	24 April 04		17 Nov. 07
John Blackmore[74]	P	23 Oct. 04	P	29 Sept. 14
Robert M'Dowall	P	24 Oct. 04		13
William Scholly		25 Oct. 04		04
Henry Francis Goldicutt	P	14 Nov. 04	D	13
Neale, M'Neale[103]	T	24 April 04	W	27 April 13
James Munday[73]	T	25 April 04	P	21 Oct. 13
James S. Tyeth[104]	P	21 Mar. 05	HP	25 Feb. 16
W. Cotter	T	25 April 05		26
Arthur Newport	T	1 May 05		10

* G. A. Armstrong promoted to an independent Majority.

A	B	C	D	E
CAPTAINS—continued.				
George M'Donnell*	T	4 Sept. 1805	PT	2 Sept. 1812
William Robinson[105]	T	5 Sept. 05	R	29 Sept. 24
Thomas Couche	P	17 Oct. 05		10
Francis Campbell[106]	T	21 Nov. 05		26
Peter Dickenson	P	27 Mar. 06	R	11
Henry Sadlier[107]	P	4 June 07	D	16
James Agnew (2 B.)	T	17 Nov. 07		14 Sept. 20
Peter Moyles (2 B.)	P	3 Feb. 09		15 Mar. 21
Edward Connor	P	20 July 09		16
J. Walter Sweetman	T	26 July 10		16
William Sall	T	23 Aug. 10		12
William Walsh	P	16 May 11	HP	25 Dec. 17
John FitzGerald[108] (2 B.)	P	6 June 11	D	5 July 35
John Bradbridge[109] (2 B.)	P	12 Sept. 11	HP	23 Dec. 17
William Hanbury Davies	T	2 July 12		25 Feb. 16
James Hardy Eustace[110] (2 B.)	P	2 Sept. 12	HP	25 Feb. 16
John Goldrisk (2 B.)	P	3 Sept. 12	HP	,, ,,
†Samuel Hooker[111]	P	13	K	5 June 13
Henry Brewster (2 B.)	P	4 Aug. 13	HP	25 Feb. 16
Thomas Cross (2 B.)	P	5 Aug. 13	HP	,, 16
Thomas Miller (2 B.)	P	12 Aug. 13		15
Edward Brown	P	24 Feb. 14	D	15
Austin Neame (2 B.)	P	10 Aug. 14	HP	25 Feb. 16
George Rawlinson	T	11 Aug. 14	HP	,, ,,
John M'Mahon[112] (2 B.)	P	29 Sept. 14	HP	,, ,,
Henry Raban (2 B.)		27 July 15	HP	,, ,,
Henry Simmonds (2 B.)	T	31 Mar. 15	HP	,, ,,
Edward F. Davis	T	18 April 16	HP	24 Dec. 17
John Tucker	T	23 May 16	R	22
William Jervois	HP	23 Dec. 17	E	22
Thomas Crosse	HP	24 Dec. 17		10 June 19
Thomas Gerrard Ball[22]	HP	25 Dec. 17	P	24 June 24
F. A. Mackenzie Fraser	T	10 June 19		21
Charles de Havilland	T	14 Sept. 20		22
David Vans Machen[113]	P	15 Mar. 21	R	7 Aug. 35
John Styles Powell	T	28 Nov. 22	P	11 July 26
William Booth	E	26 Dec. 22		31 July 23
Harris Hailes	T	31 July 23		25
Simcoe Baynes[75]	P	24 June 24	P	2 Oct. 35
James Hannay	P	30 Sept. 24		28
Malcolm Ross	P	7 April 25		28
Anthony Lyster	T	8 April 25		26
Thomas Pelling Lang	T	1 Oct. 25		26
John Horatius Maitland	T	20 April 26	R	29 Jan. 35
Thomas Hart Davies	T	8 June 26	HP	21 Feb. 33
Alexander Dirom	T	,, ,,	R	10 May 33
Charles St. Lo Malet[42]	T	,, ,,	P	10 Jan. 38
William Eleazer Pickwick	P	11 July 26	E	14 April 29

* G. M'Donnell promoted in Glengarry Fencible Light Infantry on formation of corps.

A	B	C	D	E
CAPTAINS—*continued.*				
Charles Corkran	T	24 April 1828	R	1837
Richard Henry Winchcombe Hartley[43]	T	5 June 28	P	26 Oct. 41
Thomas Kenyon	E	14 April 29	P	25 Oct. 42
Thomas Rutherford Thompson ..	P	8 Mar. 33	D	21 Nov. 37
James Byron	P	10 May 33	R	2 July 41
♣ John Longfield[44]	P	30 Jan. 35	P	19 Nov. 44
William Calder	P	6 July 35		36
William Chearnley	P	7 Aug. 35	R	4 July 45
Irwine S. Whitty	P	2 Oct. 35	R	20 Nov. 38
Richard Westenra	T	27 Jan. 37	R	8 Feb. 37
James Pringle	P	3 Feb. 37	R	27 April 38
Henry Welladvice Roper ..	P	23 June 37	P	16 Dec. 45
David Gardiner[114]	P	22 Nov. 37	R	24 June 42
Walter Ogilvy	P	10 Jan. 38	R	12 Dec. 43
♣ Edward Harris Greathed[46] ..	P	27 April 38	P	3 April 46
John Terry Liston	P	20 Nov. 38	E 3	27 Mar. 46
Cyrus Plaistow Trapaud ..	P	2 July 41	R	6 May 42
Francis Saunderson Holmes ..	P	26 Oct. 41	P	28 April 46
Stephenson Brown	P	6 May 42	D	16 Nov. 48
Alfred Augustus Malet	P	24 June 42	HP	14 Nov. 45
Frederick Douglas Lumley ..	P	25 Oct. 42	P	4 Aug. 49
J. Eldridge West	P	12 Dec. 43	R	27 Sept. 44
Coulthurst Holder	P	27 Sept. 44	D	28 May 48
Ernest Lavie	P	19 Nov. 44	R	20 Mar. 46
♣ John Hinde[46]	P	4 July 45	P	21 Oct. 57
John Long Marsden	P	14 Nov. 45	D	16 Oct. 48
Thomas Clowes	P	16 Dec. 45	R	21 April 46
James Speedy	E 3	27 Mar. 46	HP	20 July 55
C. F. B. Greville Dickenson ..	P	20 Mar. 46	E 34	28 April 46
Arthur Leslie	P	3 April 46	E 40	19 June 46
♣ James Johnston[49]	P	21 April 46	P	26 June 58
Alex. Cuningham Robertson[50] ..	E 34	28 April 46	P	24 Aug. 58
Edwin Gream Daniell[80] ..	E 55	29 April 46	P	1 July 62
Ferdinand White[115]	E 40	19 June 46	PT	21 Feb. 51
William Bayly[79]	P	29 May 48	P	27 Sept. 61
George Edward Baynes[82] ..	P	17 Oct. 48	P	9 Oct. 63
Richard Wilson Hartley ..	P	9 Feb. 49	E 94	16 Jan. 57
J. H. Edwd. de Robeck ..	P	9 Nov. 49	E 4	28 Dec. 49
Charles Stainforth Hext ..	E 4	28 Dec. 49	D	26 Jan. 55
Alfred Ingilby Garnett	P	21 Feb. 51	E 38	22 Aug. 56
Ellis James Charter	P	15 Mar. 53	E 21	2 Sept. 53
Robert Stuart Baynes[116] ..	P	,,	PT	2 Dec. 59
John Millar Bannatyne[117] ..	E 21	2 Sept. 53	HP	11 July 65

A	B	C	D	E
CAPTAINS—*continued.*				
Richard W. Woods[118]	P	12 April 1856	E 80	22 July 1856
Hon. L. W. C. A. F. Cary	E 27	15 April 56	E 96	3 Mar. 57
John Ball Campbell[119]	P	27 Jan. 55	E 27	15 April 56
Shaftoe Craster Craster	P	20 July 55	D	11 April 56
Astell Thomas Welsh[120]	E 80	22 July 56	E 109	29 May 63
De Vic Tupper[83]	E 38	22 Aug. 56	P	30 Dec. 65
Richard Raphael Meade[84]	E 94	16 Jan. 57	P	15 June 66
John Whiteside[121]	E 96	3 Mar. 57	P HP	13 Feb. 66
Thomas George Souter[122]	P	21 Oct. 57	E 51	2 April 60
*Daniel Beere[123] (2 B.)	P	,, ,,	HP	13 Feb. 63
*Erskine Nimmo Sandilands[124]	P	,, ,,	T BSC	17 Nov. 63
*Swinnerton H. Dyer[125] (2 B.)	HP	23 Oct. 57	R	20 Dec. 64
*Robert Cathcart Bruce (2 B.)	HP	,, ,,	HP	28 Aug. 63
*John Allan Macdonald (2 B.)	HP	,, ,,	R	22 April 59
*John Woods Dimond[126] (2 B.)	HP	,, ,,	R	4 Feb. 59
*R. P. Gould (2 B.)	HP	,, ,,	D	14 Nov. 57
*Owen Wynne Gray[127] (2 B.)	PT 99	,, ,,	R	4 Sept. 60
George Corry[128] (2 B.)	P	15 Nov. 57	FP	17 May 61
†§ John Vere Wm. Henry Webb[53] (2 B.)	P	11 May 58	P	2 Nov. 66
†Alex. Ross Bayly[129] (2 B.)	P	,, ,,	E 88	31 Jan. 60
†William Raymond Ximenes[130] (2 B.)	P	,, ,,	R	29 Mar. 64
†George Henry Cochrane[57] (2 B.)	PT 96	21 May 58	P	24 Mar. 75
Cha. H. Martin	HP	24 Aug. 58	R	24 Sept. 58
Fred. Bradford McCrea[85]	P	26 June 58	P	20 May 68
§ Forster Longfield[58]	P	24 Sept. 58	P	12 May 75
Robert Lewis G. M'Grigor[131] (2 B.)	P	4 Feb. 59	E 92	19 July 59
William F. Metge[132] (2 B.)	P	22 April 59	E	30 Dec. 59
William Edward Newall	E 92	19 July 59	R	15 Jan. 61
John McQueen[133] (2 B.)	HP	2 Dec. 59	T‡	1 Mar. 64
Fred. W. J. Dugmore	E	30 Dec. 59	E SFG	18 Oct. 64
Lewis John Fillis Jones[134]	E 88	31 Jan. 60	T‡	16 July 61
Robert Gordon Sanders Mason	E 51	2 April 60		66
§ Edward Tanner[56] (2 B.)	P	4 Sept. 60	P	24 Mar. 69
Reginald Whitting[86] (2 B.)	P	15 Jan. 61	P	7 Mar. 77
Fred. Anderson Stebbing[135] (2 B.)	P	17 May 61	HP	31 Oct. 71
Alfred Downie Corfield	P	16 July 61	R	30 June 63

* Appointed on formation of Second Battalion.
† Appointed on augmentation of the Second Battalion.
‡ J. McQueen and L. J. F. Jones were appointed Adjutants of Depôt Battalions.

A	B	C	D	E
CAPTAINS—continued.				
Walter John Tarte	P	27 Sept. 1861	E	16 Oct. 1863
Æneas Gordon Blair[136] (2 B.)	P	1 July 62	E 102	26 Feb. 64
Ashley George Westby (2 B.)	P	13 Feb. 63	R	6 Mar. 67
Fraser Newall	T	29 May 63	R	15 Oct. 66
James Seager Wheeley	P	30 June 63	RP	20 Aug. 79
John Cusack[137]	HP	28 Aug. 63		70
Andrew Moynihan[138] (2 B.)	P	9 Oct. 63	D	19 May 67
Hon. Somerset R. Ham. Ward[139]	E	16 Oct. 63	R	18 Oct. 64
George Campbell Ross	T	18 Dec. 63	E 20 H	19 April 64
Sydney H. Jones Parry[140] (2 B.)	E 102	26 Feb. 64	E 84	12 Sept. 65
Angus William Hall (2 B.)	T	1 Mar. 64	R	26 April 64
John William Hughes	T	29 Mar. 64	R	29 Dec. 65
John Cockerell	E 20 H	19 April 64	R	29 Nov. 64
*William Theobald Butler (2 B.)	E 26	26 April 64	PR	18 Oct. 79
Henry Farquharson	E SFG	18 Oct. 64	R	20 Sept. 71
Robert D. Forbes Shirreff (2 B.)	P	"	R	10 Nov. 65
John Coleberd Cooper	P	29 Nov. 64	R	14 Aug. 67
George Nicholl James Bradford (2 B.)	P	20 Dec. 64	R	27 Nov. 66
Philip Homer Page	P	11 July 65	R	23 Jan. 75
William Atcherley Atcherley (2 B.)	E 84	12 Sept. 65	R	23 June 75
James Q. Palmer	P	10 Nov. 65	R	26 Jan. 66
C. Dudley Ryder Madden	P	29 Dec. 65	D	7 Nov. 74
William Edward Whelan[141]	P	30 Dec. 65	R	13 June 68
William Bannatyne[57] (2 B.)	P	26 Jan. 66	P	30 Jan. 80
William James Watson	P	20 Feb. 66	R	5 Nov. 70
*Chas. Bradford Brown[142] (2 B.)	P	15 June 66	PR	8 May 80
William Hunter Baillie	P	16 Oct. 66	R	1 Aug. 68
John Randle Minshull Ford (2 B.)	P	27 Nov. 66	R	10 Nov. 69
William Albert Bridge	P	12 Feb. 67	E 21	4 Sept. 67
Edward Williams (2 B.)	P	6 Mar. 67	P	1 July 81
R. T. B. Browne (2 B.)	P	20 May 67	E 1WI	8 Aug. 68
Thomas Gorges Crawley	P	14 Aug. 67	P	1 July 81
Ernest Lewis	E 21	4 Sept. 67	HP	23 Nov. 70
Jeremy P. Jones	P	13 June 68	R	17 Apr. 80
*John Dawson[143] (2 B.)	P	1 Aug. 68	PR	23 Aug. 81
*Armar Graham Lowry[144] (2 B.)	E 1WI	8 Aug. 68	PR	18 May 81
Martin George Cole (2 B.)	P	24 Mar. 69	R	23 Mar. 1870

* Brevet-Majors Butler, C. B. Brown, Dawson, and Lowry retire with honorary rank of Lieutenant-Colonels.

A	B	C		D	E	
CAPTAINS—*continued*.						
William Willoughby Egerton	P	10 Nov.	1869	P	1 July	1881
Marmaduke Stourton	P	23 Mar.	70	T 63	3 Sept.	70
Matthew Liddon (2 B.)	P	5 Nov.	70	R	21 July	77
*Edwin Jervis[145] (2 B.)	HP	23 Nov.	70	PR	18 May	81
William Howe Hennis	P	20 Sept.	71	R	13 April	72
John Mount Batten (2 B.)	P	31 Oct.	71	HP	23 Jan.	78
Edward Emerson	P	13 April	72	FP	29 July	74
Bowland G. Moffat	P	23 April	72	R	17 July	72
Charles Fred. Malet	P	17 July	72	D	22 Nov.	77
Bennett F. Handy[88] (2 B.)	P	4 June	73	P	1 July	81
Francis James Stuart	P	14 June	73	P	,,	,,
Nash Short[89] (2 B.)	P	3 Mar.	74	P	,,	,,
*Arthur Fawkes (2 B.)	P	29 July	74	PR	7 July	80
John James Hamilton	P	8 Nov.	74	P	1 July	81
W. Stancomb Sinkins	P	23 Jan.	75	S†		
W. Toke Dooner[146]	P	24 Mar.	75	T 108	12 May	75
Thomas Blake Humfrey[147] (2 B.)	P	1 April	75	S†		
D. W. Martin[148]	HP	12 May	75	HP	27 Sept.	79
Francis Moore	P	,,	,,	E 104	22 Sept.	75
Manley C. M. Dixon	P	23 June	75	R	6 Aug.	79
Stanley N. Roberts[149] (2 B.)	E 104	22 Sept.	75	S†		
William Louis	P	21 July	77	S†		
Robert Julian Orde Jocelyn	P	23 Nov.	77	S†		
Alfred Lewis[150] (2 B.)	HP			S†		
Arthur Henry Cope[151] (2 B.)	P	24 Sept.	78	S†		
Stephen Brown	P	6 Nov.	79	S†		
Arthur Ashley Ruck[152]	P	30 Jan.	80	S†		
William Richard Orme[153]	P	17 April	80	S†		
Henry Thomas Granger (2 B.)	P	8 May	80	S†		
Lawrence C. F. Thompson	P	7 July	80	S†		
Jas. Mathew Taylor[154] (2 B.)	P	9 Feb.	81	S†		
Henry M. Wade	P	21 Mar.	81	S†		
Fred Jas. Whalley[155] (2 B.)	P	18 May	81	S†		
Henry Manley Briscoe (2 B.)	P	,,	,,	S†		
George Robert Stone	P	22 June	81	S†		

* Brevet-Major Jervis retires with honorary rank of Lieutenant-Colonel; Capt. Fawkes with honorary rank of Major.
† These Officers were serving in this rank 1st August, 1881.

CAPTAINS-LIEUTENANTS.

A	B	C		D	E	
Verny Loyd (A*)			1702			
Joachim Goudet (B)	P	16 May	07	*	*	*
George Banastre	P	5 Jan.	15	P	23 Oct.	1724
James Barry[61]		10 Mar.	15	P	7 Jan.	20
John Grey[62]	P	1 Jan.	26	P	10 Dec.	31
William Hele		1 Jan.	35	P	7 Feb.	40
Thomas Launder (D)	P	11 Sept.	36	P	12 Jan.	40
Peter Ribton	P	12 Jan.	40	P	13 May	42
Malcolm Hamilton (C)	P	13 May	42	P	15 June	43
John Lafausille[29]	P	15 June	43	P	14 July	43
Arthur Loftus[63]	P	14 July	43	P	4 Oct.	43
†John Ekins[94]	P	4 Oct.	43	P	29 Nov.	45
James Ash Lee	T	17 Feb.	45	PT	20 Oct.	46
Nehemiah Donellan	P	29 Nov.	45	P	17 Feb.	46
Richard Knight	P	10 Mar.	46	P	20 June	47
John Locket	E	20 Oct.	46	D	10 Mar.	46
Thomas Thompson[156]	P	25 June	47	HP	20 Nov.	50
Francis Wilkinson[97] (E)	P	20 Nov.	50	P	27 Aug.	53
John Corrance (F)	P	27 Aug.	53	P	26 Feb.	55
Thomas Spencer Wilson	P	26 Feb.	55	P	16 Oct.	55
Joseph Fish	P	16 Oct.	55	P	28 Aug.	56
Henry Lee	P	25 Aug.	56	P	28 Feb.	61
Robert Spence	P	20 May	61			
Richard Berr Lernoult	P	31 Jan.	66	P	15 July	67
Arent Schuyler De Peister[34]	P	15 July	67	P	23 Nov.	68
Theophilus Dame	P	23 Nov.	68	P	27 Mar.	70
Henry Hatton	P	25 Dec.	70	P	12 Oct.	71
William Potts	P	12 Oct.	71	P	22 Nov.	75
Andrew Parke	P	22 Nov.	75	P	16 Mar.	76
John Mompesson[29]	P	16 Mar.	76	P	11 May	76
Henry Bird	P	11 May	78	P	12 Dec.	81
John Burnett	P	12 Dec.	81	P	31 July	92
Thomas Bland[67]	PT	31 July	92	P	30 April	93
George A. Armstrong	P	30 April	93	P	27 Nov.	94
Thomas Fortye[70]	P	27 Nov.	94	P	17 Dec.	94
Ralph Peter Dundas	T	17 Dec.	94	P	21 Dec.	96
George J. Reeves	P	21 Dec.	96	P	5 April	1801
James Powell	P	5 April	1801	P	13 May	C2
James Ogilvie[39]	T	13 May	02	P	,,	,,

LIEUTENANTS.

A	B	C	D	E
Barnes	S	1688	P	? 1688
Fielding	S	88	P	88
Southern	S	88	P	88
Mackarty	S	88	P	88
Fletcher	S	88	P	88
Walker (A*)				
William Kerr (A)		1 Mar. 88		
Bozier (A)				
Peter De Cosne (A, B)		30 April 94		
James Adams (A)		31 May 1701		
Rupton (A)				
John Balfoure (A)		1 Aug. 02		
Henry Clavers (A)		3 Oct. 1692		
†John Morton (A, B)		10 Dec. 1702		
Joachim Goudet (A)			P	16 May 1707
Henry Whitney (*Adjutant*) (A)				
Benjamin Cuttle (A)		13 April 92	P	25 Mar. 05
Charles Townley (A)		1 Sept. 88		
Peter Ribton (B)		25 Aug. 04		
Charles Mason (*Adjutant*) (B)		25 Mar. 05		
‡John Bazire[157] (B)		25 Aug. 04		
Theophilus Nichols (B)	P	25 Mar. 05		
Bernard Smith (B)		23 June 06		
James Eaton (B)		10 June 07		
Paul Lewis (B)		4 May 07		
Thomas Redwood (B)		1 Sept. 07		
Richard Kenny (B)		16 May 07		
†John Smith (B)		25 Mar. 05		
Edward Hobart (B)	P	24 Mar. 04		
Edmund De Fisher (B)	P	15 June 08	P	09
David Mackasky (B)	P	24 Sept. 08	T	
John Turner (B)	P	23 Mar. 08		
James Barry[61]	a	20 Sept. 09	P	10 Mar. 15
George Banastre	a	23 Dec. 09	P	5 Jan. 15
John Grey[62]	a	22 Dec. 12	P	1 Jan. 26
Thomas Launder	a	25 Feb. 16	P	11 Sept. 36
Peter Ribton (D)		17 May 21	P	12 Jan. 40
Malcolm Hamilton (D)		12 Sept. 21	P	13 May 42
John Dallons[91]	a	24 Jan. 23	P	31 Aug. 33
John White (C, D)		23 Oct. 24	D	3 Dec. 42
John Lafausille[26] (C, D)		12 Nov. 26	P	15 June 43
Thomas Nugent (D)	P	Oct. 25	R	13 May 42
Charles Duterme (D)		23 Dec. 26	PT	23 Jan. 40
William Boid (D)	T	Dec. 26		20 June 39

† Grenadiers.
‡ Bazire, spelt Bezier in list of Ensigns.
a It is uncertain if these Officers served as Lieutenants in the King's.

A	B	C		D	E	
LIEUTENANTS—*continued*.						
Theophilus Cramer (D)⁶	T	10 Dec.	1731		11 July	1741
Arthur Loftus⁶³ (C, D)		23 Aug.	35	P	14 July	43
John Ekins⁹⁴ (C, D)	P	11 Sept.	36	P	4 Oct.	43
William Robinson¹⁵⁸ (C)	P	20 June	39	PT	24 Sept.	43
Nehemiah Donellan (C)	P	12 Jan.	40	P	29 Nov.	45
Charles Desclouseaux (C)	P	23 Jan.	40	P	17 Feb.	46
William Catherwood⁹³ (C)	P	11 July	41	P	,,	,,
Richard Knight (C)	P	13 May	42	P	10 Mar.	47
Henry Rogers (C)	P	,,	,,	P	17 Feb.	46
Thomas Thompson¹⁵⁶	P	15 June	42	P	25 June	47
Frank Wilkinson⁹⁷ (C)	HP	25 June	44	P	20 Nov.	50
Joseph Artiers (C)	HP	,,	,,	R	19 Feb.	47
John Cooke⁶⁴	P	4 Dec.	42	P	17 Feb.	46
William Rickson¹⁵⁹	P	14 July	43	PT	6 Mar.	47
Jacob Conway⁹⁶	P	24 Sept.	43	P	16 Aug.	50
James Walter	P	4 Oct.	43	PT	15 Oct.	44
Thomas Paske	P	15 Oct.	44	R	10 Oct.	48
Charles Hemington (E)	T 29	29 Nov.	45	P 23	22 April	52
John Corrance (E)	P	17 Feb.	46	P	27 Aug.	53
John Callaud (E)	P	17 Feb.	46	R	31 Oct.	51
John Beckwith	P	,,	,,	PT	11 June	48
John Trollop⁹⁵	P	,,	,,	P	5 Mar.	47
William Wright (E, F)	P	10 Mar.	46	R	26 Feb.	55
Thomas Troughear (E)	P	25 June	47	P 31	31 Oct.	51
Thomas Spencer Wilson (E, F)	P	19 Feb.	48	P	26 Feb.	55
James Webb⁹⁸ (E, F)	P	5 Mar.	48	P	2 Nov.	55
Joseph Fish (F)	HP	9 Feb.	48	P 3	16 Oct.	55
Colthorpe Harrington	P	6 Mar.	48	HP	9 Feb.	49
Edward Fish (E)	T	11 June	48	Red.		
H. Rogers	P	10 Oct.	48	Red.		
William Plaistow (E, F)	HP	16 Aug.	50	P 58		
John Ellis (E, F)	P	20 Nov.	50	P	31 Aug.	56
Charles Soley	HP	30 Oct.	51	E 49	17 Mar.	52
Charles Hamilton⁹⁹ (F)	P	31 Oct.	51	P	1 Sept.	56
John Carter (F)	E 49	17 Mar.	52	P 57		
Henry Lee (*Adjutant*) (F)	P	23 April	52		25 Aug.	56
Thomas Backhouse (F)	P	27 Aug.	53			
Robert Jenkinson		15 Oct.	54			
George Coghlan	P	26 Feb.	55	P 63	26 May	58
Thomas Stuart	P	31 May	55			
Richard Berrenger Lernoult	P	29 Aug.	56	P	31 Jan.	66
Robert Spence		1 Oct.	55	P	20 May	61
Grant Scott		2 Oct.	55			60
Harcourt Masters	P	3 Oct.	55	T 63	3 Oct.	55†
Christopher Brown		4 Oct.	55			
Ebenezer Warren (2 B.)	T 2	25 Aug.	56			65
Solgard Marshall (2 B.)	T 2	26 Aug.	56			
John Young (2 B.)	T 26	27 Aug.	56			

† Date of Commission in 63rd Regiment.

LIEUTENANTS—continued.

A	B	C		D	E	
John Anstruther (2 B.)	T 26	28 Aug.	1756	T 63	28 Aug.	1756*
John Phillip Adams	P	30 Aug.	56	T 63	30 Aug.	56*
George Borradale (2 B.)	P	31 Aug.	56	PT	5 April	57
Richard Dudgeon (2 B.)	T Eng.	1 Sept.	56			
William Heatly (*Adjt.*) (2 B.)		2 Sept.	56	T 63	2 Sept.	56*
Thomas Jesse (*Serjeant*) (2 B.)	T 1FG	3 Sept.	56	T 63	3 Sept.	55*
James Ward (*Serjeant*) (2 B.)	P	4 Sept.	56	T 63	4 Sept.	56*
John Ralph (*Serjeant*) (2 B.)	P	5 Sept.	56	T 63	5 Sept.	56*
George Highton (*Serjt.*) (2 B.)	P	6 Sept.	56	T 63	6 Sept.	56*
Mark Richards (*Serjeant*) (2 B.)	T 15	7 Sept.	56	T 63	7 Sept.	56*
Henry de la Doucspe (2 B.)	A	5 April	57			
Arent Schuyler de Peister[34]	T	21 Sept.	57	P	15 July	67
Theophilus Dame		22 Sept.	57	P	23 Nov.	68
Augustus Alt		25 Sept.	57			68
George Foster[100] (*Adjutant*)		26 Sept.	57	P	25 Dec.	70
Mungo Law		28 Sept.	57			60
Dick Culliford		29 Sept.	57			59
William Morrison[160]		30 Sept.	57			58
Michael Downes	P	30 Sept.	57	T 63	1 Oct.	57
William Dexter	P	2 Oct.	57	T 63	2 Oct.	57*
Mitchelbourne Knox	P	3 Oct.	57		Dec.	63
Gerard Alt	P	4 Oct.	57	T 63	4 Oct.	57*
William Reade	P	5 Oct.	57	T 63	4 Oct.	57*
James Hart	P	6 Oct.	57	T 63	6 Oct.	57*
James Wyatt	P	7 Oct.	57	T 63	7 Oct.	57*
Richard Nesbit	P	8 Oct.	57	T 63	8 Oct.	57*
Roger Parke	P	14 Oct.	59		13 April	67
Henry Savage	P	15 Oct.	59			61
Benjamin Ashe	P	27 Jan.	60			61
Charles Parke		28 Jan.	60			61
Roger Twigge		18 Mar.	60	HP		63
Richard Taylor		18 Nov.	60			61
William Marler		20 Dec.	60			61
Richard Steele		28 Feb.	61			62
James Tippet		20 May	61			61
Thomas Pennefather	P	19 Nov.	61			
James Mayne	P	6 Oct.	62			
Henry Hatton		12 Dec.	63	P	25 Dec.	70
William Potts		15 Nov.	65	P	12 Oct.	71
Timothy Edwards		31 Jan.	66		13 April	67
Andrew Parke		13 April	67	P	22 Nov.	75
John Lee	P	15 July	67		24 Dec.	70
John Mompesson	P	9 Dec.	67	P	16 Mar.	76
Henry Bird	T	22 Feb.	68	P	11 May	78
John Burnett	T	21 April	68	P	12 Dec.	81
Samuel Willoe	P	23 Nov.	68	P	6 May	77
Robert Mathews (*Adjutant*)	P	27 Mar.	70	P	7 May	77

* Dates of Commissions in 63rd Regiment.

A	B	C		D	E	
LIEUTENANTS—*continued.*						
Thomas Bennet (*Adjutant*)	P	1 Aug.	1770	P	13 Sept.	1783
Robert Clement	T	24 Dec.	70	P	39 Mar.	76
Peter Le Conte	T	25 Dec.	70		May	77
George Dame	P	26 Dec.	70		18 Nov.	74
William Highmore	P	12 Oct.	71		3 Nov.	79
Henry Yonge	P	18 Nov.	74		25 Dec.	77
Thomas Coote	T	15 Aug.	75		1 Nov.	80
John Delgarno	P	22 Nov.	75	P	26 Oct.	85
R. Leighton Kinnersley	P	23 Nov.	75		5 Jan.	80
George Clowes	P	16 Mar.	76		27 Jan.	86
Daniel Mercer	P	29 Mar.	76	P	18 Oct.	86
Daniel Showrd	P	6 May	77		6 Jan.	80
R. Bounds Brooke	P	8 May	77			90
John Caldwell	P	25 Dec.	77		29 Mar.	86
Thomas Peppyatt	P	11 May	78	P	8 Aug.	88
George Armstrong (*Adjutant*)	P	1 Mar.	79	P	17 Feb.	90
John Brock	P	3 Nov.	79			84
Durell Saumarez[66]	P	5 Jan.	80	P	31 Mar.	90
Joseph Wilmot	P	6 Jan.	80			92
Henry Stanley Monck	T	1 Nov.	80			84
Robert McDougal	P	12 Dec.	81			84
Robert Pollard (*Adjutant*)	P	13 Sept.	83	P	8 Aug.	93
Andrew Armstrong	P	2 Mar.	85		13 Dec.	86
T. St. George Armstrong	P	26 Oct.	85	P	31 Mar.	93
William Pawlett	P	27 Jan.	86			90
William Armstrong	T	29 Mar.	86			91
Daniel Bliss	P	18 Oct.	86			94
Alexander Duke[68]	T	13 Dec.	86	P	31 Mar.	93
George Strickland	P	5 Mar.	89			91
Robert Molesworth	P	31 Mar.	90			94
Bigoe Armstrong Stoney	P	2 Feb.	91			92
George Andrew Armstrong	P	2 Feb.	91	P	30 April	93
Robert Young[38]	T	4 May	91	P	29 June	93
Edward Whitehead	T	3 June	91			93
Bryce Maxwell[69] (*Adjutant*)	P	23 Nov.	91	P	26 Oct.	93
Thomas Fortye[70]	T	18 Jan.	92	P	27 Nov.	94
Philip Armstrong	P	29 Sept.	92			95
P. G. Rooke Mathews	T	31 Dec.	92			94
Bryce MacMurdo[101]	P	31 Mar.	93	P	3 April	94
James Booth[102]	P	30 April	93	K	June	94
George J. Reeves (*Adjutant*)	P	29 June	93	P	21 Dec.	97
John Armstrong	P	8 Aug.	93	P	1 July	95
John Russell	T	31 Aug.	93			94
Marcus McCausland	PT	31 Oct.	93	P	18 Nov.	95
Richard Oliver	PT	31 Dec.	93	P	19 Aug.	95
James Powell	P	28 Feb.	94	P	5 April	1801
G. Rodolphus Perdieu	PT	3 April	94			1795
Jacob Sankey	PT	3 April	94	D	13 July	96
Hon. George Annesley	PT	30 April	94			95
Arthur Beamish	PT	9 May	94			95
Joseph Davey	P	22 Oct.	94			96

LIEUTENANTS—continued.

A	B	C	D	E
Patrick Gibson ..	T	26 Nov. 1794		1798
Robert Eason[161] ..	P	27 Nov. 94		1803
H. Brough Oliver	T	10 June 95		1797
Sept. Walpole Loane	P	22 July 95	P	25 June 1803
R. Villeneuve[162] ..	P	25 Aug. 95	W	24 April 1797
John Blackmore[74]	P	1 Sept. 95	P	23 Oct. 1804
William Bluitt Sheehy ..	T	2 Sept. 95	D	10 Oct. 1796
J. R. Mont Caulfield	P	3 Sept. 95	D	,, ,,
William Gibson ..	T	4 Sept. 95		1804
John Morse	T	5 Sept. 95		04
Henry Eason	T	6 Sept. 95		1797
Trevor Stannus ..	T	7 Sept. 95		1803
James Spence ..	T	8 Sept. 95		00
Donough O'Brien[163]	T	28 Oct. 95	W	Mar. 01
Vincent Beamish	T	2 Dec. 95	D	12 Oct. 1796
James Thompson	T	23 Dec. 95		96
John J. Leith ..	T	30 Dec. 95	R	16 Nov. 96
Percy Gethin ..	P	17 Dec. 94	D*	16 June 1800
Edmund Cullen ..	P	12 Mar. 96		1796
John Church[164] ..	P	14 July 96		1802
Francis Battersby	T	10 Aug. 96	P	10 April 01
Thomas Evans[72] ..	T 93	11 Oct. 96	P	19 Nov. 03
P. Burke ..	T 93	12 Oct. 96		1797
Jenkin Francis ..	T 93	13 Oct. 96		1803
Samuel Speare ..	P	17 Nov. 96		1799
John Fitzmaurice	P	21 Dec. 96		97
Joseph Bullen ..	P	4 Jan. 97		99
Edward Cotton[71]	PT	23 Mar. 97	P	18 Nov. 1802
James M. Guffey	P	25 April 97		00
Robert M. Dowall	PT	1 Nov. 97	P	24 Oct. 04
George R. Cooke	P	8 Mar. 98		02
William Scholey	P	20 Dec. 98	D†	26 Oct. 02
Aug. (Viscount) de Mainbourg	T	14 Feb. 99		00
Zenecho Preston	T	17 Oct. 99		03
Henry Francis Goldicutt	P	2 Oct. 1800	P	14 Nov. 04
Thomas Buck ..	P	18 Sept. 00	P	16 June 03
Lord Robert Kerr	T	26 Oct. 00		03
William Henry Forsteen	T	01		01
John Ringrose Annesley	P	5 April 01		02
John Bannatyne	P	6 April 01		02
Thomas Couche ..	P	29 Nov. 01	P	17 Oct. 05
Francis Campbell	T	30 01	P	21 Nov. 05
John Graham Douglas ..	T	5 Aug. 02		03
Henry Sadlier[107] ..	P	7 Jan. 03	P	4 June 07
Richard James	T	26 May 03		04
James S. Tyeth[104]	P	25 June 03	P	21 Mar. 05
Peter Moyles (*Adjutant*)	P	19 Nov. 03	P	3 Feb. 09

* P. Gethin, shot through the heart in a duel by his brother officer, Augustus, Viscount de Mainbourg.
† W. Scholey, died at Gibraltar.

A	B	C		D	E	
LIEUTENANTS—*continued*.						
Peter Dickenson..	T	8 Dec.	1803	P	27 Mar.	1806
James Hardy Eustace[110]	T	24 April	04	P	2 Sept.	12
James Gauntlett	T	,,	,,			07
John Fitzgerald[106]	T	,,	,,	P	6 June	11
Edward Connor..	T	,,	,,	P	20 July	09
William Walsh ..	T	,,	,,	P	16 May	11
Samuel Hooker[111a]	P	11 Oct.	04	P 80		13
John Bradbridge[109]	P	12 Oct.	04	P	12 Sept.	11
Thomas Edmund Dowlin	P	24 Oct.	04		1 Dec.	04
John Goldrisk ..	T	24 April	04	P	3 Sept.	12
Andrew Liddell	P	1 Dec.	04	PT	3 Sept.	12
Henry Brewster (*Adjutant*)	T	5 Jan.	05	P	4 Aug.	13
George Browne ..	P	21 Mar.	05			06
Francis Birmingham	P	28 Mar.	05			10
Hugh Lloyd Franklin ..	T	8 May	05			10
William Scotton	P	9 May	05			08
Thomas Cross ..	P	22 Aug.	05	P	5 Aug.	13
Thomas Miller (*Adjutant*)	P	12 Sept.	05	P	12 Aug.	13
John Stanford ..	P	3 Oct.	05			07
Edward Browne..	P	14 Nov.	05	P	24 Feb.	14
Carleton Burne ..	P	5 Dec.	05	D		13
Adam Baillie	P	2 Jan.	06			09
Austin Neame ..	P	15 May	06	P	10 Aug.	14
John McMahon[113]	P	16 Oct.	06	P	29 Sept.	14
John Raymond ..	P	30 Oct.	06			09
Thomas Waring Lloyd[165]	P	6 Nov.	06	D		14
Edward Goate ..	P	8 Jan.	07			11
Henry Cooper (*Adjutant*)	P	18 June	07			14
Morton Noel[166] ..	P	22 Oct.	07	K	15 Aug.	14
George Nutall[167]	P	25 Oct.	07	W	May–June	13
Samuel Barber ..	T	14 Jan.	08			12
Charles Barstow[168]	P	15 Jan.	08	K	17 Sept.	14
Charles Ince ..	P	17 Jan.	08			10
Daniel McPherson	P	18 Jan.	08			12
William Compton	P	19 Jan.	08	R	14 Mar.	11
John Ivers	P	20 Jan.	08	D		14
William Collis ..	P	21 Jan.	08	HP	3 May	16
Andrew Gray ..	T	25 Feb.	08			11
David Home	P	25 Mar.	08	R		10
James Drummie[169]	P	5 Jan.	09	K	27 May	13
John Thorne Wayland[170]†	T	1 Mar.	09	HP	3 May	16
Herbert Raban ..	P	2 Mar.	09	P	27 July	15
Thomas Ivers ..	P	30 Mar.	09			20
Edward Finch[171]	P	20 July	09			15
James Kenny ..	P	31 Aug.	09	R		12
Roger M. Swiney	T	19 Oct.	09			19

† In Army List of 1809, and several subsequent years, *John Thorne* Wayland designated *Richard* Wayland.

LIEUTENANTS—continued.

A	B	C		D	E	
Alexander Cumming	T	8 Feb.	1810	D		1812
Caleb Eyre Powell	P	22 Feb.	10	R		13
Marshal McDermott	P	19 July	10	*	29 April	19
Charles Harris	T	16 Aug.	10			11
Malcolm Ross	P	14 Mar.	11	P	7 April	25
Jacob Ruddick	P	16 May	11	D		16
Michael Flanagan	P	6 June	11			15
Arthur Gardiner	P	11 July	11	E	14 Nov.	11
Edward Boyd[172]	P	15 Aug.	11			20
Henry Palmer Hill[173]	P	12 Sept.	11	*	10 July	32
Bernard Clarke	E	14 Nov.	11	R		14
Thomas Price (*Adjutant*)	P	30 April	12			20
Wainford Ridge	P	1 Sept.	12			14
Robert Spiers	P	2 Sept.	12	D		17
Robert Dunbar Taylor	P	3 Sept.	12			22
William Bradford	P	22 Oct.	12			17
Alexander Bourke	P	5 Nov.	12	PT	20 Feb.	35
John Lowry[174]	P	24 Dec.	12	HP	13 July	20
Richard Nicholson[175]	P	8 July	13	D.		14
Fred. William Vieth	P	3 Aug.	13			26
William Kidman	P	4 Aug.	13			17
J. G. Powell[176]	P	5 Aug.	13	R		16
Brooke Young[177]	P	6 Aug.	13			17
Alexander Greig[178]	P	7 Aug.	13	HP	25 Mar.	17
Thomas Russell	P	12 Aug.	13			17
James O. Flanagan	P	24 Feb.	14	C		15
William H. Clarence Scarman	P	22 Mar.	14			15
James Grey	P	23 Mar.	14			17
Robert Macnair[179] (2 B.)	P	24 Mar.	14			17
John Radenhurst (2 B.)	T	7 July	14			17
George R. Campsie (2 B.)	P	14 July	14	HP	25 Feb.	16
Thomas Swayne[180] (2 B.)	P	9 Aug.	14	HP	,,	,,
Samuel Garner	P	10 Aug.	14	HP	,,	16
Edward Murray† (2 B.)	P	11 Aug.	14	HP	25 Feb.	16
Charles Millar	P	29 Sept.	14	HP	,,	,,
Thomas Moyle	P	24 Nov.	14	HP	,,	,,
George Jarvis (2 B.)	P	23 Mar.	15	HP	,,	,,
Charles W. Davis (2 B.)	T	24 Feb.	14	HP	,,	,,
George Richardson (2 B.)	P	12 July	15	HP	,,	,,
Charles Howard Short (2 B.)	T	17 Aug.	15	HP	,,	,,
Henry Proctor (2 B.)	T	14 Sept.	15	HP	,,	,,
John Street (*Adjutant*)	P	26 July	15			17
Edward Murray†	T	11 Aug.	14			25
Nathan Ashurst	T	28 April	14			17
James Briscoe	T	6 Oct.	14			18
David Vans Machen[113]	T	5 Mar.	18	P	15 Mar.	21
Francis Miles	T	8 April	19			22
Simcoe Baynes[75]	T	9 Sept.	19	P	24 June	24
George Lord Bingham[181]	T	20 Jan.	20	HP	16 May	22

* H. P. Hill, appointed Paymaster. † E. Murray, the same, placed on half-pay and reappointed.

A	B	C		D	E	
LIEUTENANTS—*continued*.						
Thomas Drury (*Adjutant*)	T	20 April	1820	E	5 May	1825
Richard Spratt	T	27 April	20			24
George Forman	T	13 July	20			27
T. Rutherford Thompson	T	15 Mar.	21	P	8 Mar.	33
James Hannay	T	1 Aug.	22	P	30 Sept.	24
Archibald Machlachlan	T	5 Feb.	24	*	19 May	25
William Calder (*Adjutant*)	P	24 June	24	P	6 July	35
Charles Cotter	P	30 Sept.	24			28
William Eleazer Pickwick	P	7 April	25	P	11 July	26
Edmund Gennys	T	8 April	25			32
David Gardiner[114]	T	5 May	25	P	22 Nov.	37
William Stewart	T	9 June	25			26
Hon. Richard Hare	P	23 June	25			26
James Byron	P	17 Dec.	25	P	10 May	33
Hon. Stanhope Hawke	T	29 Dec.	25			26
William Senhouse	T	17 June	26	PT	8 Feb.	33
George Burrard	P	11 July	26	HP		29
‡ John Longfield[44]	P	26 Sept.	26	P	30 Jan.	35
John Howard	P	30 Nov.	26	R		29
Edward Hudson Clarke	T	30 April	27	R	7 Feb.	34
J. Charles Villiers Molesworth	T	14 Aug.	28			32
William Russel Lucas (*Adjt.*)	T	5 Feb.	29	†	10 Mar.	37
William Chearnley	P	15 Oct.	29	P	7 Aug.	35
Irwine S. Whitty (*Adjutant*)	P	25 June	30	P	2 Oct.	35
Ralph Cheney	P	22 June	32			34
James Pringle	T	31 Aug.	32	P	3 Feb.	37
Henry Welladvice Roper	P	21 Dec.	32	P	23 June	37
Walter Lay	P	8 Feb.	33	D	29 April	37
Walter Ogilvy	P	8 Mar.	33	P	10 Jan.	38
‡ Edward Harris Greathed[46]	P	10 May	33	P	27 April	38
John Terry Liston	P	7 Feb.	34	P	20 Nov.	38
Cyrus Plaistow Trapaud	T	19 Dec.	34	P	2 July	41
John Hilton	P	30 Jan.	35	E 4	27 Nov.	35
F. Saunderson Holmes (*Adjt.*)	P	28 Aug.	35	P	26 Oct.	41
Stephenson Browne	P	4 Sept.	35	P	6 May	42
Ant. Tisdall Sydney Plunkett	P	30 Oct.	35	R	7 June	39
Cosby William Wolseley	T	27 Nov.	35	R		37
John Eldridge West	P	3 Feb.	37	P	12 Dec.	43
Henry Capadose	T	17 Mar.	37	PT	30 April	47
Alfred Augustus Malet	P	30 April	37	P	24 June	42
‡ John Hinde[45]	P	30 June	37	P	4 July	45
Mark Pattison Seward	P	1 Sept.	37	D	30 May	42
Frederick Douglas Lumley		8 Jan.	38	P	25 Oct.	42
Coulthurst Holder	P	10 Jan.	38	P	27 Sept.	44
Hugh Hill	P	27 April	38	R	13 May	42
Ernest Lavie	P	20 Nov.	38	P	19 Nov.	44
John Long Marsden	P	7 June	39	P	14 Nov.	45
Thomas Clowes	P	2 July	41	P	16 Dec.	45

* A. Machlachlan, superseded.   † W. R. Lucas, Paymaster.

A	B	C		D	E	

LIEUTENANTS—*continued*.

A	B	C		D	E	
Charles Frederick Boughton Greville Dickenson	P	26 Oct.	1841	P	20 Mar.	1846
Arthur Leslie	P	8 May	42	P	3 April	46
₰ James Johnston[49]	P	13 May	42	P	21 April	46
William Bayly (*Adjutant*)[79]	P	23 June	42	P	29 May	48
George Augustus Young	P	24 June	42	E	30 Jan.	46
William Turnour Granville	P	25 Oct.	42	PT	28 April	46
George Ed. Baynes[82]	P	12 Dec.	43	P	17 Oct.	48
Richard Wilson Hartley	P	27 Sept.	44	P	9 Feb.	49
John Henry Ed. De Robeck	P	19 Nov.	44	P	9 Nov.	49
Alfred Ingilby Garnett	P	4 July	45	P	21 Feb.	51
John Stone	P	14 Nov.	45	R	5 Mar.	47
Ellis James Charter	P	16 Dec.	45	P	15 Mar.	53
Robert Stuart Baynes[116] (*Adjt.*)	P	27 Mar.	46	P	,,	,,
John Ball Campbell[119]	T	3 April	46	P	27 Jan.	55
Richard William Woods[118]	T	,,	,,	P	12 April	56
Thomas Geo. Souter[122]	T	,,	,,	P	21 Oct.	57
Thomas Dowse	T	,,	,,	D	12 Sept.	49
Chas. Power Cobbe (*Adjutant*)	PT	,,	,,	P 13	7 Sept.	55
Daniel Beere[123]	T 20	,,	,,	P	21 Oct.	57
Thomas Aldridge	P	3 April	46	P 60	23 Oct.	57
Erskine Nimmo Sandilands[124]	PT 42	,,	,,	P	21 Oct.	57
George Corry[128]	P	,,	,,	P	15 Nov.	57
Shaftoe Craster Craster	P	,,	,,	P	20 July	55
Ed. Rawlings Hannam	P	,,	,,	*	27 June	54
Robert Becher Stowards	T	21 April	46	R	20 July	56
William Henry Herrick	T	28 April	46	E	21 Dec.	55
Benj. Kennicott M'Dermott[132]	T 3	13 Nov.	46	R	15 May	57
McKay Rynd	P	5 Mar.	47	E 62	20 Dec.	50
Charles Covell Neame	T	30 April	47	HP	27 May	56
Horace Ximenes[133]	P	29 May	48	P 16	23 Mar.	58
John Biggs	P	17 Oct.	48	T†	31 Oct.	51
Wm. Waldegrave Pogson[134]	P	9 Feb.	49	W	17 Sept.	57
George Fuller Walker[135] (*Adjt.*)	P	13 Sept.	49	P 22	23 Mar.	58
Allan John Robertson	P	9 Nov.	49	R	15 Oct.	52
Timothy Walsh[136]	E 62	20 Dec.	50	E 29	11 Oct.	53
₰ John Vere Willm. Henry Webb[53]	P	21 Feb.	51	P	11 May	58
Edmund Bagenall	T	31 Oct.	51	D‡	24 May	53
Thomas Beattie Grierson[137]	P	15 Oct.	52	D	4 Sept.	57
Alex. Ross Bayly[129]	P	6 May	53	P	11 May	58
Wm. Raymond Ximenes[130]	P	25 May	53	P	,,	,,

* E. R. Hannam, appointed Paymaster, 60th Foot.
† J. Biggs, appointed Paymaster, 4th Dragoon Guards.
‡ E. Bagenall, killed by a tiger.

A	B	C		D	E	
LIEUTENANTS—*continued*.						
Charles Sutherland Dowson[188]	E 29	11 Oct.	1853	P 7	23 Oct.	1857
Graham E. Huddleston[189]	P	27 June	54	*	23 Mar.	55
Herbert Vervon Lillicrap	P	27 Jan.	55	R	22 Aug.	56
Fred. Bradford McCrea[65]	P	20 July	55	P	26 June	58
William Fred. Metge[132]	P	7 Sept.	55	P	22 April	59
Thomas Mackesy Vincent[190]	E 59	21 Dec.	55	K	6 Dec.	57
Fred. Anderson Stebbing[135]	P	12 April	56	P	17 May	61
William Robert Webb[191]	P	15 April	56	W	16 Sept.	57
Robert Lewis G. M'Grigor[131]	T	27 May	56	P	4 Feb.	59
⁂ Forster Longfield[58]	P	1 Aug.	56	P	24 Sept.	58
Alfred Downie Corfield (2 B.)‡	P	15 May	57	P	16 July	61
Æneas Gordon Blair[136] (2 B.)‡	P	5 Sept.	57	P	1 July	62
Andrew Moynihan[138] (2 B.)‡	P	16 Sept.	57	P	9 Oct.	63
Wm. Ed. Whelan[141] (*Adjutant*)	P	18 Sept.	57	P	30 Dec.	65
Hobart Evans Fitzgerald[192] (2 B.)‡	P 18	23 Oct.	57	R	13 Dec.	59
James Q. Palmer (2 B.)‡	PT 41	,,	,,	P	10 Nov.	65
Chas. Bradford Brown[142] (*Adjt.*) (2 B.)‡	T 63	,,	,,	P	15 June	66
F. Geo. Furlong Moore (2 B.)‡	PT 39	,,	,,	R	6 Sept.	61
James F. MacPherson (2 B.)‡	T 62	,,	,,	R	23 Mar.	61
James O'Hara (2 B.)‡	T 62	,,	,,	R	4 June	61
Charles Norris Fry[193]‡	T 18	,,	,,	R	4 June	61
William Edgeworth[194]	P	,,	,,	E 5 LD		58
Richard Thomas B. Browne	P	15 Nov.	57	P	20 May	67
⁂ Edward Tanner[56] (2 B.)	P	7 Dec.	57	P	4 Sept.	60
Ed. Thomas Pinniger	P	11 Dec.	57	R	26 May	59
Robert Yallop Stokes	P	23 Mar.	58	R		60
Reginald Whitting[86]	P	23 Mar.	58	P	15 Jan.	61
Walter John Tarte	T 31	13 July	58	P	27 Sept.	61
Henry Leeson (2 B.)§	T	23 July	58	R	16 Oct.	60
J. E. W. Black	P	30 July	58	D		58
Ashley George Westby	P	30 July	58	P	13 Feb.	63
James Seager Wheeley (2 B.)	P	20 Sept.	58	P	30 June	63
John William Hughes	T	1 Oct.	58	P	29 Mar.	64
James Magenis Lovekin	T	,,	,,	E 20		60
William Theobald Butler (2 B.)§	PT 72	,,	,,	P	26 April	64
John Evans F. Aylmer (2 B.)§	PT 33	,,	,,	HP	1 April	70
Chas. Dyneley Baynes	T	,,	,,	E 91	30 Nov.	60
Robert D. Forbes Shirreff (2 B.)§	T	,,	,,	P	18 Oct.	64

* G. E. Huddleston, appointed Paymaster in the King's Regiment.

‡ Appointed on formation of 2nd Battalion.

§ Appointed on augmentation of 2nd Battalion.

A	B	C		D	E	
LIEUTENANTS—*continued.*						
John Coleberd Cooper (2 B.)	P	26 Nov.	1858	P	29 Nov.	1864
George Nicholl Jas. Bradford (2 B.)	P	4 Feb.	59	P	20 Dec.	64
Philip Homer Page	P	22 April	59	P	11 July	65
Charles Dudley R. Madden (2 B.)	P	26 Aug.	59	P	29 Dec.	65
William Bannatyne[87] (2 B.)	P	13 Dec.	59	P	26 Jan.	66
William Unwin[195]	T	4 May	60	R	28 April	63
William J. Watson	P	4 Sept.	60	P	20 Feb.	66
W. W. Madden (2 B.)	P	16 Oct.	60	R	25 July	65
Jeremy Peyton Jones (*Adjt.*) (2 B.)	P	6 Nov.	60	P	13 June	68
Wm. Hunter Baillie (*Adjutant*)	E 91	30 Nov.	60	P	16 Oct.	66
Richard Chute	P	15 Jan.	61	R	9 Jan.	63
Theodore Henry Skinner (2 B.)	P	23 April	61	R	19 Jan.	64
Ed. Emerson	P	17 May	61	P	13 April	72
Arthur Cook	P	4 June	61	E 28	27 May	62
Wm. Albert Bridge (2 B.)	P	4 June	61	P	12 Feb.	67
Thomas Palmer Senior	P	16 July	61	*	15 May	67
John Randle Minshull Ford (2 B.)	P	6 Sept.	61	P	27 Nov.	66
Ed. Williams (2 B.)	P	27 Sept.	61	P	6 Mar.	67
Arthur Holden Turner[196]	E 28	27 May	62	R	6 Feb.	66
Thomas Picton Fleetwood	P	1 July	62	H P	21 June	70
Thomas Gorges Crawley (2 B.)	P	9 Jan.	63	P	14 Aug.	67
John Dawson[143]	P	13 Feb.	63	P	1 Aug.	68
Martin George Cole (2 B.)	P	28 April	63	P	24 Mar.	69
William Willoughby Egerton	P	30 June	63	P	10 Nov.	69
Bowland Garrard Moffat (2 B.)	P	9 Oct.	63	P	23 April	72
Charles Fredk. Malet	P	19 Jan.	64	P	17 July	72
Marmaduke Stourton (2 B.)	P	29 Mar.	64	P	23 Mar.	70
Matthew Liddon (2 B.)	P	26 April	64	P	5 Nov.	70
E. E. Granville Clayton	P	18 Oct.	64	R	26 Feb.	70
Bennett Fleming Handy[88] (2 B.)	P	29 Nov.	64	P	4 June	73
William Howe Hennis (2 B.)	P	20 Dec.	64	P	20 Sept.	71
John Mount Batten (*Adjutant*)	P	11 July	65	P	31 Oct.	71
Francis James Stuart	P	25 July	65	P	14 June	73
Nash Short[89] (2 B.)	P	10 Nov.	65	P	3 Mar.	74
Arthur Fawkes	P	29 Dec.	65	P	29 July	74
John James Hamilton (*Adjt.*)	P	30 Dec.	65	P	8 Nov.	74
William Stancomb Sinkins	P	26 Jan.	66	P	23 Jan.	75
Wm. Toke Dooner[146] (2 B.)	P	6 Feb.	66	P	24 Mar.	75
Thomas Blake Humfrey[147]	P	20 Feb.	66	P	1 April	75
Chas. J. H. Playter	P	15 June	66	R	13 Feb.	67
Alfred Mellor	P	16 Oct.	66	R	28 Oct.	68
Francis Moore (2 B.)	P	27 Nov.	66	P	12 May	75
M. C. M. Dixon (*Adjt.*) (2 B.)	P	13 Feb.	67	P	23 June	75
William Louis (*Adjutant*)	P	"	"	P	21 July	77
Robert Garnett	P	6 Mar.	67	R	16 Sept.	68

* T. P. Senior, appointed Paymaster.

A	B	C		D	E	
LIEUTENANTS—*continued.*						
George Westrenen Sawyer (2 B.)	P	20 May	1867	BoSC	17 Nov.	1869
F. B. J. Jerrard[197] (2 B.)	P	14 Aug.	67	P 91	24 June	75
George Rowan Hamilton (2 B.)	P	1 Aug.	68	H P	19 Aug.	71
Henry Webster	P	16 Sept.	68	R	25 Mar.	71
R. Julian Orde Jocelyn (2 B.) (*Adjt.*)	P	28 Oct.	68	P	23 Nov.	77
L. L. A. Wise	P	24 Mar.	69	R	22 April	71
Arthur Henry Cope[151]	P	10 Nov.	69	P	24 Sept.	78
Walter Bell Marley	P	8 Dec.	69	R	30 Nov.	70
Stephen Brown	P	26 Feb.	70	P	6 Nov.	79
Arthur Ashley Ruck[152] (2 B.)	P	23 Mar.	70	P	30 Jan.	80
John Parry Hamer	P	5 Nov.	70	R		74
James Matthew Taylor[154] (2 B.)	P	30 Nov.	70	P	9 Feb.	81
George Villiers Turner[196]	P	25 Mar.	71	P h.p.	31 Jan.	80
Herbert Henry Russell	P	22 April	71	R	27 Sept.	79
Rowland Oakeley	P	20 Sept.	71	R	25 Aug.	80
William Freeman Kelly	P	1 Nov.	71	P h.p.	31 Jan.	80
William Richard Orme[153] (2 B.)	P	"	"	P	17 April	80
Charles William Atkinson	P	"	"	E 26	30 June	74
Henry Thomas Granger (2 B.)	P	"	"	P	8 May	80
Joseph Wright Ward (2 B.)	P	"	"	R		79
H. S. A. Fuller	P	"	"	T	3 July	74
E. W. B. Hope	P	"	"	R		74
L. C. F. Thompson	P	"	"	P	7 July	80
H. N. McRae	P	"	"	BSC	28 Oct.	71
H. Meredith Wade	P	"	"	P	21 Mar.	81
W. C. F. Field	P	8 May	72	BSC		75
Fred. James Whalley[155] (*Adjt.*) (2 B.)	P	8 June	72	P	18 May	81
George Alfred Money	P	11 Sept.	72	BSC	11 Sept.	72
Ed. H. H. Montresor	P	8 May	73	BSC	8 May	73
Henry Manley Briscoe	P	12 Nov.	73	P	18 May	81
G. Robert Stone (*Adjutant*)	P	28 Feb.	74	P	22 June	81
D'Arcy Thuillier	E 26	30 June	74	BSC	28 Oct.	71
Frederick Hawkins	P	21 Sept.	74	BSC	2 Jan.	78
W. Lloyd Brereton[199]	P	"	"	S*		
Standish H. Harrison	T	2 Dec.	74	S*		
Llewellyn S. Mellor[200] (2 B.)	P	15 Jan.	75	S*		
Orestes J. H. Brooker	P	11 Feb.	75	E 2WI	24 Jan.	80
C. Blenheim Porter	P	"	"	BSC	3 Jan.	78
Chas. C. Chevenix Trench	P	"	"	BSC	1 Mar.	78
H. J. R. St. G. Richardson	P	10 Sept.	75	S*		
Henry A. Fletcher[201] (2 B.)	P	12 Nov.	75	D	26 April	81

* These Officers were serving in this rank on 1st August, 1881.

A	B	C		D	E	
LIEUTENANTS—*continued*.						
Percy Schletter[202] (2 B.)	P	13 June	1876	S*		
A. Chas. Greaves Banning[203] (2 B.)	P	10 Sept.	76	S*		
Joseph Hume Balfour[204] (2 B.)	P	6 Oct.	76	BSC	26 July	1881
Harvey Wm. de Montmorency O'Donnel Colley Grattan[205] (2 B.)	T	29 Nov.	76	R	4 Sept.	80
Edward Levien Maisey[206] (2 B.)	P	10 Mar.	77	S*		
Charles Gray Robertson[207] (2 B.)	P	22 May	77	S*		
Arthur A. W. Bright-Smith	P	11 Sep.	76	S*		
	E 2WI	24 Jan.	80	S*		
Lawrence C. Dundas[208] (2 B.)	P	30 Jan.	80	S*		
Horatio James Evans[209] (2 B.)	P	25 Feb.	78	S*		
John Burnard Edwards[210] (2 B.)	P	11 Mar.	80	S*		
Edmund H. Molyneux Seel	P	17 April	80	S*		
Valentine A. M. Fowler[211] (2 B.)	P	7 July	80	S*		
Henry J. W. Guise	P	25 Aug.	80	S*		
Gilbert T. Elliot	P	4 Sept.	80	S*		
August St. John Seton (2 B.)	P	15 Oct.	80	S*		
George Campbell	P	9 July	80	S*		
Colin A. R. Blackwell[212]	P	21 Mar.	81			
Rowland F. L. Farrer	†			S*		
Stapleton L. Cotton[213] (2 B.)	†			S*		
Lawrence E. Elliot (2 B.)	†			S*		
Arthur W. H. Tripp (2 B.)	†			S*		
Basil John Bacon (2 B.)	†			S*		
Harcourt L. Dodgson (2 B.)	†			S*		
Simpson, M. R. L'Amy	†			S*		
William Adam Cuppage (2 B.)	†			S*		
Leslie W. Shakspear (2 B.)	†			S*		
Hyde Parker	†			S*		

* These Officers were serving in this rank on 1st August, 1881.
† These Officers were transferred from the list of Second Lieutenants on 1st July 1881.

ENSIGNS.

A	B	C	D	E
Francis Stedman (A*)	A	24 Sept. 1694		
Smith (A)	S	,, 1702		
Paul Lewis (A)	S	,, ,,		
Fletcher (A)	S	,, ,,		
Gates (A)	S	,, ,,		
Mason (A)	S	,, ,,		
Burton (A)	S	,, ,,		
Emanuel Howe (A)	A	12 Feb. 01		
Theophilus Nichols (A)	A	1 June 01	P	25 Mar. 1705
Sutton (A)	S	,, 02		
Edward Hobart (A)	S	,, 02	P	24 Mar. 04
* * *	*	* *	*	* *
Savage[214]	S	04	K	2 July 04
Bezier[157]†	S	04	P	04
Henry Fletcher (B)	A	25 Aug. 04		
Robert Sutton (B)	A	,, ,,		
Ball (*Conductor*) (B)	A	25 Mar. 05		
John Turner (B)	A	,, ,,	P	23 Mar. 08
Alexander Campbell (B)	A	,, ,,		
Walter Reyner (B)	A	23 April 06		
David Mackasky (B)	A	25 June 06	P	24 Sept. 08
Edmund De Fisher (B)	A	4 May 07	P	15 June 08
John Abbington (B)	A	16 May 07		
John Chambers (B)	A	21 July 07		
James Hobart (B)	A	15 June 08		
John Lafausille[28]	‡	26 Aug. 08	P	12 Nov. 26
Francis Richardson (B)	A	24 Sept. 08		
Charles Duterme	‡	23 Feb. 09	PT	
Thomas Spencer (B)	A	25 Mar. 09		23 Jan. 40
* * *	*	* *	*	* *
Robert Wingfield (B)	A	2 May 09		
William Howe (B)	S	09		
Thomas Launder	‡	7 May 11		
John White	‡	12 July 13		
Justine Holdman[215]	S	15	W	Nov. 15
Glenkennedy[215]	S	15		
Peter Ribton	‡	5 Jan. 15		
Malcom Hamilton	‡	3 Sept. 19		
John Dallons[91]	‡	6 April 20		
Thomas Nugent	‡	Aug. 21	P	Oct. 25
Arthur Loftus[63]	‡	23 Oct. 24	P	23 Aug. 35

† Bezier, spelt Bezire in list of Lieutenants.
‡ It is uncertain if these Officers served as Ensigns in the King's Regiment.

A	B	C		D	E	
ENSIGNS—continued.						
William Robinson[158] (D)*	†	23 Dec.	1726	P	20 June	1739
John Ekins (D)[94].	†	27 April	26	P	11 Sept.	36
Nehemiah Donellan (D)	†	23 Dec.	26	P	12 Jan.	40
Charles Desclousseau (D)	†	29 May	29	P	23 Jan.	40
George Meredith (D)		1 Nov.	30	PT	4 Feb.	39
James Magrath (D)		1 Mar.	32	PT	1 Feb.	39
‡Maximilian Guerin (D)		5 July	35		13 May	42
Daniel Vanriel (D)		23 Aug.	35	PT	2 Feb.	39
Henry Lewin (D)		11 Sept.	36	D	21 Jan.	41
Osborn Jephson (D)		26 Aug.	37	PT	3 Feb.	40
Nicholas Turner..	A	12 Jan.	40	HP	18 Mar.	42
Richard Knight..	A	1 Feb.	39	P	13 May	42
John Cook[64] (C)..	A	2 Feb.	39	P	4 Dec.	42
Charles Thompson[156] (C)	A	3 Feb.	39	P	15 June	42
William Rickson[159] (C)..	A	4 Feb.	39	P	14 July	43
William Catherwood[93] ..	A	20 June	39	P	11 July	41
Henry Rodgers ..	A	24 Jan.	40	P	13 May	42
Jacob Conway[96] (C)	A	22 Jan.	40	P	24 Sept.	43
Thomas Paske (C)	A	11 July	41	P	15 Oct.	44
James Walter (C)	A	18 Mar.	41	P	4 Oct.	43
John Beckwith (C)	A	13 May	42	P	17 Feb.	46
Charles Hemington (C)	A	,,	,,	P	,,	,,
Jackson Brown (C)	A	,,	,,	R	20 April	44
Antony Wagner..	A	4 Dec.	42	R	4 June	43
John Hayward ..	A	15 Aug.	43	R	20 April	44
Richard Creswell	A	14 July	43	R	10 Oct.	44
John Trollop[95] ..	A	11 June	43	P	17 Feb.	46
John Manning ..	A	12 June	43		15 Aug.	43
William Rickman ..		14 July	43			
John Haywood ..	A	15 Aug.	43	R	20 April	44
John Corrance ..	A	24 Sept.	43	P	17 Feb.	46
J. Webbe[98] ..	A	15 Oct.	44	P	5 Mar.	48
John Callaud ..	A	4 Oct	43	P	17 Feb.	46
William Wright ..	A	20 April	44	P	10 Mar.	46
Thomas Troughear ..	A	,,	,,	P	25 June	47
Thomas Wilson[217] (C) ..	A	25 June	44	PT	19 Feb.	48
Calthorpe Harrington ..	A	,,	,,	P	6 Mar.	48
Henry Rogers ..	A	10 Oct.	44	P	10 Oct.	48
James Davison ..	A	17 Feb.	45	R	19 Mar.	46
Robert Bruce[217a] (Serjeant-Major) ..	A	,,	,,	HP	18 April	49
John Ellis ..	A	,,	,,	P	20 Nov.	50
Robert Berry ..	A	,,	,,	R	25 Feb.	48
Charles Hamilton[99] (E)..	A	5 Mar.	45	P	31 Oct.	51
Whitshed ..	A	17 July	45	E	5 Mar.	45

† It is uncertain if these Officers served as Ensigns in the King's Regiment.

‡ M. Guerin, a "minor" (note in MS. Army List of 1743, in War Office).

ENSIGNS—continued.

A	B	C		D	E	
Thomas Davenant		10 Mar.	1746	E	16 Aug.	1747
Henry Lee (E*)	T	19 Mar.	46	P	22 April	52
T. Backhouse (*Volunteer*) (E)	A	16 Aug.	47	P	27 Aug.	53
Joseph Fish	A	19 Feb.	47	PT	11 June	48
Duke Butler (E, F)	A	5 Mar.	47	CM	2 Oct.	55
Richard Middlemore (E, F)	A	6 Mar.	47	P 51	15 Oct.	54
Henry Gudgeon (*Serjeant*) (*Adj.*)	P	25 June	47		1 Sept.	47
George Coghlan (*Volunteer*) (E)	A	1 Sept.	47	P	26 Feb.	55
Edward Hosea	HP	25 Feb.	48	R	20 April	51
John Cooke	A	11 June	48	Red.		
Thomas Stewart (*Volunteer*)	A	10 Oct.	48	Red.		
Thomas Stuart (E, F)	HP	18 April	49	P	31 May	55
Grant Scott (E, F)	HP	20 Nov.	50		2 Oct.	55
Charles O'Hara (E)	A	20 April	51	T	23 Dec.	52
Harcourt Masters (F)		26 Nov.	51	P	3 Oct.	55
John Laulhi (F)		22 April	52			
Richd. Berenger Lernoult (F)		23 Dec.	52	P	29 Aug.	56
John Philips Adams (F)		27 Aug.	53	P	30 Aug.	56
George Borrowdale		12 Mar.	55	P	31 Aug.	56
Henry De la Donespe	A	18 June	55		5 April	57
Augustus Alt	A	1 Oct.	55		25 Sept.	57
George Foster[100]	A	2 Oct.	55		26 Sept.	57
Hugh Mackay	A	3 Oct.	55	R		
Mungo Law	A	4 Oct.	55	R		
Dick Culliford	A	5 Oct.	55			
William Morrison[160] (2 B.)	T 2	25 Aug.	56		30 Sept.	57
Michael Downes (2 B.)	T 2	26 Aug.	56	P	1 Oct.	57
William Dexter (2 B.)	A	27 Aug.	56	P	2 Oct.	57
Mitchelbourne Knox (2 B.)	A	28 Aug.	56	P	3 Oct.	57
Gerrard Alt	A	29 Aug.	56	P	4 Oct.	57
William Read	A	30 Aug.	56	P	5 Oct.	57
James Hart (2 B.)	A	31 Aug.	56	P	6 Oct.	57
James Wyatt (2 B.)	A	1 Sept.	56	P	7 Oct.	57
Richard Nisbet (2 B.)	A	2 Sept.	56	P	8 Oct.	57
Thomas Campbell (2 B.)	A	3 Sept.	56			
Christopher Weston	A	4 Sept.	56	T	1 Mar.	58
James Nisbet (2 B.)	A	5 Sept.	56		8 Oct.	57
Roger Parke	A	5 April	57	P	14 Oct.	59
William Russell (2 B.)	A	14 May	57			
Edmund Boyle	A	24 Sept.	57			58
W. Denholme	A	25 Sept.	57	T 63	25 Sept.	57
Henry Savage	A	26 Sept.	57	P	15 Oct.	59
Benjamin Ashe	A	28 Sept.	57		27 Jan.	60
Charles Parke	A	30 Sept.	57		28 Jan.	60
Roger Twigge	A	1 Oct.	57		18 Mar.	60
Richard Taylor	A	2 Oct.	57		18 Nov.	60
Duncan Bayne	A	3 Oct.	57			
William Brooke	A	4 Oct.	57			

A	B	C		D	E	
ENSIGNS—continued.						
John Spence	A	5 Oct.	1757	T 63	5 Oct.	1757
William Marler	A	6 Oct.	57		20 Dec.	60
Richard Steele	A	30 Dec.	58		28 Feb.	61
James Tippet	T	14 Oct.	59		20 May	61
Thomas Pennefather	A	15 Oct.	59	P	19 Nov.	61
William Southouse	T	27 Jan.	60	T	1 Nov.	64
James Mayne	A	28 Jan.	60	P	6 Oct.	62
John Lee	A	22 Aug.	60	P	15 July	67
John Mompesson	A	18 Nov.	60	P	9 Dec.	67
S. Willoe	P	7 Jan.	61	P	23 Nov.	68
Robert Mathews	A	28 Feb.	61	P	27 Mar.	70
Fred. McDowall	A	20 May	61			65
Erasmus Corbett	A	22 Mar.	62			66
George Heald	A	20 Oct.	62			66
Thomas Bennett	A	16 Nov.	64	P	1 Aug.	70
George Dame	A	4 Jan.	62	P	26 Dec.	70
John Appreece	A	18 April	66		27 May	71
William Highmore	A	2 May	66	P	12 Oct.	71
Henry Yonge	A	16 Sept.	67	P	18 Nov.	74
John Gough (*Adjutant*)	A	9 Dec.	67		27 Oct.	72
John Delgarno	A	19 Dec.	68	P	22 Nov.	75
R. Seyton Kynnersley	A	27 Mar.	70	P	23 Nov.	75
George Clowes	A	14 Sept.	70	P	16 Mar.	76
George Jennings	A	26 Dec.	70		26 Dec.	71
Daniel Showrd	A	27 May	71	P	6 May	77
William Fowke	A	10 June	71			76
Daniel Mercer	A	29 Nov.	71	Pj	29 Mar.	76
Robert Rounds Brooke	A	6 Nov.	72	P	8 May	77
John Caldwell	A	26 Dec.	74	P	25 Dec.	77
Thomas Pepyat	A	15 Aug.	75	P	11 May	78
*Walter Butler	A	22 Nov.	75			83
George Armstrong	A	23 Nov.	75	P	1 Mar.	79
John Brocke	A	24 Nov.	75	P	8 Nov.	79
Durell Saumarez[66]	A	6 April	76	P	5 Jan.	80
Joseph Wilmot	A	12 April	76	P	6 Jan.	80
George Hanbury Williams	A	26 April	76		6 Nov.	78
Robert McDougal	A	6 May	77	P	12 Dec.	81
Robert Pollard	A	8 May	77	P	13 Sept.	83
Philip Fry	A	11 May	78	HP		83
Archibald Armstrong	A	6 Nov.	78		22 Oct.	78
Anthony Kynnersley	A	15 Feb.	79		3 Nov.	79
Anthony Monin	A	21 Oct.	78		8 Aug.	88
Andrew Armstrong	A	3 Nov.	79	P	2 Mar.	85
John Armstrong	A	5 Jan.	80		25 June	81
William Armstrong	A	6 Jan.	80		11 Oct.	81
H. Hardress Lloyd	A	9 Feb.	80		17 Jan.	81
C. Nugent Armstrong	A	22 Mar.	80		23 Feb.	81
T. St. George Armstrong	A	17 Jan.	81	P	26 Oct.	85

* In the Army List of 1783, Walter Butler appears under the name of Walter Butler Sheehan, immediately after Robert Pollard, with the date of his Commission changed to 5th June, 1777.

ENSIGNS—continued.

A	B	C	D	E
William Pawlett	A	23 Feb. 1781	P	27 Jan. 1786
Donald Murchieson	A	25 June 81		84
Henry St. Germain	T	3 Sept. 81		88
Thomas Grant	T	11 Oct. 81		84
Daniel Bliss	A	13 Sept. 83	P	18 Oct. 86
George Strickland	A	30 April 84	P	5 Mar. 89
Isaac Brock	A	2 Mar. 85		90
Augustine Fitzgerald	A	16 Nov. 85		90
Robert Molesworth	A	5 April 86	P	31 Mar. 90
Bigoe A. Stoney	T	27 Oct. 86	P	2 Feb. 91
George Andrew Armstrong	A	24 Sept. 87	P	2 Feb. 91
Bryce Maxwell[69]		8 Aug. 88	P	23 Nov. 91
Thomas Rainsford	A	3 Sept. 88		90
Philip Armstrong	A	9 April 89	P	29 Sept. 92
Bryce MacMurdo[101]	A	6 Jan. 90	P	31 Mar. 93
James Booth[102]	A	17 Feb. 90	P	30 April 93
Henry Louis Dickenson	A	31 Mar. 90		93
William Russell	T	9 Feb. 91		91
George J. Reeves	A	9 Feb. 91	P	29 June 93
John Thomas Armstrong	T	30 Mar. 91	P	8 Aug. 93
William Creagh	A	13 April 91		94
Archibald MacMurdo[218]	A	23 Nov. 91		93
George Robert Stoney	A	29 Sept. 92		93
Lorenzo Toole[219]	A	28 Feb. 93	PT	3 June 94
Patrick Maxwell	A	31 Mar. 93		95
James Francis Bland	A	30 April 93		94
James Powell	A	31 May 93	P	28 Feb. 94
Robert Eason[61]	A	31 Aug. 93	P	27 Nov. 94
Pomeroy D'Arcy	A	30 Sept. 93		94
Percy Gethin	A	26 Oct. 93	P	17 Dec. 94
Joseph Davy	A	28 Feb. 94	P	22 Oct. 94
John Blackmore[74]	A	15 April 94	P	1 Sept. 95
J. R. Mont. Caulfield (Volunteer)	A	25 Aug. 94	P	3 Sept. 95
Septimus W. Loane (Volunteer)	A	27 Nov. 94	P	22 July 95
R. Villeneuve[162] (Volunteer)	A	17 Dec. 94	P	25 Aug. 95
Edmund Callen	T	1 Sept. 95	P	12 Mar. 96
George Pepyat	T	2 Sept. 95		96
Richard Burke	T	4 Sept. 95	R.	6 Sept. 96
John Babington	T	5 Sept. 95		96
John Fitzmaurice	T	6 Sept. 95	P	21 Nov. 96
Samuel Speare	A	28 Oct. 95	P	17 Nov. 96
Joseph Bullen	A	28 Oct. 95	P	4 Jan. 97
John Church[64]	A	4 Nov. 95	P	14 July 96
James McGuffy	A	12 Mar. 96	P	25 April 97
John Chapman	A	8 June 96		97
John Stotesbury	A	15 June 96		1800
Archibald Cameron	A	14 July 96		00
Richard Hungerford	A	18 Aug. 96		1799
George R. Cook	A	9 Nov. 96	P	8 Mar. 98
W. Robinson	A	9 Feb. 97		1800

A	B	C	D	E

ENSIGNS—*continued.*

A	B	C	D	E
E. H. Williams ..	A	6 Mar. 1797		1799
William Scholeley ..	A	25 April 97	P	20 Dec. 98
H. Francis Goldecutt ..	A	6 Sept. 98	P	2 Oct. 1800
Thomas Buck ..	A	11 Oct. 98	P	18 Sept. 1800
John Scafe ..	A			1799
John Ringrose Annesley ..	A	21 Feb. 99	P	5 April 1801
William Glen (*Adjutant*) ..	A	3 Oct. 99	D	18 June 01
William Leader ..	A	7 Feb. 1800		02
John Bannatyne ..	A		P	6 April 01
Thomas Couche ..	A	9 Oct. 1800	P	29 Nov. 01
James Sadlier[107] ..	A	5 April 01	P	7 Jan. 03
Jeramy ..	A	6 April 01		02
Mark Hodgson ..	A	20 Aug. 01		03
James S. Tyeth[104] ..	A	6 Nov. 01	P	25 June 03
Peter Moyles (*Adjutant*) ..	A	29 Nov. 01	P	19 Nov. 03
Samuel Hooker[111] ..	A	12 Aug. 03	P	11 Oct. 04
John Bradbridge[109] ..	A	20 Aug. 03	P	12 Oct. 04
Thomas Edmond Dowlin ..	A	27 Aug. 03	P	04
Andrew Liddell ..	A	10 Sept. 03	P	1 Dec. 04
Edward Smith ..	A	8 Dec. 03		05
George Browne ..	A	17 Dec. 03	P	21 Mar. 05
Robert Watson Gordon ..	A	31 Dec. 03		05
Francis Birmingham ..	A	7 April 04	P	28 Mar. 05
William Scotton ..	A	24 April 04	P	9 May 05
George Arden ..	A	11 Oct. 04		06
Thomas Cross ..	A	12 Oct. 04	P	22 Aug. 05
John Stanford ..	A	19 Nov. 04	P	3 Oct. 05
Edward Browne ..	A	20 Nov. 04	P	14 Nov. 05
Carieton Burne ..	A	21 Nov. 04	P	5 Dec. 05
Adam Baillie ..	A	22 Nov. 04	P	2 Jan. 06
John McMahon[112] ..	A	23 Nov. 04	P	16 Oct. 06
Thomas Miller (*Adjutant*) ..	A	24 Nov. 04	P	12 Sept. 05
Theophilus Perkins ..	A	8 Dec. 04		06
John Raymond ..	A	5 Jan. 05	P	30 Oct. 06
Thomas Waring Lloyd[165] ..	A	21 Mar. 05	P	6 Nov. 06
Austin Neame ..	A	8 May 05	P	15 May 06
Edward Goate ..	A	9 May 05	P	8 Jan. 07
G. Henry Dansey ..	A	22 Aug. 05		06
Henry Cooper ..	A	3 Oct. 05	P	18 June 07
Morton Noel[166] ..	A	4 Oct. 05	P	22 Oct. 07
William Kingsley ..	A	7 Nov. 05		06
Anthony Richards ..	A	14 Nov. 05		06
George Nutall[167] ..	A	5 Dec. 05	P	25 Oct. 07
Charles Barstow[168] ..	A	2 Jan. 06	P	15 Jan. 08
Peter Smith ..	A	20 Feb. 06		08
Charles Ince ..	A	22 May 06	P	17 Jan. 08
Daniel M'Pherson ..	A	26 June 06	P	18 Jan. 08
William Compton ..	A	3 July 06	P	19 Jan. 08
John Ivers ..	A	10 July 06	P	20 Jan. 08
William Collis ..	A	21 Aug. 06	P	21 Jan. 08
David Home ..	A	29 Oct. 06	P	25 Mar. 08

ENSIGNS—continued.

A	B	C		D	E	
James Drummie[169]	A	6 Nov.	1806	P	5 Jan.	1809
Herbert Raban	A	4 Dec.	06	P	2 Mar.	09
John Ivers	A	8 Jan.	07	P	30 Mar.	09
Charles M'Carthy (*Adjutant*)	A	12 Feb.	07			09
Edward Finch[171]	A	18 June	07	P	20 July	09
James Kenny	A	25 Sept.	07	P	31 Aug.	09
William Gubbins	A	22 Oct.	07			08
Caleb E. Powell	A	25 Oct.	07	P	22 Feb.	10
Marshal M'Dermott	A	15 Jan.	08	P	19 July	10
Gonville Bromhead	A	18 Jan.				09
Malcolm Ross	A	19 Jan.	08	P	14 Mar.	11
Jacob Ruddoch	A	20 Jan.	08	P	16 May	11
Michael Flannigan	A	19 Feb.	08	P	6 June	11
Arthur Gardiner	A	25 Mar.	08	P	11 July	11
Edward Boyd[172]	A	13 Oct.	08	P	15 Aug.	11
Andrew Black	A	20 Oct.	08			10
John Harden	A	3 Nov.	08			10
Thomas Price	A	8 Dec.	08	P	30 April	12
Anthony A. Leslie	A	2 Mar.	09	PT	3 Sept.	12
Wainford Ridge	A	23 Mar.	09	P	1 Sept.	12
Henry P. Hill[173]	A	30 Mar.	09	P	12 Sept.	11
Robert Spiers	A	27 April	09	P	2 Sept.	12
Robert Dunbar Taylor	A	20 July	09	P	3 Sept.	12
Peter Willats	A	31 Aug.	09			11
William Bradford	A	7 Mar.	10	P	22 Oct.	12
Alexander Bourke	A	8 Mar.	10	P	5 Nov.	12
John Lowry[174]	A	7 June	10	P	24 Dec.	12
Richard Powell	A	19 July	10			13
Richard Nicholson[175]	A	18 Oct.	10	P	8 July	13
Samuel Blyth	A	21 Feb.	11			13
Frederick William Vieth	A	14 Mar.	11	P	3 Aug.	13
Francis William Lamb	A	16 May	11	D		12
William Kidman	A	6 June	11	P	4 Aug.	13
Andrew Robert Charleton	A	7 June	11			12
J. G. Powell[176]	A	15 Aug.	11	P	5 Aug.	13
Daniel Frazer	A	31 Oct.	11			13
Brooke Young[177]	A	18 June	12	P	6 Aug.	13
Alexander Greig[178]	A	1 Sept.	12	P	7 Aug.	13
Thomas Russell	A	2 Sept.	12	P	12 Aug.	13
James O. Flanegan	A	3 Sept.	12	P	24 Feb.	14
Henry Clarence Scarman	A	4 Sept.	12	P	22 Mar.	14
James Grey	A	1 Oct.	12	P	23 Mar.	14
Robert Macnair[179]	A	22 Oct.	12	P	24 Mar.	14
George Campsie	A	5 Nov.	12	P	14 July	14
Thomas Swayne[180]	A	24 Dec.	12	P	9 Aug.	14
Samuel Garner	A	28 Jan.	13	P	10 Aug.	14
Luke Vipont	A	25 Feb.	13	R		15
Edward Murray	A	28 April	13	P	11 Aug.	14
Augustus Keily	A	29 April	13			14
Charles Millar	A	24 June	13	P	29 Sept.	14
Thomas Moyle	A	8 July	13	P	24 Nov.	14

A	B	C	D	E
ENSIGNS—*continued.*				
George Jarvis	A	3 Aug. 1813	P	23 Mar. 1815
George Richardson	A	4 Aug 13	P	12 July 15
A. Thompson	A	5 Aug. 13		24
H. Francis	A	6 Aug. 13		20
Donald Æ. Macdonald[220]	A	7 Aug. 13		15
John Hilton	A	12 Aug. 13		14
John Street (*Adjutant*)	A	21 Oct. 13	P	26 July 15
George Augustus McDermott	A	2 Dec. 13		20
Richard Shaw	A	24 Feb. 14		20
John Mathieson[221] (2 B.)	A	25 Feb. 14		17
John Farnam (*Adjutant*) (2 B.)	A	26 Feb. 14	HP	25 Feb. 16
William Wainwright	A	22 Mar. 14	HP	27 Jan. 20
Charles Barry	A	23 Mar. 14	T 60	16 Feb. 15
Rutherford Thompson	T	24 Mar. 14		21
William Calder (2 B.)	A	14 July 14	P	24 June 24
Charles Cotter	A	9 Aug. 14	HP	25 Feb. 16
War-Lut. Pur. Moriarty (2 B.)	A	10 Aug. 14	HP	,, ,,
Robert Mawdsley (2 B.)	A	29 Sept. 14	HP	,, ,,
James White (2 B.)	A	24 Nov. 14	HP	,, ,,
William Robinson (2 B.)	A	16 Feb. 15	HP	,, ,,
William Constantine (2 B.)	A	23 Mar. 15	HP	,, ,,
George Surtees (2 B.)	A	25 May 15	HP	,, ,,
Robert Young (2 B.)	A	27 July 15	HP	,, ,,
Robert Mawdesley	T	29 Sept. 14		22
Robert Minty	A	21 May 18		22
William Curtis	T	13 Jan. 20	D	23
Charles Cotter	HP	27 Jan. 20	P	30 Sept. 24
William Eleazer Pickwick	T	18 May 20	P	7 April 25
Vere Essex Ward	T	10 Aug. 20	R	22
Honourable Richard Hare	T	10 Jan. 22	P	23 June 25
Charles Rainsford	T	12 Sept. 22		25
Charles Clark	A	8 July 24		30
James Byron	T	5 Aug. 24	P	17 Dec. 25
Edward Newton	A	30 Sept. 24		25
Irwine S. Whitty (*Adjutant*)	A	8 April 25	P	25 June 30
George Burrard	A	21 April 25	P	11 July 26
John Longfield[44]	A	23 June 25	P	26 Sept. 26
John Howard	A	12 Nov. 25	P	30 Nov. 26
William Chearnley	A	26 Nov. 25	P	15 Oct. 29
W. Laton Worthington	A	17 Dec. 25		28
John Singleton	A	17 June 26		27
George Murphy	A	26 Sept. 26		28
Charles Ben Caldwell	A	10 Oct. 26		29
John James Edward Hamilton	A	7 Dec. 26		29
Ralph Cheney	A	31 Dec. 27	P	22 June 32
Edward Orme	A	19 June 28	R	21 Sept. 32
Henry Welladvice Roper	A	21 Nov. 28	P	21 Dec. 32
Walter Lay	A	4 Aug. 29	P	8 Feb. 33
Clement Thomas Baldwin	A	14 Oct. 29	R	30
Walter Ogilvy	A	15 Oct. 29	P	8 Mar. 33
Henry Lomax	A	13 June 30	R	27 Feb. 35

A	B	C	D	E
ENSIGNS—*continued.*				
Godfrey Baldwin	T	2 Nov. 1830		1832
¶ Edward Harris Greathed[46]	A	22 June 32	P	10 May 33
John Terry Liston	A	27 July 32	P	7 Feb. 34
John Hilton	A	21 Sept. 32	P	30 Jan. 35
Austin John Bewes	A	21 Dec. 32	D	,, ,,
Fra Saunderson Holmes	A	8 Feb. 33	P	28 Aug. 35
Stephenson Browne	A	8 Mar. 33	P	4 Sept. 35
Antony Tisdall Sidney Shawe Plunkett	A	10 May 33	P	30 Oct. 35
John Eldridge West	A	7 Feb. 34	P	3 Feb. 37
Alfred Augustus Malet	A	30 Jan. 35	P	30 April 37
William St. Leger	A	27 Feb. 35	D	1 Dec. 36
¶ John Hinde[48]	A	28 Feb. 35	P	30 June 36
Charles Harte	T	4 Sept. 35	R	26 Feb. 36
Mark Pattison Seward	A	30 Oct. 35	P	1 Sept. 37
Hugh Hill	A	24 Nov. 35	P	27 April 38
Coulthurst Holder	A	22 Jan. 36	P	10 Jan. 38
George Langton Marshall	A	26 Feb. 36	R	20 Oct. 37
Ernest Lavie	A	3 Feb. 37	P	20 Nov. 38
John Long Marsden	A	17 Feb. 37	P	7 June 39
Robert Frederick Turner	A	30 June 37	R	6 Dec. 39
William Montagu S. McMurdo[22]	A	1 July 37	P 22	5 Jan. 41
Thomas Clowes	A	1 Sept. 37	P	2 July 41
William Seymour	A	20 Oct. 37	R	6 Dec. 39
Chas. F. B. Greville Dickenson	A	10 Jan. 38	P	26 Oct. 41
Pennant Athelwold Iremonger	A	27 April 38	P 84	20 May 42
Arthur Leslie	A	20 Nov. 38	P	8 May 42
¶ James Johnson[49]	A	7 June 39	P	13 May 42
William Bayly[79] (*Adjutant*)		6 Dec. 39	P	23 June 42
George Augustus Young	A	6 Dec. 39	P	24 June 42
William Turnour Granville	A	8 Jan. 41	P	25 Oct. 42
George Edward Baynes[112]	A	2 July 41	P	12 Dec. 43
Richard Wilson Hartley	A	26 Oct. 41	P	27 Sept. 44
John Henry Ed. De Robeck	A	6 May 42	P	19 Nov. 44
Alfred Ingilby Garnett	A	13 May 42	P	4 July 45
John Stone	A	20 May 42	P	14 Nov. 45
Thomas Aldridge	A	21 May 42	P	3 April 46
John Hudson (*Serjeant-Major*)	A	25 June 42	R	28 July 43
Ellis James Charter	A	25 Oct. 42	P	16 Dec. 45
Robert Stuart Baynes[116]	A	28 July 43	P	27 Mar. 46
Charles Lennox Maher	A	12 Dec. 43	T 61	26 July 44
George Curry[124]	A	26 July 44	P	3 April 46
Shaftoe Craster Craster	A	27 Sept. 44	P	,, ,,
Edmund Loder	A	19 Nov. 44	R	11 Nov. 45
Ed. Rawlings Hannam	A	4 July 45	P	3 April 46
William Parker Howell	A	11 Nov. 45	R	1 Dec. 46
Edmund David Lyon	A	14 Nov. 45		3 April 46
M'Kay Rynd	A	16 Dec. 45	P	5 Mar. 47
William Huddlestone Macadam	A	23 Jan. 46	R	29 Dec. 48
Horace Ximenes[183]	A	27 March 46	P	29 May 48
William Waldegrave Pogson[184]	A	3 April 46	P	9 Feb. 49

A	B	C	D	E
ENSIGNS—*continued.*				
John Biggs	A	3 April 1846	P	17 Oct. 1848
Fred. Dickenson Bourne	A	5 April 46	E 28	27 Dec. 47
George Fuller Walker[185]	A	14 April 46	P	13 Sept. 49
Allan John Robertson	T 78	5 Mar. 47	P	9 Nov. 49
¶ John Vere Wm. Henry Webb[53]	T CMR	5 Mar. 47	P	21 Feb. 51
Thomas Beattie Grierson[187]	T 28	27 Dec. 47	P	15 Oct. 52
Alexander Ross Bayly[129]	T	15 Aug. 48	P	6 May 53
William Raymond Ximenes[130]	A	29 Dec. 48	P	25 May 53
Graham Egerton Huddleston[189]	A	30 Dec. 48	P	27 June 54
Herbert Vernon Lilicrap	A	9 Feb. 49	P	20 July 55
Frank McPherson	T	20 Sept. 49	D	15 July 52
John McNamee	T	9 Nov. 49	T StHB	3 Aug. 55
Charles Geo. Mackenzie	T	21 Feb. 51	P 28	13 Feb. 55
William Frederick Metge[132]	T	16 July 52	P	7 Sept. 55
William Cole Hamilton	A	23 Nov. 52	P 88	30 Mar. 55
Fred. Bradford McCrea[85]	A	27 June 54	P	20 July 55
Fred. Anderson Stebbing[135]	A	18 May 55	P	12 April 56
William Hext Mountsteven[223]	A	3 Aug. 55	W	10 July 57
William Robert Webb[191]	A	7 Sept. 55	P	15 April 56
Æneas Gordon Blair[196] (2 B.)	A	7 March 56	P	5 Sept. 57
¶ Forster Longfield[55]	T	24 April 56	P	1 Aug. 56
Andrew Moynihan[138] (*Serjeant-Major*)	PT 90	2 May 56	P	16 Sept. 57
Robert B. Moorhead		8 July 56	E 12	17 Feb. 57
Alfred Downie Corfield		1 Aug. 56	P	15 May 57
William Ed. Whelan[141]	E 12	17 Feb. 57	P	18 Sept. 57
William Edgeworth[194]	A	22 May 57	P	23 Oct. 57
R. T. B. Browne	T 33	23 Oct. 57	P	15 Nov. 57
¶ E. Tanner[56]	T 33	,, ,,	P	7 Dec. 57
E. T. Pinniger	T 28	,, ,,	P	11 Dec. 57
R. T. Stokes	T 48	,, ,,	P	23 Mar. 58
B. Whitting[86]	T 62	,, ,,	P	,, ,,
J. E. W. Black	T 41	,, ,,	P	30 July 58
A. G. Westby	T 63	,, ,,	P	,, ,,
J. S. Wheeley (2 B.)	T 97	,, ,,	P	20 Sept. 58
R. D. F. Shirreff (2 B.)	T 94	,, ,,	P	1 Oct. 58
J. C. Cooper (2 B.)		30 Oct. 57	P	26 Nov. 58
Ed. Emerson (*Serjeant-Major*) (*Adjutant*) (2 B.)	T 96	6 Nov. 57	P	17 May 61
Richard Chute	A	17 Nov. 57	P	15 Jan. 61
Thomas P. Senior (2 B.)	A	18 Nov. 57	P	16 July 61
Thomas P. Fleetwood (2 B.)	A	19 Nov. 57	P	1 July 62
G. N. J. Bradford (2 B.)	A	20 Nov. 57	P	4 Feb. 59
W. J. Watson	A	21 Nov. 57	P	4 Sept. 60
Arundel Hill Cotter	A	11 Dec. 57	R	16 July 61
Philip Homer Page	A	12 Dec. 57	P	22 April 59
John George Brown	A	13 Dec. 57	R	61
Arthur Cook		16 Mar. 58	P	4 June 61

A	B	C		D	E	
ENSIGNS—*continued.*						
William John Cooper (2 B.)	A	23 Mar.	1858	R	4 July	1860
Charles Blandford Crease	A	24 Mar.	58	R	15 Jan.	62
Charles Dudley Ryder Madden (2 B.)		30 Mar.	58	P	26 Aug.	59
William Bannatyne (2 B.)[87]	T 24	21 May	58	P	13 Dec.	59
William W. Madden (2 B.)	A	2 July	58	P	16 Oct.	60
Jeremy Peyton Jones	A	3 July	58	P	6 Nov.	60
Robert Handcock	A	8 Oct.	58	R	28 Jan.	62
Walter Mowbray Johnston	A	28 Jan.	59	R		63
Charles Thomas Fred. Blair (2 B.)	A	29 Jan.	59	R	29 May	63
Theodore Henry Skinner (2 B.)	A	1 April	59	P	23 April	61
William Albert Bridge	A	3 June	59	P	4 June	61
John Randle Minshull Ford (2 B.)	A	21 Oct.	59	P	6 Sept.	61
Ed. Williams (2 B.)	A	6 Jan.	60	P	27 Sept.	61
Bowland Garrard Moffat	A	4 July	60	P	9 Oct.	63
Thomas Gorges Crawley	A	5 July	60	P	9 Jan.	63
John Dawson[143]	A	21 Sept.	60	P	13 Feb.	63
Martin George Cole	A	21 Dec.	60	P	28 April	63
William Willoughby Egerton	A	8 Feb.	61	P	30 June	63
Charles Fred. Malet	A	9 Feb.	61	P	19 Jan.	64
Marmaduke Stourton	A	17 May	61	P	29 Mar.	64
Matthew Liddon	A	16 July	61	P	26 April	64
Richard Aylmer	A	17 July	61	R	14 Jan.	62
Ed. Everard Granville Clayton	A	23 July	61	P	18 Oct.	64
John James Hamilton	A	6 Aug.	61	P	30 Dec.	65
Bennett Fleming Handy[88] (2 B.)	A	7 Aug.	61	P	29 Nov.	64
William Howe Hennis (2 B.)	A	27 Sept.	61	P	20 Dec.	64
Henry Champanté Crespin	A	3 Dec.	61	R	8 Aug.	62
John Mount Batten	A	31 Dec.	61	P	11 July	65
Francis James Stuart	A	14 Jan.	62	P	25 July	65
Charles James Holman Playter	A	15 Jan.	62	P	15 June	66
Nash Short[89]	A	28 Jan.	62	P	10 Nov.	65
Arthur Fawkes	A	8 Aug.	62	P	29 Dec.	65
Ambrose William Humphrys (2 B.)	A	5 Sept.	62	R	7 Mar.	65
William Stancomb Sinkins	A	9 Jan.	63	P	26 Jan.	66
William Toke Dooner[146] (2 B.)	A	30 Jan.	63	P	6 Feb.	66
Walter Cowan	A	13 Feb.	63	T 60	13 Feb.	63
Thomas Blake Humfrey[147] (2 B.)	A	21 April	63	P	20 Feb.	66
Alfred Mellor (2 B.)	A	28 April	63	P	16 Oct.	66
Francis Moore (2 B.)	A	29 May	63	P	27 Nov.	66
Berkeley Aug. Fonblanque (2 B.)	A	30 June	63	R	29 Mar.	67
Manley C. Matthew Dixon	T 101	9 Oct.	63	P	13 Feb.	67
William Louis	A	19 Jan.	64	P	13 Feb.	67
Robert Garnett	A	29 Mar.	64	P	6 Mar.	67
George Westrenen Sawyer (2 B.)	A	28 June	64	P	20 May	67

A	B	C	D	E
ENSIGNS—*continued.*				
Fred. Bart. Joseph Jerrard[197] (2 B.)	A	18 Oct. 1864	P	14 Aug. 1867
George Rowan Hamilton (2 B.)	A	29 Nov. 64	P	1 Aug. 68
Robert Julian Orde Jocelyn (2 B.)	A	20 Dec. 64	P	28 Oct. 68
Robert Lionel Fisher (2 B.)	A	10 Mar. 65	*	12 Oct. 67
Arthur C. C. Plunket	A	11 July 65	R	7 Mar. 67
Henry Webster	A	8 Aug. 65	P	16 Sept. 68
Lewis Lovat Ayshford Wise	A	10 Nov. 65	P	24 Mar. 69
Walter Bell Marley	A	29 Dec. 65	P	8 Dec. 69
Arthur Henry Cope[151]	A	26 Jan. 66	P	10 Nov. 69
Stephen Brown	A	6 Feb. 66	P	26 Feb. 70
Arthur Ashley Ruck[152] (2 B.)	A	7 Feb. 66	P	23 Mar. 70
John Parry Hamer (2 B.)	A	20 Feb. 66	P	5 Nov. 70
Frederic Martyn	A	15 June 66	D†	3 Aug. 70
James Matthew Taylor[154] (2 B.)	T 48	16 Oct. 66	P	30 Nov. 70
George Villiers Turner[196] (2 B.)	T 73	27 Nov. 66	P	25 Mar. 71
Rowland Oakeley	A	13 Feb. 67	P	20 Sept. 71
Ponsonby McM. Shaw	A	14 Feb. 67	D	6 Nov. 69
Herbert Henry Russell	A	6 Mar. 67	P	22 April 71
William Freeman Kelly	A	7 Mar. 67	P	1 Nov. 71
Edm. O'Donnell O'Kelly (2 B.)	A	30 Mar. 67	R	22 April 71
John William Nott Bower (2 B.)	A	13 July 67	R	21 Aug. 69
William Richard Orme[153] (2 B.)	A	1 Aug. 68	P	1 Nov. 71
Charles William Atkinson	A	16 Sept. 68	P	,, ,,
Henry Thomas Granger (2 B.)	A	28 Oct. 68	P	,, ,,
William George Wolfe Macbay	T 57	24 Mar. 69	T	14 Sept. 70
Joseph Wright Ward (2 B.)	T 82	21 Aug. 69	P	1 Nov. 71
Sidney Jervis Hammet	T 63	10 Nov. 69	R	19 Feb. 70
H. S. A. Fuller	A	8 Feb. 70	P	1 Nov. 71
E. W. B. Hope	A	14 Sept. 70	P	,, ,,
L. C. F. Thompson	A	5 Nov. 70	P	,, ,,
H. N. M'Rae	A	25 Mar. 71	P	,, ,,
H. M. Wade	A	23 Sept. 71	P	,, ,,

Appointment of Ensigns discontinued.

* R. L. Fisher, superseded. † F. Martyn, drowned at Bombay

SUB-LIEUTENANTS.

A	B	C		D	E	
William C. F. Field	A	8 May	1872	P	8 May	1872
Fred. J. Whalley[155] (2 B.) ..	A	8 June	72	P	8 June	72
George Alfred Money	A	11 Sept.	72	P	11 Sept.	72
Llewellyn-Salusbury Mellor[200] (2 B.)	A	15 Jan.	73	P	15 Jan.	75
E. H. H. Montresor	A	8 May	73	P	8 May	73
H. M. Briscoe	A	12 Nov.	73	P	12 Nov.	73
Henry A. Fletcher[201] (2 B.) ..	A	"	"	P	12 Nov.	75
George R. Stone	A	28 Feb.	74	P	28 Feb.	74
Percy Schletter[202] (2 B.) ..	A	13 June	74	P	13 June	76
Fred. Hawkins (2 B.)	A	21 Sept.	74	P	21 Sept.	74
Willm. Lloyd Brereton[199] (2 B.)	A	"	"	P	21 Sept.	74
O. J. H. Brooker	A	11 Feb.	75	P	11 Feb.	75
Charles Blenheim Porter ..	A	"	"	P	"	"
C. C. Chenevix-Trench	A	"	"	P	"	"
E. L. Maisey[206] (2 B.)	A	22 May	75	P	22 May	77
H. J. R. St. G. Richardson ..	A	10 Sept.	75	P	10 Sept.	75
A. C. G. Banning[203] (2 B.) ..	A	"	"	P	10 Sept.	76
J. H. Plunkett	A	"	"	T	29 Nov.	76
Joseph Hume Balfour[204] (2 B.)	A	6 Oct.	75	P	6 Oct.	76
O'Donnel Colley Grattan[205] (2 B.)	A	10 Mar.	75	P	10 Mar.	77
And. H. G. J. Hervey	A	12 Feb.	76	D	25 Oct.	76
Charles Gray Robertson[207] (2 B.)	A	11 Sept.	76	P	16 Feb.	78

Appointment of Sub-Lieutenants discontinued.

SECOND LIEUTENANTS.

A	B	C		D	E	
George Kenrick Moore	A	5 Sept.	1877	P 24	12 April	1879
Lawrence C. Dundas[208] (2 B.) ..	A	30 Jan.	78	P	30 Jan.	80
Horatio James Evans[209] (2 B.) ..	A	"	"	P	25 Feb.	78
Hugh O'Donnell	A	30 Jan.	78	T 24	26 Mar.	79
Henry Seaton (2 B.)	A	"	"	D	23 May	78
John Burnard Edward[210] (2 B.)	T 13	24 July	78	P	11 Mar.	80
John D. M. Williams	A	21 Aug.	78		Mar.	79
Edmund H. Molyneux-Seel ..	A	4 Dec.	78	P	17 April	80
John M. Longe	A	21 June	79	R	11 Feb.	80
Valentine A. M. Fowler[211] (2 B.)	A	13 Aug.	79	P	7 July	80
Henry J. W. Guise	A	"	"	P	25 Aug.	80
Gilbert T. Elliot	A	"	"	P	4 Sept.	80
Augustus St. John Seton ..	A	11 Oct.	79	P	15 Oct.	80
George Campbell	A	14 Jan.	80	P	9 Feb.	81
Colin A. R. Blackwell[212] (2 B.)	T 92	24 Jan.	80	P	21 Mar.	81
Rowland F. L. Farrer	A	25 Feb.	80	*		
Stapleton L. Cotton[213] (2 B.) ..	A	"	"	*		

* On 1st July, 1881, these Officers were transferred to the list of Lieutenants, and the appointment of Second Lieutenants was discontinued.

A	B	C	D	E
SECOND LIEUTENANTS— *continued.*				
Francis H. Smalpage (2 B.)	A	25 Feb. 1880	R	13 April 1880
Lawrence E. Elliott (2 B.)	A	11 Aug. 80	*	
Arthur W. H. Tripp (2 B.)	A	,, 80	*	
Basil John Bacon (2 B.)	A	22 Jan. 81	*	
Harcourt L. Dodgson (2 B.)	A	,, ,,	*	
Simpson M. R. L'Amy	A	,, ,,	*	
Willm. Adam Cuppage (2 B.)	T 99	,, ,,	*	
Leslie Wm. Shakspear	T 75	,, ,,	*	
Hyde Parker	A	23 April 81	*	

* On 1st July, 1881, these Officers were transferred to the list of Lieutenants, and the appointment of Second Lieutenants was discontinued.

ADJUTANTS.

A	B	C		D	E	
Henry Whitney (A*)	A	30 May	1696			
Charles Mason (B)						
Henry Gudgeon (E, F)	A	1 Sept.	1747	PT	29 Oct.	1754
Henry Lee (E)	A	29 Oct.	54	T	4 Feb.	60
W. Heatly (2 B.) Serjt.-Maj.	P SFG	25 Aug.	56	T 63	25 Aug.	56
Richard Berr Lernoult	A	4 Feb.	60	P	31 Jan.	66
George Foster[100]	A	2 May	66	P	4 Oct.	70
John Gough	A	4 Oct.	70		27 Oct.	72
James Webb	T	27 Oct.	72		10 April	75
Robert Mathews	A	10 April	75	P	22 Dec.	78
Thomas Bennet	A	22 Dec.	78	P	30 Sept.	82
George Armstrong	A	30 Sept.	82	P	17 July	90
Robert Pollard	A	17 Feb.	90	P	31 July	93
Bryce Maxwell[69]	A	31 July	93	P	26 Oct.	93
John Raw (2 B.)	T	31 Oct.	93		27 Aug.	94
Marcus McCausland	A	27 Aug.	94	P	18 Nov.	95
George J. Reeves	A	21 Dec.	96		29 Aug.	98
William Glen	T	29 Aug.	98	D	18 June	1801
Peter Moyles	A	3 Sept.	1801		12 Feb.	07
Thomas Miller (2 B.)	A	24 Nov.	04		12 Nov.	07
Charles M'Carthy (2 B.)	A	12 Feb.	07		3 Feb.	09
‡Peter Moyles		12 Nov.	07	P		09
Henry Cooper	A	17 Aug.	09		26 Feb.	14
Henry Brewster	A	25 Aug.	09		21 Oct.	13
John Street (2 B.)	P	21 Oct.	13		31 July	17
John Farnam (2 B.)	P	26 Feb.	14	HP	25 Feb.	16
Thomas Price	A	31 July	17		20 April	20
Thomas Drury	A	20 April	20	E	5 May	25
William Calder	A	5 May	25		28 June	27
Irvine S. Whitty	A	28 June	27	P	30 Oct.	35
William Russel Lucas	A	30 Oct.	35	†	10 Mar.	37
Francis Saunderson Holmes	A	10 Mar.	37	P	14 Dec.	41
William Bayly[79]	A	14 Dec.	41	P	29 May	48
Robert Stuart Baynes[116]	A	29 May	48	P	15 Mar.	53
Charles Power Cobbe	A	6 May	53	PT	10 April	55
George Fuller Walker[185]	A	10 April	55	P	30 April	58
Edward Emmerson (2 B.)	A	6 Nov.	57	R	16 July	58
William Edward Whelan[141]	A	30 April	58	P	30 Dec.	65
Chas. Bradford Brown[142] (2 B.)	A	16 July	58	P	15 June	66
William Hunter Baillie	A	1 Feb.	66	R	4 Dec.	66
Jeremy Peyton Jones (2 B.)	A	15 June	66	P	13 June	68
John James Hamilton	A	4 Dec.	66	P	8 Nov.	74

† W. R. Lucas, appointed Paymaster.
‡ P. Moyles, re-appointed.

A	B	C	D	E
ADJUTANTS—*continued*.				
John Mount Batten (2 B.)	A	13 June 1868	P	31 Oct. 1871
Manley C. M. Dixon (2 B.)	A	15 Nov. 71	P	23 June 75
William Louis	A	1 Jan. 75	P	21 July 77
Robert Julian O. Jocelyn (2 B.)	A	7 Aug. 75	R	26 Aug. 76
Fred. James Whalley[155] (2 B.)	A	26 Aug. 76	S*	
William Freeman Kelly	A	12 Sept. 77	PT	17 April 80
George Robert Stone	A	26 May 80	S*	

* These Officers held the Appointment of Adjutant on 1st January, 1881.

INSTRUCTORS OF MUSKETRY.

A	B	C	D	E
William James Watson	A	17 Feb. 1859	P	20 Feb. 1866
J. Evans Freke Aylmer (2 B.)	A	30 May 59		4 June 61
T. Picton Fleetwood (2 B.)	A	4 June 61		16 Aug. 65
J. P. Jones (2 B.)	A	16 Aug. 65	*	15 June 66
William A. Bridge	A	1 Mar. 66	P	12 Feb. 67
John Mount Batten (2 B.)	A	15 June 66	*	13 June 68
John Francis Stuart	A	12 Feb. 67	P	31 Dec. 72
Manly C. M. Dixon (2 B.)	A	13 June 68	*	15 Nov. 71
F. B. J. Jerrard (2 B.)[197]	A	15 Nov. 71	P 91	24 June 75
William Louis	A	31 Dec. 72	R	1 Jan. 75
William Freeman Kelly	A	1 Jan. 75	*	12 Sept. 77
P. K. Whalley (2 B.)[155]	A	24 June 75	*	26 Aug. 76
Arthur Ashley Ruck (2 B.)[182]	A	6 Sept. 76	P	30 June 80
Herbert Henry Russel	A	17 Jan. 78	R	1 Aug. 79
H. Meredith Wade	A	1 Aug. 79	P	21 Mar. 81
O'Donnell C. Grattan (2 B.)[206]	A	29 April 80	S†	
Llewellyn Salusbury Mellor	A	21 Mar. 81	S†	

* Appointed Adjutant.
† These Officers were serving as Instructors of Musketry on 1st August, 1881.

PAYMASTERS.

A	B	C	D	E
George Ridge		1 Feb. 1798		24 Dec. 1802
Michael Toler Kingsley ..		24 Dec. 1802		17 Mar. 14
Mark Hodgson (2 B.)		5 Jan. 05		29 April 19
Henry Howe		17 Mar. 14	HP	25 Feb. 16
Marshall Mac Dermott.. ..		29 April 19		28 Sept. 30
Sampson Hugh Cox		28 Sept. 30		20 July 32
Henry Palmer Hill[173]	A	20 July 32	D	26 May 36
William Russell Lucas	A	10 Mar. 37	T	17 Dec. 41
Bartholomew Hartley[224] ..	T 48	17 Dec. 41	D	9 Sept. 54
G. E. Huddlestone[185]	A	23 Mar. 55	E 52	6 Sept. 61
John Falls (2 B.)[225]	A	4 Dec. 57	P	1 April 78
F. W. Fellows	E 52	6 Sept. 61	HP	15 May 67
Thomas Palmer Senior	A	15 May 67	T	80
Fras. Gilbert Hamley (*Assistant Paymaster in Army*)		22 Sept. 73	S*	
Thos. R. W. Davidson (2 B.) (*Paymaster Pay Department*)	A	5 Jan. 80	S*	

* These Officers were serving as Paymasters on 1st August, 1881.

QUARTERMASTERS.

A	B	C	D	E
Benjamin Cuttle (A*)		1 Sept. 1697		
†John Bulfoure (B)				
John Norman (E)		24 Jan. 1749	HP	16 Jan. 1752
Donald Valentine (F)	HP	16 Jan. 52	T	28 June 56
Grant Scott (E)..	A	28 June 56		4 Feb. 60
Harcourt Masters (2 B.) ..	A	25 Aug. 56	T 63	25 Aug. 56
Thomas Stewart..	A	4 Feb. 60		1 Jan. 62
Richard Taylor	A	1 Jan. 62		19 Oct. 63
Roger Parke	A	19 Oct. 63		11 May 67
A. Schuyler de Peister[34] ..	A	11 May 67	P	13 April 68
William Potts	A	13 April 68		7 April 79
Patrick Gibson	A	7 April 79		16 Jan. 1800
Mark Hodgson	A	16 Jan. 1800	†	5 Jan. 05
William Lewis (2 B.)	A	12 Oct. 04		1 Nov. 13
Charles McCarthy	A	5 Jan. 05	‡	12 Feb. 07
George Shaw (2 B.)	A	12 Feb. 07		1 May 17
George Kiernan (2 B.).. ..	A	1 Nov. 13	HP	25 Feb. 16
William Only	A	21 Oct. 19	D	14 Jan. 29
Samuel Brodribb	A	15 Jan. 29	HP	10 Feb. 37
Job Aldridge (Q.M.-Serjt.) ..	A	10 Feb. 37	D	18 Oct. 42
John Ross[26]	A	8 Nov. 42	D	20 June 57
Thos. Massey Chadwick (2 B.) .	HP	17 Nov. 57	T	1 Jan. 77
Joseph Hamilton[27]	HP	16 April 58	D	22 Sept. 59
John Keatinge[228] (Serjt.-Major)	A	23 Sept. 59	E 19	25 Feb. 62
Charles Usherwood[229]	E 19	25 Feb. 62	HP	20 May 64
Alfred Berry[230] (Serjt.-Major)	A	20 May 64	E 3	30 Jan. 66
George Russel Holt White[231] ..	E 3	30 Jan. 66	HP	5 July 73
William Rowe (Serjt.-Major)..	A	18 Oct. 73	S§	
Philip Spencer[232] (Q.-M. Serjt.) (2 B.)	A	31 Jan. 77	S§	

† M. Hodgson, appointed Paymaster.
‡ C. McCarthy, appointed Adjutant.
§ These Officers were serving in this rank on 1st June, 1881.

SURGEONS.

A	B	C	D	E
Chirurgeon John Chambers (A, B*)	A	30 May 1696		
Robert Miller (E, F)		13 Sept. 1745		19 Feb. 1762
John Morgan		24 Sept. 1857		
Joseph Goldie		19 Feb. 62		15 July 67
James Latham		15 July 67		18 Aug. 75
Robert M'Causland		18 Aug. 75		9 July 89
Edward Smith		9 July 89		25 April 99
Francis Manson..		25 April 99		25 Dec. 1806
Samuel Cathcart		25 Dec. 1806		28 Sept. 09
William Hacket..		25 Nov. 08		6 Jan. 14
John Moore (2 B.)	P	28 Sept. 09		16
Charles Waring (2 B.).. ..		6 Jan. 14		16
Perkins V. Crofton	T	4 May 09		25 Sept. 18
Thomas Cartan, M.D.		25 Sept. 18		23 Feb. 26
Henry Thornton Mostyn ..		23 Feb. 26	T 47	14 Jan. 30
James Hinton Cardiffe, M.D...	T	14 Jan. 30	D	5 Dec. 36
Peter Fraser	P	6 Dec. 36	HP	3 Dec. 41
John Maitland, M.D.		3 Dec. 41	E 83	8 April 42
William Gardiner	E 83	8 April 42	E 69	20 Mar. 46
John Chas. Graham Tice, M.D.	E 69	20 Mar. 46	E 21	11 July 51
Francis Charles Annesley[233]	F 21	11 July 51	T	11 Sept. 60
John Madden[234] (2 B.)† ..	PT 43	2 Oct. 57	HP	9 Dec. 75
John Irvine, M.D.[235]† ..	T	11 Sept. 60	T	14 April 63
Thomas Clark Brady[236]† ..	T	14 April 63	T	24 April 69
Grahame Auchinleck, M.D.[237]†	T	24 April 69	P	2 July 76
Frederick Robert Wilson† ..	A	Mar. 76		Aug. 78

† In the Army Lists from March to June, 1873, Surgeons Madden and Auchinleck are designated *Surgeons-Major*: from July, 1873, to August, 1878, Surgeon-Major Madden and those who follow are designated *Medical Officers*; in August, 1878, the appointment of Medical Officers to regiments was discontinued.

ASSISTANT-SURGEONS.

A	B	C	D	E
Boyd (*Surgeon's Mate*)..	E	25 June 1739		
William Morlen..	A	1 Feb. 98		25 June 1801
John Brown	A	25 June 1801		5 Mar. 07
Thomas Sandall..	A	17 May 03		08
John Moore	A	9 May 05	P	28 Sept. 09
John Barlow	A	5 Mar. 07		08
John Cocks	A	11 Feb. 08		13
Charles Waring	A	6 July 09		
Lucas Pulsford	A	17 May 10	T 18 D	28 Mar. 11
Charles I. Ingham	A	16 Aug. 10		19

A	B	C	D	E
ASSISTANT-SURGEONS— *continued.*				
Walter D. Irwin	T 78	28 Mar. 1811		1813
William Steele	*	18 May 12		18
John Douglas (2 B.)	T	17 June 13	HP	25 Feb. 16
Richard Crofton (2 B.)		9 Nov. 15	HP	,, ,,
William Steele	*	18 May 12		4 April 22
George Scott, M.D.		4 April 22		27 Jan. 25
John Ferguson		27 Jan. 25		20 Aug. 29
John Knightley Adams		20 Aug. 29	D	25 Sept. 34
Peter Fraser	T	18 June 30	P	6 Dec. 36
Gideon Dolmage	T	26 Sept. 34		15 Jan. 36
John Charles Graham Tice	A	15 Jan. 36	E	29 Jan. 43
Isodore Anthony Blake	A	15 Sept. 37	E	25 Feb. 42
James Richard Ffennell	E	29 Dec. 43	E 79	12 April 50
Richard Domenichetti, M.D.		3 April 46	P 75	10 June 57
Henry Clinton Martin		21 April 46	E 94	12 Sept. 56
Henry Day Fowler	E 79	12 April 50	P	26 Feb. 56
William Henry Yates[238]		26 Feb. 56	T	1 July 62
Thomas James Biddle[239]	E 94	12 Sept. 56		61
Thomas Smith Hollingsworth		4 Sept. 57		11 Feb. 59
William Jay (2 B.)		23 Mar. 58	T	5 May 63
Joseph Edw. O'Loughlin (2 B.)		10 Sept. 58		61
R. Westrop Saunders, M.D.	A	11 Feb. 59		60
Isaac Hoysted	A	1 July 62	E 13	26 Jan. 66
†William George Ross, M.D.	A	5 May 63	T	April 73
John Stuart	E 13	26 Jan. 66	T	15 Feb. 68
Henry Joseph O'Brien, M.B	T	15 Feb. 68	T	25 Jan. 71
†James Saltus Conyers, M.D.[240] (2 B.)	A	31 Mar. 68	T	April 73
Albert Halahan L'Estrange	T	25 Jan. 71	T	12 Feb. 72
†R. Blood, M.D.	T	12 Feb. 72	T	April 73

* W. Steele reappointed.
† In the Army List of March, 1873, the Assistant Surgeons Ross, Conyers, and Blood are designated *Surgeons*.

CHAPLAINS.

A	C	E
*George Powell (A, B)	30 May 1696	
George Hatfield	5 Aug. 1747	29 May 1761
Benjamin Thornton	29 May 61	18 Nov. 67
Philip Rosenhagen	18 Nov. 67	31 Aug. 93
William Archibald Armstrong	31 Aug. 93	97

Appointment of Chaplains discontinued.
* From MS. Army List of 1702, in War Office.

Appendix 2

BIOGRAPHICAL NOTICES AND ABSTRACTS OF WAR SERVICES OF OFFICERS WHO HAVE SERVED IN THE KING'S REGIMENT*.

N.B.—The succession numbers correspond with the reference numbers in Appendix I.

INDEX.

Name.	Number.	Name.	Number.
A.		Bazire, Lt. J.	157
		Beaumont, Col. J.	3
Airey, Lt.-Col. G.	36	Beere, Capt. D.	123
Annesley, Surg. F.	233	Berry, Qr.-Mr. A.	230
Armstrong, Col. B.	14	Berwick, James Duke of,	
Armstrong, Maj. T.	65	Col.	2
Auchinleck, Surg. G.	237	Biddle, Asst.-Surg. T. J...	239
Auckland, Lt.-Col. D.	30	Bingham, Lieut. Lord G..	181
		Blackwell, Lt. C. A. R.	212
		Blackmore, Maj. J.	74
B.		Blair, Capt. Æ. G.	136
		Bland, Maj. T.	67
Balfour, Lt. J. H.	204	Bolton, Lt.-Col. M.	32
Ball, Col. T. G.	22	Booth, Capt. J.	102
Bannatyne, Maj. W.	87	Boyd, Lt. E.	172
Bannatyne, Capt. J. M...	117	Bradbridge, Capt. J.	109
Banning, Lt. A. C. G.	203	Brady, Surg. T. C.	236
Barrington, Col. The Hon.		Brereton, Lt. W. L.	199
J.	11	Brooke, Maj. J. C.	77
Barry, Maj. J.	61	Brown, Capt. C. B.	142
Barstow, Lieut. C.	168	Bruce, Ensign J...	217a
Bathe, Lt.-Col. Sir W.			
P. De, Bart.	41	**C.**	
Bayly, Col. Sir H.	17		
Bayly, Maj. W.	79	Caldwell, Lt.-Col. J.	31
Bayly, Capt. A. R.	129	Campbell, Capt. F.	106
Baynes, Maj. S.	75	Campbell, Capt. J. B.	119
Baynes, Maj. G. E.	82	Cathcart, Lt.-Col. Hon. G.	40
Baynes, Capt. R. S.	116	Catherwood, Capt. W.	93

* In compiling these notices, the Editor of HART's *Army List* has kindly permitted me to make extracts from his work, and most of the information given respecting the war services of the officers who were gazetted to the regiment subsequent to 1840 has been obtained from this source.

Name.	Number.	Name.	Number.
Church, Lt. J.	164	Fortye, Maj. T.	70
Cochrane, Lt.-Col. G. H.	57	Foster, Capt. G.	100
Colman, Lt.-Col. W. F. A.	52	Fowler, Lt. V. A. M.	211
Conway, Capt. J.	96	Fry, Lt. C. N.	193
Conyers, Asst.-Sur. J. S.	240		
Cook, Maj. J.	64		
Cope, Capt. A. H.	151	**G.**	
Cornwallis, Maj. F.	59		
Corry, Capt. G.	128	Gardiner, Capt. D.	114
Cotton, Maj. E.	71	Glenkennedy, Ensign	216
Cotton, Lt. S. L.	213	Grattan, Lt. O'D. C.	205
Cusack, Capt. J.	137	Gray, Capt. O. W.	127
		Greathed, Lt.-Col. E. H.	46
D.		Greig, Lt. A.	178
		Grey, Maj. J.	62
		Grierson, Lt. T. B.	187
Dallons, Capt. J.	91	Grogan, Lt.-Col. C. E.	55
Daniell, Maj. E. G.	80		
Dawson, Lt.-Col. E.	35		
Dawson, Capt. J.	143	**H.**	
Dimond, Capt. J. W.	126		
Dooner, Capt. W. T.	146	Haines, Lt.-Col. F. P.	47
Dowson, Lt. C. S.	188	Handy, Maj. B. F.	88
Drew, Lt.-Col. F. B.	54	Hanmer, Maj.	60
Drummie, Lt. J.	169	Hamilton, Maj. T. de C.	81
Drummond, Col. Sir G.	18	Hamilton, Capt. C.	99
Duffy, Col. J.	19	Hamilton, Qr.-Mr. J.	227
Duke, Major A.	68	Hartley, Lt.-Col. B. H. W.	43
Dundas, Col. R.	15	Hartly, Paymr. B.	224
Dundas, Lt.-Col. A.	33	Hill, Lt. H. P.	173
Dundas, Lt. L. C.	208	Hinde, Lt.-Col. J.	48
Dyer, Capt. S. H.	125	Hoghton, Lt.-Col. D.	37
		Holdman, Ens. J.	215
		Hooker, Capt. S.	111
E.		Hotham, Col. Sir C., Bart.	6
		Huddleston, Paymr. G. E.	189
Eason, Lt. R.	161	Humfrey, Capt. T. B.	147
Edgeworth, Lt. W.	194		
Edwards, Lt. J. B.	210		
Ekins, Capt. J.	94	**I.**	
Eustace, Capt. J. H.	110		
Evans, Maj. T.	72		
Evans, Lt. H. J.	209	Irvine, Surg. J.	235
F.		**J.**	
Falls, Paymr. J.	225	Jerrard, Lt. F. B. J.	197
Ferrars, Lord R.	1	Jervis, Capt. E.	145
Finch, Lt. E.	171	Johnston, Lt.-Col. J.	49
Fitzgerald, Capt. J.	108	Jones, Capt. L. J. F.	134
Fitzgerald, Lt. H. E.	192		
Fletcher, Lt. H. A.	201		

Name.	Number.	Name.	Number.
K.		**N.**	
Keatinge, Qr.-Mr. J.	228	Nicholson, Lt. R.	175
Keightly, Lt.-Col. G.	26	Noel, Lt. M.	166
		Nutall, Lt. G.	167
L.			
		O.	
Lafausille, Lt.-Col. J.	28		
Lenoe, Col. C.	8	O'Brien, Lt. D.	163
Lewis, Capt. A.	150	Ogilvie, Lt.-Col. J.	39
Lloyd, Capt. L.	90	Onslow, Col. R.	9
Lloyd, Lt. T. W.	165	Orme, Capt. W. R.	153
Loftus, Maj A.	63		
Longfield, Lt.-Col. J.	44		
Longfield, Lt.-Col. F.	58	**P.**	
Lowry, Capt. A. G.	144		
Lowry, Lt. J.	174	Parry, Capt. S. H. J.	140
		Peister, Lt.-Col. A. S. de.	34
		Pocock, Col. J.	7
M.		Pogson, Lt. W. W.	184
		Powell, Lt. J. G.	176
McCrea, Maj. F. B.	85		
McDermot, Lieut. B. K.	182		
Macdonald, Ens. D. Æ.	220	**R.**	
McGregor, Capt. R. L. G.	131		
McMahon, Capt. J.	112	Ramsay, Lt.-Col.	23
Machen, Capt. D. V.	113	Ramsay, Lt.-Col. L. De	25
MacMurdo, Capt. B.	101	Rickson, Lt. W.	159
MacMurdo, Ens. A.	218	Roberts, Capt. S. N.	149
MacMurdo, Ens. W. M. S.	222	Robertson, Lt.-Col. A. C.	50
McNair, Lt. R.	179	Robertson, Lt. C. G.	207
Macneil, Col. Sir R.	20	Robinson, Capt. W.	105
McNeale, Capt. N.	103	Robinson, Lt. W.	158
McQueen, Capt. J.	133	Ross, Qr.-Mr. J.	226
Madden, Surg. J.	234	Ruck, Capt. H. A.	152
Maisey, Lt. E. L.	206		
Malet, Lt.-Col. C. St. L.	42		
Martin, Lt.-Col. E.	27	**S.**	
Martin, Capt. D. W.	148		
Matthiesen, Ens. J.	221	Sadlier, Capt. H.	107
Maxwell, Maj. B.	69	Sandilands, Capt. E. N.	124
Meade, Maj. R. R.	84	Saumarez, Maj. D.	66
Metge, Capt. W. F.	132	Savage, Ens.	214
Mellor, Lt. L. S.	200	Schletter, Lt. P.	202
Migott, Capt. R.	92	Short, Maj. N.	89
Mompesson, Lt.-Col. J.	29	Souter, Capt. T. G.	122
Monins, Col. E.	21	Spencer, Qr.-Mr. P.	232
Morrison, Col. H.	5	Stanwix, Col. J.	12
Morrison, Lt. W.	160	Stebbing, Captain F. A.	135
Mountsteven, Ens. W. H.	223	Stevens, Col. E.	16
Moyniham, Capt. A.	138	Sutton, Lt.-Col. R.	24
Munday, Maj. J.	73	Swayne, Lt. T.	180

Name.	Number.	Name.	Number.
T.		Webb, Col. J. R.	4
		Webb, Col. D.	13
Tanner, Lt.-Col. E.	56	Webb, Lt.-Col. J. V. W.	
Taylor, Capt. J. M.	154	H.	53
Thompson, Capt.-Lt. T. C.	156	Webb, Capt. J.	98
Toole, Ensign L.	219	Webb, Lt. W. R.	191
Trollop, Capt. J.	95	Welsh, Capt. A. T.	120
Tupper, Maj. De V.	83	Whalley, Capt. F. J.	155
Turner, Maj. C. B.	76	Wheatstone, Maj. J. B.	78
Turner, Lt. A. H.	196	Whelan, Capt. W. E.	141
Turner, Lt. G. V.	198	White, Capt. F.	115
Tyeth, Capt. J.	104	White, Qr.-Mr. G. R. H.	231
		Whiteside, Capt. J.	121
		Whitting, Maj. R.	86
U.		Wilkinson, Capt. F.	97
		Wilson, Lt.-Col. T. M.	45
Unwin, Lt. W.	195	Wilson, Ens. T.	217
Usherwood, Qr.-Mr. C.	229	Wolfe, Col. E.	10
		Woods, Lt.-Col. H. G.	51
V.		Woods, Capt. R. W.	118
Villeneuve, Lt. R.	162		
Vincent, Lt. T. M.	190	**X.**	
		Ximenes, Capt. W. R.	130
		Ximenes, Lt. H.	183
W.			
Walker, Lt. G. F.	185	**Y.**	
Walsh, Lt. T.	186		
Wayland, Lt. J. T.	170	Yates, Asst.-Surg. W. H.	238
Ward, Capt. The Hon. S.		Young, Lt.-Col. R.	38
R. H.	139	Young, Lt. B.	177

COLONELS.

(The notices of the first sixteen colonels are reprinted from the first edition.)

No. 1. Robert Lord Ferrars, a descendant of the ancient and honourable family of Shirley, was born during the usurpation of Cromwell, while his father, Sir Robert Shirley, Bart., was a prisoner in the Tower of London, on account of his loyalty to King Charles I. In 1677, he obtained a confirmation to himself and his heirs, of the ancient barony of Ferrars of Chartley, which had been in abeyance from the time of the decease of Robert Devereux, Earl of Essex, in September, 1646. He held the appointments of master of the horse and steward of the household to Queen Catherine, consort of King Charles II.; and on the breaking out of the rebellion of James Duke of Monmouth, in June, 1685, he raised a company of infantry for the service of King James II., and on 19th June of that year was appointed colonel of the corps, which was then styled "The Princess Anne of Denmark's Regiment" and now bears the distinguished title of The King's Regiment of Foot.

In the following year his lordship's regiment was given to James Fitz-James, afterwards Duke of Berwick. He adhered to the principles of the revolution of 1688; was a member of the privy council in the reigns of King William III. and Queen Anne, and was advanced to the dignity of Viscount Tamworth and Earl Ferrars in September, 1711. He died in 1717.

No. 2. James Fitz-James, natural son of King James II., by Miss Arabella Churchill, was educated on the Continent, and in 1686, he served with the imperialists at the siege of Buda. At the end of the campaign he returned to England, and on 1st November of that year was appointed Colonel of the Princess Anne's, now The King's (Liverpool) Regiment of Foot. In 1687, he was created Duke of Berwick. In the same year His Grace had the command of an Austrian regiment of *cuirassiers*, and served in the Imperial Army against the Turks. On his return to England he was made governor of Portsmouth. In the spring of 1688, he obtained the colonelcy of the Royal Regiment of Horse Guards; and when Lord Churchill joined the Prince of Orange, the Duke of Berwick was promoted to the command of the third troop of Life Guards. Having been educated in the Roman Catholic religion, he adhered to his father at the revolution in 1688, and accompanied His Majesty in his flight to France.

In the following year he attended King James to Ireland, and was appointed colonel of a troop of Irish Life Guards. From this period the Duke of Berwick was constantly engaged in hostility to his country; and he appears to have acted from principle. Being distinguished for a comprehensive mind and a sober judgment, which he assiduously employed in obtaining a knowledge of the profession of arms, the politics of courts, and the tempers and dispositions of men, these acquirements, united with exalted rank, personal bravery, success in war, candour, and affability, procured him the attachment of armies and the esteem of kings, and he may be said to have become a truly great man.

In April, 1689, he signalised himself in an affair with King William's troops at Cladisford; was afterwards engaged in the siege of

Londonderry; and subsequently defeated some Inniskilling militia at Donegal, where he obtained a considerable booty of cattle. In July, of the same year, he defeated another party of militia, near Trelick. In 1690, he was engaged at the Battle of the Boyne, and in the defence of Limerick; but returned to France in the following spring. In 1691, he accompanied Louis XIV. into Flanders,—was employed in the siege of Mons,—and in the attack upon the allies near Catoir. In the following year he was at the Battle of Steenkirk; and in 1693, he was appointed lieutenant-general in the French Army, and was at the Battle of Landen.

In the latter engagement he led a French corps to the charge with great gallantry; but advancing too far into the English lines, his retreat was cut off; he then pulled the white cockade out of his hat, drew the brim over his face, and endeavoured to pass through the army unobserved. But his uncle, Brigadier-General Churchill, recognising the person of the duke's *aide-de-camp,* was induced to look round for the principal, whom he soon discovered and made prisoner. The Duke of Berwick, after having been exchanged for the Duke of Ormond, served with the French Army in the subsequent campaigns in Flanders, until the peace of Ryswick; and was frequently engaged in operations of importance. On the 4th of May, 1698, he was appointed colonel of an Irish regiment in the French service.

On the breaking out of the war, in the reign of Queen Anne, he served the two first campaigns in the Netherlands, and in 1704, was sent with eighteen battalions of infantry, and nineteen squadrons of cavalry, into Spain, where he received the appointment of captain-general of the Spanish forces. In his operations against the Army of Portugal, he had the most distinguished success. By great perseverance he was enabled to advance before the Portuguese were prepared to take the field, and from his skilful operations, Salvatierra and Castello-Branco were taken; the castles of Segura, Rosmarines, and Mont-Santo were delivered up; two Dutch battalions were made prisoners near Formosa; Portalegre was taken by storm; and Castel-de-Vide and Marvao surrendered; but at the end of the campaign the Duke of Berwick was recalled to France, and the reason assigned was,—*He is a devil of an Englishman who will have his own way.*

In 1705, he commanded in Languedoc, where he crushed the rebellion of the Camisards, which was partly of a religious character, and such cruelties were practised by both parties, that the bare recital of them is calculated to cause humanity to shudder. At the close of the campaign he took the city of Nice. In February, 1706, he was advanced to the rank of a marshal of France, and again sent into Spain, where he displayed extraordinary talents in manoeuvring a few troops so as to retard the advance of a large army. After receiving reinforcements from France, Marshal Berwick was enabled to act on the offensive, and, having regained a considerable portion of territory, he concluded the campaign by taking Carthagena.

On Easter Monday, in 1707, he was attacked near Almanza, by the allied English, Dutch, and Portuguese Armies, commanded by the Marquis las Minas and the Earl of Galway, over whom he gained a complete victory; near five thousand men were killed; whole battalions of English were taken prisoners; one hundred and twenty colours and standards, all the artillery, and most of the baggage, fell into the hands of the French. Such was the result of an engagement in which an Englishman commanded the French, and a Frenchman the English Army; and it has been asserted that the slaughter of the English on this occasion would have been much greater, but for the attachment of Marshal Berwick to his countrymen.

After this victory, Requeña and Cuenca were taken; Saragossa surrendered; all Arragon submitted; Xativa was carried by storm, the city reduced to ruins, and the few inhabitants who survived were exiled for their resistance. Alcire, Mirabet, and Monzon, subsequently surrendered; Valencia was taken possession of; and this successful campaign was concluded by the taking of Lerida. The King of Spain, to reward such distinguished skill and bravery, erected the towns of Liria and Xérica, with their dependencies, into a dukedom, which he gave to Marshal Berwick, with the title of *grandee* of the first class.

In 1708, Marshal Berwick served in the Low Countries. In the following year he commanded in Provence and Dauphiny, and the great ability with which he recovered that frontier was rewarded by the gift of the territory of Warty, and a dukedom in France. In the four subsequent years he commanded on the frontiers of Italy with great success; and in 1714, he was sent to besiege Barcelona, which he took by storm. For several years after the restoration of peace, the Duke of Berwick commanded in Guyenne; and in 1719, he led a French Army against Spain, with his usual success. He subsequently led a very retired life until the year 1733, when he was called upon to command the French Army on the Rhine; and in the following year he was killed by a cannon-ball at the siege of Phillipsburg. From him descended the two noble families of the Dukes of Liria and Xérica in

Spain, and of the Dukes of Fitz-James in France.

No. 3. John Beaumont served in the army in the reign of King Charles I.; and on the breaking out of the rebellion of James, Duke of Monmouth, he raised a company of foot for the service of King James II., who promoted him to the Lieutenant-Colonelcy of The Princess Anne's Regiment, which now bears the distinguished title of The King's Regiment of Foot. Being of staunch Protestant principles, he beheld the attempts made by King James II. to subvert the religion and laws of Great Britain, with grief and indignation; and when required to receive a number of Irish Roman Catholic recruits into his corps, he resolved to brave the anger of the king, and to stand boldly forward as the champion of the civil and religious liberties of his country, in which he was supported by several captains. He was brought to trial, and had not the political events, then transpiring, intimidated the Jesuitical counsellors of King James II., this brave patriot would, probably, have lost his life; but he escaped with a sentence of dismissal from the service. On 31st December, 1688, the Prince of Orange gave him the colonelcy of the regiment, with which he served until 1695, when he disposed of his commission. He was governor of Dover Castle several years. His decease occurred on the 3rd of July, 1701.

No. 4. John Richmond Webb was an officer in the Queen's (now Third) Regiment of Dragoons, in the reign of King James II.; and during the wars of King William III., he became so distinguished for his personal bravery, and for constant attention to all the duties of his station, that on 26th December, 1695, His Majesty promoted him to the Colonelcy of the Princess Anne's (now the King's) Regiment or Foot. During the wars of Queen Anne, he served under the great Duke of Marlborough, and distinguished himself on several occasions, particularly at the storming of Venloo in 1702. In January, 1704, he was promoted to the rank of brigadier-general; in 1705, he commanded a brigade at the forcing of the French lines at Helixem, &c.; and soon after the victory at Ramilies in 1706, he was promoted to the rank of major-general.

In 1708, he distinguished himself at the Battle of Oudenarde; and during the siege of the celebrated fortress of Lisle, he commanded the convoy of an immense quantity of stores from Ostend to the besieging army. The fate of Lisle depended on the success of this enterprise. The troops under his orders amounted to about eight thousand men; twenty-two thousand French and Spaniards under Count de la Motte advanced to attack the convoy; and Major-General Webb formed the few men he had with him in the wood of Wynendale; placing a battalion in ambush on each side of the road, he drew up the remainder in an open space at the end of the defile. Thrice the enemy penetrated the wood; but was driven back with severe loss, and eventually the French and Spaniards were forced to relinquish the contest and retire. Major-General Webb's conduct on this occasion was highly commended, and he received the thanks of Her Majesty Queen Anne, and of Parliament, for his skill and bravery.

★★★★★★

"*Lunae 13° die Decembris; Anno 7° Annae Reginae*, 1708.
Resolved, Nemine contradicente,—'That the thanks of this House be given to Major-General Webb for the great and eminent services performed by him at the Battle of Wynendale.'
"And Major-General Webb being then in the House, Mr. Speaker gave him (in his place) the thanks of the House accordingly, as followeth:—
'Major-General Webb,—'Tis with pleasure, Sir, I receive the commands of the House to return you their thanks for the great and eminent services performed by you at the Battle of Wynendale,
'We are all sensible, how much the reducing of the fortress of Lisle is owing to your courage and conduct.
'I wish a more early notice than the motion now made, had been given me, that I might have expressed myself more suitably to the occasion; though at the same time I am very sensible, I should then have wanted expressions.
'One of the greatest honours we are capable of conferring, is due to your merits; and as such, in obedience to command, I now give you the unanimous thanks of the House for your great services performed.'
"Upon which Major-General Webb said;
'Mr. Speaker,—I return my hearty thanks to this honourable House for the great honour they have been pleased to do me. The success I had at Wynendale, is owing to the great courage and resolution, which the officers and soldiers showed in that action.
'I have always endeavoured to deserve the good opinion of the House, and 'tis the greatest pleasure to me imaginable, that I have served my queen and my country, to their satisfaction.'

******

On the 1st of January, 1709, he was promoted to the rank of lieutenant-general; and at the Battle of Malplaquet, on the 11th of September following, he highly distinguished himself and was dangerously wounded. In 1712, he was advanced to the rank of general and placed in the command of the troops in South Britain, under the Duke of Ormond, Captain-General of Her Majesty's forces.

In 1715, political events occasioned his removal from all his commands; but his former services were rewarded with the government of the Isle of Wight. He died on the 5th of September, 1724.

No. 5. Henry Morrison served many years in the second regiment of Foot Guards, and was promoted to the command of a company in December, 1694. He served under King William III. in the Netherlands, and was taken prisoner at the storming of the outworks of the fortress of Namur in July, 1695. He continued to serve in the Foot Guards in the reign of Queen Anne; obtained the rank of colonel in the army in 1704, that of brigadier-general in 1710, and in April, 1711, he was appointed second major of the regiment. On 5th August, 1715, he purchased the Colonelcy of The Queen's (now The King's) Regiment of Foot, which he retained until his decease in 1720.

No. 6. Charles Hotham, eldest son of the Rev. Charles Hotham, rector of Wigan, succeeded to the dignity of baronet on the decease of his uncle in 1691. He served with distinction in the wars of King William III., and also under the great Duke of Marlborough in the reign of Queen Anne. In 1705, he obtained the colonelcy of a regiment of foot, with which he proceeded to Spain in 1706, and was in garrison at Alicant when the unfortunate Battle of Almanza was fought. Sir Charles served with reputation daring the remainder of the war; but his regiment, having suffered severely in the defence of several fortified towns, was disbanded in Catalonia in 1708. He was appointed brigadier-general in 1710; and shortly after the accession of King George I., he was commissioned to raise a regiment of foot, which, after the suppression of the rebellion of the Earl of Mar, was sent to Ireland, and disbanded in the following year. Sir Charles was afterwards appointed colonel of a newly-raised regiment of dragoons, which was disbanded in November, 1718.

On the 7th of July, 1719, the Colonelcy of the Thirty-Sixth regiment of Foot was conferred on Sir Charles Hotham; he was removed to the Eighth Foot on 3rd December, 1720; and in April following to the Royal Dragoons. His decease occurred on the 8th of January, 1720.

No. 7. John Pocock obtained a commission in a regiment of foot in June, 1695; and having signalised himself in the wars of Queen Anne, he was promoted to the rank of colonel in the army in 1707. In 1710, he succeeded William Lord Strathnaver in the colonelcy of a regiment of foot, with which he served in Flanders under the great Duke of Marlborough, and afterwards under the Duke of Ormond. At the peace of Utrecht his regiment was disbanded; and in 1715, he was commissioned to raise a regiment of foot for the service of King George I. After the suppression of the rebellion of the Earl of Mar, this regiment was sent to Ireland, where it was disbanded in 1718: and in December, 1720, he was appointed to the colonelcy of the Thirty-Sixth foot, from which he was removed on 21st April, 1721, to The King's Regiment. On the expectation of England becoming involved in a war, in 1727, he was promoted to the rank of brigadier-general. He died in April, 1732, at his house in Leicester Fields, London.

No. 8. Charles Lenoe entered the army in the reign of Queen Anne; his first commission bearing date the 4th of December, 1704; and he served under the Duke of Marlborough. In 1721, he was promoted to the colonelcy of the Thirty-sixth Foot, and on 8th May, 1732, he was honoured with the command of the Eighth, or The King's Regiment, which he retained until his decease in December, 1738.

No. 9. Richard Onslow entered the army in 1716; and in 1733, he was promoted to the rank of colonel. In November, 1738, King George II. appointed him to the colonelcy of the Thirty-Ninth Regiment; and on 6th June, 1739, gave him the colonelcy of The Eighth Regiment. He was promoted to the rank of major-general in 1743, and was removed to the first troop of Horse Grenadier Guards in 1745: he obtained the rank of lieutenant-general in 1747. He continued at the head of the first troop of Horse Grenadier Guards until his decease in 1760.

No. 10. Edward Wolfe obtained his first commission on the breaking out of the war in the year 1702, and he was actively engaged in the several campaigns until the peace of Utrecht. He rose to the rank of major in Stanwix's (Twelfth) Regiment; and afterwards held the commission of captain and lieutenant-colonel in the Third Foot Guards. On the breaking out of the war with Spain, in 1739, he was appointed colonel of a corps which was numbered the Forty-Fourth

Foot, or First Marines; and was employed in the expedition against Carthagena, in 1741. In 1743, he was promoted to the rank of brigadier-general, and on 25th April, 1745, King George II. rewarded his services at the head of the First Marines with the command of The King's Regiment: in the following month he was promoted to the rank of major-general, and in 1747, to that of lieutenant-general. He died 27th March, 1759.

No. 11. The Honourable John Barrington, third son of John, first Viscount Barrington, served in the Third Foot Guards, and in 1746, he obtained the commission of captain-lieutenant in the Second Foot Guards; in which corps he was promoted to the rank of captain and lieutenant-colonel in 1748. In 1756, he was promoted to the rank of colonel, and appointed *aide-de-camp* to King George II. In 1758, His Majesty gave him the colonelcy of the Sixty-Fourth Regiment,— then formed of the Second Battalion of the Eleventh; promoted him to the local rank of major-general in the West Indies, and sent him second in command of an expedition against the French West India Islands. Major-General Hopson dying in the West Indies, the command of the troops devolved on Major-General Barrington, who succeeded in reducing the valuable island of Guadaloupe. In June, 1759, he was removed to the Fortieth Regiment; and on 24th October of the same year, to the Eighth, or The King's: he was also appointed Governor of Berwick. He died at Paris, on the 2nd of April, 1764.

No. 12. John Stanwix was appointed ensign in a regiment of foot in 1706, and served in the army thirty-nine years before he obtained the rank of lieutenant-colonel (4th October, 1745). He was for several years lieutenant-colonel of the Seventy-First Foot; which corps was disbanded in 1749. He was subsequently deputy quarter-master-general, and in 1755, he was appointed colonel-commandant of a battalion of the Sixtieth Regiment. He was promoted to the rank of major-general in 1759, and to that of lieutenant-general in 1761: on 11th April, 1764, he was removed to the colonelcy of The King's Regiment. In 1766, he was drowned on his passage from Ireland.

No. 13. Daniel Webb, having chosen the profession of arms, purchased a commission as ensign in a regiment of foot, on the 20th of March, 1720. He was promoted to the majority of the Eighth Horse, now Seventh Dragoon Guards, in 1742, and served at the battle of Dettingen, in 1743, where his regiment highly distinguished itself. In April, 1745, he succeeded Lieutenant-Colonel Francis Ligonier (who was promoted to the colonelcy of the Forty-Eighth Foot) in the lieutenant-colonelcy, and the Eighth Horse, under his command, acquired additional honours at the Battle of Fontenoy. He was promoted to the colonelcy of the Forty-Eighth Foot, in 1755: obtained the rank of major-general in 1759; that of lieutenant-general in 1761; on 18th December, 1766, he was removed to the Eighth, or The King's Regiment, and on 22nd October, 1772, to the Fourteenth Light Dragoons, which he retained until his death on 11th November, 1773. (As mentioned at the beginning of Appendix 1, the name of any officer who entered the regiment after 1st January, and left it before 31 at December of the same year, will most probably not be found in the Army List).

No. 14. Bigoe Armstrong, after a progressive service in the subordinate commissions, with reputation to himself and advantage to his country, was promoted to the lieutenant-colonelcy of the Eighteenth Foot, on the 25th of November, 1752; and in 1760, his excellent conduct on all occasions was rewarded with the colonelcy of the Eighty-Third—a corps raised in Ireland, in 1758, and disbanded in 1763. In 1762, he was promoted to the rank of major-general, and on 20th October, 1771, he was appointed Colonel of the Eighth, The King's Regiment; in 1772, he was promoted to the rank of lieutenant-general, and in 1783, to that of general. He died at his house in Upper Wimpole Street, Cavendish Square, on the 24th of July, 1794.

★★★★★★

General Bigoe Armstrong held the appointment of colonel of the King's Regiment from 20th October, 1771, to 24th July, 1794. During the twenty-three years fourteen officers of the name of Armstrong served in the regiment; of these, one entered as a chaplain, and ten as ensigns; ultimately two became majors, three captains, and eight left the service or exchanged before they attained the rank of captain. One of the fourteen. Major Thomas Armstrong, was killed at the capture of Guadaloupe, June, 1794, another. Major George Armstrong, held the appointment of adjutant from 30th September, 1782, to 17th July, 1790. (For dates of the commissions held by these officers, *vide* Appendix No. 1.)

★★★★★★

No. 15. Ralph Dundas was appointed Cornet in the Fourth Dragoons in 1755, and in February, 1762, he obtained the command of a troop in the Eleventh Dragoons, then serving in Germany under Prince Ferdinand of Brunswick. His regiment returned to England in the following year; in 1770, he was appointed to the majority, and in 1775, to the lieutenant-colonelcy of that distinguished corps. His zealous attention to all his duties, as commanding-officer of the Eleventh Dragoons, was rewarded in 1781, with the rank of colonel; in 1790, with that of major-general; and on 30th July, 1794, with the colonelcy of the Eighth, or The King's Regiment of Foot. He was promoted to the rank of lieutenant-general in 1797, and to that of general in 1802: he was also rewarded with the government of Duncannon Fort. He died on the 7th of February, 1814.

No. 16. Edmund Stevens procured, in April, 1760, a commission of cornet in the Twenty-First Dragoons, or Royal Foresters, then raised by the Marquis of Granby, and disbanded in 1763. In November, 1760, he was removed to the Royal Dragoons, and in 1761, to the Second Foot Guards, in which corps he served as adjutant several years, and was promoted to the rank of lieutenant and captain in 1768. In 1776, he was appointed major of brigade to the Foot Guards in North America; and he served at the reduction of Long Island, at the Battles of Brandywine, and German-town, in 1777; and at Monmouth in the following year. In May, 1778, he was promoted to the rank of captain and lieutenant-colonel, in the First Foot Guards, in which corps he obtained a majority in 1792, and a lieutenant-colonelcy in 1795.

He was promoted to the rank of major-general in 1793; was appointed governor of Fort William in 1795, and colonel of the Sixty-Fifth Regiment in 1797. He served on the staff at the camp at Warley, under General the Marquis Cornwallis, in 1795; in London, and afterwards at Winchester and Portsmouth, in 1797. In 1798, he was promoted to the rank of lieutenant-general; and he served on the staff at various encampments in England, until 1802; in 1803, he was promoted to the rank of general. On 8th February, 1814, His Royal Highness the Prince Regent conferred on the veteran General Edmund Stevens, the colonelcy of the Eighth, or The King's Regiment of Foot, which he retained until his decease in 1825.

No. 17. Sir Henry Bayly, G.C.H., was appointed ensign in the Eighty-Fifth Foot on 12th April, 1782. In 1873, the Eighty-Fifth was disbanded, and he was placed on half pay. (The details of Sir H. Bayly's services are extracted from the records of the Coldstream Guards, and were communicated to me by Colonel Fremantle.—A. C R.)

On 27th October, 1790, he was appointed ensign in the Coldstream Guards, and posted to the Second Battalion. In May, 1793, he was transferred to the First Battalion, which was then serving in Holland. He was present at the Battle of Famars (23rd May), siege of Valenciennes (23rd May to 26th July), and at the Battle of Lincelles, where he was wounded (18th August, 1793). On 28th August, 1793, he was promoted lieutenant and captain in Second Battalion then serving in England. From this date until March, 1794, he was on sick leave, and from March until November employed in recruiting duties.

In April, 1798, he was transferred to the First Battalion, and served with it under the Duke of York in the expedition to the Helder from August to October, 1799. On 5th September, 1799, he was promoted to captain and lieutenant-colonel in the Second Battalion. In June, 1804, he was transferred to the First Battalion, and in January, 1805, again transferred to the Second Battalion. On 25th October, 1809, he was promoted colonel, and on 1st January, 1812, major-general. From July, 1813, to March, 1814, he was on the staff of the Home District, from which he was transferred to the command of a brigade of Provisional Militia in the South of France. On 25th July, 1814, he ceased to be borne on the strength of the Coldstreams. On 27th May, 1825, he was promoted lieutenant-general, and on 13th September of the same year appointed Colonel of the King's Regiment. In 1834, he was made a G.C.H., and 23rd November, 1841, promoted general. He died on 23rd April, 1846.

No. 18. Sir Gordon Drummond, G.C.B., the fourth son of Colin Drummond, Esq., of Concraig and Megginch Castle, county of Perth, was born 27th September, 1772, and educated at Great Braddon, Essex. (This notice has been revised and corrected by Sir Gordon Drummond's daughter, the Right Honourable the Countess of Effingham.—A. C. R.)

The dates of his commissions and transfers are:—21st September, 1789, ensign. First Royal Scots; 31st March, 1791, lieutenant, promoted into Forty-First Regiment; 31st January, 1792, captain. Forty-First Regiment; 28th February, 1794, major, promoted into Twenty-Third Regiment; 22nd April, 1794, promoted lieutenant-colonel in the King's Regiment, on the strength of which he continued to be borne in this rank until 28th July, 1814; 25th October, 1809, colonel (by brevet); 1st January, 1805, major-general; 4th June, 1811, lieutenant-general; 27th May, 1825, general.

On 8th February, 1814, he was appointed colonel of the Ninety-Seventh, afterwards Ninety-Sixth (or the Queen's Own Regiment); which regiment having been reduced in 1818, on 11th March, 1819, he was appointed colonel of the Eighty-Eighth Regiment; on 16th January, 1824, transferred to the Seventy First Highland Light Infantry; on 21st September, 1829, to the Forty-Ninth Regiment; and on 24th April, 1846, to the King's Regiment. He was made a K.C.B. in 1814, and a G.C.B. in 1817.

In 1792, he served as A.D.C. on the staff of Lord Westmoreland.

In 1794-95, he served in the Twenty-Third Regiment with the army in Holland under the Duke of York, and distinguished himself at the siege of Nimeguen.

In 1801, he embarked for Egypt as Lieutenant-Colonel of the King's Regiment. He commanded the regiment at the landing, at the battles of 8th, 13th, and 21st March, at the action of Ramanieh, and at the surrender of Cairo and Alexandria. For these services he received the Egyptian medal. In 1804, he was appointed brigadier-general on the staff in England; from 1805, to 1807, he served under Sir Eyre Coote in the West Indies; in 1808, he was transferred to the Canadian, and in 1811, to the Irish staff. He continued to serve in Ireland in command of the south-eastern district until 1813, when he was sent to Canada as second in command under Sir George Prevost. He commanded the troops employed at the capture of Fort Niagara, at the actions of Black Rock, Buffalo, and Oswego, at the Battle of Lundy's Lane, and at the attack on Fort Erie; at Lundy's Lane he was severely wounded in the neck, and had a horse shot under him.

******

For an account of General Drummond's operations in Canada, *vide* Allison's Europe, vol. x; *vide* also despatches in the *Annual Register* for 1814, vol. lvi, describing capture of Fort Niagara, Expedition against Oswego, the action of the Falls of Niagara, repulse of sortie of garrison of Fort Erie.

******

On the recall of Sir George Prevost, he was made commander of the forces, and entrusted with the administration in chief of the province of Canada. These duties he performed until 1816, when he was relieved, at his own request, and returned to England.

On 17th October, 1807, he married Margaret, youngest daughter of W. Russel, Esq., of Brancepeth Castle, county of Durham.

His death took place at his house in Norfolk-street, Parklane, on

10th of October, 1854; he was then in his 82nd year, and was senior general of the army. He was buried at Kensal Green Cemetery.

His eldest son, Gordon, on the 10th June, 1826, was appointed ensign in the Coldstream Guards; he commanded the brigade of Guards at the fall of St. Sebastopol, and died on 17th November, 1856, when in command of the First Battalion of the Coldstreams.

No. 19. John Duffy, C.B., K.C., was appointed ensign on 21st October, 1795. On 6th January, 1796, he was promoted to a lieutenancy in the Tenth Foot, and on 13th July, 1797, appointed adjutant. On 12th August, 1804, he was promoted to a company in the Forty-Third Light Infantry, and in the same regiment to a majority on 17th June, 1813, and to a lieutenant-colonelcy 22nd November, 1813. On 21st September, 1815, he was transferred to the Rifle Brigade, and on 9th September, 1819, to the King's Regiment. On 20th March, 1828, he retired on half pay.

He was promoted to be colonel on 22nd July, 1830; major-general on 23rd November, 1841; and lieutenant-general 11th November, 1857. On 18th May, 1849, he was appointed colonel of the Twenty-Eighth Foot, and on 10th October, 1854, transferred to the King's Regiment.

He was a Companion of the Bath and a Knight of the Crescent.

In 1796, he served in the West Indies under Sir Ralph Abercromby, and afterwards in the Winter Expedition to the coast of Holland.

In 1799, he served in the East Indies with the force under Sir David Baird.

In 1801, he served in Egypt under Sir Ralph Abercromby, and received a medal.

In 1807, he served with the Forty-Third at the siege and capture of Copenhagen, and at the Battle of Kioge.

In 1808-9, he served with the Forty-Third in Spain under Sir John Moore.

From 1809, to 1813, he again served in Spain with the Forty-Third, and was present at the actions of Condeixa, Pombal, Redinha, and Sabugal; at the Battle of Fuentes d'Onor and at the siege of Ciudad Rodrigo, where he commanded the storming party at the assault of the outwork of Fort Raymond; at the siege and assault of Badajos; at the Battle of Vittoria, where he received a wound in the head; at several skirmishes in the Pyrenees and on the Bidassoa; at the action of the heights of Vera, and at the Battles of the Nivelle and Nive. He received a gold medal for Badajos and the silver Peninsular War medal with six clasps for Fuentes d'Onor, Ciudad Rodrigo, Vittoria, Pyrenees, Nivelle, and Nive.

He died on 14th October, 1854.

******

This notice is compiled from Hart's *Army List* and from the records of the King's and Forty-Third Regiments. Previous to 1811, General John Duffy is designated in the Army List "James."—A. C. B.

******

No. 20. Roderick M'Neill was appointed ensign in the Fifty-Second Light Infantry on 17th March, 1808. The dates of his subsequent promotions, exchanges, and transfers are: 9th May, 1809, lieutenant Fifty-Second. In 1818, he was placed on half-pay; 1st December, 1814, captain Sixtieth Rifles; 1st July, 1819, exchanged to First Life Guards; 9th August, 1821, major First Life Guards; 29th December, 1821, exchanged to Eighty-Fourth Foot; 25th June, 1822, lieutenant-colonel Eighty-Fourth; 17th June, 1828, placed on half-pay; 15th April, 1842, appointed to Seventy-Eighth Highlanders; 10th January, 1837, colonel; 9th November, 1846, major-general; 20th June, 1854, lieutenant-general; 21st December, 1862, general.

He was appointed Colonel of the King's on 8th March, 1855; and was transferred to the Seventy-Eighth Highlanders on 3rd June, 1860.

In 1809, he served with the Fifty-Second in the Peninsula under Sir John Moore, and received the Peninsular War medal, afterwards he was present with his regiment during the Walcheren Expedition.

In 1813, he served in Sweden and Pomerania.

In 1813, he served in Holland with the Sixtieth, and was present at the attack on Bergen-op-Zoom.

In 1815, he was present at the Battle of Waterloo, and received the medal. (This abstract is entirely taken from Hart's *Army List*.—A. C. R.)

He died on 22nd October, 1863.

No. 21. Eaton Monins, son of John Monins, Esq., was born at Canterbury in the year 1795, and was educated at Charterhouse. (This notice has been revised and corrected by the widow of Major-General Monins.—A. C. R.)

The dates of his commissions and exchanges are:—1st December, 1814, ensign, Fifty-Second Light Infantry; 9th September, 1819, lieutenant; 23rd June, 1825, captain; 8th April, 1826, exchanged to Sixty-

Ninth Regiment; 19th November, 1830, major; 2nd October, 1835, lieutenant-colonel; 9th November, 1846, colonel by brevet; 20th June, 1854, major-general; 3rd June, 1860, appointed Colonel of the King's Regiment.

In 1815, while an ensign in the Fifty-Third, he was present at the Battle of Waterloo and received the medal. After his promotion to his lieutenancy he held the appointment of adjutant of the Fifty-Second Light Infantry from 10th January, 1822, to 29th May, 1823. He served with the Sixty-Ninth Regiment in the West Indies (1836-40), in North America (1840-42), in Malta (1847-48), and on the 10th November, 1848, he retired on half-pay, after which he did not return to regimental duty or hold any staff appointment.

On 21st October, 1824, he married Margaret, daughter of Thomas Newsham, Esq.

His death took place on the 16th June, 1861, at his residence, Wellesley House, Upper Walmer, Kent. He was buried in the parish church of St. Mary, Walmer, in the tower of which church a memorial turret clock was placed by his widow.

No. 22. Thomas Gerrard Ball, the son of Abraham Ball, Esq., of the city of Chester, was born in Chester, on 24th January, 1791, and educated at Chester. (This notice has been revised and corrected by General Ball.—A. C R.)

In August, 1801, (being then in his 11th year), he entered the Royal Navy, as midshipman, on board the *Saturn*, line-of-battle ship, commanded by Rear-Admiral Tottie, which ship formed part of the squadron employed in the blockade of Brest. At the conclusion of the Peace of Amiens, he returned home, but was soon afterwards sent to the West Indies. Subsequently, when war again broke out, he served in the *Magicienne* and *Fortuneé* frigates, commanded by Captain Henry Vansittart, which were employed in blockading the French, Dutch, and Spanish ports.

After serving about six years in the navy, during the last three of which he was on the West India station, on the 17th September, 1807, he was appointed ensign in the Thirty-Fourth Regiment; he was promoted in it lieutenant on 1st December, 1808, and captain, 7th April, 1814. On 25th June, 1817, when the second battalion of the Thirty-Fourth was reduced, he was placed on half-pay, but on 25th December of the same year he was reappointed to the command of a company in the King's. He was promoted major on 24th June, 1824, and lieutenant-colonel, 20th October, 1855. In this rank he continued to serve until 25th October, 1842, when he retired on half-pay.

The dates of his other commissions are:—Colonel (by brevet), 9th June, 1846; major-general, 20th June, 1854; lieutenant-general, 7th March, 1862; general, 10th June, 1870. On 24th April, 1860, he was appointed colonel of the Forty-Sixth Regiment, and on 17th June, 1861, was transferred to The King's Regiment.

From June, 1809, until November, 1813, he served in the Peninsula with the Second Battalion of the Thirty-Fourth Regiment, he was present at the Battle of Busaco, siege of Badajoz, Battle of Albuera, actions at Arroyo-de-Molinos and Almiraz, Battle of Vittoria, and action of the pass of Maya. At the Battle of Vittoria he was wounded in the head, and at the pass of Maya, severely wounded in the left leg. For these services he received the Peninsular medal with three clasps.

He married first, Elizabeth, daughter of the Honourable Edward Massey, of Chester; second, Charlotte, daughter of —— Mason, Esq., of Sheffield; third, Catherine, youngest daughter of the Reverend Canon Jones, Rural Dean and Vicar of Llanrhaiadr, North Wales.

LIEUTENANT-COLONELS.

No. 23. —— Ramsay, on the dismissal of Lieutenant-Colonel John Beaumont, (September, 1688), was appointed his successor. (*Vide* Records part 1.)

(I have not been able to ascertain how long he commanded the regiment, or what other officers served with it in the rank of lieutenant-colonel between 1688, and 1702.—A. C. R.)

No. 24. Richard Sutton commanded the King's for about five years and eight months (from 10th December, 1702, until 25th March, 1708); during this period the regiment was serving in the Low Countries and Germany with the Duke of Marlborough, and was present at the great Battles of Blenheim and Ramilies, and at many sieges and minor actions. Lieutenant-Colonel Sutton was promoted colonel by brevet on 1st January, 1706.

No. 25. Louis de Ramsay succeeded to the command of the regiment on 25th March, 1708; during the five preceding years he had served with it in the rank of major with great distinction; he had given repeated proofs of valour and ability, and had been promoted lieutenant-colonel by brevet on 1st January, 1706.

He was killed at the Battle of Malplaquet on 11th September,

1709, while in command of the regiment. (*Vide Records* part 1.)

There is no record of the names of the lieutenant-colonels of the King's between 11th September, 1709, and 1st February, 1731.

No. 26. George Keightly entered the service as ensign in 1703, was promoted captain in 1700, major in 1708, and Lieutenant-Colonel of the King's Regiment on 1st February, 1731. He commanded the regiment for fourteen years, and served with it in the campaigns in Germany and the Low Countries of 1743, 44, and 45.

On 26th June, 1748, he was wounded at the Battle of Dettingen; and on 11th May, 1745, he was again wounded at the Battle of Fontenoy.—*Vide Records*, part 1.

No. 27. Edmund Martin entered the service as ensign in 1703, was appointed Captain in the King's 17th March, 1718; promoted major 6th December, 1730; promoted to be lieutenant-colonel, and transferred to Price's Regiment 7th February, 1741; again transferred to the King's on 1st May, 1745. He commanded the regiment for the next four years until his death on 26th April, 1740. During his period of command the regiment was serving in the Netherlands, and was present at the Battles of Roucoux and Val; at the latter battle (1st July, 1847), Lieutenant-Colonel Martin received a wound.—*Vide Records*, part 1.

No. 28. John Lafausille received the commission of ensign 26th August, 1708. The dates of his other commissions are: lieutenant 12th November, 1726; captain-lieutenant 15th June, 1743; captain 14th July, 1743; major 17th February, 1746; lieutenant-colonel 27th April, 1740.

In the MS. Army List of 1743, his name appears as fourth in the list of lieutenants, so from that date until he succeeded to the command of the regiment in 1740, his promotion was rapid. He held command for upwards of nine years until 24th August, 1758, when the Second Battalion of the King's was constituted the Sixty-Third Regiment. Lieutenant-Colonel J. Lafausille was then promoted to be colonel of the Sixth-Sixth Regiment, and continued to command it until his death on 19th January, 1763.

He served in the King's during the campaigns of 1742, 43, 45, including the Battles of Dettingen, Fontenoy, Falkirk, Culloden, Roucoux, and Val. In the last of these battles he received a wound.—*Vide Records,* part 1.

No. 29. John Mompesson was transferred on 28th August, 1758, to the King's Regiment from the Fiftieth, in which regiment his lieutenant-colonel's commission was dated 16th December, 1755. He commanded the King's for ten years, during which period the regiment served in the campaigns of 1760, 61-62, and was present at the Battle of Warbourg, surprise of Zierenberg, Battles of Campen, Kirch-Denkern, and Groebenstein.—*Vide Records*, part 1.

No. 30. Dudley Auckland was transferred from the Thirty-Sixth Regiment and promoted to a majority in the King's Regiment on 24th June, 1767. He was then a brevet lieutenant-colonel (date 11th July, 1762); the date of his captain's commission was 1st October, 1755. On 23rd November, 1768, he succeeded to the command of the regiment, which he held for the next four years until 27th October, 1772.

During his term of command, the regiment was quartered in Canada, and was not engaged in any military operation.—*Vide Records*, part 1.

No. 31. John Caldwell's commission of captain is dated 20th December, 1755. He was then serving in the Seventh Fusiliers, of which regiment he was promoted to be major on 18th July, 1766. He was promoted to be lieutenant-colonel, and transferred to the King's on 27th October, 1772. He commanded the regiment for four years, and retired from the service on 11th November, 1776. During this period the regiment was quartered in Canada, and, in the campaign of 1776, it took part in the operations for expelling the Americans from Canada.—*Vide Records* part 1.

No. 32. Mason Bolton's commission of lieutenant is dated 2nd October, 1755. He was then serving in the Ninth Foot, and in that regiment was promoted captain on 23rd March, 1764, and major 31st May, 1773. On 11th November, 1776, he was promoted lieutenant-colonel, and transferred to the King's.

He commanded the regiment for four years, until he retired from the service on 1st November, 1780. The King's was serving in Canada, where the chief duty assigned to it was the protection of the frontier.— *Vide Records* part 1.

No. 33. Alexander Dundas was transferred from the Thirty-Fourth Regiment on 1st November, 1780. The dates of his commissions in the Thirty-Fourth are:—Captain 25th August, 1762; major, 6th January, 1776. He commanded the King's for rather less than three years, and retired from the service on 13th September, 1783. During his period of command the regiment was quartered in Canada.— *Vide*

Records part 1.

No. 34. Arent Schuyler De Peister was born in 1726, and was promoted to the Lieutenant-Colonelcy of the King's on 13th September, 1783. (I am indebted to the Reverend John Paton, minister of St. Michael's Church, Dumfries, for the details subsequent to Colonel S. de Peister's retirement.)

The dates of his other commissions in the regiment are:—Major, 6th May, 1777; captain, 3rd November, 1768; lieutenant, 21st September, 1757. During the campaigns in Germany of 1760-61-62, he served as lieutenant; and in the American War, from 1776, to 1782, first as captain, afterwards as major. He commanded the King's for upwards of ten years, during which time the regiment was quartered in England and Ireland, and retired from the service on 3rd April, 1794.

He then settled in Dumfries, and married Rebecca Blair, whose father had been provost of the town in the years 1790-91-92. After his marriage he purchased Mavis Grove, an estate on the banks of the Nith, about three miles from Dumfries. He was appointed Colonel of the Dumfries Volunteers, which regiment he continued to command until his death, on 26th November, 1822, at the age of 96. He was buried in the churchyard of St. Michael's Church. The funeral was a public one, and a tombstone was erected to his memory, on which were inscribed some verses written by himself.

★★★★★★

He possessed considerable poetical talent, and was an intimate friend of the poet Burns, as were also his wife and his wife's sister. Burns' verses beginning,—

My honoured Colonel, deeply I feel
Your interest in the poets' weal—

were addressed to Colonel S. de Peister. Jean and Philadelphia McMurdo, his wife's nieces, are also celebrated in several of Burns' songs,

★★★★★★

Two nephews and a grand nephew of Mrs. Schuyler De Peister have served in the King's Regiment, namely, Captain Bryce McMurdo (No. 101), his brother Archibald (No. 218), and William Montagu, son of Archibald (No. 222).

Mrs. McMurdo, of Mavis Grove, widow of Colonel J. McMurdo, the elder brother of Sir William, possesses a very interesting portrait of Colonel Schuyler de Peister, dressed in the uniform worn by the

King's in 1790, and General Sir Wm. M. S. McMurdo possesses an excellent copy of this portrait. Another good portrait of Colonel S. de Peister, not dressed in uniform, is now in possession of Major Greig, C.B., Chief of the Liverpool Police.—*Vide Records*, part1.

No. 35. Edward Dawson was appointed ensign in the Fourth Regiment 1st April, 1782, promoted to be lieutenant 28th February, 1785; to be captain, and transferred to Fifty-First Regiment 5th March, 1791; to be major, and transferred to the King's, 31st August, 1793. He succeeded to the lieutenant-colonelcy of the regiment on 3rd April, 1794, and, after commanding it for two years, retired from the service on 1st March, 1796.

The King's during his term of command was serving in Holland, and for a short time took part in the defence of Nimeguen in November, 1794.—*Vide Records*, part 1.

No. 36. George Airey, son of George J. Airey, Esq., a landed proprietor in Northumberland, was born at Newcastle-on-Tyne in 1759, and was educated there. (This notice has been revised by General Lord Airey.)

The dates of his commissions and exchanges are:—6th December, 1779, ensign in Ninety-First Regiment; 6th July, 1781, lieutenant; 2nd January, 1782, exchanged to Forty-Eighth Regiment; 19th November, 1788, captain; 1st May, 1796, major, and transferred to Sixty-Eighth Regiment; 4th May, 1798, lieutenant-colonel, and transferred to Eighth, the King's Regiment; 25th April, 1808, brevet colonel; 4th June, 1811, major-general; 19th July, 1821, lieutenant-general; 28th October, 1823, colonel of Thirty-Ninth Regiment.

He was knighted in 1821, and in 1824, was made a Knight Commander of the Royal Hanoverian Guelphic Order.

In 1794, he commanded a company in a battalion composed of light companies of regiments which formed part of the force under the command of Lieutenant General Sir Charles Grey, and was present at the capture of the Islands of Martinique and Guadaloupe. The same year he served as *aide-de-camp* on the staff of Lieutenant-General Tonyn.

In 1795, he was appointed assistant adjutant-general in the West Indies. In 1798, he accompanied the King's Regiment to Minorca, but was soon afterwards appointed deputy quartermaster-general at Malta on the staff of Major-General Fox.

In 1801, he was detached on special service to the Island of Elba, where he assumed command of three hundred English soldiers, eight hundred Tuscan troops, and four hundred Corsicans, in the pay of Great Britain. This insignificant force was inspired by its commander with so determined a spirit that it successfully defended the town of Port Ferrajo against the French for full five months, from July, 1801, until hostilities were suspended and the town handed over to the French in accordance with the preliminary conditions of the Peace of Amiens.

The successful resistance of a handful of men to the troops who had vanquished the greatest military monarchies of Europe excited (says Alison) a great sensation both in England and on the Continent.

★★★★★★

Vide History of Europe, 3rd Edition, Edinburgh, 1839, vol. iv, chap. xxxii, concerning this service, the following passage occurs in the *Annual Register* for 1802, (vol. xliv):—"It is much to be regretted that the particulars of the gallant and glorious defence of Elba by a handful of troops under the command of Colonel Airey of the Eighth has never yet come in a satisfactory form before the public." See also Dumas' *Precis des Evénemens Militaires* (Edition Paris, 1817), vol. v, and *Victoires Conquêtes des Francais* (Edition Paris, 1835), vol. vii, chap. xix.

Dumas says:—"The Governor, Lieutenant-Colonel Airey, a brave man whose name deserves to be remembered, could neither be deceived nor seduced by any proposal of the enemy.

"A rich merchant having dared to advise the surrender of the place, Lieut.-Colonel Airey caused him to be shot .... It was, indeed, a strange spectacle to see a single small town, situated in an island almost touching the Continent, easy of access, and already occupied by our troops, arresting the conquerors of Europe and filling them with astonishment by its obstinate resistance."

★★★★★★

At the termination of the war Colonel Airey resumed the duties of deputy quartermaster-general on the staff of Major-General Fox, whose division was then at Minorca; he was afterwards transferred to the Irish staff, and, after serving some time on it, returned to the staff of Major-General Fox at Gibraltar as military secretary.

In 1807, he served in Egypt as acting deputy adjutant-general during the operations from 17th, to 21st March, which resulted in the capitulation of Alexandria (mentioned in despatches).

In 1808, he was appointed deputy adjutant-general to the army in Sicily, and in 1810, in addition to his staff duties, he was appointed to the command of a brigade which formed part of the force held in readiness to repel the threatened invasion of Murat. After his promotion to the rank of major-general on 4th of June, 1811, he still continued to serve in Sicily until the month of December of that year, when he was appointed to the command of the troops in the Ionian Islands. In 1813, he was relieved of this command by Lieutenant-General Campbell, and on 25th of December of that year, he was appointed quartermaster-general of the forces in Ireland, which appointment he held until 1822.

In October, 1797, he married the Honourable Catherine Talbot, third daughter of Margaret, first Baroness Talbot de Malahide.

★★★★★★

Three of his sons, Richard, James Talbot, and Dionysius, entered the army; Dionysius, who was then a captain in the Royal Artillery, died on 28th October, 1845.

Richard and James are still, (1881), serving: Richard, who in 1876 was created a baron, and who is Colonel of the Seventh Royal Fusiliers, and a G.C.B., with the rank of general; and James, who is a K.C.B., with the rank of lieutenant-general.

★★★★★★

His death took place at Paris, on 13th February, 1833. He was buried in the cemetery of Pere-la-Chaise, where a monument was erected to his memory.

No. 37. Daniel Hoghton was appointed major in the Ninety-Seventh Regiment on its formation, 8th February, 1794, on 12th August, 1795, he was transferred to the Sixty-Seventh Regiment, and promoted brevet lieutenant-colonel on 3rd May, 1796. On 22nd November, 1804, when a second battalion was added to the establishment of the King's, he was transferred from the Sixty-Seventh and given command of the new battalion. During the first five years of his term of command, the battalion was quartered at home, during the last two in New Brunswick and Nova Scotia. He was promoted colonel by brevet on 1st January, 1805, and major-general 25th July, 1810. He died in the following year, 1811.—*Vide Records*, part 1.

No. 38. Robert Young received his first commission of ensign in the Eighty-Third Regiment in 1783. The same year the Eighty-Third was disbanded, and he remained on half-pay until 4th May, 1791, when he was appointed lieutenant in the King's. He was promoted to be captain 29th June, 1793, major 4th January, 1797, brevet lieutenant-colonel 29th April, 1802, and lieutenant-colonel in the King's 27th April, 1809. He was made colonel by brevet on 4th June, 1811, and, after commanding the first battalion of the regiment for six years, was promoted to the rank of major-general on 4th June, 1814. He died in the following year.

He served in Canada during the campaigns of 1812, 13, and 14. On 28th May, 1813, he commanded the right division of the expedition against Sackett's Harbour; for this service his name was mentioned in orders. During the summer of 1814, he was appointed to command the station of Kingston.—*Vide Records*, part 1.

No. 39. James Ogilvie was appointed lieutenant in the Seventh Fusiliers 22nd August, 1800; promoted captain, and transferred to the King's 13th May, 1802; promoted major 4th June, 1807; brevet lieutenant-colonel, 4th June, 1813, and succeeded to the command of the first battalion 28th July, 1814. He retired from the service on 20th February, 1816.

He served in Canada as major in the first battalion during the campaigns of 1813-14; in the defence of Fort George on 27th May, 1813, and subsequent retreat; he commanded five companies of the regiment. At the surprise of the American camp at Stoney Creek on 5th June, he commanded the same five companies; was wounded; mentioned in despatches. At the attack on Black Rock and Buffalo on 29th December, he commanded a detachment of the regiment numbering two hundred and forty rank and file; and was again wounded, and again mentioned in despatches.—*Vide Records*, part 1.

No. 40. The Honourable George Cathcart, son of the first Earl Cathcart, was born in London, 12th May, 1794. He received the commission of cornet in the Second Life Guards on 10th May, 1810. The dates of his other regimental commissions and of his unattached and brevet promotions are:—Lieutenant Sixth Dragoon Guards, 1st July, 1811; captain unattached, 24th December, 1818; Seventh Hussars, 16th December, 1819; major Twenty-Second Foot, 8th April, 1820; lieutenant-colonel, unattached, 13th May, 1826; Thirty-Seventh Foot, 24th July, 1828; the King's, 20th March, 1828; half-pay, 25th September, 1835; First Dragoon Guards, 11th May, 1838; half-pay, 19th January, 1844; brevet-colonel, 23rd November, 1841; major-general, 11th November, 1851.

He served as A.D.C. to his father during the campaigns of 1813-

14, and was present at the Battles of Lutzen, Bautzen, Dresden, Leipzic (for which he received the Fourth Class of the Order of St. Wladimir), Brienne, Bar-sur-Aube, Arcis and Fère Champenoise. In the campaign of 1815, he was A.D.C. to the Duke of Wellington, and was present at the Battles of Quatre Bras and Waterloo (medal). He commanded the King's for seven years, from 1828, to 1835. During this time the regiment was quartered in Ireland, Nova Scotia, and Jamaica. He afterwards commanded the First Dragoon Guards for six years (1838-44). From 1846, to 1853, he held the appointment of deputy-lieutenant of the Tower of London. In 1853, he was made adjutant-general of the army and a Knight Commander of the Bath. After holding this appointment for about a year he received command of a division of the army in the Crimea, and was killed at the battle of Inkerman on 5th November, 1854. On 16th December, 1824, he married the Lady Georgiana Greville, daughter of the Countess of Mansfield.

No. 41. Sir W. P. de Bathe, Bart., exchanged from half-pay with Lieutenant-Colonel the Honourable G. Cathcart on 25th September, 1835, and retired from the service on the 2nd of the following month. His connection with the King's Regiment was, therefore, merely nominal.

No. 42. Charles St. Lo Malet, son of Sir Charles Warre Malet, Bart., of Wilbury House, Wilts, was born at Hartham Park. Corsham, Wilts, and was educated at the Royal Military College of Sandhurst. (This notice has been revised by Colonel Malet.) He was appointed a cornet in the Eleventh Light Dragoons in January, 1819. Exchanged into the Twenty-First Light Dragoons and, after serving with them in India, to the Eighth Hussars on 3rd July, 1823; promoted to be lieutenant 26th May, 1825. On 8th June, 1826, he obtained his company, and exchanged to the King's. On 10th January, 1838, he was promoted to be major, and on 25th October, 1842, lieutenant-colonel. He commanded the regiment for three years, during which it was quartered in Ireland and England. On 16th December, 1845, he retired on half-pay.

He married first, Jane St. Lo, daughter of John Clark, Esq., and Elizabeth St. Lo, heiress of the St. Lo family; second, Caroline Emilia, daughter of J. T. Anstey, Esq., late Madras Civil Service. Two of his sons received commissions in the army; William St. Lo, who served in the Eighth Hussars from 1863, to 1875, when he retired with the rank of captain; and Alexander George William, now, (1881), serving as a captain in the Thirty-Ninth Regiment. A third son, Thomas St. Lo, holds the commission of captain in the Dorsetshire Militia; he was attached to the Twenty-Fourth Regiment during the Zulu War, and received the medal.

His brother, Captain Alfred Augustus Malet, served in the regiment from 30th January, 1835, until 14th November, 1845, and his nephew, Captain Charles Fred Malet, from 9th February, 1861, until 22nd November, 1877, when he died in India.—*Vide Records*, part 1.

No. 43. Richard Henry Winchcombe Hartley, the son of Winchcombe Henry Hartley, Esq., and of the Lady Louisa Lumley, eldest daughter of Richard, fourth Earl of Scarborough, was born in 1801. On 10th September, he was appointed ensign in the Twenty-Fourth Foot, and promoted to be lieutenant in it on 1st October, 1820; on 1st September, 1823, he exchanged into the Thirty-Seventh Regiment; on 1st October, 1825, he received an unattached company, and was placed on half-pay; on 5th June, 1858, he exchanged into the King's, and in it was promoted to be major 26th June, 1841, and lieutenant-colonel 16th December 1845. His brevet promotions are dated, major, 28th June 1838; colonel, 20th June, 1854.

In May, 1857, when the news of the Meerut outbreak reached Jellundur, he was in temporary command of the station, and, in anticipation of orders soon afterwards received from Headquarters, took the measures necessary for seizing and securing the fort and magazine of Phillour. A few days after the regiment joined the force besieging Delhi, he was appointed to command the Umballa brigade; some months later he was transferred to Jellundur, where he died in command of the station on 25th June, 1858, after having been Lieutenant-Colonel of the King's for twelve years and a half.

A monument was erected to his memory in the parish church of Great Malvern.

For details of his services *vide Records*, part 1.

No. 44. John Longfield, C.B., the son of Colonel John Longfield, of Longueville, County of Cork, was born at Dublin 18th September, 1804. He was appointed ensign in the King's Regiment on 28th June, 1825, and served in it continuously until 1st June, 1860, when he retired on half-pay. The dates of his other regimental commissions are:—Lieutenant, 26th September, 1826; captain, 30th January, 1835; major, 19th November, 1844; lieutenant-colonel, 3rd April, 1846.

He was promoted to be colonel by brevet 20th June, 1854; major-general, 3rd August, 1860; lieutenant-general, 5th September, 1869; and general, 19th July, 1876.

On 19th April, 1868, he was appointed colonel of the Twenty-Ninth Foot.

He commanded brigades in Bengal from May, to 22nd November, 1855; from 4th April, to 30th December, 1856; and from 29th June, 1857, to 9th April, 1859.

In 1857, he was present with the regiment when the Native troops mutinied at Jellundur, and at the siege of Delhi, on the arrival of the regiment, he was appointed to the command of the second brigade. After the capture of the city he was left there in command of the station.

For his services during the mutiny campaigns he was mentioned in despatches, made a Companion of the Bath (21st January, 1858), and received a medal and one clasp. He retired on half-pay on 31st August, 1860, and on 30th May, 1862, he was granted a good service pension.

On 29th April, 1861, he married Frances Patience, daughter of the Rev. Mountford Longfield, rector of Desertserges, County of Cork.

For details of his services *vide Records*, part 1.

No. 45. Thomas Maitland Wilson was the son of General John Wilson, who was Lieutenant-Governor of Ceylon when Sir Thomas Maitland was Governor. He was born at Colombo in Ceylon, on 15th September, 1806, educated at the Royal Military College of Sandhurst, and was appointed ensign in the Seventy-Eighth Highlanders on 15th April, 1824. The dates of his subsequent commissions, transfers, and exchanges are:—Lieutenant Seventy-Eighth, 13th May, 1826; captain, unattached, 23rd December, 1831; Ninety-Sixth Regiment, 20th January, 1832; brevet major, 9th November, 1846; Ninety-Sixth Regiment, 18th August, 1848; lieutenant-colonel Ninety-Sixth, 15th June, 1849; half-pay, 4th April, 1846.

On 21st October, 1857, when a second battalion was added to the establishment of the King's, he was transferred from half-pay, and appointed lieutenant-colonel of the new battalion, which he continued to command until 27th September, 1861, when he again retired on half-pay. He was promoted to be brevet-colonel 28th November, 1854; major-general, 7th January, 1864; lieutenant-general, 23rd April, 1872; general, 1st October, 1877. He was appointed colonel of the Sixty-Third Regiment on 22nd August, 1873, and on 15th October, 1877, transferred from the Sixty-Third to the Ninety-Sixth, in which he had passed the greatest part of his regimental service. While a captain in the Ninety-Sixth he held the Staff appointments of assistant military secretary, Ceylon, from 11th January, 1839, to 5th April, 1841, and of deputy assistant adjutant-general, Ceylon, 1st June, to 21st September, 1841.

The Second Battalion of the King's during the four years it was commanded by Colonel Wilson was stationed first in Ireland, and afterwards at Gibraltar.—*Vide Records*, part 2.

No. 46. Edward Harris Greathed, son of E. H. Greathed, Esq., of Uddens, Dorset, was born on 8th June, 1812. He was educated at Westminster School.

On 22nd June, 1832, he was appointed Ensign the King's Regiment, and after serving in it continuously for twenty-seven years, retired on half-pay 28th October, 1859.

The dates of his regimental commissions are:—Lieutenant, 10th May, 1833; captain, 27th April, 1838; major, 3rd April, 1846; lieutenant-colonel, 26th June, 1858. His brevet promotions are dated: lieutenant-colonel, 20th June, 1854; colonel, 19th January, 1858; major-general, 6th March, 1868; lieutenant-general, 1st October, 1877; general, 1st July, 1880. On 28th January, 1880, he was appointed colonel of the One Hundred and Eighth Regiment.

While a Lieutenant-Colonel in the King's, he was deputy adjutant-general of the Bombay Army from 23rd October, 1857, to 2nd February, 1859. After retiring on half-pay he was assistant quartermaster general Northern District from 5th September, 1861, to 5th May, 1863; assistant adjutant-general Dublin District 1st September, 1863, to 27th July, 1864, and major-general commanding the Eastern District from 2nd April, 1872, to 31st March, 1877.

In 1857, during the Indian Mutiny Campaign, he commanded the regiment at the siege of Delhi from 29th June until all resistance ceased, and the capture of the city was completed on 20th September. He was then appointed to the command of a moveable column, and was ordered to clear the Doab and to reopen communications with Cawnpore. In performing this service, he attacked and dispersed considerable hordes of the enemy at Bulandshahr and Alighur, and on 10th October inflicted a signal defeat on a large force of mutineers, who made a sudden and unexpected attack on the troops under his command immediately on his arrival at Agra after a forced march of forty-four miles.

During Sir Colin Campbell's operations for the relief of Lucknow in November, 1857, and subsequently at the action of the 30th November and battle of 6th December near Cawnpore, and at the action

GENERAL SIR E. H. GREATHED, K.C.B.

Presented by ten Officers of the King's who served under him during the Indian Mutiny.

of Khuda Gunj on 2nd January, 1858, he commanded a brigade. For the details of these and his other services, *vide Records*, part 1.

He was five times mentioned in despatches, received the brevet of colonel and a good service pension. He was gazetted a Companion of the Bath on 1st January, 1858, and subsequently on 28th March, 1865, was made a Knight Commander of the Order. He also received the honorary degree of D.C.L. of Oxford.

Since the formation of the regiment in 1685, until the present time, Sir Edward Greathed is the only officer of the King's who has received his first commission in the regiment, who has served in it through all the ranks from ensign to lieutenant-colonel, and who has commanded in the field first the regiment and afterwards larger bodies of troops, of which the regiment formed part.

He married first, in 1854, Louisa Frances, daughter of the Venerable Archdeacon Hartwell.

Second, in 1860, Ellen Marj, daughter of the Rev. George Tufnell.

Third, in 1869, Charlotte Frederica Caroline, eldest daughter of Sir George Osborn, Bart., of Chicksands Priory.

No. 47. Frederick Paul Haines, son of Gregory Haines, Esq., C.B., Commissary-General, was born 10th August, 1811, at Kirdford, Sussex. (This notice has been revised by Sir F. P. Haines.)

He was educated at Midhurst, Brussels, and Dresden.

On 21st June, 1839, he received the commission of ensign in the Fourth (the King's Own). The dates of his subsequent regimental commissions and brevet and unattached promotions are:—Lieutenant Fourth Foot, 15th December, 1840; captain Tenth Foot, 16th May, 1846; Twenty-First Fusiliers, 31st March, 1847; major (brevet), 7th June, 1849; Twenty-First Fusiliers, 15th November, 1854; lieutenant-colonel, brevet, 2nd August, 1850; unattached, 24th April, 1855; The King's, 28th October, 1859; half-pay, 1st July. 1862; colonel, brevet, 28th November, 1854; major-general, 25th November, 1864; lieutenant-general, 23rd May, 1873; general, 1st October, 1877. He was appointed colonel of the One Hundred and Fourth Foot 16th May, 1874.

He has held the following Staff appointments and commands:— A.D.C to Commander-in-Chief East Indies from 20th November, 1844, to 22nd May, 1846; military secretary. Headquarters, East Indies, 23rd May, 1846, to 7th May, 1849; commandant Balaclava, 10th December, 1854, to 17th January, 1855; assistant adjutant-general, Aldershot, 20th June, 1855, to 31st January, 1856; military secretary Madras,

10th June, 1856, to 24th June, 1860; brigadier-general (Acting), Aldershot, 28th December, 1861, to 30th June, 1862; deputy adjutant-general. Headquarters, Ireland, 1st July, 1862, to 22nd March, 1863; brigadier-general, Ireland, 8th March, 1864, to 31st December, 1864; major-general, Bengal, 28th March, 1865, to 27th March, 1870; special duty in quartermaster-general's department. Army Headquarters, 6th August, 1870, to 31st October, 1870; quartermaster-general, Army Headquarters, 1st November, 1870, to 31st March, 1871; commander-in-chief, Madras, 22nd May, 1871, to 24th December, 1875; commander-in-chief in India, 10th April, 1876, to 7th April, 1881.

In the Sutlej Campaign of 1845, he served as A.D.C. and officiating military secretary to the Commander-in-Chief, Sir Hugh Gough, and was present at the Battles of Moodkee and Ferozeshah; at the latter battle he had his horse killed under him, and was himself severely wounded by a grape shot. For his services in this campaign he was promoted to a company without purchase in the Tenth Foot, and received a medal with two clasps.

In the Punjab Campaign of 1848-49, while serving as military secretary to the commander-in-chief, he was present at the action of Ramnugger, at the passage of the Chenab, and at the Battles of Chillianwallah and Goojerat; for this campaign he received the brevet of major and a medal and two clasps. In the campaign in the Crimea of 1854-55, he served with the Twenty-First Fusiliers, and was present at the Battles of Alma, Balaclava, and Inkermann, and at the siege and fall of Sebastopol. At the Battle of Inkermann, after Colonel Ainslie was wounded, as senior officer present, he commanded the right wing of the Twenty-First Fusiliers together with other regiments belonging to the fourth division; for this campaign he received a medal with four clasps, the Turkish medal, and the 5th class of the Medjidie. He directed the military operations of the Afghan campaigns of 1878-79-80, and on 5th May, 1881, received the thanks of both Houses of Parliament.

On 20th May, 1871, he was made a Knight Commander, and on 2nd June, 1877, a Knight Grand Cross of the Bath, and on 29th July, 1879, he was made a Knight Grand Commander of the Order of the Star of India.

On 11th September, 1856, he married Charlotte Jane Sophia, daughter of Major-General Edward Evory Miller, Madras Army.

His son, Gregory Sinclair, is now, (1881), serving as lieutenant in the Fifty-Fourth Regiment, and his son Evan Paul Arbuthnot as second lieutenant in the Second Royal Cheshire Militia.

No. 48. John Hinde, eldest son of the Reverend John Hinde Vicar of Ludford, Lecturer of Ludlow, and Head Master of Ludlow Grammar School, Shropshire, was born at Yoxley, Hants, on 2nd August, 1814, and was educated at Ludlow Grammar School. (This notice has been revised by the widow of Major-General Hinde).

On 28th February, 1835, he was appointed Ensign in the King's, and, after thirty-one years' continuous service in the regiment, during the last five years of which he commanded a battalion, on 10th June, 1866, he retired on full-pay with the honorary rank of major-general.

The dates of his regimental commissions are:—Lieutenant 30th June, 1837; captain, 4th July, 1845; major, 21st October, 1857; lieutenant, colonel, 27th September, 1861. His brevet promotions are dated:—Major, 5th July, 1857; lieutenant-colonel, 19th January, 1858.

In 1857, he was present with the regiment when the Native troops mutinied at Jullundur on 7th June. He was left at Phillour in command of a detachment, and did not rejoin the regiment at Delhi until 20th September, the day on which the siege terminated.

He commanded the regiment during the subsequent operations, including the actional Bulandshahr, the affair of Allyghur, the Battle of Agra, the action of Dilkooska, the relief of Lucknow, the affair of the 2nd, and action of 6th December, near Cawnpore, and the action of Khuda Gunj, on 2nd January, 1858.

For these services he was four times mentioned in despatches; he was promoted to the brevet rank of lieutenant-colonel, and gazetted a Companion of the Bath.

After retiring on full pay, he was appointed Lieutenant-Colonel of the First Warwickshire Rifle Volunteers. He continued to command this corps until his death, which took place at the Hermitage, Powick, near Worcester, on 1st March, 1881. On 11th June, 1845, he married Frances, daughter of Richard Gould, Esq., of Manchester.

Two of his sons received the commissions of ensign. John Henry Edward in the Twenty-Eighth Foot, who is now, (1881), a captain in the Thirty-Fourth Foot, and Charles William in the Eighty-Third Foot; he was transferred to the Bombay Staff Corps, on 25th October, 1871, and, while holding the appointment of adjutant of the First Bombay Grenadiers, was killed on 20th July, 1880, at the Battle of Maiwand.

For details of his services, *vide Records*, part 1.

No. 49. James Johnston, son of Lieutenant-General Sir Wm. Johnston, K.C.B., Colonel of the Sixty-Eighth Light Infantry, was born in Quebec, 24th December, 1820. He was educated at Dr. Barney's school, Gosport; was appointed ensign in the Eighth, the King's Regiment, on 7th June, 1839, and after twenty-three years of continuous service in the regiment, obtained the rank of lieutenant-colonel 1st July, 1862. The dates of his intermediate commissions are:—Lieutenant, 13th May, 1842; captain, 21st April, 1846; major, 26th June, 1858.

He commanded the Second Battalion for three years, during which it was quartered at Gibraltar and Malta.

He died at Malta on 29th January, 1865, and a marble monument was erected to his memory in the garrison cemetery by his brother officers.—*Vide Records*, parts 1 & 2.

No. 50. Alexander Cuningham Robertson, eldest son of Lieutenant David Robertson, Royal Marines, was born at Edinburgh on 8th February, 1816. He was educated at the High School and University of Edinburgh, and in 1842-43, studied at the Senior Department of the Royal Military College of Sandhurst.

On 15th February, he was appointed ensign in the Thirty-Fourth Regiment, promoted in it to be lieutenant on 30th August, 1841, and captain on 11th November, 1845; on 28th April, 1846, he exchanged into the King's Regiment, and in it was promoted to be major on 23rd July, 1858, and lieutenant-colonel on 30th December, 1865. He commanded the Second Battalion of the regiment for nine years, and retired on half-pay on 24th March, 1875.

The dates of his brevet promotions are:—Major, 19th January, 1858; lieutenant-colonel, 20th July, 1858; colonel, 15th December, 1864; major-general, 1st October, 1877 (with antedate to 8th February, 1870).

The same day that he retired on half-pay (24th March, 1875), he was gazetted lieutenant-colonel of the Second Royal Lancashire Militia, and commanded its second battalion until 2nd October, 1876, when he was selected for the command of the Thirteenth and Fourteenth Brigade Depots, which appointment he held until February, 1878, four months after his promotion to the rank of major-general. On 1st July, 1881, he was placed on the retired list with the honorary rank of lieutenant-general.

On 18th February, 1834, he was present at the Battle of Santarem as a volunteer in the army of Field Marshal the Duke of Saldanha.

From July, 1835, to June, 1837, he served in the British Auxiliary

Legion of Spain first as a lieutenant and afterwards as a captain.

He was present at the relief of San Sebastian 5th May, 1836, at the Battles of Alza 6th June, 1836; of the heights of Ametza, 1st October, 1836, (where he was severely wounded by splinters from a round shot); of Ametzagana and Oriamendi 15th and 16th March, 1838, and at the attack and capture of Irun 17th May, 1837. For these services he received the Cross of the 1st Class of the Order of San Fernando and two medals.

In 1855-56, he held the appointment of assistant engineer in the Indian Department of Public Works. In 1857, he served with the King's at the siege of Delhi from 2nd July, to 11th September. He was present at the repulse of the sorties of the 9th, and 14th July, and was in command of the regiment at the repulse of the sortie of the 18th July. On 12th August, he commanded a detachment of the King's and Sixty-First Regiments at the capture of four guns in front of advanced piquet.

In December he acted as deputy assistant quartermaster-general to Brigadier-General Seton's column, and was present at the actions of Gungeree, Puttiala, and Mynpooree. On 1st January, 1858, he was appointed assistant adjutant-general to General Wyndham's division, but the division being broken up on the 9th, he was transferred to Judge Advocate's Department, and held the appointment of Deputy Judge Advocate from 10th January, 1858, until 21st January, 1859. He then rejoined the regiment, and as senior officer present, commanded the First Battalion from 22nd January, 1859, until it disembarked at Gosport on 5th September, 1860.

For his services during the mutiny campaigns he was mentioned in despatches, received the brevet of lieutenant-colonel and a medal and two clasps. When he succeeded to the command of the Second Battalion it was stationed in Malta, afterwards, during his term of command, it was quartered at Aldershot, Bury, Manchester, Preston, the Curragh and Cork.

On 2nd June, 1877, he was gazetted a Companion of the Bath, and on 24th March, 1880, appointed honorary colonel of the Fifteenth Lancashire Rifle Volunteers.

He was married first, (in 1853), to Mary Ann Jean, eldest daughter of Brigadier-General A. Manson, C.B., Bombay Artillery.

Second (in 1880), to Annie, eldest daughter of Richard Walker, Esq., of Bellevue, Bury, Lancashire.

His only son, Charles Gray (No. 207), was appointed sub-lieutenant in the King's on 11th September, 1876, and is still serving in it,—*Vide Records*, part 1.

No. 51. Henry George Woods, son of Henry George Woods, assistant-surgeon. Ninety-Fourth Regiment, was born 6th August, 1825, at Totness, Devon, and educated at the Grammar School of Helston in Cornwall.

He was appointed ensign in the Ninety-Seventh Foot on 6th August, 1843, and continued to serve in it until 21st December, 1855, when he received an unattached majority. The dates of his intermediate commissions were:—Lieutenant, 20th October, 1848, captain, 29th December, 1854.

From 29th July, 1853, to 28th December, 1854, he held the appointment of adjutant, and on 2nd November, 1855, he was made a brevet major. On 15th October, 1861, he exchanged from half-pay into the King's, and on 15th June, 1866, on the retirement of Colonel Hinde, was promoted to the vacant lieutenant-colonelcy. He commanded the First Battalion for thirteen years and a half until 30th January, 1880, when he was made a major-general.

From 20th July, 1850, to 12th June, 1851, he held the appointment of A.D.C. to the major-general commanding in Jamaica, and from 29th July, 1853, to 28th December, 1854, that of assistant military secretary in Ceylon.

He served with the Ninety-Seventh Regiment in the Crimea from 20th November, 1854, and commanded the Grenadiers at the storming of the Redan 8th September, 1855, when he was wounded. He was present at the fall of Sebastopol, and received the brevet of major, a medal with clasp, the 5th Class of the Medjidie, and the Turkish medal. He commanded the First Battalion of the King's throughout a complete tour of Indian service, embarking with the colours at Malta on 10th May, 1878, and disembarking with them at Portsmouth on 23rd January, 1879. Soon afterwards he received a good-conduct pension.—*Vide Records*, parts 1 & 2.

No. 52. William Frederick Adams Colman, the son of Captain George Francis Charles Colman, Thirty-First Foot, was born at Plymouth in 1826, and educated at Devonport Grammar School and the Royal Academy, Woolwich.

On 15th June, 1843, he was appointed ensign in the Eightieth Regiment, promoted lieutenant in it on 10th March, 1845; captain in the Fifty-Third Foot, 15th March, 1853, and major in the Fifty-Third 19th April, 1864. In November, 1864, he exchanged to half-pay, and, on 22nd May, 1866, again exchanged into the King's, in which he was promoted to be lieutenant-colonel on 24th March, 1875; he was posted to the Second Battalion, but, without joining it, on the 12th of May he retired from the service with the honorary rank of colonel.

In November, 1844, he was wrecked in the transport *Briton* on the Lesser Andamans, and remained on the island fifty-one days, suffering very severe hardships.

During the Sutlej campaign of 1845-46, he served with the Eightieth Regiment, and was present at the Battles of Moodkee, Ferozeshah, and Sobraon, at which latter battle he killed a standard bearer in single combat. For this campaign he received a medal and two clasps.—*Vide Records*, part 1.

No. 53. John Vere William Henry Webb, the son of Captain John Wynne Webb, Seventy-Ninth Highlanders, was born at Bath 2nd May, 1830.

He was educated at Dr. Steele's school. Isle of Man.

On 29th January, 1847, he received his first commission in the Cape Mounted Rifles; on 5th March, 1847, he was transferred to the King's, and, after a continuous service of twenty-eight years in the regiment, succeeded Lieutenant-Colonel Colman in command of the Second Battalion on 12th May, 1875.

The dates of his intermediate regimental commissions are:—Lieutenant, 21st February, 1851; captain, 11th May, 1858; major, 2nd November, 1866.

In 1857 he served with the regiment at the siege of Delhi from 6th June, until 20th September. He was present at the repulse of the sorties of 9th, and 14th July; at the attack on the enemy's outpost and capture of four guns on 12th August, and at assault on 14th September, and fighting in the city on the six following days. In the subsequent operations he was present at the action of Bolundshahr, affair of Allyghur, Battle of Agra, action of Dilkoosha, relief of Lucknow, affair of 2nd and action of 6th December, 1857, near Cawnpore, and at the action of Khuda Gunj on 2nd January, 1858.

After commanding the Second Battalion two years, during which it was stationed at Fermoy, the Curragh, and Aldershot, he retired on full-pay with the honorary rank of colonel on 7th March, 1877.

On 13th October, 1859, he married Laetitia Annie, daughter of George Llewhellin, Esq.—*Vide Records*, parts 1 & 2.

No. 54. Francis Barry Drew, the son of Francis Drew, of Drew's

Court, Limerick, was born at Drew's Court, on 29th September, 1825, and educated at Limerick and at Trinity College, Dublin.

He was appointed ensign Twenty-Eighth Foot 28th May, 1845. On 12th February, 1847, he exchanged to the Fortieth, was promoted lieutenant 17th August, 1848, and held the appointment of adjutant from 11th February, 1848, to 20th November, 1851, when he was promoted captain. On 16th January, 1852, he exchanged into the Sixty-Fourth Foot; on 16th January, 1853, into the Eleventh Foot; on 26th January, 1855, into the Ninety-Fourth Foot, and on 23rd August, 1859, into a depot battalion. On 23rd August, 1865, he was placed on half-pay as a major unattached; on 2nd September, 1868, he exchanged from half-pay into the King's, in which he was appointed lieutenant-colonel on 7th March, 1877. After commanding the Second Battalion for two years, he exchanged into the Fourteenth Foot on 13th September, 1879, which regiment he now, (1881), commands.

His brevet promotions are dated:—Major, 27th July, 1863; lieutenant-colonel, 25th October, 1873; colonel, 23rd October, 1878.

He held the appointment of commandant of the Schools of Instruction of the Auxiliary Forces at Manchester, from 1st February, 1871, to 16th July, 1872, and at Aldershot from 25th August, 1876, to 24th March, 1877.

He commanded the King's during the Afghan campaign of 1878, and was present at the action of 28th November, and at the forcing of the Peiwar Kotal, during which engagement, when Brigadier Cobbe was wounded, he succeeded to the command of the brigade; he was also present at the action of Matan.

For his services in this campaign he was three times mentioned in despatches, was nominated a Companion of the Bath on 19th July, 1879, and received a medal and clasp.

He married, first, on 2nd September, 1848, Anne Charlotte, daughter of John Cator, Esq., of Woodbastwick Hall, Norfolk.

Second, on 31st August, 1854, Henrietta, daughter of John Hunter, Esq., of Ormley Lodge, Surrey.

Third, on 18th June, 1867, Adelaide Emma, daughter of the Reverend George Tyrhitt Drake, rector of Malpus, Cheshire.—*Vide Records*, parts 1 & 2.

No. 55. Charles Edward Grogan, the son of Colonel George Grogan, of Seafield House, county of Dublin, was born at Dublin on 2nd November, 1826, and educated by a private tutor.

He was appointed cornet in the Seventh Hussars on 16th April, 1847, and on the 3rd of September, same year, transferred to the Twelfth Lancers. He was promoted lieutenant on 28th April, 1848, and on 17th January, 1851, exchanged into the Fourteenth Foot, in which regiment he was promoted to be captain 29th December, 1854; major, 14th January, 1864, and lieutenant-colonel, 15th August, 1877. He exchanged into the King's on 13th September, 1879, and at present commands the Second Battalion of the regiment. The dates of his brevet promotions are:—Lieutenant-colonel, 6th January, 1864; colonel, 6th January, 1869.

He served with the Second Battalion during the Afghan campaign of 1879-80. He commanded the Lower Kurrum Brigade from 11th August, 1880, until the brigade was broken up in November.—*Vide Records*, part 2.

No. 56. Edward Tanner, son of Joseph Bouverie Hussey Tanner, Esq., of Wexcombe, Wilts, was born at Salisbury on 30th January, 1839, and educated at King's College, London.

He was appointed ensign in the Thirty-Third Foot on 30th November, 1855, and was transferred to the King's on 23rd October. After a little over twenty-two years' service in the regiment, on 30th January, 1880, he was promoted to be lieutenant-colonel, and at present commands the First Battalion.

The dates of his intermediate regimental commissions are:—Lieutenant, 7th December, 1857; captain, 4th September, 1860; major, 24th March, 1869; and on 1st October, 1877, he was promoted to the brevet rank of lieutenant-colonel.

He served with the Second Battalion in the Afghan campaigns of 1878, 79, 80, and was present at the action of 28th November, at the forcing of the Peiwar Kotal on 2nd December, 1878. In the middle of the action, after Brigadier Cobbe was wounded, the command of the battalion devolved upon him, and from that time until 13th September, 1880, when relieved by Colonel Grogan, he continued in temporary command.

For his services in these campaigns he was mentioned in despatches, was nominated a Companion of the Bath on 22nd February, 1881, and received a medal and clasp.

On 3rd September, 1867, he married Georgina, daughter of Major-General George Wm. Powlett Bingham, C.B.—*Vide Records*, part 2.

No. 57. George Henry Cochrane, son of Lieutenant-Colonel G. Cochrane, Ceylon Rifles, born in Ceylon, on the 24th Discerner, 1829, and educated at the Royal Military College of Sandhurst. The dates of his commissions are:—Ensign Eighty-Third Foot, 2nd August; Ninety-Sixth Foot, 18th August, 1848; lieutenant Ninety-Sixth Foot, 13th December, 1851; captain Eighth (the King's), 21st May, 1868; major, 24th March, 1875; brevet lieutenant-colonel, 25th April, 1880.

He served with the Second Battalion during the Afghan campaign of 1878, and when General Roberts' column advanced to attack the Peiwar Kotal, was left in command of the post of Kurrum.

On 5th July, 1866, he married Rose Noble, daughter of—Cole, Esq.—*Vide Records*, parts 1 & 2.

No. 58. Forster Longfield, son of the Rev. Mountford Longfield, vicar of Desertserges, county of Cork, and cousin of Colonel John Longfield (No. 44), was born at Church Hill, near Bandon, on 28th February, 1829. and was educated by a private tutor and at Bandon School. He received the commission of ensign in the Fifth Fusiliers on 15th January, 1856, was transferred to the King's on 24th April same year, and from that time continued to serve in the regiment (for dates of commissions *vide* Succession Lists, Appendix No. 1).

He accompanied the force under Major R. Stuart Baynes, which surprised and secured the fort and magazine of Phillour on 13th May, 1857. Served at the siege of Delhi; present at repulse of sorties on 9th, 14th, 18th, 23rd July; at attack of outpost and capture of four guns on 12th August, 1857. He was also present at the action at Dilkoosha and relief of Lucknow, at the actions on 2nd and 6th December, 1857, at Cawnpore, and at the action of Khuda Gunj. During the Oude campaign of 1858-59, he acted as brigade quartermaster to Brigadier Hale's column, and was present at the capture of the fort and town of Sandee (Mutiny medal with two clasps). He was promoted to be a brevet lieutenant-colonel on 19th May, 1880.—*Vide Records*, parts 1 & 2.

MAJORS.

No. 59. Frederick Cornwallis served with the regiment in the campaign of 1704, and was killed at the Battle of Blenheim.—*Vide Records*, part 1.

No. 60. Brevet Lieutenant-Colonel Hanmer was at the Battle of Dunblane 11th November, 1715, when the regiment was broken by the charge of the Highland clans; he was surrounded, and after holding his opponents at bay for some time, was overpowered and killed.—*Vide Records*, part 1.

No. 61. James Barry. The dates of his commissions are:— Lieutenant 20th September, 1709; captain-lieutenant 10th March, 1715; captain 7th January, 1720; major 7th February, 1741. He served with the regiment in the campaign of 1743, and at the Battle of Dettingen on 27th June received a wound of which he died.—*Vide Records*, part 1.

No. 62. John Grey. The dates of his commission are:—Ensign 17th February, 1709; lieutenant 22nd December, 1712; captain-lieutenant 1st January, 1727; major 14th July, 1743.

He served with the regiment as a captain in the campaign of 1743. At the Battle of Dettingen, after Lieutenant-Colonel Keightley and Major Barry were wounded, the command of the regiment devolved on him, and for his services on this occasion he was promoted to the vacancy caused by the death of Major Barry.—*Vide Records*, part 1.

No. 63. Arthur Loftus. His commissions are dated:—Lieutenant 23rd August, 1735; captain-lieutenant 14th July, 1743; captain 4th October, 1743; major 27th April, 1749. He served as captain in the regiment during the campaign of 1745, and on 11th May, was wounded at the Battle of Fontenoy. He died on 25th August, 1753.—*Vide Records*, part 1.

No. 64. John Cook. The dates of his commissions are:—Ensign 2nd February, 1739; lieutenant 4th December, 1742; captain 17th February, 1746; major 25th August, 1756.

During the campaign in the Netherlands of 1745, he served with the regiment as a lieutenant; and on 1st May of that year was wounded at the Battle of Fontenoy.—*Vide Records*, part 1.

No. 65. Thomas Armstrong served in a battalion of flank companies, under Sir Charles Grey, at the capture of Guadaloupe. He was killed between 19th June, and 2nd July. In the casualty return annexed to Sir Charles Grey's despatch, dated 8th July, 1794, his name appears as Captain Armstrong, the news of his promotion (which is dated 3rd April, 1794) had not therefore reached him at the time of his death. *Vide* note No. 14 of this Appendix.

No. 66. Durell Saumarez was appointed ensign in the regiment on 6th April, 1776, and after serving in it as lieutenant and captain, attained the rank of major in 1794. In the MS. master roll for the last half of that year he is marked "killed in the West Indies" (no date given), and in the *London Gazette* of 17th March, 1795, T. Bland is promoted major, *vice* Saumarez, deceased, but I have not succeeded in finding any despatch or casualty list in which Major Saumarez's death is mentioned. The date of the major's commission of his successor is 17th December, 1794.

No. 67. Thomas Bland was appointed ensign in the Twenty-Eighth Regiment on 26th October, 1775. The dates of his subsequent commissions are:—Lieutenant Twenty-Eighth, 19th August, 1778, captain and transferred to the King's 31st July, 1792; major, 17th December, 1794. He retired from the army on 4th June, 1797.

In the campaign of 1794, in Flanders and Holland, he served with the regiment as a captain; and on the 4th November of that year, during the defence of Nimeguen in a sortie made by the garrison, he received a wound.—*Vide Records*, part 1.

No. 68. Alexander Duke was promoted to be a lieutenant on 28th August, 1781; he was afterwards placed on half-pay, from which he was transferred to the King's on 13th December, 1786. He was promoted to be captain on 31st March, 1793, and major on 10th July, 1799. He retired from the service in 1804.

He served with the regiment as major in the expedition to Egypt in 1801, and was wounded in the battle fought near Alexandria on 13th March.—*Vide Records*, part 1.

No. 69. Bryce Maxwell was appointed ensign in the King's on 8th August, 1788. For the dates of his other commissions, *Vide* Appendix No. 1. He held appointment of adjutant from 31st July to 26th October, 1793.

In 1809, he commanded the regiment in the expedition against Martinique, and on 2nd February was killed in storming the heights of Surirey.—*Vide Records*, part 1.

No. 70. Thomas Fortye. The dates of his commissions in the regiment are:—Lieutenant 18th January, 1792; captain, 27th November, 1794; major, 24th October, 1804. In the Egyptian campaign of 1801, he served with the King's as captain, and was wounded on 13th March at the Battle of Mandora. On 18th April, 1805, he was transferred to the 1st Royal Veteran Battalion; from 1827, to 1832, he held the appointment of barrack master in Guernsey, and in 1834, he retired from the army.—*Vide Records*, part 1.

No. 71. Edward Cotton entered the King's as a lieutenant 23rd March, 1797; was promoted captain 18th November, 1802, and major, 3rd February, 1809. He served with the regiment in Canada during the campaign of 1813-14; on 27th May, 1813, he was present at the defence of Fort George, and received a wound. A few months afterwards he died from the effects of the severe exertions he had undergone.—*Vide Records*, part 1.

No. 72. Thomas Evans, son of Richard Evans, Esq., was born near Wolverhampton in March, 1776.

In 1793, he enlisted one hundred and fifty men for the service, and entered the army as a volunteer.

On 3rd December, 1794, he was appointed ensign in the One Hundred and Thirteenth Regiment; after its reduction on 11th October, 1796, he was transferred as lieutenant to the King's; promoted in it to be captain 19th November, 1803; major 6th February, and brevet lieutenant-colonel 13th October, 1812. In this year he was also made a Companion of the Bath.

On 24th December, 1815, the establishment of the King's was reduced to a single battalion, and on 14th March, 1816, he was appointed major in the Seventieth Foot; on 24th September, 1829, he was promoted to be its lieutenant-colonel, and continued to command it for the next nine years. On 22nd July, 1830, he was made colonel by brevet. On 28th June, 1838, after having served forty-five years as a regimental officer, only two of which were spent in England, he was promoted to be major-general; on 11th November, 1851, to be lieutenant-general; and on 18th May, 1855, to be general.

On 12th July, 1847, he was appointed colonel of the Eighty-First Regiment.

In 1794-95, he served in the West Indies.

In 1796, he was present at the capture of Demerara and Berbice; in returning home after that service he was captured, and kept a close prisoner in France until 1797.

In 1798-99, he served in Minorca and Guernsey; in 1800, on the coast of Spain in Malta and Marmorice; in 1801, he served with the King's in Egypt as lieutenant, and for some weeks performed the duties of adjutant.

He was present at the battles of 8th March, at Aboukir, and of 13th and 21st March, near Alexandria; also, at the action of Ramanieh, and at the surrender of Cairo and Alexandria.

******

A journal kept by Lieutenant Thomas Evans, which commences on 1st May, 1799, and ends on 3rd September, 1801, is now, (1881), in possession of his son. Colonel C. R. O. Evans, R.A., who kindly allowed me to read it and to make extracts from it.—A. C. R.

******

In 1804, 5, and 6, he served in the West Indies as captain in the King's, and A.D.C. to Sir Gordon Drummond. In 1807-8, he served in Nova Scotia; in 1809-10, in Canada as A.D.C. and Military Secretary to Sir Gordon Drummond. During the campaigns in Canada of 1812, 13, 14, he, for part of the time, held the appointment of brigade-major, discharging the duties of deputy assistant adjutant-general, and for part of the time was in command of the King's.

He superintended the preparation of the force detached to operate against Detroit and Michilimacinac; he was present at the defence of Fort George, and destruction of the enemy's batteries; at the assault on Sackets Harbour, where he was wounded in three places; at the attack on the force at Forty Mile Creek; at the Battle of Chippawa; at the night attack on the force investing Fort George, when the American General Swift was killed; at the Battle of Lundy's Lane, where his sword was shivered in his hand; at the siege and assault of Fort Erie, where the piquets under his command on 5th and 12th August, 1814, repulsed two sorties, and inflicted severe loss on the enemy, and where he received a contusion, and had his horse shot under him. During the months of January, February, and March, 1814, he was detached to New Brunswick, in order to conduct the Second Battalion of the King's and a party of seamen through the wilderness to Quebec.

For these services his name was mentioned in despatches on ten different occasions; he received the brevet of lieutenant-colonel, and was made a Companion of the Bath.

He married Harriet Lawrence, daughter of Judge Ogden, of Montreal.

He died on 11th February, 1863, at Three Rivers, Canada, and a memorial chapel was erected at London, Canada West, to commemorate his name and services.

Four of his sons received commissions in the army: Thomas, appointed ensign in the Forty-First Foot in 1839, and killed in Afghanistan in 1841; Charles Richard Ogden, appointed lieutenant in the Royal Artillery on 17th June, 1843, now brigadier-general commanding at Agra; Gordon, appointed ensign in the Sixty-Ninth Foot in 1842, retired in 1848; Richard John, appointed ensign in the Twenty-Ninth Regiment in 1846, retired in 1864 with the rank of major.—*Vide Records*, part 1.

No. 73. James Munday (or Mundy) was appointed captain in the King's on the addition of a second battalion to the establishment in 1804; he was promoted major on 21st October, 1813. (He appears never to have served in the ranks of ensign or lieutenant; his name is not to be found in the Army List previous to 1805.) He served with the regiment in the American campaign of 1813, and on 5th June of that year was wounded while commanding a company at the surprise of the American camp at Stoney Creek. He retired from the army in 1816.—*Vide Records*, part 1.

No. 74. John Blackmore was appointed ensign in the King's on 15th April, 1794; for the dates of his other commissions, *vide* Appendix No. 1. After serving twenty-two years in the regiment, he was placed on half-pay on 25th February, 1816; promoted to be lieutenant-colonel on 10th February, 1837; and died in 1845.

He served with the regiment as captain in the American campaign of 1813; and in the attack on Sackett's Harbour on 29th May, he was wounded and taken prisoner.—*Vide Records*, part 1.

No. 75. Simcoe Baynes. The dates of his commissions are:—Ensign Royal Corsican Rangers, 24th June, 1812; lieutenant Royal Corsican Rangers, 28th December, 1815; captain the King's, 24th June, 1824; major the King's, 2nd October, 1835; lieutenant-colonel, unattached, 26th October, 1841. His brevet promotions are dated colonel 11th November, 1851; major-general 26th October, 1858; lieutenant-general 28th August, 1865; general 14th December, 1873.

He was appointed colonel of the Thirty-Fifth Foot, 27th March, 1863.

He served three years as a midshipman in the Royal Navy, and in 1809, was present at the capture of Ischia, Zante, Cephalonia and Cerigo. On the 3rd May, 1810, he was in the action of the *Spartan* frigate in the Bay of Naples. From 1812, to 1817, he served in the Ionian Islands, and was present at the capture of Paxo in 1813, and at the occupation of Corfu on the evacuation by the French in 1814. On 21st October, 1821, he was with a detachment defending a Turkish man-of-war from an attack made by the Greeks, and in the disarmament which followed, he was specially and actively employed. In 1834, he served in the West Indies during the emancipation of the slaves, and in 1839-40. in North America during the settlement of the Boundary Question.

He died at Malta on 13th September, 1874. Two of his nephews, George Edward Baynes and Robert Stuart Baynes, received commissions in the King's, *vide* Nos. 82 and 116 of this Appendix.

******

Colonel Baynes, who commanded a force, of which a detachment of the King's formed part, and which attacked Sackett's Harbour on 29th May, 1813, was an uncle of Major Simcoe Baynes.—*Vide Records*, part 1.

******

No. 76. Charles Barker Turner received his first commission in the Twenty-Sixth Regiment on 11th September, 1806; he was promoted to a lieutenancy in the Eleventh Regiment on 12th March; to a company 15th October, 1812; to a majority 16th March, 1826; and he continued to serve in it until 9th November, 1830, when he received the brevet of lieutenant-colonel, and was appointed inspecting field officer in New Brunswick. On 3rd February, 1837, he was appointed major in the King's, but he only remained in the regiment until 9th January of the following year. From January, 1838, until 4th September, 1843, he was employed on particular service; he was then placed on half-pay, and retired from the army by the sale of his commission in 1845.

In 1807 he was present as a subaltern of the Eleventh at the capture of Madeira, and he served with the Eleventh in the Peninsula from August, 1809, until January, 1814. He was present at the Battles of Busaco and Fuentes D'Onor, at the action of El Bodon, at the second siege of Badajoz, at the siege and storming of Ciudad Rodrigo, at the action of St. Christobal, Battle of Salamanca and capture of Madrid, at the siege of Burgos, investment of Pampeluna, Battles of the Pyrenees on 28th, 29th, and 30th July, 1813, and at the Battle of the Nivelle; he was also present at twenty-eight minor actions and skirmishes.

At the Battle of the Nivelle he led the attack of the Sixth Division and brought the light companies of his brigade out of action; in the afternoon of that day, while pressing the enemy's rear guard, he received a wound in the shoulder from a musket bullet. For these services he was decorated with a cross of honour by the King of Portugal, and made a Knight of the Royal Hanoverian Guelphic Order 18th January, 1832.

No. 77. James Croft Brooke. (This notice was revised by the widow of Major-General Brooke.) The dates of his commissions are:—Ensign (Thirty-First Foot), 31st October, 1831; lieutenant, (Thirty-First Foot), 2nd September, 1833; captain (Thirty-First Foot), 31st March, 1846; major (Thirty-First Foot), 2nd October, 1849; exchanged to the King's 11th December, 1849; lieutenant-colonel (brevet), 14th April, 1857.

He served with the Thirty-First Regiment under General Pollock in the Afghan campaign of 1842, and was present at the actions of Mazeena, Tezeen, and Jugdulluck, at the occupation of Cabul, and the various engagements which preceded the occupation. He commanded a company during the campaign, and received a wound at Jugdulluck while protecting some guns attached to the rear guard (medal).

In 1857, he served as major with the King's Regiment during the siege of Delhi, and was present at the repulse of the sorties on 9th and 14th July; he commanded the regiment at the repulse of the sortie of 23rd July, and was one of the four field officers who commanded in the trenches from 7th to 13th September. He was present and severely wounded at the assault of the city on the 14th September. Medal and clasp.

He retired on half-pay on 15th October, 1861, was promoted to be brevet-colonel on 11th November, 1861, and major-general on 6th March, 1868.

On 24th May, 1873, he was appointed a Companion of the Bath, and on 19th November, 1870, he was granted a good service pension. He died at St. Heliers, Jersey, on 27th April, 1875. He was buried in the cemetery of Rickmansworth, Herts, where a tombstone was erected by his widow.—*Vide Records*, part 1.

No. 78. John Butler Wheatstone served as captain in the Forty-Fifth Foot during the Kaffir campaigns of 1846, 51, 52, 53 (medal); he retired on full-pay with the rank of lieutenant-colonel on 23rd August, 1858.

No. 79. William Bayly was born at Drogheda on 20th February, 1796. He enlisted in the King's Regiment as a drummer on 25th November, 1807; on 11th January, 1828, he was appointed sergeant-major of the regiment, and on 26th May, 1839, he received the commission of ensign in the Second West India Regiment. On 6th December the same year he was transferred to the King's, (he never joined the Second West India Regiment, but was allowed to remain with the depot companies until transferred to the King's); for the dates of his other commissions *vide* Appendix No. 1. He held the appointment of adjutant from 14th December, 1841, to 29th May, 1848.

During the Indian Mutiny of 1857, he served with the regiment as captain, and was present at the outbreak of the *sepoy* troops at Jellundur on 7th June. He accompanied the regiment to Delhi, and was present at the repulse of the sorties of 9th, 14th, 18th, and 23rd July. On the 23rd he was in command of the two flank companies. For these services he received a medal and clasp. He retired on full-pay with the rank of lieutenant-colonel on 9th October, 1863, and died at Hastings on 16th December, 1874.

His only son, Alex. Ross Bayly, received the commission of ensign in the regiment (*vide* No. 129 of this Appendix), and his brother-in-law, John Ross, served in it as quartermaster (*vide* No. 226).—*Vide Records*, part 1.

No. 80. Edwin Gream Daniell. The dates of his commissions are:— Ensign (Fifty-Fifth Foot), 2nd October, 1835; lieutenant (Fifty-Fifth Foot), 7th September, 1838; captain (Fifty-Fifth Foot), 25th March, 184.5; exchanged to the King's 26th April, 1846. Major by brevet 19th January, 1858.

In 1841, he served with the Fifty-Fifth Regiment in China, and was present at the actions of Amoy, Chusan, and Chinhae, including repulse of night attack; present also at the expedition up the Ningpo River to You-You (medal). In 1857, served with the King's Regiment at the siege of Delhi, and was severely wounded at the repulse of the sortie on 9th July (medal and brevet-major). He exchanged to half-pay on 23rd January, 1863, was promoted to be lieutenant-colonel on 27th December, 1868, and retired from the service by the sale of his commission in 1872.—*Vide Records*, part 1.

No. 81. Thomas de Courcy Hamilton, V.C. The dates of his regimental commissions are:—Ninetieth Light Infantry, 30th September, 1842; lieutenant Ninetieth, 10th April, 1847; exchanged to Sixty-Eighth Light Infantry in 1848; captain Sixty-Eighth Light Infantry, 20th December, 1854. He held the appointment of adjutant of the Sixty-Eighth from 23rd August, 1850, to 27th August, 1855; major (by brevet), 10th March, 1857; major unattached, 27th November, 1857; exchanged to the King's Regiment 23rd January, 1863; brevet-colonel, 20th May, 1873; promoted lieutenant-colonel and transferred to Sixth-Fourth Regiment 20th May, 1868.

In 1846-47, served with Ninetieth Regiment in Kaffirland (medal). In 1854-55, served with Sixty-Eighth Light Infantry in the Crimea;

present at the Battles of Alma, Balaclava, and Inkermann; served during siege, and present at the fall of Sebastopol f medal and four clasps, Knight of the Legion of Honour, and Turkish medal). On 11th May, 1855, with a small party of men he charged a large body of Russians, who during a sortie had captured a battery, and for his gallantry and distinguished conduct on that occasion he received the Victoria Cross.

He retired on full pay with the rank of major-general 21st January, 1874.

No. 82. George Edward Baynes, son of Sir Edward Baynes, K.C.M.G., Her Majesty's Agent and Consul-General at Tunis, nephew of Major Simcoe Baynes, and brother of Captain R. Stuart Baynes (*vide* No. 75 and No. 116 of this Appendix). For dates of his commissions in the King's from ensign to major, *vide* Appendix No. 1. In 1857, he was with the regiment at Jellundur when the Native troops mutinied on the night of 7th June; he afterwards served with it at the siege of Delhi, and was present at the repulse of the sorties of 9th, 14th, 18th, and 23rd July; at the assault of the city on 14th September he commanded the storming party of the second column; for these services he was mentioned in despatches, received a brevet majority and medal and clasp.

On 1st April, 1866, after twenty-five years' service in the regiment, he retired on half-pay with the rank of lieutenant-colonel unattached. From 30th March, 1867, to 11th April, 1872, he held the appointment of assistant quartermaster-general, and from 12th to 22nd April, 1872, that of assistant military secretary in Nova Scotia. From 3rd June, 1872, to 4th January, 1878, he was assistant military secretary at Malta, and on 10th November, 1877, he was selected for the command of the Forty-Second Brigade Depot (Oxford), which he still holds.

He was promoted to the rank of brevet-colonel on 30th March, 1872.—*Vide Records*, part 1.

No. 83. De Vic Tupper. The dates of his commissions are:—Ensign in Thirty-Eighth, 15th October, 1852; lieutenant Thirty Eighth, 11th August, 1854; captain Thirty-Eighth, 15th January, 1856; exchanged into the King's 22nd August, 1856; major, The King's, 30th December, 1865. In 1854-55, served with the Thirty-Eighth Regiment in the Crimea; present at the Battles of Alma and Inkermann, at the siege of Sebastopol, attack and capture of the cemetery 18th June, and at the fall of the city (medal and three clasps). In 1857, was present with the regiment at Jellundur at the outbreak of the mutiny, and was afterwards engaged in various field services in the Punjab (medal). He retired on half-pay on 22nd May, 1866, and on 14th April, 1875, was promoted to the rank of lieutenant-colonel.—*Vide Records*, part 1.

No. 84. Richard Raphael Meade. The dates of his commissions are:—Ensign Ninety-Fourth Foot, 6th October, 1848; lieutenant Ninety-Fourth Foot, 6th October, 1851; captain Ninety-Fourth Foot, 31st August, 1855; exchanged into the King's 16th January, 1857; major, 15th June, 1866. He held the appointment of adjutant of the Ninety-Fourth from 29th October, 1852, until his promotion to captain 31st August, 1855. He served as a volunteer with the artillery in an action at Agra, on 5th July, 1857, and with the regiment, as captain, at the relief of Lucknow; at the affair of 2nd and action of 6th December at Cawnpore, and at the action of Khuda Gunj. During the campaign in Oude of 1858-59, he was in temporary command of the regiment.

He exchanged to half-pay on 2nd September, 1868, and died in 1873.—*Vide Records*, parts 1 & 2.

No. 85. Frederick Bradford M'Crea. For dates of commissions in the regiment from ensign to major, *vide* Succession Lists, Appendix No. 1.

He served with the regiment during the mutiny of 1857, and was present at the two days' fighting in the city 19th and 20th September; at the actions of Bulandshahr and Allyghur, at the affair of Akrabad and Battle of Agra, at the affair of Kanouje and advance into Oude; at the actions of Mariganj, Alumbagh, and Dilkoosha, and at the relief of Lucknow. At the actions near Cawnpore on the 2nd and 6th December, 1857, and at the action of Khuda Gunj, 2nd January, 1858.

During the months of August, September, and October, 1858, he was stationed at Meerun-ke-Serai in command of detachments, consisting of the Grenadier and A Companies and upwards of 1,500 Native troops, and was employed in watching about sixteen miles of the course of the Ganges, to prevent the rebel bands crossing from Oude to the Agra district. On 1st November the greater number of the troops were withdrawn from Meerun-ke-Serai, and the detachment of the King's rejoined headquarters, which were then in Oude attached to Brigadier Hale's column; to this column he for some time acted as brigade-quartermaster (medal and clasp).—*Vide Records,* part 1.

No. 86. Reginald Whitting received the commission of ensign in Sixty-Second Regiment on 26th December, 1856. He was transferred to the King's Regiment on 23rd October, 1857, and from that date continued to serve in the regiment (for dates of commissions, *vide* Succession Lists, Appendix No. 1).

In the Indian Mutiny campaign of 1858-59, he acted as staff adjutant to a detachment at Sasseram, and was engaged in the operations against the rebels in the jungles of Jugdespore, under Sir E. Lugard, May, 1858.

He also served with the regiment during the Oude campaign of 1858-59, and was present at the capture of the fort and town of Sandee. During these operations he acted as adjutant to wing of the regiment, and from 16th to 28th January, 1859, as field quartermaster to Brigadier-General Hale's column (medal).—*Vide Records*, parts 1 & 2.

No. 87. William Bannatyne (younger brother of Captain J. Millar Bannatyne, *vide* No. 117 of this Appendix) was appointed ensign in the Twenty-Fourth Regiment 27th April, 1858, and transferred to the King's on 21st May, 1858 (for dates of his other commissions, *vide* Appendix No. 1).

During the campaign in Afghanistan of 1880, he served with the Second Battalion from 31st May, 1880, until the end of the campaign, and on 11th August, on Colonel Grogan being appointed to the command of the Lower Kurrum brigade, he succeeded to the temporary command of the battalion (medal).—*Vide Records*, part 2.

No. 88. Bennett Fleming Handy. (For dates of commissions from ensign to major, *vide* Appendix No. 1.) He served as captain with the Second Battalion during the Afghan campaign of 1879-80 (medal).

No. 89. Nash Short. (For dates of commissions from ensign to major, *vide* Appendix No. 1.) He served as captain with the Second Battalion during the Afghan campaign of 1879 (medal).—*Vide Records*, part 2.

CAPTAINS.

No. 90. Leonard Lloyd served with the regiment during the campaign of 1704, and on 13th August was wounded at the Battle of Blenheim.—*Vide Records*, part 1.

No. 91. John Dallons served with the regiment during the campaign of 1745, and on 11th May was wounded at the Battle of Fontenoy. He died on 16th February, 1746.—*Vide Records,* part 1.

No. 92. Richard Miggot (or Magott) served with the regiment in the campaign of 1747, and on 2nd July of that year was killed at the Battle of Val.—*Vide Records*, part 1.

No. 93. William Catherwood served with the regiment in the campaign of 1747, and on 2nd July of that year he was wounded at the Battle of Val.—*Vide Records*, part 1.

No. 94. John Ekins (or Atkins) served in the regiment as a captain-lieutenant during the campaign of 1745, and on 11th May of that year was wounded at the battle of Fontenoy. He died on 15th August, 1750.—*Vide Records*, part 1.

No. 95. John Trollop served with the regiment in the campaign in the Netherlands of 1746, and on 11th October of that year was wounded at the Battle of Roucoux. He was promoted to be major in the Sixty-Third Foot, and was killed at the taking of Guadaloupe.—*Vide Records*, part 1.

No. 96. Jacob Conway served with the regiment as a lieutenant during the campaign in the Netherlands of 1747; on 2nd July of that year he was wounded at the Battle of Val. He died on 21st April, 1752.—*Vide Records*, part 1.

No. 97. Francis Wilkinson served with the regiment as a captain during the campaign in Germany of 1760, and on 31st July of that year was wounded at the Battle of Warbourg.—*Vide Records*, part 1.

No. 98. James Webb served as ensign with the regiment in the campaign in the Netherlands of 1747, and was wounded at the Battle of Val (1st July).—*Vide Records*, part 1.

No. 99. Charles Hamilton served as ensign with the regiment during the campaign in the Netherlands of 1747, and was wounded at the Battle of Val.—*Vide Records*, part 1.

No. 100. George Forster served in the regiment as a captain during the campaign in America of 1776. On 19th May, at the head of a detachment of two subalterns and thirty-eight non-commissioned officers and privates of the King's, reinforced by one hundred and twenty Indians and some Canadian Volunteers, he captured the American fort of the Cedars, defended by three hundred and ninety officers and soldiers, who surrendered as prisoners of war. On the 20th he surprised and made prisoners an American detachment advancing from Montreal to reinforce the post, and on the 27th repulsed an expedition of seven hundred men in boats, sent from Montreal, under the command of Colonel Arnold, to endeavour to recover the fort. For these brilliant exploits he was promoted to be major in the Twenty-first North British Fusiliers (5th November, 1766). He became a brevet lieutenant-colonel on 20th November, 1782, and on 31st December, 1784, lieutenant-colonel of the Sixty-Sixth Regiment, which he continued to command until 23rd October, 1787, when his name disappears from the Army List.—*Vide Records*, part 1.

No. 101. Bryce MacMurdo was born in 1773. (For dates of his commissions from ensign to captain, *vide* Appendix No. 1.) In the muster-rolls of 1794-95, he is returned as a prisoner of war. He served with the regiment as a captain in the Egyptian campaign of 1801, and at the battle fought near Alexandria on 13th March of that year, received a wound. After leaving the army he resided at his estate of Mavis Grove, near Dumfries, and was appointed colonel of the Dumfriesshire Yeomanry Cavalry. He died on 11th September, 1838, and was buried in the churchyard of St. Michael's Church, Dumfries, where a monument was erected to his memory. He was the nephew of the wife of Colonel Schuyler De Peister (*vide* No. 34), from whom he inherited the estate of Mavis Grove. His younger brother, Archibald, was appointed ensign in the regiment on 23rd November, 1791, (*vide* No. 218), and his nephew, William M. McMurdo on 1st July, 1837 (*vide* No. 222). *Vide Records*, part 1.

No. 102. James Booth served in a battalion of flank companies under Sir Charles Grey, at the capture of Guadaloupe, where he was killed between 9th June and 2nd July, 1794. In the casualty return annexed to Sir Charles Grey's despatch of 8th July, 1794, his name appears as Lieutenant Booth, and in the Annual Army List his name does not appear as a captain; but the *London Gazette* of 27th January, 1795, P. T. Robertson, from the Thirty-Eighth Regiment, is promoted to be captain in the King's, *vice* Booth, deceased.

No. 103. Neale M'Neale served with the regiment in the American campaign of 1813. On 27th April of that year, while in command of the Grenadier Company, he was mortally wounded in opposing the attack on York, the capital of Upper Canada, made by an American force under Major-General Pike.—*Vide Records*, part 1.

No. 104. James S. Tyeth served with the regiment during the American campaign of 1813. At the attack on the American post of Sackett's

Harbour (29th May, 1813) he was wounded and taken prisoner.

No. 105. William Robinson served with the regiment during the American campaigns of 1813-14. At the attack on Black Rock and Buffalo, on 30th December, 1813, after Lieutenant-Colonel Ogilvie was wounded, the command of a detachment of two hundred and forty rank and file of the King's devolved on Captain Robinson. Major-General Riall, who commanded the expedition, reported "that by a judicious movement to the right with three companies he made a considerable impression on the left of the enemy's position." He was afterwards appointed to the command of a corps of provincial militia, with the local rank of lieutenant-colonel, and on 25th July, 1814, when in command of that corps, he was present at the Battle of Lundy's Lane, and received a wound. He was promoted to be a brevet major on 19tb December, 1813. He commanded a detachment of three companies sent to reinforce the garrison of Santa Maura, and on 4th October, 1819, was present at an attack made by Lieutenant-Colonel Sir Frederick Stovin on the insurgent inhabitants of that island.

He retired from the army in 1824.—*Vide Records*, part 1.

No. 106. Francis Campbell served with the regiment during the American campaigns of 1813-14. He had a horse shot under him, and highly distinguished himself at the battle of Lundy's Lane. In Lieutenant-General Gordon Drummond's despatch his name was honourably mentioned.—*Vide Records*, part 1.

No. 107. Henry Sadlier served with the regiment during the campaign in America of 1813-14. He commanded the Light Company in the attempt made by Major Evans on the night of 12th July, 1814, to carry off the general commanding the American troops encamped near Fort George. He died in 1816.—*Vide Records*, part 1.

No. 108. John Fitzgerald received the commission of ensign in the Irish Brigade on 18th January, 1798; on its reduction he was placed on half-pay, from which he was transferred to the Ninety-sixth on 23rd July, 1803. On 24th April, 1804, he was promoted and transferred to the King's, in which he obtained his company on 6th June, 1811. He died of fever at Spanish Town, Jamaica, on 5th July, 1831, having served thirty-one years in the regiment, and no less than twenty-one years in the rank of captain. He was made a brevet-major on 22nd July, 1830.

He served with the regiment as a lieutenant in Hanover from October, 1805, until February, 1806; in the Copenhagen Expedition 1st August to 1st December, 1807; at the capture of Martinique, February, 1809; and as a captain during the campaigns in America of 1813-14.

No. 109. John Bradbridge served with the regiment during the American campaigns of 1813-14. He was present at the siege of Fort Erie (August and September, 1814), and was made prisoner while opposing a sortie made by the garrison on the 17th September.—*Vide Records*, part 1.

No. 110. James Hardy Eustace served with the regiment during the campaign in America of 1813. At the attack made on Ogdenberg on 13th February, 1813, he commanded a company of the King's, which carried a fort at the point of the bayonet, and captured two stand of colours. His conduct was highly commended in despatches.—*Vide Records*, part 1.

No. 111. Samuel Hooker received the commission of ensign in the King's on 12th August, 1803, and was promoted to be lieutenant on 12th October, 1804. He served with the First Battalion of the Regiment in Canada during the campaigns of 1812-13, and was killed in the night attack on the American camp of Stoney Creek, 5th June, 1813. In the Army List of 1813, his name stands first of the lieutenants, but in the list of casualties appended to the Army List of 1814, he is returned as a captain. He must, therefore, have been promoted to a company sometime between 1st January and 25th June, 1813,—*Vide Records* part 1.

No. 112. John M'Mahon served with the regiment during the campaign in America of 1813. He received a wound on 27th May, 1813, when opposing the attack made by the Americans on Fort George.—*Vide Records*, part 1.

No. 113. David Vans Machen received the commission of ensign in the Ninety-First Regiment on 3rd September, 1812; was promoted lieutenant 27th July, 1814; transferred to the Fifty-Second Light Infantry on 13th April, 1815; placed on half-pay 25th March, 1817; transferred to the King's 5th March, 1818; and promoted captain in it 15th March, 1821. He served as ensign in the Ninety-First Regiment at the unsuccessful assault on Bergen-op-Zoom, 8th March, 1814. He retired from the service on 7th August, 1835.

No. 114. David Gardiner served as a subaltern with the Eighty-

Eighth Regiment in the Peninsula during the campaigns of 1812-13, and 14. He made prisoner an officer of the French Eighty-Eighth. He was placed on half-pay as a lieutenant on 25th March, 1816, and appointed to the King's on 5th May, 1825. He retired from the service on 12th December, 1848.

No, 115. Ferdinand White, C.B. (Son of José Maria Blanco, commonly called Blanco White, whose interesting autobiography was edited by J. H. Thorn, and published in London, 1845.) In 1841-42, he served as captain in the Fortieth throughout the operations in Afghanistan (medal). He was afterwards present with the fortieth at the Battle of Maharajpore (medal).

For his services in Afghanistan he was made a Companion of the Bath, and promoted to be a brevet major. He exchanged into the King's on 19th June, 1846, and on 21st February, 1851, he was promoted to be an unattached lieutenant-colonel, and placed on half-pay. He died in 1856.

No. 116. Robert Stuart Baynes, nephew of Major Simcoe Baynes, and elder brother of Major George Edward Baynes (No. 75 and 82 of this Appendix), was appointed ensign in the King's on 28th July, 1843, and after 16 years' continuous service in the regiment, during five of which he held the appointment of adjutant, he retired on half-pay with the rank of major unattached on 4th November, 1859. The dates of his subsequent promotions are: Lieutenant-colonel, 17th June, 1859; colonel, 7th September, 1865; major-general, 1st October, 1877, (antedated, 26th March, 1870).

He served in the Crimea as military magistrate at Headquarters. For his services in this campaign he was promoted to be brevet major (25th December, 1856), and received the British and Turkish medals.

During the Indian Mutiny campaign of 1857, he served with the regiment as captain. He commanded the detachment which on the night of 12th May was dispatched from Jellundur to secure the fort and magazine of Phillour. He was present at the siege of Delhi, and on the day of the assault (14th September), commanded the loading company of the King's, was severely wounded and had his leg amputated.

After retiring on half-pay he held the following appointments:— Member of the Ordnance Select Committee; deputy assistant adjutant-general for militia. Headquarters of the army from 1st May, 1860, to 31st March, 1861; military magistrate, Gibraltar, from 1861, to 1868; secretary to Government, Gibraltar; appointed 1868, and still holds the appointment.

No. 117. John Millar Bannatyne was appointed ensign Ninety-Third Highlanders, 17th December, 1847; promoted lieutenant, Ninety-Third, 10th January, 1851; adjutant, Twenty-First North British Fusiliers, 4th March to 21st April, 1853; captain, Twenty-First, 22nd April, 1853; exchanged to the King's, 2nd September, 1853; exchanged to half-pay, 11th July, 1865; was promoted brevet major 19th January, 1858, and brevet lieutenant-colonel, 27th December, 1868. He retired from the service by the commutation of his retiring allowances in December, 1870.

In 1857, he served with the King's regiment at the siege, assault, and capture of Delhi; was present at repulse of sorties on 9th, 14th, and 18th July; at the assault on 14th September and six days' subsequent fighting in the city; commanded the regiment at the capture of Burn bastion on the night of 19th September, and the infantry of the column which occupied the Great Mosque on the following day; served as brigade major to Colonel Greathed's column; present at action of Bulandshahr, affair of Allyghur and Battle of Agra. Served as brigade major of Third Infantry Brigade at action of Dilkoosha and relief of Lucknow; at affair of 2nd and action of 6th December near Cawnpore, and at the action of Khuda Gunj (six times mentioned in despatches. Brevet major; medal and two clasps).—*Vide Records*, parts 1 & 2.

No. 118. Richard William Woods served in the Buffs at the Battle of Punniar (bronze star). He exchanged into the Eightieth Regiment, afterwards, (on 1st December, 1862), he was appointed staff officer of Pensioners. He retired from the army with the rank of lieutenant-colonel on 25th August, 1880.

No. 119. John Ball Campbell served with the Forty-Ninth Regiment in China from May, 1842, until the end of the war.

No. 120. Astell Thomas Welsh exchanged from the Eightieth Foot to the King's as captain on 22nd July, 1856. In 1852-53, served with the Eightieth Regiment in the Burmese war. Present at bombardment of Rangoon, capture of the great Dagon Pagoda (with the storming party), bombardment and capture of Prome (specially thanked by Governor-General in Council), repulse of night attack on camp at Prome, and expedition into the Poungdey district in February and March, 1852 (medal). During the Mutiny campaign of 1857, he served with the King's Regiment as captain (medal).—*Vide Records*, part 1.

No. 121. John Whiteside enlisted as private in the Ninth Regiment, on 16th January, 1831; was appointed sergeant-major on 1st March, 1843, and received the commission of ensign in it on 19th December, 1845, and of lieutenant on 12th November, 1847; he afterwards exchanged, first into the Twenty-Second, and soon afterwards into the Ninety-Sixth Regiment, in which he was promoted to a company on 11th March, 1856. Exchanged into the King's, 3rd March, 1857. In 1842, served with the Ninth Regiment as quartermaster-sergeant in the Afghan campaign under General Pollock (medal). In 1845-46, served with the Ninth Regiment during the Sutlej campaign; as sergeant-major at the Battles of Moodkee and Ferozeshah, and as ensign at the Battle of Sobraon (medal and clasps). In 1858-59, served as captain with the King's during the Oudh campaign, and was for part of the time in command of the regiment; present at the attack and capture of the fort and town of Sandee. He was promoted to an unattached majority on 13th February, 1866, and retired on full pay with the honorary rank of lieutenant-colonel on 11th November, 1866.—*Vide Records,* part 1.

No. 122. Thomas George Souter, son of Captain T. A. Souter Forty-Fourth Regiment, the only officer who survived the massacre of Jugdullack, 13th January, 1842, and who saved one of the regimental colours; he served with the Buffs at the action of Punniar, 29th December, 1843 (medal), and in the King's Regiment at the siege of Delhi in 1857; present at the repulse of the sorties of 14th, 18th, and 23rd July (medal and clasp). He exchanged, first into the Fifty-First Regiment, and afterwards into the Bengal Staff Corps, in which he attained the rank of major; he died in London while on furlough, on 30th December 1864.—*Vide Records,* part 1.

No. 123. Daniel Beere served in the King's Regiment at the siege of Delhi, and was wounded at the assault of the city on 14th September, 1857 (medal and clasp), he exchanged to half-pay on 1st January, 1863. He is now, (1833), a lieutenant-colonel, and holds the appointment of staff officer of Pensioners.—*Vide Records,* parts 1 & 2.

No. 124. Erskine Nimmo Sandilands, was appointed ensign Forty-Second, 21st May, 1842, promoted on 3rd April, 1846, to be lieutenant in the King's; captain 21st October, 1857; transferred to Bengal Staff Corps on its formation in 1861, and employed in Department of Public Works until 23rd November 1879, when he retired with the honorary rank of major-general.

In 1857, served with the King's at the siege of Delhi; present at repulse of sorties on 14th, 18th, and 23rd July, wounded by a splinter of a shell on 10th August, and again severely wounded at the assault on the city on 14th September when in command of the Light Company; notwithstanding this wound he did not quit the ranks for several hours, and after recovering from it he rejoined the regiment on 13th October, and served with it at the relief of Lucknow by Lord Clyde, and subsequent operations; present at the action of Dilkoosha; at affair of 2nd and action of 6th December near Cawnpore, and at the action of Khuda Gunj (medal and two clasps).—*Vide Records*, part 1.

No. 125. Swinnerton Halliday Dyer. In 1855, served with Nineteenth Regiment at siege of Sebastopol from 2nd January; present at assaults of the Redan on 18th June and 8th September; was also present at bombardment and surrender of Kinburn (medal and clasp; Third Class of the Medjidie, and Turkish medal).

No. 126. John Woods Dimond served in the Kafir war of 1851, in the Royal Navy on board Her Majesty's ship *Hermes* (medal).

No. 127. Owen Wynne Gray served with the Thirty-Ninth at the affair of Gorapore, near Kurnool, on 18th October, 1839, and also at the Battle of Maharajpore 29th December, 1843 (medal).

No. 128. George Corry in 1857-58, served with the King's Regiment during the Indian Mutiny campaign; present at the defeat of the mutineers on the banks of the Chumbul and at the attack and capture of the villages of Bhujah and Seorale by Brigadier Showers, when he was in command of a detachment of two hundred men of the regiment.—*Vide Records*, parts 1 & 2.

No. 129. Alexr. Ross Bayly, son of Major Wm. Bayly (*vide* No. 79), appointed ensign in the King's, 2nd April, 1847. (For other regimental commissions *vide* Succession List.) Exchanged to Eighty-Eighth Foot on 31st January, 1860; transferred to Bengal Staff Corps at its formation in 1861; employed in Department of Public Works until 1st September, 1877, when he retired with the honorary rank of colonel.

Served with the King's during the Indian Mutiny campaign of 1857; present at the siege of Delhi; at the repulse of the sorties of the 9th, 14th, 18th, and 23rd July; at the night attack on advanced piquet and capture of four guns on 12th August; at the assault and six days' subsequent fighting; at the action of Bulandshahr, affair of Allyghur, and Battle of Agra; at the action of Dilkoosha and relief of Lucknow;

at the affair of 2nd and action of 6th December, near Cawnpore, and at the action of Khuda Gunj (medal and clasps).—*Vide Records*, part 1.

No. 130. William Raymond Ximenes, younger brother of Lieutenant Horace Ximenes (No. 183). (For commissions from ensign to captain *vide* Succession List.) In 1855, he served as A.D.C. to his uncle. Brigadier D. F. Evans, commanding Fourth Brigade Ottoman Contingent (Turkish medal). In 1857, served with the King's Regiment from 18th September until close of the campaign; present at the action of Bulandshahr, affair of Allyghur, and Battle of Agra; at the action of Dilkoosha and capture of Lucknow; at the affair of 2nd and action of 6th December, near Cawnpore and at the action of Khuda Gunj (medal and two clasps). He retired from the army by the sale of his commission, on 29th March, 1864, and died on 30th November, 1880,—*Vide Records*, part 1.

No. 131. Robert L. Grant M'Grigor served with the King's during the Indian Mutiny campaign of 1857, Present at the siege of Delhi (slightly wounded); at the assault and fighting in the city during the six subsequent days; at the action of Bulandshahr, affair of Allyghur, and Battle of Agra; at the action of Dilkoosha and relief of Lucknow; at the affair of 2nd and action of 6th December, near Cawnpore, and at the action of Khuda Gunj (medal and two clasps).—*Vide Records*, part 1.

No. 132. William Frederick Metge served with the King's Regiment at the siege of Delhi in 1857. Present at the repulse of the sorties on 9th, 14th, and 18th July; was with the storming party of the left attack at the assault of the city (wounded). Afterwards served in command of the Police Cavalry with General Whitelock's column in Bundelcund (medal and clasp).

No. 133. John M'Queen, ensign. Ninth Regiment, 5th November, 1854, lieutenant 8th March, 1865; adjutant, 15th February, 1855, to 7th October, 1879; captain, 23rd September, 1859. In 1854-55 served with the Ninth Regiment in the Crimea. Present at Battles of Alma, Balaclava, and Inkermann; at the siege of Sebastopol; repulse of sortie on 6th October; assault on the cemetery on 18th June, and at the fall of the city (wounded in left arm; medal and clasps, Fifth Class of the Medjidie and Turkish medal).

No. 134. Lewis John Fillis Jones, ensign (Seventh Fusiliers), 14th July, 1854; lieutenant (Seventh Fusiliers), 8th December, 1854; captain (Eighty-Eighth Foot) 27th May, 1856. Exchanged to the King's

31st January, 1860. Major (by brevet) 16th April, 1861, served in the Crimea with the Seventh Fusiliers from 20th October, 1854; present at the siege of Sebastopol, at the Battle of Inkermann (wounded); at the repulse of the sorties of 26th October, 1854, 5th April, 1855, (wounded) and 9th May, 1855; at the attack and capture of the quarries on 7th June (wounded), and at the attack on the Redan on 18th June, when he was severely wounded in three places.

He was also wounded in the trenches on 27th March, 1855 (medal and clasp, and Fifth Class of Order of Medjidie). In 1857-58, he served with the Eighty-Eighth Regiment in the Mutiny campaign, was present at the actions near Cawnpore of General Windham's force in November, 1857, also at the action of Bloognapore, the capture of Calpee, and the subjugation of Oudh (medal and clasps). On 16th July, 1861, he was appointed adjutant of a depot battalion, and on 21st January, 1872, he retired from the service with the honorary rank of lieutenant-colonel; his brother, Jeremy Peyton Jones, served in the regiment from 3rd. July, 1858, until 17th April, 1880, (*vide* Appendix No. 1).

No. 135. Frederick Anderson Stebbing. (For date of commission from ensign to captain, *vide* Succession List.) Served with the regiment at the siege and assault of Delhi, and at the six days' subsequent fighting in the city: present at the actions of Gungeree, Puttialee, and Mynpooree (medal with clasp). He retired on half pay on 31st October, 1871, and was promoted to major (by brevet) on 8th July, 1874.

No. 136. Aneas Gordon Blair was present at Jellundur at the outbreak of the *Sepoy* troops, on the night of 17th June, 1857 (medal).

No. 137. John Cusack enlisted as private in the Ninety-Seventh on 23rd August, 1839; was appointed sergeant-major of it in August, 1854, and received the commission of lieutenant in the Land Transport Corps on 14th June, 1855. He was transferred to the 24th as quartermaster of the Second Battalion on 13th April, 1858; was appointed adjutant of it 3rd February, 1860; promoted to an unattached company 6th February, 1863, and exchanged to the King's on 28th August, 1863.

He served as sergeant-major of the Ninety-Seventh Regiment in the Crimean campaign of 1854-55, and was present at the taking of the quarries; at the assaults on the Redan on 18th June and 8th September, and at the fall of Sebastopol (wounded). (Medal with clasp, medal for distinguished conduct in the field, and Turkish medal.)

No. 138. Andrew Moynihan, V.C, was born on 1st January, 1830; enlisted as private in the Ninetieth Regiment on 11th September, 1848; was appointed sergeant-major of it 29th January, 1856, and received the commission of ensign in the King's 2nd May, 1856. (For commissions from ensign to captain, *vide* Succession Lists, Appendix No. 1.)

In 1854-55, he served as corporal with the Ninetieth Light Infantry during the Crimean campaign and siege of Sebastopol; was present at capture of quarries 7th June, and at the assaults on the Redan on 18th June, and 8th September; on 8th, belonged to storming party, and was the first man who entered the work; was made prisoner while endeavouring to carry off the body of Lieutenant Swift, but was soon after rescued after receiving two bayonet wounds; was one of the last men to leave the Redan; after the troops had retired into the trenches he recrossed the open ground, and under a terrific fire rescued a wounded officer who had fallen near the Redan (medal and clasp, mentioned in despatches, and Victoria Cross, French war medal, and Turkish medal). In 1858, present with detachment of the regiment at defeat of rebels in ravines of Chumbul, and at the capture of Bhujah and Seorale. In the Oudh campaign of 1857-58, he served with the regiment, and was present at capture of the town and fort of Sandee. He died of fever at Malta on 19th May, 1867.—*Vide Records,* part 2.

No. 139. The Honourable Somerset R. H. Ward, ensign, Seventy-Second Highlanders, 8th November, 1850; lieutenant, Seventy-Second Highlanders, 11th November, 1853; captain, Seventy-Second Highlanders, 10th September, 1858; exchanged to King's 16th October, 1863. In 1855 served in the Crimea with the Seventy-Second Highlanders; present at the expedition to Kertch and at the fall of Sebastopol (medal and clasp and Turkish medal). In 1857-58 served as adjutant Seventy-Second Highlanders, with the Rajapootana Field Force, and subsequently throughout the operations in Central India and pursuit of the rebel forces under Tantia Topee and Rao Sahib; present at the siege, assault, and capture of Kotah (medal and clasp).

No. 140. Sidney H. Jones Parry, ensign. First Madras Fusiliers, 20th February, 1849; lieutenant 8th January, 1853; captain 11th June, 1859; exchanged to King's 26th February, 1864. In 1852-53, served with the Madras Fusiliers in the Burmese campaigns; present at investment and subsequent defence of Pegu (medal with clasp). In 1854-55, served in the Crimea as assistant quartermaster-general of the Second Infantry Division of the Turkish Contingent (medal). In 1857-58, served with Sir

H. Havelock's column at the relief of Lucknow; present at storming of Secundrabagh, Shah Nujeef, and Tara Kotee; afterwards served with Outram's force during occupation of the Alumbagh, and at the capture of Lucknow, and subsequent campaign in Oudh (medal with two clasps).

No. 141, William Edward Whelan. (For commissions from ensign to captain, *vide* Succession Lists, Appendix No. 1.) In June, 1858, served with a detachment of the regiment during operations against the rebels in the ravines of the Chumbul; present at attack and capture of the villages Bhujah and Seorale. During the Oudh campaign of 1857-58, served as adjutant of the regiment, and was present at the attack and capture of the fort and town of Sandee (medal). He retired from the service on 13th June, 1868, and now holds the appointment of resident magistrate at Portadown, Ireland.—*Vide Records*, part 1.

No. 142. Charles Bradford Brown was appointed ensign in the Sixty-Third Foot on 15th March, 1855, and transferred to the King's Regiment as lieutenant, 16th November, 1857. He held the appointment of adjutant of the Second Battalion from 16th July, 1858, until promoted captain on 15th June, 1866; promoted major by brevet on 13th April, 1879.

He served as a subaltern with the Sixty-Third Regiment in the Crimea, and was present at the assault of the Redan, at the bombardment and surrender of Kinburn, and at the fall of Sebastopol (medal with clasp and Turkish medal). On 24th September, 1879, he embarked with a draft of the Second Battalion for service in Afghanistan, but shortly after landing in India his constitution was shattered by a sunstroke, and on 8th May, 1880, he retired from the service with the honorary rank of lieutenant-colonel.—*Vide Records*, part 1.

No. 143. John Dawson served with the Second Battalion during the Afghan campaigns of 1878, 79, 80, was present at the action of 28th November, and at the Battle of the Peiwar Kotal.—*Vide Records*, part 2.

No. 144. Armar Graham Lowry, nephew of Lieutenant John Lowry (No. 174), served with the Forty-First Regiment throughout the Crimean campaign of 1854-55, was present at the Battles of Alma and Inkermann, at the assault of the Redan, 8th September (twice wounded), at the repulse of the sortie of 26th October, 1854, and at the fall of Sebastopol. (Medal with three clasps, Turkish medal, and Fifth Class of the Medjidie.) On 7th September, 1856, he retired from the service as captain in the Forty-First. On 23rd April, 1866, he again entered the army as ensign in the First West Indian Regiment; he exchanged into the King's as captain, on 8th August, 1868, and on 18th May, 1881, retired with the honorary rank of lieutenant-colonel.

No. 145. Edwin Jervis served with the Thirty-Third Regiment during the Abyssinian campaigns of 1867-68. He was present at the storming of Magdala (medal). During the Afghan campaigns of 1878-79-80, he served as a captain in the Second Battalion, and was present at the action of 28th November, at the Battle of Peiwar Kotal, and at the repulse of an attack on the camp at Ali-Kheyl. He was mentioned in despatches, promoted to a brevet majority (1st March, 1881), and received & medal and clasp. On 18th May, 1881, he retired from the service with the honorary rank of lieutenant-colonel.—*Vide Records*, part 2.

No. 146. William Toke Dooner. (For dates of commissions from ensign to captain, *vide* Appendix No. 1.) In 1872, he passed the final examination of the Staff College of Sandhurst; from 12th September, 1873, until 24th March, 1874, he was employed under Sir Garnet Wolseley in special service on Gold Coast; he trained and commanded throughout the Ashantee war the Opobo company of Russell's regiment; was present at capture of Adubrassie, Battle of Amoaful, capture of Becquah, advanced guard action of Jarbinbah, skirmishes between Adwabon and the River Ordah, Battle of Ordahsu, and capture of Coomassie; surveyed for the Intelligence Department part of the road between Cape Coast and the Prah. (Mentioned in despatches; medal with clasp.) On 12th May, 1875, he exchanged into the One Hundred and Eighth Foot, and now holds the appointment of brigade major at Aldershot.

No. 147. Thomas Blake Humfrey commanded a company of the Second Battalion during the Afghan campaign of 1879-80 (medal).—*Vide Records*, part 2.

No. 148. David William Martin. In the Indian Mutiny campaign of 1857-58, while holding the commission of subaltern in the Seventy-Fifth Foot, was employed as assistant field engineer during the siege of Delhi. At the Battle of Budlee-ke-Serai, he acted as orderly officer to the chief engineer (medal with clasp); on 27th September, 1879, he retired on a pension with the honorary rank of lieutenant-colonel.—*Vide Records*, part 1.

No. 149. Stanley Napier Roberts served as captain with the Second Battalion during the Afghan campaigns of 1878-79, 80; he was present at the action of 28th November, and at the Battle of the Peiwar Kotal (medal and one clasp).—*Vide Records*, parts 1 & 2.

No. 150. Alfred Lewis served with the Sixtieth Rifles in the Indian Mutiny campaign of 1858 (medal). In 1862, while serving in the Fourth Battalion of the Sixtieth, he volunteered to go after some men who had deserted with their arms and ammunition; these deserters he succeeded in capturing, after they had fired several times on his party; for this service he was mentioned in general orders by Sir F. Williams, and recommended for promotion. During the Afghan campaigns of 1878-79-80, he served as captain with the Second Battalion of the King's (medal).—*Vide Records,* part 2.

No. 151. Arthur Henry Cope commanded a company of the Second Battalion during the Afghan campaigns of 1878-79, 80. On 10th April, 1879, he commanded a party of eight officers and privates, who pursued and attacked twenty Afghans, who had murdered a native follower; five of the Afghans were killed and several wounded; for this service the party was thanked in divisional orders (medal).—*Vide Records*, part 2.

No. 152. Arthur Ashley Ruck served as musketry instructor with the Second Battalion daring the Afghan campaigns of 1878-79-80 (medal).—*Vide Records*, part 2.

No. 153. William Richard Orme served as a subaltern in the Second Battalion daring the Afghan campaigns of 1878-79, 80 (medal).— *Vide Records*, part 2.

No. 154. James Mathew Taylor served with the Second Battalion daring the Afghan campaigns of 1878-79-80. He was present at the action of 28th November, and at the battle of the Peiwar Kotal (medal and clasp).— *Vide Records*, part 2.

No. 155. Frederick James Whalley served as adjutant with the Second Battalion daring the Afghan campaigns of 1878-79, 80. He was present at the action of 28th November, and at the battle of the Peiwar Kotal, and was one of four officers who did duty continuously with the battalion, from 21st November, 1878, the day it entered Afghanistan, until it recrossed the frontier, on 21st October, 1880. He was one of a party of eight officers and privates who, under command of Captain Cope, pursued and attacked twenty Afghans, who, on 10th April,

1879, had murdered a camp follower; five of the Afghans were killed and several others wounded.

For this service the party were thanked by the major-general commanding the division. He held the appointment of Station Staff Officer at the Peiwar Kotal from 16th February, 1879, until the station was evacuated in September, 1880 (medal and clasp).—*Vide Records*, part 2.

CAPTAINS LIEUTENANTS.

No. 156. Thomas (or Charles) Thompson served as a subaltern in the campaign in the Low Countries of 1745; on the 11th May he was wounded at the battle of Fontenoy.—*Vide Records*, part 1.

LIEUTENANTS.

No. 157. John Bazire (or Bezier) served with the regiment in the campaign of 1704, was wounded on 2nd July at the storming of the heights of Schellenberg, and again on 13th August, at the Battle of Blenheim.— *Vide Records*, part 1.

No. 158. William Robinson served with the regiment in the campaign in Flanders of 1743, and on 26th June, he was wounded at the Battle of Hanan.— *Vide Records*, part 1.

No. 159. William Rickson served with the regiment in the campaign in the Netherlands of 1746, and was wounded on 11th October at the Battle of Roucoux.— *Vide Records*, part 1.

No. 160. William Morrison served with the regiment in the campaign in the Netherlands of 1760, and was wounded on 16th October at an attack on the Convent of Campen, near Rhineberg.— *Vide Records*, part 1.

No. 161. Robert Eason served with the regiment in the campaign in Egypt of 1801, and on 13th March was wounded in the attack on the French position near Alexandria.

No. 162. Robert Villenuve served as brigade-major on the staff of Brigadier-General Hompesch, during the operations which resulted in the capitulation of Trinidad on 18th February, 1797. While performing this duty he received a wound of which he died on the 24th April following. His wound was the only casualty recorded. *Vide* in *Bulletins of the Campaigns*, a despatch of Sir R. Abercrombie, dated Trinidad, 27th February, 1797.

No. 163. Donough O'Brien served with the regiment in the campaign in Egypt of 1801. On 13th March, in the attack of the French position near Alexandria, he received a wound, of which he died a few days afterwards.—*Vide Records*, part 1.

No. 164. John Church served with the regiment in the campaign in Egypt of 1801. He was wounded oh 13th of March, in the attack of the French position near Alexandria.—*Vide Records*, part 1.

No. 165. Thomas Warring Lloyd served with the First Battalion during the campaign in America of 1813. He was wounded on 27th May, in the action near Fort George.—*Vide Records*, part 1.

No. 166. Morton Noel served the First Battalion during the campaigns in America of 1813-14. He was wounded on 27th May, 1813, at the action near Fort George; was present at the Battle of Lundy's Lane, 23rd July, 1814, and at the siege of Fort Erie. He was killed on 15th August, 1814, in an unsuccessful attempt made during that siege to turn the American position between Snake Hill and the lake;—*Vide Records*, part 1.

No. 167. George Nutall served with the First Battalion during the American campaign of 1813. He died of a wound received at the attack of Sackett's Harbour, on 29th May, 1813.—*Vide Records*, part 1.

No. 168: Charles Barstow served with the First Battalion during the campaign in America of 1813-14. On 11th July, 1813, he commanded a detachment which formed part of the force of Lieutenant-Colonel Bishopp, in the attack on Black Rock. He was killed on 17th September, 1814, in a sortie made by the garrison during the siege of Fort Erie.

No. 169. James Drummie served with the First Battalion during the campaign in Canada of 1813. He was killed on 27th May, in the action fought near Fort George.—*Vide Records*, part 1.

No. 170. John Thorne Wayland served with the First Battalion in the campaigns in America of 1813-14. Was present at the actions of Fort George, and was severely wounded on the night of 5th June, 1813, at the surprise of the American camp at Stoney Creek. He was placed on half-pay 3rd May, 1816. Subsequently he served as a captain in the Canadian Rifles (13th March, 1827). He was promoted brevet-major 23rd November, 1841, and retired from the army in 1850. In the Army List of 1809, and of several subsequent years, his Christian name is stated to be Richard,—*Vide Records*, part 1.

No. 171. Edward Finch served with the First Battalion during the campaigns in America of 1813-14. After the surprise of the American camp at Stoney Creek, 5th June, 1813, he was twice employed in carrying despatches.—*Vide Records*, part 1.

No. 172. Edward Boyd served with the First Battalion during the campaigns in America of 1813-14. He was wounded on the night of 5th June, 1813, at the surprise of the American camp at Stoney Creek, and again on 5th July, 1814, at the action near Chippawa.—*Vide Records*, part 1.

No. 173. Henry Palmer Hill, in 1809, served with the regiment as ensign at the capture of Martinique. In 1813-14, served with the First Battalion in Canada as lieutenant, and was present at the actions at York Town, Sackett's Harbour, Stoney Creek, Chippawa, Landy's Laue, and at the siege of Fort Erie. He was appointed paymaster of the regiment on 10th July, 1832, and died of inflammation in the bowels at Up Park Camp, Jamaica, on 26th May, 1836.

No. 174. John Lowry served with the First Battalion during the campaigns in America of 1813-14, and was present at the actions of Prescot, Sackett's Harbour, Chippawa, Lundy's Lane, assault on Fort Erie, and repulse of sortie. He was shot through the body on 29th May, 1813, at the attack on Sackett's Harbour, received a contusion at Lundy's Lane, and was severely wounded during the siege of Fort Erie, at the sortie made by the garrison on 17th September, 1814. He was placed on half-pay on 13th July, 1820. He is at present, (1881), and has been for many years past, a resident in Dublin.

His nephew, Armar Graham Lowry (No. 144), served in the regiment as a captain from August, 1868, to May, 1881.—*Vide Records*, part 1.

No. 175. Richard Nicholson served with the First Battalion daring the campaigns in America of 1813-14. He was wounded and taken prisoner on 27th May, 1813, in the action fought near Fort St. George.—*Vide Records*, part 1.

No. 176. J. G. Powell served as ensign with the First Battalion during the campaign in America of 1813; was wounded at the attack on Ogdenberg, 13th February, 1813.—*Vide Records*, part 1.

No. 177. Brooke Young served with the First Battalion during the campaigns in America of 1813-14. He was wounded on the attack on

Black Rock on 30th December, and again on 15th August, 1814, at the attack made by the flank companies for the purpose of turning the position between Snake Hill and the lake, during the siege of Fort Erie.—*Vide Records*, part 1.

No. 178. Alexander Greig served with the First Battalion during the campaigns in America of 1813-14. He was wounded on 29th May, 1818, at the attack on Sackett's Harbour. He was mentioned in the public despatches of General Fisher, for his zeal and conduct at the storming of Oswego on 6th May, 1814; again by Major-General Riall, for having distinguished himself at the action of 5th July, 1814, on the plains of Chippawa, and again in general orders, for the capture of Colonel Stainton, of the United States Army, at the Battle of Lundy's Lane, 25th July, 1814. He held the appointment of staff adjutant to Colonel Pearson. He was placed on half-pay 25th March, 1817; appointed paymaster of the Eighty-Third Regiment 10th April, 1823, and retired from the service in 1826.—*Vide Records*, part 1.

No. 179. Robert MacNair served with the First Battalion during the campaign in America of 1814; was present at the siege of Fort Erie, and was made prisoner during the sortie of the garrison, on 17th September.—*Vide Records*, part 1.

No. 180. Thomas Swayne served as ensign with the First Battalion during the campaign in America of 1814. He was wounded at the Battle of Lundy's Lane, 26th June, 1814;—*Vide Records*, part 1.

No. 181. George Charles Lord Bingham (afterwards third Earl of Lucan, G.C.B.) was appointed ensign in the Sixth Foot, 29th August, 1816; exchanged into Third Foot Guards on the 24th, and to half-pay on 25th December, 1818; exchanged into the King's on 20th January, 1820, and after serving two years in the regiment, again exchanged to half-pay on 16th May, 1822. Subsequently he served in the First Life Guards, in the Seventy-Eighth and Thirty-First Foot, and in the Seventeenth Light Dragoons, which regiment he commanded from 9th November, 1826, till 14th April, 1833. He attained the rank of major-general on 11th November, 1851, of lieutenant-general, 24th December, 1858, and of general, 28th August, 1865. He was appointed colonel of the Eighth Light Dragoons, 17th November, 1855, and of the First Life Guards, 22nd February, 1865.

From 21st February, 1854, till 18th August, 1855, he served in the Crimea, during the last six months of which period he was in command of the cavalry division.

No. 182. Benjamin Kennicott M'Dermott served with Third Buffs at the Battle of Punniar. (Bronze star.)

No. 183. Horace Ximenes (elder brother of W. Raymond Ximenes, *vide* No. 130). (For dates of commissions, *vide* Appendix No. 1.) He served with the regiment as a subaltern during the Indian Mutiny campaign of 1857, and acted as orderly officer to Colonel Greathed at the actions of Bulandshahr and Allyghur, at the Battle of Agra, at the action of Dilkoosha and relief of Lucknow, at the actions near Cawnpore on 2nd and 6th December, 1857, and at Khuda Gunj on 2nd January, 1858 (medal and clasp). On 23rd March, 1858, he was promoted, without purchase, to a company in the Sixteenth Regiment; he retired from the service on 2nd November, 1866, and died 18th June, 1868.—*Vide Records*, part 1.

No. 184. William Waldegrave Pogson served with the regiment during the Mutiny campaign of 1857. He was present at the outbreak of the Native troops at Jellundur on the night of 7th June, at the march from Jellundur to Delhi (14th to 28th June), at the repulse of the sorties of 9th, 14th, 18th, and 23rd July, and at the assault of the city on 14th September. On the 23rd he received a slight wound. On the day of the assault he was attached to the storming party, received a severe wound from a grape shot, had his leg amputated, and died three days afterwards, on 17th September.—*Vide Records*, part 1.

No. 185. George Fuller Walker was appointed ensign in the King's on 14th April, 1856; promoted lieutenant, 13th September, 1849; and appointed adjutant, 10th April, 1855; which appointment he held until promoted to a company in the Twenty-Second Foot, on 17th March, 1858.

He served with the regiment as adjutant during the Mutiny campaign of 1857-58. Was present at the outbreak of the Native troops at Jellundur on the night of 7th June; at the march from Jellundur to Delhi (14th to 28th June); at the repulse of the sorties of 9th, 14th, 18th, and 23rd July, and at the assault of the city on 14th September. He had his horse shot under him on the 9th, and on the day of the assault received a severe wound in the arm, notwithstanding which he did not quit the ranks for several hours. After the capture of the city, though still suffering from his unhealed wound, he marched with the regiment, and was present at the actions of Bulandshahr and Alighur;

at the battle of Agra, relief of Lucknow, actions near Cawnpore on 2nd and 6th December, and at the action of Khuda Gunj, 2nd January, 1858 (medal and two clasps).

After leaving the regiment he served, first in the Twenty-Second, and afterwards in the Twelfth Foot, to the command of the First Battalion of which regiment he succeeded on 3rd April, 1878. He served with it in the Afghan campaigns of 1878-79-80, until appointed to the command of a brigade.—*Vide Records*, part 1.

No. 186. Timothy Walsh enlisted as a private in the Forty-Eighth Regiment on 17th November, 1825, was transferred to the Fifty-Fifth Regiment 1st August, 1834, of which regiment he was appointed sergeant-major on 1st February, 1842. On 22nd November, 1845, he received the commission of ensign in the Seventy-Eighth Highlanders, from whence he was transferred first to the Sixty-Second, and afterwards to the King's Regiment.

In 1834, he served as corporal in the Forty-Eighth in the campaign against the Rajah of Coorg; and in 1841 as sergeant-major Fifty-Fifth in the Chinese War; he was present at the capture of Amoy, capture of Chusan, capture of Chinhae, repulse of night attack on Chinhae 10th October, 1841, capture of Chapoo, Woosung, and Shanghae, and at the escalade of Heling Kiang (medal). On 11th October, 1853, he exchanged with the quartermaster of the Twenty-Ninth Regiment.

No. 187. Thomas Beattie Grierson served with the regiment during the siege of Delhi, and was present at the repulse of the sorties of 9th, 14th, 18th, and 23rd July. He died of dropsy at Umballa on 4th September, 1857.—*Vide Records*, part 1.

No. 188. Charles Sutherland Dowson served in the Twenty-Ninth Regiment during the campaign in the Punjab of 1848-49. He was present at the affair of Ramnugger, at the passage of the Chenab, and at the Battles of Chillianwallah and Goojerat (medal and two clasps).

No. 189. Graham Egerton Huddleston served with the King's during the Mutiny campaign of 1857. He was present at the siege, assault, and capture of Delhi, at the action of Bulandshahr, affair of Alighur, Battle of Agra, affair of 2nd and action of 6th December, near Cawnpore, and at the action of Khuda Gunj (medal and clasp).

On 6th September, 1861, he exchanged into the 52nd Regiment, in which he served as paymaster until 1869.

Afterwards (in 1871) he was appointed paymaster in the Seventieth

Foot, and continued to serve in it until his death, on 15th February, 1877.

No. 190. Thomas Mackesey Vincent served in the navy with a combined naval and military force, which on 23rd May, 1855, attacked and destroyed the town of Malageat, on the West Coast of Africa; in performing this service he was dangerously wounded. In the Indian Mutiny campaign of 1857, he joined the regiment the day before it reached Delhi, but was shortly afterwards invalided to Mussooree, and did not rejoin until the return of the regiment to Cawnpore, after the relief of Lucknow, on 29th November. He was killed in the action fought near Cawnpore, on 6th December.— *Vide Records*, part 1.

No. 191. William Robert Webb served with the regiment during the Indian Mutiny campaign of 1857. He was present at the outbreak of the *sepoys* at Jellundur, on the night of 7th June; at the march from Jellundur to Delhi, 14th to 28th June; at the repulse of the sorties of 9th, 14th, 18th, and 23rd July, and at the assault of the city on 14th September. He was mortally wounded during the advance from the breach to the Moree bastion, and died on the following day.— *Vide Records*, part 1.

No. 192. Hobart Evans Fitzgerald served in the Crimea in 1854-55, with the Fifth Dragoon Guards. He was present at the battles of Balaklava, Inkermann, and Tchernaya, and at the siege and fall of Sebastopol (medal and three clasps).

No. 193. Charles Norris Fry served with the 18th Royal Irish in the Crimea.

No. 194. William Edge worth (of Edgeworrthstown), grandnephew of Maria Edgeworth, served with the regiment during the Mutiny campaign of 1857. He was present at the siege and assault of Delhi, and did duty with the artillery, to which he was attached as a volunteer. He was severely wounded in the action of Bulandshar, 27th September, 1857. Shortly afterwards he exchanged into the Fifth Royal Irish Light Dragoons, and was promoted captain the Third Dragoon Guards, 12th March, 1861. He died of cholera at Bombay, on 25th June, 1863.

No. 195. William Unwin enlisted a private in the Twentieth Regiment, on 15th November, 1839, was appointed quartermaster sergeant, 1st January, 1856, and received the commission of ensign in it on 8th April, 1858, was promoted lieutenant, 11th April, 1859, and was transferred to the King's, 4th May, 1860. In 1854-55, he served in the Crimea with the Twentieth Regiment as quartermaster sergeant, present at the Battles of Alma, Balaklava, and Inkermann, siege of Sebastopol, assaults of Redan on 18th June, and 8th September, and at the fall of the city; present also at the capture of Kinburn (medal with four clasps, and Turkish medal). In 1857-58, served with the Twentieth Regiment, first as quartermaster sergeant, afterwards as ensign, in the Indian Mutiny campaign; present at the actions of Chanda, Ameerpore, and Sultanpore; at the capture of Lucknow, and subsequent operations in Oudh, including affairs of Churda, fort of Musjerdia, and Banhee (medal and clasp). He also received a medal for long service and good conduct.

No. 196. Arthur Holden Turner served in 1859 with the 28th Regiment, at the storming of the forts on Beyt Island, and at the siege and capture of Dwarka.

No. 197. Frederick Bartholomew Joseph Jerrard held an appointment in the Transport Service during the Ashantee war of 1873-74. During the five days preceding the capture of Coomassie, he was employed in protecting communications north of the Prah (medal). On 24th June, 1875, as a reward for his services, he was promoted to a company in the Ninety-First Foot. Soon afterwards he exchanged into the Thirty-Third Foot. He now holds the appointment of inspector and adjutant of the East India Rifle Volunteer Corps.

No. 198. George Villiers Turner served with the Second Battalion during the Afghan campaigns of 1878-79-80. He was attached as orderly officer to the staff of Brigadier Thelwall, and was present at the action of 28th November, and at the Battle of the Peiwar Kotal. In the month of November, 1879, his company formed part of the force under Genera] Tytler, during his operations in the Zymukt Valley (medal and clasp). On 24th January, 1880, he was promoted to an unattached company, and on 7th July appointed to One Hundred and Fifth Foot, in which he is at present (1881), serving.—*Vide Records*, part 2.

No. 199. William Lloyd Brereton served with the Second Battalion during the Afghan campaigns of 1878-79-80. He was present at the action of 28th November, and at the Battle of the Peiwar Kotal, and was one of four officers who served with the battalion continuously from the 21st November, 1878, the day on which it entered Afghanistan, until it recrossed the frontier on 21st October, 1880 (medal and clasp).—*Vide Records*, part 2.

No. 200. Llewellyn Salusbury Mellor served with the Second Battalion during the Afghan campaigns of 1878-79-80, and was present at the action of 28th November, and at the Battle of the Peiwar Kotal (medal and clasp).—*Vide Records*, part 2.

No. 201. Henry Arthur Fletcher served with the Second Battalion during the Afghan campaigns of 1878-79-80. He was present at the action of 28th November, and at the Battle of the Peiwar Kotal (medal and clasp). He died on 26th April, 1881.—*Vide Records*, part 2.

No. 202. Percy Schletter served with the Second Battalion during the Afghan campaigns of 1878-79-80 (medal).—*Vide Records*, part 2.

No. 203. Arthur Charles Greaves Banning served with the Second Battalion during the Afghan campaigns of 1878-79-80. He was present at the action of 28th November, and at the Battle of the Peiwar Kotal (medal and clasp).—*Vide Records*, part 2.

No. 204. Joseph Hume Balfour served with the Second Battalion during the Afghan campaigns of 1878-79-80. He was present at the action of the 28th November, and at the battle of the Peiwar Kotal (medal and clasp).—*Vide Records*, part 2.

No. 205. O'Donnell Colley Grattan served with the Second Battalion during the Afghan campaigns of 1878-79-80; he was present at the action of 28th November, and at the Battle of the Peiwar Kotal and at the action of All Kheyl (medal and clasp).—*Vide Records*, part 2.

No. 206. Edward Lieven Maisey served with the Second Battalion during the Afghan campaigns of 1878-79-80. He was attached as orderly officer to the staff of Brigadier Cobbe, and was present at the action of 28th November, and at the Battle of the Peiwar Kotal (medal and clasp).—*Vide Records*, part 2.

No. 207. Charles Gray Robertson (son of Lieutenant-Colonel A. Cuningham Robertson, *vide* No. 50) served with the Second Battalion during the Afghan campaign of 1878, and was present at the action of the 28th November, and at the battle of the Peiwar Kotal. During the campaigns of 1879-80, he served in the Transport Department, and was attached to the force of Sir Frederick Roberts. He was present at the action of Karez Kila 10th December, 1879; at the actions near Kabul and defence of Sherpur 12th to 23rd December, 1879; at the repulse of the attack on Colonel Jenkyn's detachment near Charassia 25th April, 1880; at Sir F. Robert's march from Kabul to Candahar 8th to 31st August, 1880, and at the Battle of Bala Wali 1st September, 1880, when he acted as orderly officer to General Baker (star and medal with two clasps).—*Vide Records*, part 2.

No. 208. Lawrence Charles Dundas served with the Second Battalion during the Afghan campaigns of 1878-79-80. He was present at the action of 28th November, and at the battle of the Peiwar Kotal, and was one of a party of eight officers and privates who on 10th April, 1879, pursued and attacked twenty Afghans, killing five of them and wounding several others. For this service the party was thanked in divisional orders (medal and clasp).—*Vide Records*, part 2.

No. 209. Horatio James Evans served with the Second Battalion during the Afghan campaigns of 1878-79-80. He was present at the action of 28th November, and at the Battle of the Peiwar Kotal and at the action of Ali Kheyl; he was one of four officers who did duty continuously with the battalion from 21st November, 1878, the day on which it entered Afghanistan, until it recrossed the frontier on 21st October, 1880 (medal and clasp).—*Vide Records*, part 2.

No. 210. John Burnard Edwards served with the Second Battalion during the Afghan campaigns of 1878-79-80. He was present at the action of the 28th November, and at the battle of the Peiwar Kotal, and he was one of the four officers who did duty continuously with the battalion from 21st November, 1878, the day on which it entered Afghanistan, until it recrossed the frontier on 2lst October, 1880 (medal and clasp).—*Vide Records*, part 2.

No. 211. Valentine Augustus Milman Fowler served with the Second Battalion during the Afghan campaign of 1879-80 (medal).

No. 212. Colin Alex. Robertson Blackwell served (as second lieutenant) with the Second Battalion during the Afghan campaign of 1879-80 (medal).

No. 213. Stableton Lynch Cotton served with the Second Battalion during the Afghan campaign of 1879-80 (medal).

ENSIGNS, SUB-LIEUTENANTS AND SECOND LIEUTENANTS.

No. 214. — Savage served with the regiment in the campaign in

Germany of 1704, and was killed on 2nd July at the storming of the heights of Schellenburg.—*Vide Records*, part 1.

No. 215. Justine Holdmann was mortally wounded and taken prisoner at the Battle of Dunblane (12th November, 1715). He was a young officer of great promise and conspicuous for his personal valour.—*Vide Records*, part 1.

No. 216. — Glenkennedy was taken prisoner at the Battle of Dunblane (12th November, 1718).—*Vide Records*, part 1.

No. 217, Thomas Wilson served with the regiment during the campaign in the Netherlands of 1747, and was wounded at the Battle of Val.— *Vide Records*, part 1.

No. 217a. John Bruce, after serving as a non-commissioned officer and attaining the rank of sergeant-major, received the commission of ensign on 17th February, 1745, He was severely wounded at the Battle of Culloden, 16th April, 1745, and retired on half-pay on 18th April, 1749.— *Vide Records*, part 1.

No. 218. Archibald McMurdo, brother of Bryce McMurdo, and father of W. M. S. McMurdo (No. 101), was born in 1775; he was appointed ensign in the King's 23rd November, 1791, and after serving in it about two years was promoted and transferred to the Fifty-Third (20th November, 1793). On the 11th July, 1796, he attained his company in the Twenty-Seventh Enniskillings, in which regiment he was promoted major on 8th May, 1801, He retired from the service in 1803.

In 1799, he served with the Twenty-Seventh in the expedition to Holland, and in the battle near Bergen on 2nd October, he received a severe wound, from the effects of which he never thoroughly recovered.

After retiring from the army, he was appointed lieutenant-colonel of the Dumfriesshire Militia. He died in Dumfries on 11th October, 1829.

No. 219. Lorenzo Toole received a wound at the capture of Martinique, 1793, the expenses attending the cure of which are charged in the account of Extraordinary Expenses presented to the House of Commons from 25th December, 1795, to 25th December, 1796 (note in MS. Volume, Library, Royal U.S. Institution).

No. 220. Donald Aeneas Macdonald was wounded at the Battle of Lundy's Lane 25th July, 1814.— *Vide Records*, part 1.

No. 221. John Mathiesen was made prisoner during the sortie

made by the garrison at Fort Erie on 17th September, 1814.—*Vide Records*, part 1.

No. 222. William Montagu Scott McMurdo, son of Archibald McMurdo, who served as ensign in the regiment in the years 1791-92-93, (*vide* No. 218), and nephew of Captain Bryce McMurdo (*vide* No. 101), was appointed ensign in the King's on 1st July, 1837. He was promoted to be a lieutenant in the Twenty-Second Foot on 5th January, 1841. He was subsequently promoted to a company in the Twenty-Eighth and exchanged to the Seventy-Eighth Foot, and commanded the Military Train from 1st April, 1857, until February, 1860. He was gazetted major-general on 27th March, 1868; lieutenant-general on 19th February, 1878, and general on 20th May, 1878.

Between December, 1842, and January, 1865, he held the following Staff appointments:—Assistant quartermaster-general in Scinde; A.D.C. to the Commander-in-Chief in the East Indies; officiating assistant adjutant-general, Bengal; assistant adjutant-general, Dublin; director-general of transport, Crimea; inspector of volunteers and inspector-general of volunteers. Between 1st October, 1866, and 4th March, 1873, he held the following commands:—Brigadier-General Dublin District, and major-general commanding a division of the Bengal Army. He was appointed A.D.C. to the Queen 11th December, 1856; Companion of the Bath on 2nd January, 1857, and Knight Commander of the Bath in May, 1881. On 19th July, 1876, he was appointed colonel of the Sixty-Ninth Foot, and on 23rd August, 1877, transferred to the Fifteenth Foot, which appointment he still holds.

During the campaign in Scinde in 1843, he served as assistant quartermaster-general of the army, under Sir Charles Napier. He was present at the Battle of Meeanee, in which his horse was shot under him; at an affair with the enemy, while conducting Major Stark's brigade from Muttaree to Hydrabad, and at the Battle of Hydrabad, where he received a sabre wound in the right breast (medal).

In 1845, he again served as assistant quartermaster-general to Sir Charles Napier, during the campaign against the mountain and desert tribes on the right bank of the Indus. In 1851-52, he served as assistant adjutant-general of Queen's troops in the expedition against the Afreedies, and was present at the forcing of the Kohat Pass (medal). In the Crimean campaign he served as director-general of the Land Transport Corps (medal and clasp for Sebastopol, officer of the Legion of Honour, 4th class of the Medjidie, and Turkish medal).

No. 223. William Hext Mountsteven served with the regiment during the Indian Mutiny campaign of 1857. He was present at the outbreak of the *sepoys* at Jellundur on the night of 7th June, and at the march from Jellundur to Delhi 14th to 21st June; on the 9th July he was mortally wounded, and died the next day.— *Vide Records*, part 1.

Paymasters.

No. 224. Bartholomew Hartley served as lieutenant in the Royal York Rangers at the surrender of Martinique and taking of Guadaloupe in 1815. His son Richard Wilson Hartley was appointed ensign in the regiment on 26th October, 1841, and served in it until 16th January, 1857, when he exchanged into the Ninety-Second Regiment. He is now, (1881), serving in the Dublin County Militia with the rank of captain and honorary major.

No. 225. John Falls served during the Crimean War as paymaster of the Turkish Contingent (Turkish medal). He died in 1881.

Quartermasters.

No. 226. John Ross enlisted as private in the King's Regiment on 7th March, 1826, on 25th of December of the same year he attained the rank of sergeant; on 15th November, 1840, he was appointed quartermaster-sergeant, and on 8th November, 1842, received the commission of quartermaster. He served with the regiment during the Mutiny campaign of 1857, and was present at the outbreak of the *sepoy* troops at Jellundur on the night of the 7th June. On the march from Umballa to Delhi he was found dead in a *doolie*, having died of sunstroke during the night of 20th June, 1857. He was brother-in-law of Major W. Baillie, No. 79, and uncle of Captain A Ross Baillie, No. 129.

No. 227. Joseph Hamilton enlisted in the Royal Artillery as a gunner and driver on 4th May, 1843, was appointed colour-sergeant 31st August, 1854, and received the commission of lieutenant in the Land Transport Corps on 6th July, 1855, from which he was transferred to the King's Regiment as quartermaster on 16th April, 1858.

He served as a company sergeant R.A. in the trenches before Sebastopol from 17th October, 1854, until the fall of the town, 8th September, 1855. He was present at the Battle of Inkermann, and was wounded on 17th June, 1855, while doing duty in the trenches. He received the Crimean medal with two clasps, also a medal for distinguished conduct in the field. In November, 1858, he served in the

Mutiny campaign with detachments of the Forty-Second and Seventy-Ninth under Brigadier Douglas (medal). He died at Futtehghur on 22nd September, 1859.

No. 228. John Keatinge enlisted as private in the King's on 7th April, 1846; was appointed quartermaster-sergeant 19th November, 1858, and received the commission of quartermaster in it on 23rd September, 1859. He served with the regiment as a colour-sergeant during the Indian Mutiny campaign of 1857-58-59. Was present at the siege, assault, and capture of Delhi; at the battle of Agra and other actions of Colonel Greathed's column; at the relief of Lucknow; at the actions near Cawnpore on 2nd and 6th December; at the action of Khuda Gunj 2nd January, 1858, and at the operations in Oudh between 18th October, 1858, and 2nd February, 1859 (medal and two clasps).

No. 229. Charles Usherwood served in the Crimea in 1854-55, with the Nineteenth Regiment. He was present at the affairs of Bulganack and McKenzie's farm, Battles of Alma and Inkermann, capture of Balaklava, and at the siege and fall of Sebastopol (medal and three clasps and Turkish medal).

No. 230. Alfred Berry enlisted in the King's Regiment on 11th October, 1852, was appointed its sergeant-major on 2nd April, 1862, and received the commission of quartermaster on 20th May, 1864. He served as a non-commissioned officer with the regiment during the Mutiny campaigns of 1857-58-59, and was present at Jellundur when the *Sepoy* troops mutinied on the night of 7th June; at the siege, assault, and capture of Delhi; at the battle of Agra and other actions of Colonel Greathed's column; at the relief of Lucknow; at the actions near Cawnpore on 2nd and 6th December, 1857; at the action of Khuda Gunj 2nd January, 1858, and at the operations in Oudh between 18th October, 1858, and 2nd February; 1859.

No. 231. George Russel Holt White served as a non-commissioned officer with Ninth Lancers during the Sutlej campaign of 1845-46; present at the battle of Sobraon (medal); during the Punjab campaign of 1848-49; present at the passage of the Chenab, and at the Battles of Chillianwallah and Goojerat (medal with two clasps), and during the Indian Mutiny campaigns of 1857-58-59; was present at the Battle of Budlee-ke-Serai; at the siege, assault, and capture of Delhi; with Colonel Greathed's column at the actions of Bulandshahr, Agra, and Kanouge; at the relief of Lucknow; Battle of Cawnpore, 6th December, 1857; actions at Serai-ghat and Khuda Gunj; at the siege and capture of Lucknow; at the summer campaign of 1858, in Oudh and Rohilcund; present at actions of Rhodamore, Aligunj, Bareilly, and Shahjehanpoor; at the pursuit to Mahumdee; passage of the Gogra at Fyzabad; operations on the Nepaul frontier, and actions at Muckleegaum and Kumdekote (medal with two clasps). He also served as quartermaster with the Third Buffs during the China campaign of 1860 (medal).

No. 232. Philip Spencer enlisted as private in the King's Regiment on 26th April, 1858; he attained the rank of sergeant on 17th February, 1863, was appointed orderly room clerk, 20th October, 1866, and quartermaster-sergeant on 7th December, 1870. On 31st January, 1877, he received the commission of quartermaster, in which rank he served with the Second Battalion during the Afghan campaigns of 1878-79-80. He was present at the action of 28th November, and at the Battle of the Peiwar Kotal (medal and clasp.)

SURGEONS.

No. 233. Francis Charles Annesley served with the regiment as surgeon in medical charge of the regiment during the siege, assault, and capture of Delhi in 1857 (medal and clasp).

No. 234. John Madden served as assistant surgeon with the Forty-Third Light Infantry during the Kaffir war of 1851-53, and on the death of the surgeon succeeded to the medical charge of the regiment (medal.)

No. 235. John Irvine, M.D. In 1857-58, served with General Havelock's column, in medical charge of Royal Artillery; present at actions of Futtehpore, Aoung, Pandoo Nuddee, Cawnpore, Oonac, Busseerut Gunj, Mungawara, Alumbagh, and relief and defence of the residency of Lucknow (mentioned in despatches); served with General Ontram's force in the Alumbagh from November, 1857, to March, 1858; present at capture of Lucknow (medal and two clasps.)

No. 236. Thomas Clark Brady served in the Fifty-Seventh Regiment during the campaign in the Crimea of 1854-55; he was present at the Battles of Balaklava and Inkermann, at the attack on the Redan on 18th June, and at the siege and fall of Sebastopol; he was also present at the bombardment and the surrender of Kinburn (mentioned in despatches; medal, clasp, and Turkish medal).

No. 237. Grahame Auchinleck served as assistant surgeon in the Burmese war of 1852-53 (medal with clasp for Pegu); also, in the Euzoofzie expedition of 1858 (medal with clasp); was present at Mean Meer in 1857, when General Renny disarmed one regiment of native cavalry, and three regiments of native infantry.

Assistant Surgeons.

No. 238. William Henry Yates. In 1857, served with the regiment at the siege of Delhi, and was in medical charge of the regiment during the subsequent operations; present at action of Bulandshahr; affair of Allyghur, Battle of Agra, action of Dilkoosha, relief of Lucknow; affair of 2nd and action of 6th December, near Cawnpore, and at the action of Khuda Gunj (medal and two clasps).

No. 239. Thomas James Biddle served with the Forty-Ninth regiment in the Crimea from 13th September to 23rd December, 1854 (medal and clasp). Served with the King's Regiment in 1857; at the siege, assault, and capture of Delhi.

No. 240. James Saltus Conyers served with the force under Sir Garnet Wolseley during the Ashantee war of 1873-74. He was present at the battle of Amoaful, attack and capture of Becquah, Battle of Ordahsu and capture of Coomassie (medal and clasp).

List of Volunteers, Non-commissioned Officers, and Privates whose Names are mentioned in the Records,

Volunteers. D. McLean and H. P. Hill (part 1).

Sergeant-Major. Snowdon (part 1).

Colour-Sergeants. Walker (part 1); W. Junes (part 2).

Drum-Majors. Byrne (part 1); Owen Cuningham (part 2).

Sergeants. Thorn (part 1); James Howard, C. J. S. Savage (part 2).

Privates. No. 2041 John Brown (part 1); Peter Murphy (part 1); W. Lynch (part 1); James Ball (part 1); J. Burgess, L. Jones, R. Jones, C. Delaney (part 2).

Appendix 3

A. *Establishment of the Non-Commissioned Officers, Drummers, and Privates, King's Regiment, at various periods from 1802 to 1881. Extracted from War Office Returns.*

1st Battalion.

	Companies.	Serjeants.	Drummers.	Corporals.	Privates.
December 25th, 1802, Gibraltar	10	35	22	40	710
„ 1804, Home	10	44	22	40	760
„ 1807 do.	10	54	22	50	950
„ 1811, Canada	10	55	22	50	950
„ 1813 do.	11	63	22	58	950
July 25th, 1815, Home	10	55	22	50	950
September 25th, 1816 do.	10	45	22	40	760
October 25th, 1818, Malta	10	35	22	30	620
August 25th, 1821, Ionian Islands	8	29	12	24	552
December 25th, 1824, Home	8	30	12	24	551
„ 1825 do.	10	42	14	36	704
January 1st, 1831, Nova Scotia	10	43	14	36	703
August 12th, 1839 do.	10	47	14	40	760
April 1st, 1843, Home	10	47	17	40	760
„ 1846 do.	10	58	21	50	950
July 24th, 1857, India	12	67	25	60	1,140
April 1st, 1858 do.	12	66	25	60	1,140
July 3rd, 1860, at sea	12	67	25	60	1,140
September 5th, 1860, Home	12	57	25	50	900
February 14th, 1862 do.	12	57	25	50	850
April 1st, 1863 do.	12	58	25	50	750
„ 1865 do.	12	56	25	50	710
„ 1866, Malta	12	57	25	50	710
„ 1867 do.	12	59	25	50	750
„ 1868 do.	12	59	25	50	860
„ 1870, India	10	56	21	48	872
„ 1872 do.	10	55	19	50	870
„ 1873 do.	8	49	17	40	780
August 1st, 1878, Aden	8	41	17	40	560
April 1st, 1879, Home	8	42	16	40	440
August 1st, 1881 do.	8	42	16	40	440

2ND BATTALION.

Formation ordered 25th December, 1804.

	Companies.	Serjeants.	Drummers.	Corporals.	Privates.
December 25th, 1804, Home..	10	23	22	20	380
June 15th, 1809 do. ..	10	34	22	30	570
December 25th, 1811, Nova Scotia ..	10	35	22	30	570
„ 1812 do.	10	45	22	40	760
„ 1813 do.	11	53	22	48	760
„ 1814, Canada	11	43	22	38	570
July 25th, 1815, Home ..	10	35	22	30	570

Reduced 24th December, 1815.

Formation ordered 24th July, 1857.

	Companies.	Serjeants.	Drummers.	Corporals.	Privates.
July 24th, 1857, Home	8	39	17	32	608
April 1st, 1858 do.	12	54	25	48	902
„ 1859, Gibraltar ..	12	56	25	50	900
July 3rd, 1860 do.	12	57	25	50	900
February 14th, 1862 do.	12	57	25	50	850
April 1st, 1863 do.	12	58	25	50	750
„ 1867, Malta	12	59	25	50	570
„ 1868, Home	10	49	21	40	560
„ 1869 do.	10	49	21	40	520
„ 1870 do.	10	49	21	40	460
August 15th, 1870, Home ..	10	49	21	40	660
February 1st, 1871 do.	10	49	21	40	560
April 1st, 1872 do.	10	47	19	40	480
„ 1873 do.	8	41	17	40	480
„ 1876 do.	8	41	17	40	780
October 1st, 1877 do.	8	49	17	40	780
January 1st, 1881, India ..	8	50	16	40	780
August 1st, 1881 do.	8	50	16	40	780

B. *Extracts from Annual Reports of the Inspector-General of Musketry, showing results of the Musketry Instruction of both Battalions for each year from* 1859 *to* 1881.

Year.	Battalion.	No. in order of merit.	Figure of merit.	Percentage of 1st class shots.	Marks-men.	Non-exer-cised.	Stations.
1858–59	I		not exercised				India.
	II	75	27·92	23	4	..	Home.
1859–60	I		not exercised				India.
	II	53	34·81	23	4·50	1	Gibraltar.
1860–61	I	105	33·53	..	..	18	India, Home.
	II	45	40·08	40	12	0·50	Gibraltar.
1861–62	I	91	39·03	34	11	1·50	Home.
	II	55	41·25	37	11·75	2·25	Gibraltar.
1862–63	I	52	43·46	45	18·25	1·44	Home.
	II	74	41·93	44	14·95	2·34	Gibraltar, Malta.
1863–64	I	49	43·38	50	20·28	1·53	Home.
	II	122	38·29	18	2·53	1·25	Malta.
1864–65	I	16	88·56	40	7·90	2·34	Home.
	II	100	50·91	18	0·86	1·70	Malta.
1865–66	I	22	82·69	39	7·13	1·67	Home.
	II	51	69·06	24	3·47	0·45	Malta.
1866–67	I	78	76·28	31	6·26	2·34	Home.
	II	112	66·00	22	4·28	2·68	Malta.
1867–68	I	47	105·42	52	12·37	1·31	Malta.
	II	22	117·12	58	16·49	5·57	Malta, Home.
1868–69	I	118	96·93	45·73	20·26	2·56	Malta, India.
	II	31 (b)	121·89	62·79	15·84	3·87	Home.
1869–70	I	122	81·80	41·60	13·00	7·10	India.
	II	23	121·34	59·81	12·86	3·38	Home.
1870–71	I	115	91·02	48·31	13·25	9·37	India.
	II	10	136·15	70·13	18·18	1·54	Home.
1871–72	I	120	92·55	49·05	11·66	5·80	India.
	II	39	122·70	59·90	19·04	1·12	Home.
1872–73	I	102	67·54	52	13·21	1·65	India.
	II	67	75·36	55	11·83	1·16	Home.
1873–74	I	55	84·80	66	24·93	3·02	India.
	II	36	88·53	61	25·92	3·69	Home.
1874–75	I	16	94·39	77	38·37	1·28	India.
	II	88	77·20	51	14·05	2·06	Home.
1875–76	I	7	98·48	79	35·69	14·61	India.
	II	110	69·39	29	8·68	2·00	Home.
1876–77	I	11	86·83	66	19·81	1·28	India.
	II	109	53·46	30	7·89	3·01	Home.
1877–78	I	9	119·04	52	38·98	0·89	India, Aden.
	II	131	80·02	12	6·51	0·41	Home.
1878–79	I	2	125·67	63	47·80	2·44	Aden, Home.
	II		not exercised				Home, Afghan[n].
1879–80	I	36	101·50	38·57	18·42	2·16	Home.
	II		not exercised				Afghanistan.
1880–81	I	48	104·16	34·86	21·10	1·35	Home.
	II	67	100·23	31·46	20·85	7·29	India.

Appendix 4

NOTES ON THE COSTUME AND EQUIPMENT OF THE EIGHTH, THE KING'S REGIMENT.
Contributed by S. M. Milne, Esq.

Comparatively little authentic is known regarding the early costume or equipment of the regiment.

Some information may be culled from the pages of Grose, and other military antiquarians of lesser note, concerning the uniform of the infantry in general, but very little as regards the peculiarities which distinguished one corps from another.

Towards the year 1742, however, some degree of regularity seems to have prevailed, for at that date a book was produced, probably by the King's order, giving coloured illustrations of private soldiers in every regiment; the voluminous skirts of the Queen Anne period were now permanently buttoned back, and were becoming smaller; the lapels across the chest, of regimental facing, were conspicuous; the coat collar, however, was as yet absent. From this work the uniform of the King's Regiment appears to have been as follows (*vide* Plate 3, fig. 1):

Hat:—Cocked, with white lace round the edge, and a flat black cockade on the left side.

Coat:—Scarlet, blue lapels, fastened back with ten white lace loops and buttons, also a button on the shoulder to keep the top of the lapel back, an edging of lace round the outside of the lapels, the coat fastened at the waist, below the lapels, with three buttons having lace loops; the skirts cut very large, edged with lace, and buttoned back; straight slit pockets in the skirts, with four buttons and lace loops, very large cuffs of blue cloth to the sleeves (opening outward), four buttons and loops up the sleeve; regimental lace round the outside of the blue cuff.

Waistcoat:—Scarlet, very long, edged at the bottom with lace, and showing when the coat skirts were buttoned back.

Breeches:—Blue, with white gaiters coming above the knee, fastening below the knee with a buff strap.

Pouch:—Black, hung very low in front of the right thigh by a broad buff shoulder-belt, the sword and bayonet suspended in a frog from a broad waist-belt with a buckle in front.

The regimental lace shown in this illustration is white with a wavy blue stripe. At this period there seems to have been no very strict regulation as regards the lace; in all probability it varied from time to time to suit the taste of the colonel, though it constituted a very great distinction between regiments, and indeed continued to do so until comparatively recent times.

Gradually some kind of order must have been attained, as the Army List for 1767, gives, for the first time, the different patterns of lace as worn and apparently authorised; that for the King's Regiment was of white worsted, about half an inch wide, with a blue and a yellow stripe down one edge, and this pattern was adhered to by the rank and file through many a change in the coat until 1836, when white tape was substituted, coloured lace being still worn by the drummers. But at some period the drummers' lace was changed; for, when all regimental laces were abolished in 1866, and the universal pattern adopted, the drummers of the King's Regiment were wearing a white worsted lace with blue *fleur de lys* woven thereon.

Not only did every regiment have its own distinct pattern of lace, but the loops (lace sewn round the button-holes) were of different forms: some being square-headed, some pointed, and others frog loops; some regiments had their loops set on at equal distance; others by twos, so that at any period between 1768, and 1836, a person conversant with the various patterns of lace and with the different colours of the facings, could tell to what regiment a man belonged without closely examining the small pewter buttons for the regimental number; the King's Regiment wore square-headed loops at equal distances.

About the middle of the last century a strong desire seems to have been manifested by the authorities to enforce stricter regularity in the uniform and equipment of the army at large, and in consequence the Royal Warrant of 1751, was issued, giving the following details having reference to the regiment. (A Royal Warrant, dated September,

Plate 3

1742　　1768　　1792　　1792

Recorded by Lieutenant-Colonel G.P. Baynes

1743, had previously appeared, but on a much smaller scale than that of 1751):—

> No colonel to put his arms, crest, device, or livery on any part of the appointments, nor any part of the clothing to be altered, but by the King, or by the captain-general's permission.

As regards the Colours and Standards:—The King's or first colour to be the great union throughout; the second colour to be blue, with the union in the upper canton, in the centre of each to be painted or embroidered the White Horse on a red ground within the garter, surmounted by the crown; in the three corners of the second colour the King's cypher and crown, the rank of the regiment being shown in the upper corner; cords and tassels crimson and gold, mixed.

Drummers to wear the royal livery, *viz.*, red, lined, faced and lapelled on the breast with blue, and laced with royal lace. The front of the grenadiers' caps to be blue, with the King's cypher and the crown over it, embroidered, the little flap (in front) to be red, with White Horse, and the motto "*Nec aspera terrent*," back of cap red, the turn-up blue.

The front part of the drums to be painted blue, having the White Horse within the garter, the rank of the regiment below.

The cloth grenadier caps were abolished by the Warrant of July, 1768, which states that "black bearskin caps be supplied"' to the fusilier regiments, companies of grenadiers and drummers, as often as shall be necessary."

The next general clothing warrant was issued in December, 1768, but in the meantime a great change had taken place in the fashion and cut of the uniform; the turned-down collar or cape, as it was then called, appeared, the coat gradually became scantier, and only met across the chest, the waist being quite exposed; the lapels were now simply ornaments, the skirts turned well back, and lined with white; coat pockets much smaller, and the length of the waistcoat shortened; the large cuffs entirely disappeared, and smaller and neater ones, without any slit, took their place; the sword was dispensed with, except for the sergeants and grenadiers, the latter, being picked men, were probably considered strong enough to carry the sword as well as musket and bayonet.

The costume of the regiment at this period, 1768 (*vide* Plate 3, fig. 2), was as follows:—

Officers:—Scarlet coats, lapelled blue to the waist, the lapels three inches wide, fastened back by gilt buttons, having the regimental number thereon, placed at equal distances, the button-holes laced round with narrow gold lace loops, the cape of blue cloth turned down and fastened by one button and loop at each end; small round blue cuffs, three and a half inches deep, without slit, thereon four lace loops and buttons, cross pockets (in line with the waist) with four buttons and short loops, two loops and one button on each side of the slit behind, skirts lined and turned back, white.

Officers of grenadiers had an epaulette of gold lace and fringe on each shoulder; battalion officers one on the right shoulder only; waistcoat and breeches white, black linen gaiters with black buttons and small stiff tops, black garters. The sash crimson, and tied round the waist; gorget gilt, with the King's arms and the regimental badge engraved thereon, and fastened to the neck by blue rosettes and ribbons; sword hilt gilt, with a crimson and gold-striped sword knot; hats laced with gold, black cockades. The officers of the grenadier company wore black bearskin caps, on the front the King's crest with the regimental badge and motto in gilt metal on a black ground; they carried fusils, and had white shoulder-belts and pouches. The other officers carried espontoons, a light steel-headed pike with a small cross-bar just below the blade, about seven feet in length.

Sergeants:—Coats similar to those worn by the officers, excepting that the buttons were of white metal and the loops of white braid; hats laced with silver, crimson worsted sashes with a stripe of blue; swords and halberts were carried, the latter a light ornamental kind of battle-axe, with a long handle or shaft.

Grenadiers:—Coats with wings of red cloth on the point of the shoulder, having six loops of regimental lace, and a border of the same round the bottom, black bearskin caps, the cap-plate having the same badges as the officers' caps in white metal on a black ground; height of cap without bearskin twelve inches; grenadiers alone among the privates wore swords.

Corporals and Private Men:—Coat laced with the regimental lace, as before described, buttons white metal with regimental number, the loops square-headed and placed at equal distances in the same positions as the officers' lace loops were placed; the corporals distinguished by a silk epaulette on the right shoulder; breadth of shoulder-belt two and three-quarter inches, that of waist-belt (supporting the bayonet) being two inches.

Drummers and Fifers:—Being a royal regiment, wore red coats, faced and lapelled blue, laced with royal lace, in other respects they were dressed like the private men, excepting that they wore bearskin caps with a plate in front, thereon the King's crest of silver-plated metal on a black ground, with trophies of colours and drums, the regimental badge on the back part; a short sword with a scimitar blade.

Pioneers:—Each had an axe, a sword, and an apron, a cap with a leather crown, and a black bearskin front, on which was displayed the King's crest, together with a saw and an axe in white, on a red ground, the regimental badge at the back.

Regimental Colours:—Still as described in the Warrant of 1751, the size being six feet six inches flying and six feet deep on the pike; length of pole, spear, and ferril included, being nine feet ten inches.

Towards the end of the century, the gaiters became shorter; the collar, probably following the French fashion of the day, began to be worn turned up, the lace loop and button which had been used to fasten it down was attached to the new front, and became simply an ornamental pendage, and so remained for more than half a century; in the illustration of the uniform in 1792 (*vide* Plate 3, figs. 3 and 4) this may be observed, and also that the coat was becoming more scanty and the waistcoat shrinking up to the waist. A very correct idea can now be formed of the regimental breast-plate; that for the officers was oval, gilt, with a beaded edge, the White Horse in silver with a garter, surmounted by the crown; that worn by the privates was simply square, of brass, with the figure 8 and the words "The King's Regiment" engraved thereon.

Another peculiarity may be also observed for the first time at this date, one very trivial in itself, but alone confined to the regiment, and as such worthy of remark, and that is, a narrow red piping was worn straight up the front ends of the blue collar; this distinction was kept up carefully for a long period, and only disappeared upon the adoption of the new coatee in 1829.

The Warrant of 1796, authorised a considerable change in the fashion and cut of the coat; according to it the lapels were to be continued down to the waist, but to be made either to button over occasionally, or to clasp close with hooks and eyes all the way down to the bottom; the collar was ordered to stand up, and was made very high and roomy to admit the large neckcloth then in vogue, the light infantry jacket was to be made shorter in the skirt, and the pocket flaps placed thereon in a slanting direction, and not level with the waist, as in the long coats.

The illustration for 1800, (Plate 4, fig. 1), shows an officer with his coat buttoned, but having (as was then fashionable) the top of the lapels doubled back, disclosing two or three of the highest gold loops; whilst this fashion obtained, it was very usual to have only the top of the lapel so ornamented.

A change was now impending in the head-dress of the infantry, for the last twenty-five years of the eighteenth century, the light infantry had worn leather helmets or caps of various shapes and patterns; by a General Order dated February, 1800, the use of hats was discontinued, and a cylindrical shako with a peak introduced; this head-dress was made of lacquered felt, and was ornamented with a large brass oblong plate in front about six inches high and four inches broad, thereon displayed, as far as the Eighth Regiment was concerned, the White Horse within a garter surmounted by the crown and the number of the regiment, and surrounded by trophies of arms and standards, underneath the lion of England.

As far as can now be ascertained, the worsted red-and-white tuft was fixed in the front rising from a small black cockade; the warrant states that the grenadiers may wear these shakos when not using their grenadier caps, their tuft being white, that for the light infantry being green, the regimental button was worn in the centre of the black cockade, the grenadiers using a grenade instead. The officers still, however, retained their old cocked hats, those of the grenadier companies had to wear bearskins when the men wore theirs, but the light infantry officers always wore caps like the men.

In 1801, the want of great coats was constantly pressed upon the authorities. James in his *Regimental Companion* states that:

> It had been proposed in 1798, to allow this article to every soldier, instead of making a few ragged great coats to go through a species of fatigue drill in guard-mounting in more regiments than one.

In April, 1801, a warrant was issued authorising each man of the Foot Guards and infantry of the line, who was not then possessed of a good serviceable great coat, should be provided with one.

Apparently the lacquered shako did not answer all requirements, for by the warrant of October, 1806, it was abolished and a felt one introduced, "the leather parts and brass plates to be supplied every two years, and the felt crown and tuft annually." This cap was probably copied from one then used by the Austrian infantry; it was light and well fitted to the head, and was worn by the infantry throughout

Plate 4.

Presented by Major William Bannatyne

the Peninsular and Waterloo Campaigns; the brass plate in front was smaller than the last, oval in shape, with the crown on the top: the worsted tuft was fixed at the side, rising from a black cockle as in the last, and suspended across the front hung a crimson and gold twisted cord with tassels for the officers, and the same in white or green worsted for the non-commissioned officers and privates of the battalion Or of the light infantry companies respectively. (By a General Order dated July, 1808, the queues were abolished, and the hair of the private soldiers ordered to be cut short in the neck.)

In 1812, the general costume of the regiment was as follows (*vide* Plate 4, figs. 3 and 4):—

Officers:—Cap as above described, jacket of scarlet cloth cut short in the skirt (the long coats we're reserved for full dress occasions), double breasted, the blue gold-laced lapels generally worn buttoned across, so as to hide the lace, the gorget not invariably worn, the shirt collar and black neck-cloth showing above the high coat collar, on each side of which were two gold loops and buttons, the front edge showing the distinctive red piping, the turn-backs of the skirts white, laced with gold, and edged with a blue piping. The skirt ornaments at the corners being gold half sprays on blue cloth, the back skirts and side edges laced, two lace holes and one button each side of the back-appearing just under the sash, the slashed pockets having four small loops and buttons; blue cuffs with four loops and buttons at equal distances; pantaloons of grey cloth with ankle gaiters, the breeches and leggings being reserved for home duties.

A long straight sword, black leather scabbard, gilt mounting, with crimson and gold sword knot, suspended from a frog; shoulder-belt of white buffalo leather, ornamented with the regimental breast-plate, which at this period was of gilt metal, nearly square, the angles slightly rounded off. The White Horse within an oval garter having its proper motto, surmounted by a crown. Just underneath the latter a small label bearing the word "King's." The officers of the light infantry company carried the curved light infantry sabre suspended by slings from the shoulder-belt.

Officer's rank was distinguished by the epaulette (see General Order, February, 1810). Field officers wore two epaulettes, a colonel having a crown and a star on the strap, a lieutenant-colonel a crown, a major a star; captains and subalterns, including the quartermaster, wore one epaulette only on the right shoulder, the officers of flank companies wore two wings with grenades or bugles thereon respectively;

the adjutant wore in addition to his epaulette an epaulette strap on his left shoulder. The epaulettes of field officers and captains, together with the wings of captains of flank companies, were edged with bullion, those of subalterns with fringe. The paymaster and surgeons wore the regimental coat, but without epaulettes or sash, the sword being suspended by a plain waist-belt, worn under the coat.

The private soldiers wore short single-breasted jackets laced across the breast with loops of regimental lace four inches long, square headed, at equal distances, white pewter buttons, lace round the high square cut collar, showing the frill attached to the stock, blue shoulder-straps edged with lace, and terminated by a small white worsted tuft; in the flank companies by a wing of red cloth trimmed with diagonal stripes of lace edged with a large overhanging wing of white worsted; trousers grey with black ankle gaiters. The sergeants were dressed like the privates, but in probably finer cloth, and had the chevrons of their rank on the arm, their sash was crimson with a blue stripe; they carried a sword suspended by a shoulder-belt, and a halbert, the latter very similar to the espontoon formerly carried by the officers, the old fashioned battle-axe headed halbert having fallen into disuse a considerable time, in fact, since 1792.

★★★★★★

The sergeants' great coats had cuffs and collars of blue cloth, and wore their chevrons on the arm—chevrons being first introduced in consequence of a General Order dated July, 1802, which ordered that the sergeant-majors should be distinguished by four, the sergeants by three, and the corporals by two chevrons on the right arm made of the lace worn on the coats, thus superseding the epaulettes and shoulder knots, which hitherto had been the distinctive mark of the non-commissioned officers.

★★★★★★

The jacket was made pretty easy, perhaps in consequence of a General Order in April, 1810, which:

> Calls attention to the evils occasioned by the coat of the infantry being so tight and short in front, occasioning a corresponding shortening of the waistcoat, making the latter article totally useless for what it is primarily intended, namely, a fatigue dress in barracks during summer.

No sooner had Waterloo been gained, than the authorities determined to change the infantry head-dress from the neat and serviceable felt cap to the broad-topped heavy shako then common in all continental armies. It was eleven inches in diameter at the top, seven and a half deep, brass chin scales, which could be fastened up to the black cockade, and upright white feather twelve inches high, and a brass plate in front with regimental devices; a cap cover of "prepared linen" was worn in wet weather. The officers' shako had gold lace, two inches broad round the top, and a three-quarter inch lace round the bottom; a green feather was worn by the light infantry, and the bearskin caps were retained for the grenadiers with a brass plate, and leather peak in front, and white feather—gold tassels for the officers and white ones for other ranks.

Short coats for all ranks were abolished in 1820, and in 1822, the breeches and leggings. The same year a circular was issued calling attention to the fact that:

> The gorget formed a part of the officers' equipment, and must be worn on occasions of duty.

Evidently that ancient ornament was gradually falling into disuse.

June, 1823. Bluish-grey trousers took the place of the darker grey ones; white linen trousers also introduced instead of a second pair of cloth ones for the rank and file.

1826. The private soldier's coat altered in cut, the lace taken off the collar, and a single loop placed on each side, the loops across the chest made broad at the top, tapering down narrower towards the bottom; the lace taken off the coat skirts, except the loops on the slashed pockets.

1827. Officers' costume was as follows (*vide* Plate 4, fig. 2):—

Shako as described for 1816, but half an inch higher, and the gold lace round the top increased to two and a quarter inches in breadth. A scarlet coat with long skirts, two lace loops each side the collar, the distinctive red edging to it still preserved, the gorget, gold lace loops on the blue lapels showing when they are buttoned back, four buttons and lace loops on the cuffs, skirts with white turn-backs laced, and also edged blue. Skirt ornaments, blue garter edged gold with "proper" motto in gold, surmounted by a crown, the White Horse within the garter, on a scarlet ground, two loops and one button each side of back, the side seams laced, the pockets cut across the coat, not slashed, with four small loops and buttons.

Greyish-blue or white trousers according to the season of the year; though not regulation, for full dress, a broad gold lace stripe was worn down the outside seam of the trousers. Field officers wore two epaulettes with the usual distinction of ranks, captains and subalterns one, on the right shoulder, the adjutant an epaulette strap on the left shoulder in addition; officers of the flank companies, wings with grenades or bugles respectively. To the regimental breastplate was added the word "Niagara" on a label below the garter. The light infantry officers wore black caplines, the crimson rifle sash with cords and tassels, together with whistles and chains.

A blue great coat, otherwise frock coat, quite plain, single breasted, with regimental buttons, was authorised for undress; the crimson sash was worn with it, and the sword was suspended in a frog from a black leather waist-belt with gilt clasp; as an undress covering for the head, the shako was worn without feather, covered with oilskin. The cloak was blue cloth, lined with scarlet shalloon. The paymaster, quartermaster, and surgeon, and assistant-surgeons wore single breasted coats with ten buttons and loops across the chest on the scarlet, regimental cuffs and collars, black leather sword-belt under the coat; no epaulettes or sash; all wore cocked hats, the paymaster and quartermaster with gold loop and tassels, the former without a feather, surgeons plain black silk loop and button without feather.

The sergeants still carried the halbert, for which fusils, however, were substituted in 1830 (*vide* Plate 5, fig. 1).

In December, 1828, another change was ordered to be made in the shako, the one used in the Prussian Army being closely copied (*vide* Plate 5, fig. 2). The gold lace was stripped off, the height reduced to six inches, a large gilt star plate with regimental device was adopted in the front, gilt scales to fasten under the chin, and caplines were introduced, the latter to be worn on parade occasions only, wound round the cap across the front in a heavy braided festoon, and then hung down, terminating in two tassels which were looped up to one of the coat buttons, made of gold lace for the officers, of white worsted for battalion companies, and of green worsted for the light infantry. A month afterwards the feather was ordered to be white for the whole of the infantry (light infantry excepted), but still twelve inches high.

Probably with a view of dispensing with the great quantity of lace worn by some regiments, notably by the Eighth, the authorities determined to introduce a uniform of a much neater description. The result was the Warrant of February, 1829, which introduced and authorised the well-known coatee (*vide* Plate 5, fig. 3), which remained, with scarcely any alteration, the dress of the infantry officer until the Crimean War. It was double-breasted, the buttons placed at equal distances, two gold lace loops with two small buttons each side the collar, scarlet slashed flaps to the blue cuffs, thereon four small square lace loops and buttons, white turnback to the skirts, with the regimental skirt ornaments as before, slashed scarlet pockets, with square loops and buttons.

A universal pattern epaulette was adopted for the whole of the infantry, with stripes of the colour of the facings upon the strap for captains and subaltern officers (previously every regiment had its own peculiar pattern); the distinctions of rank on the strap remained as before, all ranks of officers wearing a pair, there being a little difference in the length of the fringe for the various ranks. The new "Oxford mixture" substituted, as a colour, for the old bluish-grey trousers; a forage cap was authorised for the first time, that for the regiment being of blue cloth, with a large flat stiffened top having a band and welt of scarlet cloth; a plain scarlet shell jacket was ordered to be worn, as uniform, by officers in certain climates, unauthorised shell jackets of fantastic design had been previously worn by many regiments; shoulder cords of gold were added to the plain blue frock coat, and the sword was ordered to be worn with it, suspended in the white shoulder-belt with regimental breast-plate instead of the black waist-belt, the crimson sash still being worn round the waist.

1830. A red fatigue jacket was substituted for the old white one hitherto worn by the rank and file, which had originally in its turn sprung from the old waistcoat with sleeves.

The accession of William the Fourth was marked by considerable changes, as far as the regiment was concerned. The Warrant of August, 1830, discontinued the caplines and tassels so lately introduced; the feather was shortened to eight inches, and a green ball tuft for the light infantry adopted; the band was ordered to be dressed in white coatees with blue facings; and lastly, the gorget, after forming an ornamental appendage for more than a century, was abolished. For some time the mounted officers had worn their swords suspended by slings from a white shoulder-belt; but in 1832, the field officers were ordered to wear swords suspended by slings from a white waistbelt with gilt clasp, having regimental devices thereon; the scabbard was to be of brass instead of black leather; the adjutant was to wear a steel scabbard, and to retain the old method of carrying his sword.

1834. A new forage cap for the officers authorised of blue cloth, with a scarlet band, and as a particular mark of distinction, the White Horse was to be embroidered on the front. The undress now present-

1827   1831   1845   1864

Presented by Major General Le Rene Xavier Sandilands

ed a handsome appearance, for the blue frock coat was ornamented with blue cloth shoulder-straps, laced with regimental gold lace, and terminating with gilt metal crescents. The different ranks of field officers were distinguished by crowns and stars, as on the epaulettes; the grenadier officers wore a silver grenade, and the light infantry officers a silver bugle within the crescent, the sword being carried once more in the frog of a black patent leather waist-belt, field officers wearing slings. About this period the tall feathers in the shakos disappeared, and were replaced by white worsted ball-tufts, the light infantry wearing green ones (*vide* Plate 5, fig. 3).

1836. By General Order, this year the coloured regimental lace so long worn by the men was abolished, and plain white tape lace took its place; but the peculiar mode of wearing it was retained; that is, square-headed loops across the chest, at equal distances; the sergeants were directed to wear double-breasted coats without any lace on the chest, white epaulettes, and wings for those of flank companies; coloured lace was still worn by the drummers, the *fleur de lys* pattern being used.

In 1842, the new percussion muskets were generally introduced, and next year the bearskin caps of the grenadiers were discontinued.

1844. A new shako, sometime called the Albert hat, was adapted for the infantry, six and three-quarter inches deep, one quarter less in diameter at top than at bottom, thus completely altering the shape. Officers had a gilt star ornament with crown over, four and a half inches in diameter; the men retained the brass plate they had worn with the large-topped shako; a chin chain and ball tuft completed it; the latter two-thirds white and one-third red at bottom for battalion and field officers; all white for grenadiers; green for light infantry.

The same year new regulations were issued regarding the colours:

Forbidding any regimental record or device being placed on the Queen's colour, other than the number of the regiment in gold characters, surmounted by the imperial crown.

1845. The blue and red-striped sashes of the sergeants were discontinued, and a plain crimson one, two and a half inches wide, substituted.

1848. The blue frock coat with shoulder scales was abolished, a plain shell jacket being worn as uniform, with a black patent leather sling sword-belt; a grey great coat, like that worn by the men, was prescribed for the officers in lieu of the blue cloak.

1850. A plain shoulder-belt without breast-plate to carry the pouch authorised, the bayonet being hung in a frog from a waistbelt.

The experiences of the Crimean War, or the general favour in which the frock coat was held by Continental troops, hastened the end of the old coatee; and in 1855, the double-breasted tunic was first authorised; the white tape lace, with the regimental method of wearing it, disappeared altogether, except for the drummers, who continued to wear the *fleur de lys* lace. The general effect, however, of the red and blue was relieved by white piping, now for the first time introduced into the infantry uniform; brass buttons and dark blue trousers, with a red welt down the outer seam, were adopted; the shako was made much smaller and lighter, and officers and sergeants' sashes were worn over the shoulder.

With the coatee, the officers lost the handsome epaulettes and wings; their tunic was made very similar to that worn by the men, excepting that the lapels were made to fold down at the top, thus showing the regimental facing which lined the coat; a little gold lace on the collar (with distinctive badges), on the cuffs and slashes of the cuffs, and on the skirts, was all the ornament they obtained; a perfectly plain blue frock coat had been authorised in 1852, not, however, to be worn on parade or duty, but now a double-breasted coat was adopted for undress, with regimental buttons, and a plain stand-up collar, the crimson sash to be worn over it, the sword to be carried in the white sling waist-belt; the coloured tuft on the shako was the only distinction of the flank companies; indeed, that difference did not last long, for these companies were broken up in 1862, and the whole regiment dressed alike (*vide* Plate 5, fig. 4).

1858. A Royal Warrant was issued altering the colours; they were to be only three feet nine inches flying, and three feet deep, ornamented with gold and crimson fringe for the Queen's, and blue and gold for the regimental colour; the poles to be surmounted with the crest of England instead of the ornamental spear-head; cords and tassels three feet long of crimson and gold.

1866. Steel scabbards replaced the officers' black leather ones, and by a General Order the peculiar drummer's lace of the *fleur de lys* pattern was discontinued, and the universal drummer's lace for the army adopted in its place.

1867. Officers' patrol jacket introduced instead of the blue frock coat.

1868. The slashed cuff on the tunic abolished, and pointed cuffs with distinctions for the various ranks introduced; a gold and crimson sash, gold laced trousers and sword-belt for levees, &c., authorised; the shako was ornamented with gold lace, and the old star plate replaced by a garter with number inside, surrounded by a wreath of laurel in high relief, the whole surmounted by a crown. Two years afterwards the red ball tuft, authorised for all Royal Regiments, was substituted for the red and white tuft previously worn, and on the 10th of August, 1880, (in consequence of the shako having been superseded by the helmet), a circular was issued authorising the King's and other Royal Regiments to place a piece of red cloth under the helmet plate, as a means of perpetuating the distinction that was indicated by the red ball tuft.

Previous to 1859, the coatee (afterwards tunic) was the only authorised mess dress of infantry officers, but for many years it had been customary to wear the shell jacket open, exposing a waistcoat, the material and pattern of which was determined solely by the authority of the lieutenant-colonels commanding battalions. In the King's Regiment the waistcoat of the 1st Battalion had a rolling collar and buttons, the second a standing collar and studs. It was probably because commanding officers occasionally made unnecessary and injudicious changes in the patterns of the mess jacket and waistcoat that a circular was issued in February, 1872, establishing as the mess dress to be worn on all ordinary occasions a scarlet jacket with distinctions of rank on the cuffs and collar, and a blue waistcoat of a uniform pattern for all infantry regiments.

With the introduction of the helmet in 1878 (*vide* Plate 10), these notes of the costumes of the regiment come to a conclusion. Changes during the last twenty years have only been superficially glanced at; in all probability they are well known to those who take interest in the matter, and therefore need not be detailed at length.

It may not be out of place here to mention that the regiment received authority to bear the Sphinx with the word "Egypt" on their colours and appointments on the 6th July, 1802. The word "Niagara," 19th May, 1815. "Martinique," 28th September, 1816. "Delhi" and "Lucknow," 3rd September, 1863. "Peiwar Kotal" and "Afghanistan," 1878-80, on 1st June, 1881.

Although the White Horse had been the regimental badge for a very long period, it was not until the 8th of August, 1840, that the Hanoverian motto (*Nec aspera terrent*) was authorised to be displayed upon the colours. The authorities, after a considerable correspondence with the officers of the regiment, acceded to their claim for this distinction, and on that date " a drawing of the colours bearing the

motto "*Nec aspera terrent*," in addition to the other insignia, and badges of the "Royal Cypher and the White Horse, was submitted to the Queen and received the Royal Sign Manual."

The "motto and badge" had formerly been worn upon the cap-plates of the grenadiers as detailed, but this distinction was common to the grenadier companies of all infantry regiments.

Appendix 5

Description of the Memorial Cross erected at Chelsea Hospital to commemorate the Services and Death of the Officers Non-commissioned Officers, and Privates lost by the Regiment during the Indian Mutiny Campaigns of 1857-58; also of the Tablet erected at Delhi in the Cemetery near the Cashmere Gate.

The Chelsea Memorial is in the form of the old Irish cross, with gable top. The shaft is of Sicilian marble, with carved gable moulding. The upper part of the shaft, above the gloria, contains a figure in relief of the Saviour; the lower part three reliefs illustrating "the Bivouac," "the Battle," "the Burial."

The base of the cross is of Sicilian, with bands of coloured marbles. The real base is of red Mansfield, and the sub-base of Greenmorr stone; granite palisades; red Mansfield posts. The height of the memorial is 22 feet.

The following is a copy of the inscriptions and of the names cut on the memorial: —

> This cross commemorates the services' and death of 243 officers, n-.c. officers, and privates lost by the 8th the King's Regiment while engaged in suppressing the great Sepoy Mutiny of 1857-58. some died in battle, some of wounds, some of disease, all in the devoted performance of duty.
> On three sides of the base are inscribed the words Delhi captured—Agra defended—Lucknow relieved.

The names are:—
Officers.—Colonel R. H. W. Hartley. Lieutenants W. W. Pogson, T. B. Grierson, T. M. Vincent, W. R, Webb, J. E. W. Black. Ensign W. H. Mountsteven. Quartermaster J. Ross.
Sergeants.—D. Jones, M. Devette, G. Ketton, G. Cox, H. Shar-

rocks, J. Paulden, G. Holmes, J. Dyson, C. Dundas, J. Harris, J. F. Edwards, S. Brewer, C. Kelly, J. Smith, J. Clarkson, D. Prior, B. Perry, B. Walters, H. Wright.
Corporals.—J. Farrell, W. Robinson, P. Lee, W. Ridsdale, J. Murphy, J. Stockard, F. Blake, J. Farnan, L. Fletcher, W. James, G. Candler, J. W. Jones, A. Robertson, C. Lampett, P. Kelleher.
Drummers.—F. Gay, J. Greenall, T. Mara, J. Moore.
Privates.—G. Bishop, J. Gallagher, J. Donovon, P. Crawley, J. Keatinge, W. Murphy, J. McGuire, P. M'Girvie, A. Bain, M. McCarthy, M. Jordan, W. Collis, J. Bailey, W. Grives, W Bolton, J. Dooling, T. McKay, A. Noah, J. Millan, T. Regan, J. Biss, G. Elms, W. Shapter, L. Cousins, T. McSweeney, S. Bratby, W. Dumerick, J. Malone, R. Ranger, F. Tudgay, D. Shea, C. Davis, J. Bridges, P. Weedon, C. Curren, H. Williamson, J. Bryan, W. Johnson, J. Mitten, W. Roberts, T. Hardern, P. Connor, C. Barthrupt, James Turner, John Turner, T. Taylor, P. Bryan, B. McGuire, M. Dahey, W. Spikesman, T. Hanlon, M. Canahan, S. Marsden, J. Bryant, T. Downey, D. Twine, D. Shanahan, H. Baker, J. Field, D. White, H. Podgers, W. Salter, J. Beal, S. Pinnell, T. Lawless, W. Russell, W. Walsh, E. Corcoran, J. Hardern, C. Bryant, E. Morgan, C. Little, J. Smith, W. Rollston, J. Smith, R. Clowser, J. Dennison, J. Hishnell, H. Foley, J. H. White, A. Nelson, W. Brumade, J. Middlecolt, J. McColley, W. Yendell, P. Hennessey, J. Halloran, W. Dunn, J. Healey, J. Rattan, C. Mills, H. McKeown, H. James, M. Keough, R. Peters, P. Clarke, T. Ford, J. Bartlett, J. G. Crump, T. Flinn, J. Morcombe, W. Boundford, R. Sayers, C. Fuller, C. Kidney, J. Raynard, T. Davis, J. Bray, W. Curtis, W. Ray, G. Thomas, J. Gough, J. Finn, J. Holmes, B. Markham, B. Davis, J. Barry, D. Funkie, J. May, W. Watters, W. Gretorix, C. Hazel, W. Taft, H. McGill, J. Cunningham, T. Robinson, W. Sidebottom, T. Mount, J. Mitchell, P. McMahon, T. Lucas, S. Bidder, T. Smith, J. Mahoney, W. M'Farlane, O. Murphy, E. Hughes, J. Garlick, T. Burrows, J. Roach, C. Keleher, W. Hall, W. Kirwin, J. Medstone, E. McKee, G. Wortley, G. King, J. Shackleton, J. Mitchell, T. Sellers, R. Uglow, W. Waring, M. Dwyer, W. Jones, M. Shea, W. Lee, G. Lee, W. Brown, W. Ramsey, D. Price, G. Highton, J. Constable, W. Bullough, P. Attwood, T. Riley, J. Irwin, J. Russell, E. Whiteway, G. Mills, G. Hooper, W. Jenkins, W. Radford, W. S. Robinson, G. Trim, P. Whelan, T. Collins, J. Barrett, W. Sher, F. Parker,

F. Wint, W. Ellis, A. Milligan, W. Jones, C. Wright, H. Harris, H. Salt, G. Discombe, W. Dowse, D. Sullivan, W. Hinds, J. Jacobs, W. Armston, W. White, W. Gage, A. Harrod, F. Hart, R. McLeod

The Delhi monument is a mural tablet, 30 inches by 15, of white Jyepoor marble, set in a Gothic frame of red sandstone, and fixed in the wall of the cemetery near the entrance gate.

It bears the following inscription:—

Erected by the 8th the King's Regiment in memory of Lieut. Pogson, Lieut. Webb, Ensign W. Hext Mountsteven, and of forty-one non-commissioned officers and privates killed at Delhi between 30th May and 30th September, 1857.

MEMORIAL CROSS ERECTED AT CHELSEA HOSPITAL.

Appendix 6

Abstract of the Services of "The Second Royal Lancashire Militia" (The Duke of Lancaster's Own).

Section 1.—Disembodied from the 1st of March, 1797, to the 10th of March, 1878.

The regiment was raised on the 1st of March, 1797, and designated the First Royal Lancashire Supplementary Militia. It was divided into six divisions, and each division in succession was embodied at Wigan for twenty-one days' training and exercise, the first division commencing its course of instruction on the 21st of March, and the last on the 10th of July.

Section 2.—Embodied from the 10th of March, 1798, to the 29th of April, 1802.

The regiment was embodied for continuous service at Preston on the 10th of March, 1798, at which date its effective strength was fourteen officers, and seven hundred and eighty-six non-commissioned officers and privates.

The following is a statement of the number of miles marched and the names of the stations where it was quartered during this period of its embodied service:—

Date.	Days.	Route.	No. of Divisions.	Marches.	Miles.	Average.
7th to 17th April, 1798	11	Preston to Durham.	3	8	132	16·5
27th July, 1798	1	Durham to Sunderland	1	1	13	13
9th and 10th Aug., 1798	2	Sunderland to Blythe Camp	2	2	27	13·5
8th October, 1798	1	Blythe Camp to Newcastle-on-Tyne	1	1	16	16
16th March, 1798	1	Newcastle to Tynemouth	1	1	9	9
19th April to 4th May, 1799	16	Tynemouth to Liverpool	4	12	165	13

Date.	Days.	Route.	No. of Divisions.	Marches.	Miles.	Average.
2nd to 27th May, 1799.	26	Liverpool to Portsmouth	2	19	251	13·2
31st May to 1st June, 1799	2	Portsmouth to Isle of Wight (by sea)	2	—	—	—
21st April to 9th May, 1801	19	Isle of Wight to Plymouth	3	11	153	13·9
2nd to 23rd Nov., 1801	22	Plymouth to Newcastle-under-Lyne	4	16	259	16·2
8th to 12th April, 1802	5	Newcastle to Liverpool	3	4	55	13·7
	106	Total		75	1,080	14·4

In the month of June, 1798, the strength of the regiment was augmented to twelve companies, and its establishment fixed at one colonel, one lieutenant-colonel, two majors, nine captains, fourteen lieutenants, ten ensigns, two adjutants, one quartermaster, one surgeon, fifty sergeants, twenty-six drummers, forty-eight corporals, and one thousand one hundred and fifty-two privates; total, forty-one officers, and one thousand two hundred and seventy-six non-commissioned officers and men. The regiment was then quartered at Durham, and it received there its first colours. On the 17th of August of the same year an order was received from Mr. Dundas changing the appellation of the regiment, and directing it to be called "The Second Royal Lancashire Militia;" about the same time the accoutrements were changed from black to buff.

On the 14th of November the establishment of the regiment was reduced to ten companies, and its strength fixed at thirty-three officers and six hundred and ninety-four non-commissioned officers and privates. On the 15th of December, 1800, in consequence of the Union of Ireland with Great Britain, an alteration was ordered to be made in the colours of the regiment. On the 13th of August, 1801, a company was added to the establishment, but on the 25th of February, 1802, this company was again reduced.

On the 27th of March, 1802, a definitive Treaty of Peace with France was signed at Amiens; and on the 29th of April, the regiment was disembodied at Liverpool, one adjutant, twenty-seven sergeants, twenty-seven corporals, and twelve drummers being retained as its peace establishment.

Section 3.—Disembodied from the 29th of April, 1802, to the 4th of March, 1803.

Section 4.—Embodied from the 4th of March, 1803, to the 16th March, 1816.

A War Office order for the embodiment of the Militia forces of the kingdom was issued on the 14th of March, 1803, and on the 4th of April the regiment assembled at Liverpool, the establishment being fixed at ten companies, thirty-seven officers, and nine hundred and eighteen non-commissioned officers and privates.

The following is a statement of the number of miles marched by the regiment, and of the names of the places where it was quartered during this period of its embodied service:—

Date.	Days.	Route.	No. of Divisions.	Marches.	Miles.	Average.
23rd to 16th June, 1803	20	Liverpool to Chelmsford (in 3 divisions)	3	17	251	14·8
19th July, 1803	1	Chelmsford to Dunbury Camp	1	1	5	5
24th November, 1803	1	Dunbury Camp to Chelmsford	1	1	5	5
19th to 28th Dec., 1803	10	Chelmsford to Woodbridge	2	4	55	16·2
6th and 7th Aug., 1804	2	Woodbridge to Lexden Heath	1	2	27	13·5
25th October, 1804	1	Lexden Heath to Colchester	1	1	1	1
4th to 23rd July, 1805	20	Colchester to Sunderland	3	17	263	14·9
6th October, 1806	1	Sunderland to North and South Shields	1	1	9	9
8th October, 1806	1	North and South Shields to Sunderland	1	1	9	9
	1	Sunderland to Tynemouth	1	1	9	9
2nd May, 1807	1	Tynemouth to Newcastle	1	1	9	9
9th May, 1807	1	Newcastle to Sunderland	1	1	13	13
16th May, 1807	1	Sunderland to Newcastle	1	1	13	13
8th to 19th June, 1807	12	Newcastle to Liverpool	3	11	178	16·2
26th Oct. to 4th Nov., 1807	10	Liverpool to Hull	2	9	145	16·1
29th May to 24th June, 1809	27	Hull to Crediton	3	24	341	14·5
27th to 29th June, 1809	3	Crediton to Plymouth	3	3	48	16
26th and 27th April, 1813	2	Plymouth to Dartmoor	2	1	16	16

Date.	Days.	Route.	No. of Divisions.	Marches.	Miles.	Average.
29th May to 24th June, 1809	27	Hull to Crediton ...	3	24	341	14·5
27th to 29th June, 1809	3	Crediton to Plymouth	3	3	48	16
26th and 27th April, 1813	2	Plymouth to Dartmoor	2	1	16	16
21st and 22nd May	2	Dartmoor to Plymouth	2	1	16	16
15th April to 2nd May, 1814	18	Plymouth to Monkstown (by sea)				
2nd and 3rd May, 1814	2	Monkstown to Mallow	—	2	21	10·5
7th to 10th May, 1814	4	Mallow to Limerick	4	3	35	11·7
1st and 2nd Sept., 1814	2	Limerick to Birr....	—	2	41	20·5
31st Oct. and 1st Nov.,	2	Birr to Mullingar...	—	3	39	19·5
24th to 27th Feb., 1816	4	Mullingar to Dublin	2	2	38	19
29th Feb. and 3rd Mar., 1816	4	Dublin to Liverpool (by sea)				
		Total...........		109	1,587	14·5

During this period the number of volunteers given by the regiment was: to the navy in 1803, thirty-three; to the line in 1805, one hundred and eighty-three; in 1807-8, three hundred and seventy; in 1809-10, two hundred and eighty-six; in 1811, two hundred and seven; in 1812, one hundred and seven; in 1813, two hundred and twenty-two; in 1814, fifteen. Total number of volunteers to the army and navy from 1803, to 1814, one thousand four hundred and twenty-eight.

On the 20th of June, 1803, the establishment was augmented to twelve companies, fifty-five officers, and one thousand three hundred and sixty-eight non-commissioned officers and privates; and on the 9th of July a circular was received authorising two lieutenant-colonels, two adjutants, and two sergeant-majors to be borne on the establishment, thereby increasing the total strength of the officers to fifty-seven, and the non-commissioned officers and privates to one thousand three hundred and sixty-nine.

On the 31st December, 1803, a letter from His Majesty King George the Third, dated Windsor, 25th December, was communicated to the Earl of Derby, authorising the regiment and also the other Lancashire Militia Corps to bear on their colours the Red Rose, the ancient badge of the County Palatine.

On the 27th January, 1804, permission was given to form two rifle companies.

On the 12th of July, 1805, the extra lieutenant-colonel, adjutant, and sergeant-major were struck off the strength, and the establishment reduced to ten companies, thirty-seven officers, and nine hundred and eighteen non-commissioned officers and privates.

In March, 1808, the establishment of non-commissioned officers and privates was increased to one thousand one hundred and thirty-two, but no change was made in the number of officers. On the 11th of October, 1811, the establishment of non-commissioned officers and privates was again reduced to nine hundred and eighteen.

On the 13th of April, 1814, orders having been received that the regiment (which had been stationed at Plymouth for nearly four years) was to embark for Ireland, Major-General Browne, who commanded the garrison, published a farewell order from which the following is an extract:

> The major-general regrets the departure of the regiment, because in all points it was an example to other corps both as to interior management and outward soldierlike appearance. To Colonel Wilson, their worthy and excellent commander, the major-general requests the acceptance of his warmest acknowledgemonts.

On the 28th of May, 1814, Major-General Darby commanding at Limerick, after finishing the inspection of the troops under his command, published an order in which the following words occur:—

> The fine appearance of the Lancashire Regiment was conspicuous, its movements were well executed, exact and steady. The conduct of that corps in the field, particularly with regard to its correctness in its movements, is worthy of imitation.

The regiment was disembodied at Liverpool on the 15th of March, 1816. The adjutant, paymaster, quartermaster, surgeon, sergeant-major, drum-major, twenty-seven sergeants, twenty-seven corporals, and twelve drummers, were retained on the peace establishment.

In a letter dated the 8th of March, from Lord Palmerston, Secretary of State, giving instructions respecting the disembodiment of the regiment, his lordship said:

> I am commanded to express to you the very great satisfaction which His Royal Highness (the Prince Regent) has received from the exemplary and meritorious services of the corps.

Lord Stanley, the colonel of the regiment, also received a letter dated Horse Guards, 6th March, 1816, in which the Adjutant-General, Sir Harry Calvert, says:

I have received the commander-in-chief's commands to desire that your lordship will express to the officers, non-commissioned officers and private soldiers of the regiment, the just sense which His Royal Highness entertains of the zeal with which they have continued in the performance of their military duties, after the period when the termination of hostilities on the Continent enabled the prince regent to dispense with the services of the greater part of the militia forces. The commander-in-chief desires to offer this testimony of his approbation in addition to that which the Second Royal Lancashire Regiment shares in common with the militia force of the United Kingdom, for the services performed during the late eventful war.

Section 5.—Disembodied from the 16th of March, 1816, till the 18th of December, 1854.

On the 11th of May, 1829, the establishment of the regimental staff was reduced to one adjutant, one sergeant-major, twenty sergeants, one drum-major, and seven drummers.

On the 28th of April, 1831, a letter was received from Lord Melbourne, Secretary of State, signifying His Majesty's pleasure that the three regiments of Royal Lancashire Militia should for the future be called the Duke of Lancaster's Own Regiment of Militia.

On the 30th of April, 1833, a circular was issued notifying that lots had been drawn at the Palace of St. James's, in presence of the king, to determine finally and permanently the precedency of militia regiments, and that one hundred and thirteen had been the number drawn for the regiment.

On the 8th of November, 1854, a letter was addressed by Lord Palmerston, Secretary of State, to the Earl of Sefton, Lord Lieutenant of the County of Lancaster, permitting the regiment to become a rifle corps, and authorising a change of uniform from red to green at the next issue of clothing.

Between 1816, and 1852, the regiment was only once called out for training, *viz.*, in 1832, when it was embodied at Liverpool for twenty-eight days.

In each of the years, 1852, 1853, and 1854, it was assembled for twenty-eight days' training, headquarters during that time being at Rupert House, Liverpool.

Section 6.—Embodied from the 18th of December, 1854, to the 22nd July, 1856.

In consequence of the exigencies of the Crimean War the regiment was embodied for service at Liverpool on the 18th of December, 1854. During this period it was stationed at Glasgow, and gave about five hundred men as volunteers to the line: while quartered there barracks for the permanent staff and store rooms were erected by the county at St. Domingo Road, Liverpool, in which the Headquarters of the corps was established, at the termination of its embodied service on the 22nd of July, 1856.

Section 7.—Disembodied, 22nd July, 1856, to 27th September, 1858.

The regiment assembled at Liverpool for training and exercise:—

In 1857, no training.
On 27 Sept., 1858, for 28 days.
,, 4 July, 59, ,, 21 ,,
,, 23 April, 60, ,, 27 ,,
,, 22 April, 61, ,, 27 ,,
,, 8 May, 62, ,, 21 ,,
,, 29 April, 63, ,, 21 ,,
,, 18 April, 64, ,, 21 ,,
,, 1 May, 65, ,, 27 ,,
,, 16 April, 66, ,, 27 ,,
,, 29 April, 67, ,, 27 ,,
,, 20 April, 68, ,, 27 ,,
,, 26 April, 69, ,, 27 ,,
,, 25 April, 70, ,, 27 ,,

On 1 May, 1871, for 27 days.
,, 6 May, 72, ,, 27 ,,
,, 5 May, 73, ,, 27 ,,
,, 4 May, 74, ,, 27 ,,
,, 3 May, 75, ,, 27 ,,
,, 1 May, 76, ,, 27 ,,
,, 5 Mar., 77 (recruits), for 83 days.
,, 30 April, 77 (regiment), for 27 days.
,, 4 Mar., 78 (recruits), for 83 days.
,, 29 April, 78 (regiment), for 27 days.

On the 19th of December, 1878, the Headquarters and permanent staff of the regiment were removed from St. Domingo Militia Barracks, Liverpool, to Oxford Barracks, Warrington, the headquarters of the Thirteenth Brigade Depot. (*Vide* Records, parts 1 & 2.) Instructions were given that a detachment of non-commissioned officers, under the superintendence of the adjutant, should proceed to Liverpool, three days in each week to carry on recruiting.

On 1st July, 1881, the 2nd Royal Lancashire was incorporated with the Eighth, the King's Regiment, and its two battalions were designated the third and fourth battalions of The King's (Liverpool Regiment). At the same time the number of the sub-district was altered from the Thirteenth to the Eighth.—(*Vide* Records part 2.)

The regiment was embodied at Warrington for training and exercise—

In 1879. Recruits, on 28th April, for 63 days; regiment, on 9th June, for 20 days.
„ *1880.   „   „ 26th April, for 69 days;   „   „ 7th June, for 27 days.
„ *1881.   „   „ 25th April, for 69 days;   „   „ 6th June, for 27 days.

A	B	C	D	E	F
## SUCCESSION LIST OF COLONELS.†					
‡Edward Lord Stanley	A	1 Mar. 1797	R	8 May 1847	
Hon. Thomas Stanley	A	June 1847	R	1 Mar. 48	
Hon. Charles James Fox Stanley	A	1 Mar. 48	R	1 Mar. 42	Gren. Gds.
Sir Thomas Hesketh, Bart.	P	1 Mar. 52	D	20 Aug. 1872	
Nicholas Blundell	P	25 Sept. 72			
## SUCCESSION LIST OF LIEUTENANT-COLONELS.					
Henry Richmond Gale	A	1 Mar. 1797	R	Dec. 1799	
Edward Wilson	P	11 Dec. 99	D	12 Feb. 1823	
William Horton	P	24 July 1803	D	15 April 16	
Robert Entwistle	P	23 May 23			
Nicholas Blundell	P	9 Nov. 70	R	26 July 81	
Hon. Frederick A. Stanley	P	16 May 74	T	16 May 74	Gren. Gds.
A. Cuningham Robertson	A	24 Mar. 75	P	2 Oct. 76	8th Ft. (the King's)
Charles S. Garraway	P	28 Oct. 76	S		
Richard Geo. Bomford Bolton	P	27 July 81	S		R. H. Gds.
## SUCCESSION LIST OF MAJORS.					
Sir Thomas Hesketh, Bart.	A	1 Mar. 1797	R	25 June 1798	
Edward Wilson	P	26 June 98	P	11 Dec. 99	
James Starkey	P	17 Oct. 98	P	Dec. 99	
Edward Brooks	P	17 Dec. 99	R		
William Horton		22 Oct. 1802	P	24 July 1803	
Thomas Ashton	P	8 Mar. 03	R	Sept. 11	
William Nicholson	P	26 July 03	R	05	
George Bigland	P	27 Sept. 11	R	20	
Robert Entwistle	P	14 May 17	P	23 May 23	
Hon. Edward Stanley		20 Oct. 20	R		

* In 1880 and 1881 the training of the regiment, and the last twenty-seven days of the recruits' training, was carried out under canvas, at Altcar.

† For explanation of entries in Columns A, B, C, D, and E, *vide* Appendix No. I, p. 208; in Column F are entered the regiments of the regular forces in which the officer formerly served.

‡ Lord Stanley of Knowsley, afterwards 13th Earl of Derby.

A	B	C	D	E	F

SUCCESSION LIST OF MAJORS—*continued.*

A	B	C	D	E	F
James Hilton	P	16 April 1825			
E. G. Hornby	P	6 Dec. 27			
Sir Thomas Hesketh, Bart.		21 Feb. 46	P	1 Mar. 1852	
James Wardlaw	A	4 Oct. 52	D	3 Oct. 67	
Nicholas Blundell	P	3 Nov. 52	P	25 Sept. 72	
Robert Johnson	P	30 Oct. 67	R	24 Aug. 69	
Hon. Frederick A. Stanley	A	27 April 70	P	16 May 74	Gren. Gds.
Alexander T. Knight	P	19 Nov. 72	R	21 April 76	
Charles S. Garraway	P	16 May 74	P	28 Oct. 76	
Richard Geo. Bomford Bolton	P	16 May 74	P	27 July 81	R. H. Gds.
Henry S. Beresford Bruce	P	16 Oct. 75	R	30 June 81	Rifle Brig.
George C. Bancroft	P	3 Mar. 77	R	12 Sept. 79	
George T. Bolton	P	29 Oct. 79	S		Roy. Navy
Sir Thomas G. F. Hesketh, Bart.	P	27 July 81	S		
Thomas Gardner	P	27 July 81	S		

SUCCESSION LIST OF ADJUTANTS.

A	B	C	D	E	F
John Phillips	A	1 Mar. 1797	P	26 June 1803	
William Mingay	A	16 July 98			
James Atherton	A	13 July 1803	D	29 April 34	
John Wilde	A	21 May 04	R	15 Mar. 16	
James Weir	A	7 Feb. 46	R	10 July 62	
Henry S. B. Bruce	A	20 June 62	P	21 April 76	Rifle Brig.
Reginald Whitting	A	21 April 76	PT	20 April 77	8th Ft. (the King's)
Manly C. M. Dixon	A	20 April 77	R	6 Aug. 79	,, ,,
John James Hamilton	A	6 Aug. 79			,, ,,

www.ingramcontent.com/pod-product-compliance
Lightning Source LLC
Chambersburg PA
CBHW030216170426
43201CB00006B/103